WESTMAR COLLEG

SOCIALISM AND FASCISM
1931-1939

SOCIALISM AND FASCISM

1931 – 1939

BY

G. D. H. COLE

NEW YORK

ST MARTIN'S PRESS INC

1960

Copyright © Margaret Cole 1960

MACMILLAN AND COMPANY LIMITED
London Bombay Calcutta Madras Melbourne

THE MACMILLAN COMPANY OF CANADA LIMITED
Toronto

ST MARTIN'S PRESS INC
New York

PRINTED IN GREAT BRITAIN

PREFACE

G. D. H. COLE died suddenly in January 1959. The draft of this, the last volume projected in his *History of Socialist Thought*, had been completed and typed a little while previously; but owing largely to an accident in which he broke his arm, he was unable to subject it to the close revision and scrutiny by other authorities which he had employed in the case of the earlier publications. The draft showed, therefore, some overlapping and some errors which he would certainly have removed; furthermore, two projected chapters, on Israel and India, and the bibliography, except for the section on China, were too obviously incomplete to be published as they stood. His death came too suddenly for last-minute instructions; I have therefore omitted these (the section of the bibliography dealing with China being appended to Chapter XII) and with the help of our son, Humphrey Cole, and of Julius Braunthal, who writes the Introduction, have removed redundancies and such minor errors as we could detect. In other words, I have edited the book so far as I am able, and ask the indulgence of critics for any blemishes which remain. For the rest, the book remains as he wrote it. At one time, as the preface to Volume III indicates, he had thought of bringing the story down to 1945. This he did only in part; much of the narrative now ends with the outbreak of war. But the last long chapter shows clearly that this was to be the last of the series, and that he had finished what he had to say.

For the reasons given above, this Preface does not contain, as did those in earlier volumes, a long list of names to whom thanks are due; and those, who must be many, who did contribute information, particularly on foreign countries, while the book was in preparation, must please accept this generalised acknowledgment of their services. I must, however, specifically thank a few: Humphrey Cole, who worked extensively on the necessary revisions; Julius Braunthal, who went through the proofs in detail and made many valuable suggestions; Nuffield

College, which provided invaluable assistance with the typing; and Miss Brotherhood of Nuffield, who with astonishing accuracy coped with the task of reading extremely difficult handwriting.

MARGARET COLE

KENSINGTON, 1960

CONTENTS

		PAGE
	PREFACE	v
	INTRODUCTION	ix
	LIST OF PRINCIPAL CHARACTERS OF THE PERIOD	xv
CHAP.		
I.	THE WORLD IN THE 1930s	1
II.	THE ECLIPSE OF SOCIALISM IN GERMANY	32
III.	GREAT BRITAIN IN THE 1930s	64
IV.	FRENCH SOCIALISM	93
V.	THE CIVIL WAR IN SPAIN	119
VI.	THE ECLIPSE OF AUSTRIAN SOCIALISM	150
VII.	SCANDINAVIA AND FINLAND	170
VIII.	BELGIUM, HOLLAND, AND SWITZERLAND	187
IX.	EASTERN EUROPE	195
X.	THE UNITED STATES — CANADA — LATIN AMERICA	207
XI.	THE SOVIET UNION FROM THE BEGINNING OF THE FIRST FIVE-YEAR PLAN	230
XII.	COMMUNISM IN CHINA IN THE 1930s	264
XIII.	LOOKING BACKWARDS AND FORWARDS	292
	INDEX OF NAMES	339
	GENERAL INDEX	343

INTRODUCTION

BY

JULIUS BRAUNTHAL

I AM very grateful to Mrs. Margaret Cole for having asked me to read the galley proofs of the late G. D. H. Cole's posthumous volume of his *History of Socialist Thought* and to write a brief Introduction to it. This great honour of having been invited to associate my name with this most important contribution to the history of international Socialism touches me deeply.

G. D. H. Cole's work is an immense achievement, never before attempted by any scholar of any country. When he contemplated the scope of the study he had in mind he intended to limit it to a history of Socialist thought only — as he stated in the Preface to the first volume of his work; he considered writing a comprehensive history of Socialism as 'an impossible task for any single author'. Yet the impossible he has accomplished. He has given more than he promised. His work is indeed the fullest history of modern Socialism ever written in any language, an encyclopaedia of the international Socialist movement no less than of Socialist thought.

This achievement is all the more remarkable because it was carried out under the handicap of increasing ill-health. As a sufferer for very many years from diabetes, he knew that in all probability he would not live to a great age; and from time to time, contemplating the size of the task he had set himself, he wondered, as in the Preface to the fourth volume, published at the end of 1958, whether he would live to finish it. By a tremendous effort of will-power he succeeded in writing the half-thousand pages which form the present volume, and so brought the study of world Socialism to the second world war and to some extent beyond it.

G. D. H. Cole gave to this volume the title *Socialism and Fascism*. But in fact it encompasses more than the title indicates. The story of the tragedy of European Socialism is unfolded in its fullness, and the nature of Fascism is perspicaciously analysed in a fresh approach to that phenomenon. The upsurge of the American Labour movement, stirred up by the great depression in the early 'thirties, and the changes in the power position of the working class in the United States produced by the New Deal, are surveyed and evaluated. The peculiar character of the social revolution in Mexico and the social movements in the other Latin American countries are described and explained. Yet Communism retains the central place in this study. In investigating the primary forces which produced the eclipse of European Socialism and the triumph of Fascism, the significance of the Bolshevik revolution, its ideology, and the economic development of the Soviet Union from the beginning of the first Five-Year Plan up to almost the eve of the Twentieth Congress of the Russian Communist Party are thoroughly re-examined. And, finally, the philosophy of Chinese Communism and its rise to power are discussed in a fascinating chapter.

Moreover, G. D. H. Cole concluded the study with a chapter transcending the scope of the volume as indicated by its title. In 'Looking Backwards and Forwards', he attempted to assess the present position of Socialism and to estimate its prospects. Thus this volume expresses in many respects his last word on ideas and events. He retraces the development of Socialist thought from its very beginnings at the end of the eighteenth century up to our days, showing what became of them in the process of interaction of ideas and circumstances. He then turns to highly stimulating reflections on the crucial problem of present-day Socialism, the problem of how the disastrous gulf that lies between Social Democrats and Communists can possibly be bridged. He discusses the essence of the values which Social Democracy is striving to realise—civil rights, political rights, and social and economic security, arising from the basic claim to individual equality—and the values of the Communist societies, arising from a basic collectivism that denies the priority of individual rights. In conclusion, he saw no way of transcending this fundamental difference.

G. D. H. Cole was, however, neither a Communist nor a Social Democrat, because he considered both Communism and Social Democracy to be creeds of centralisation and bureaucracy, while he felt, as he said in the concluding words of the study, 'that a Socialist society that is to be true to its equalitarian principles of human brotherhood must rest on the widest possible diffusion of power and responsibility'.

This conception of Socialism, first theoretically formulated by G. D. H. Cole in his writings on Guild Socialism four decades ago, guided his creative work throughout his life. It also inspired the survey of various schools of Socialist thought in these volumes, especially the discussion of Proudhonism and some aspects of Bakuninism, of César de Paepe's version of Socialism and some aspects of French Syndicalism. In particular he was attracted by two types of contemporary Socialism which appeared to him the nearest approach to the ideal for which he stood: the Israeli Socialism based on the Kibbutzim and the Histadrut, and the Indian philosophy of Savordaya as propagated by Vinova Bhave and Jayprakash Narayan and embodied in the Bhoodan movement.

In spite of its incompleteness, G. D. H. Cole's monumental work will remain the standard work on the history of Socialism for many years to come. With this work he has added to his renown as the historian of the British working-class movement the distinction as the most prodigious historian of the international Socialist movement.

G. D. H. Cole was a great figure of international Socialism no less than of British Socialism. It is naturally most difficult to estimate the full extent and depth of his influence upon the international Socialist movement. Alone the amazing range of languages into which his books have been translated—Japanese, Chinese, Hebrew, Italian, Spanish, Polish, Serbian and, of course, German, Swedish, Norwegian, and Dutch—has placed him in the first rank of Socialist scholars known to Socialists all over the world. G. D. H. Cole is respected in the international Socialist movement in the first place as the most outstanding historian of his time of the British working class. His *Short History of the British Working Class Movement*, translated into Japanese, Hebrew, and Italian, has been chosen as a text-book by universities of many a country. His admirable essay on Marx's economic thought with which he introduced the Everyman's edition of *Capital* and, still more, the lucid exposition of Marxism in his famous book *What Marx Really*

Meant (republished in 1948 under the title *The Meaning of Marxism*) are major contributions to the dissemination and understanding of Marx's philosophy. But some of his books, if I may speak from my own experience, exerted an immediate influence upon the international Socialist movement. For example, his *Self-Government in Industry*, published in 1917, and translated into German and Swedish, was a source of inspiration for the architects of Socialist reconstruction in Germany and Austria when the revolutionary upsurge at the end of the first world war posed the problem of socialisation of industries in these countries. Rudolf Hilferding, one of the outstanding leaders of the German working class and a member of the Commission for Nationalisation set up by the Socialist German Government, wrote an Introduction to the German version of the book, and Otto Bauer's *Weg zum Sozialismus* (The Road to Socialism), published in 1919, was greatly influenced by Cole's ideas. So was Otto Neurath's scheme of nationalisation which he worked out for the then Socialist governments of Saxony and Bavaria.

Far more immediate and, indeed, far more decisive was, however, G. D. H. Cole's influence as a teacher. In his first years as a tutor at the University, and in the working-class education movement, he profoundly influenced many of the young men and women who were instrumental in building the post-war world. Later, when he became Professor and devoted most of his time to post-graduate teaching, he had many students from America, from the Commonwealth, and from Asia. Students of the social movements in the Asian countries as they emerged after the second world war have often explained the phenomenon of the amazing spread of Socialist aspirations all over Asia—indeed one of the most astonishing phenomena of contemporary history—by the prevalence of Socialist trends of thought among Asian intellectuals. This observation I found confirmed in my conversations with intellectuals in Tokyo and Hong Kong, in Djakarta, Singapore, Rangoon, and Delhi, whether they were active in the Labour movement or teachers at universities or working in the administration of their countries. To them the name of Cole as well as those of Laski and Tawney are household words, and their teachings and writings are gratefully remembered as their source of Socialist inspiration.

INTRODUCTION

G. D. H. Cole believed in Socialism as a living creed. To him it was not merely a beautiful idea fit for the contemplation of scholars, but a stern moral challenge to be met by the utmost endeavour to realise it. In his early years he was research officer to the A.S.E. (later the Amalgamated Engineering Union) and one of the principal founders of the National Guilds League and the Fabian (later Labour) Research Department; he was also the first research secretary of the Labour Party and continuously one of the most important leaders of the Workers' Educational Association. Between the wars he was active in many Socialist organisations, and was the chief architect of the New Fabian Research Bureau, which at the beginning of the war galvanised the Fabian Society into new and influential life; he was the Society's President when he died. In his closing years, in his endeavour to revive the crusading spirit in the Socialist movement, he inspired the formation of the International Society for Socialist Studies.

The idea that moved him in the last of his achievements in the realm of Socialist action is a noble testament to the idealism with which he was imbued. Disillusioned by the impasse of Socialism, as he confessed in two remarkable articles in the *New Statesman*, he saw no prospect of rescuing it from its imprisonment within national frontiers, except by re-creating an international Socialist movement, not as a federation of national parties, but rather as a crusade of a devoted minority in every country. He suggested the establishment of a World Order of Socialists individually pledged to put first their duty to Socialism as a world-wide cause. For Socialism, he insisted, is in essence an international gospel of humanism, the vision of a world made alive by the sense of human fellowship, a faith in social equality not only of one's own countrymen but of the whole of mankind.

This wonderful spirit of Socialist internationalism is not the smallest part of the rich legacy which G. D. H. Cole has bequeathed to the international Socialist movement. He was indeed a great Socialist.

JULIUS BRAUNTHAL

September 1959

THE PRINCIPAL CHARACTERS
OF THE PERIOD

	CHAP. REF.		CHAP. REF.
KAUTSKY, 1854–1938 [1], [2]	2	NYGAARDSVOLD, 1879–1952 [2]	7
LANSBURY, 1858–1940 [1], [2]	3	JOUHAUX, 1879–1952 [1], [2]	4
B. WEBB, 1858–1943 [1], [2]	3	STALIN, 1879–1953 [2]	11
S. WEBB, 1859–1947 [1], [2]	3	AZAÑA, 1880–1940	10
BRACKE, 1861–1955 [2]	4	TRANMAEL, 1879– [2]	7
VLIEGEN, 1862–1947 [2]	8	TROTSKY, 1879–1940 [1], [2]	11
HENDERSON, 1863–1935 [1], [2]	3	TAWNEY, 1880– [2]	3
JOWETT, 1864–1944 [1], [2]	3	O. BAUER, 1881–1938 [2]	6
SNOWDEN, 1864–1937 [1], [2]	3	BEVIN, 1881–1951 [2]	3
MACDONALD, 1866–1937 [1], [2]	3	FIMMEN, 1881–1943 [2]	8
VANDERVELDE, 1866–1938 [1], [2]	8	FOSTER, 1881– [2]	10
ADDISON, 1869–1951 [2]	3	GRIMM, 1881–1958 [2]	8
CACHIN, 1869–1958 [2]	4	RYKOV, 1881–1938 [2]	11
GANDHI, 1869–1948 [2]	—	V. TANNER, 1881– [2]	7
KRUPSKAIA, 1869–1939 [2]	11	VOROSHILOV, 1881– [2]	11
LARGO CABALLERO, 1869–1946 [2]	10	WIGFORSS, 1881– [2]	7
DE LOS RIOS, 1870–1949	10	DIMITROV, 1882–1949 [2]	9
DE MAN, 1871–1947 [2]	8	ATTLEE, 1883– [2]	3
PIECK, 1871– [2]	2	COMPANYS, 1883–1940	10
HUYSMANS, 1871– [2]	6	KAMENEV, 1883–1936 [2]	11
BLUM, 1872–1950 [2]	4	PRIETO, 1883–	10
SAVAGE, 1872–1940 [2]	—	VYSHINSKY, 1883–1955 [2]	11
BRAILSFORD, 1873–1958 [2]	3	ZINOVIEV, 1883–1936 [2]	11
RAKOVSKY, 1873–? [2]	11	SHINWELL, 1884– [2]	3
STAUNING, 1873–1942 [2]	7	SANDLER, 1884– [2]	7
J. H. THOMAS, 1873–1949 [1], [2]	3	N. THOMAS, 1884– [2]	10
KALININ, 1875–1946 [2]	11	V. AURIOL, 1884– [2]	4
LITVINOV, 1876–1951 [2]	11	HANSSON, 1885–1946 [2]	7
SCULLIN, 1876–1953 [2]	—	RADEK, 1885–? [2]	11
J. LONGUET, 1876–1938 [2]	4	CHU TEH, 1886–	12
U. SINCLAIR, 1878– [2]	10	BELA KUN, 1886–1936 [2]	9
F. ADLER, 1879–1960 [2]	6	P. MURRAY, 1886–1952 [2]	10
		BEN GURION, 1888– [2]	—

[1] Discussed also in Volume III.
[2] Discussed also in Volume IV.

	CHAP. REF.		CHAP. REF.
THAELMANN, 1886–1944 [2]	2	KHRUSHCHEV, 1894–	11
DALTON, 1887– [2]	3	EVATT, 1894– [2]	—
KAROLYI, 1887–1955 [2]	—	BULGANIN, 1895– [2]	11
MORRISON, 1888– [2]	3	HAYA DE LA TORRE, 1895– [2]	10
SOKOLNIKOV, 1888–? [2]	11	MIKOYAN, 1895– [2]	11
BUKHARIN, 1889–1938 [2]	11	ZHUKOV, 1895–	11
NEHRU, 1889– [2]	—	LI LI-SAN, 1896–	12
COLE, 1889–1959 [2]	3	P'ENNG PAI, 1896–1929	12
NEGRÍN, 1889–1956	10	GOTTWALD, 1896–1953	9
CRIPPS, 1890–1952 [2]	3	BEVAN, 1897– [2]	3
HO CHI MINH, 1890–	—	CHOU EN-LAI, 1898– [2]	12
MOLOTOV, 1890– [2]	11	BERIA, 1899–1953	11
POLLITT, 1890– [2]	3	CHANG WAN-TIEN, 1900–	12
TITO, 1890– [2]	9	A. PHILIP, 1901–	4
BRAUNTHAL, 1891– [2]	6	STRACHEY, 1901–	3
NENNI, 1891– [2]	—	DÍAZ, 1902–1940	10
RAKOSI, 1892– [2]	9	ORWELL, 1903–1950 [2]	3
NIN, 1892–1937	5	CH'EN SHAO-GÜ, 1904–	12
MAO TSE-TUNG, 1893– [2]	12	GAITSKELL, 1906– [2]	3
LASKI, 1893–1950 [2]	3	DURBIN, 1906–1948	3
GOLLANCZ, 1893–	3	SILONE, 1906–	—
LOMBARDO TOLEDANO, 1893– [2]	10	CH'IN PANG-HSEIN, 1907–1946	12
TOGLIATTI, 1893– [2]	—	REUTHER, 1907– [2]	10

[1] Discussed also in Volume III.
[2] Discussed also in Volume IV.

CHAPTER I

THE WORLD IN THE 1930s

THE period to be dealt with in the present section of my study is that of the 1930s — or, more exactly, of the years between the economic disaster of 1931 and the outbreak of the second world war eight years later. It was a period of sensational political and economic change, and also of rapid shifts in social attitudes and beliefs. Within these eight years Fascism, in its German Nazi form, became the absolute master in Germany and Austria and a powerful influence over a large part of Europe, extinguishing the once powerful German and Austrian working-class movements even more ruthlessly than Italian Fascism had already overturned the working-class movement in Italy. The United States underwent an economic and social cataclysm of unparalleled severity, from which it emerged, thanks to the New Deal, with a Trade Union movement incomparably stronger than before, and enjoying a measure of public and social recognition that it had never previously known. The Soviet Union carried through the successive stages of its economic plans under a growingly dictatorial system of police rule, and to the accompaniment of a series of sensational trials in which many of the leading figures of the Revolution were made away with to gratify Stalin's intensely suspicious and inordinate lust for power and worship. In Great Britain, the Labour Party went down in 1931 to a defeat so disastrous that there had been no full recovery from it even in 1939. In France, where the economic crisis developed later than elsewhere, the left rallied its forces to launch, in 1936, what came to be known as 'l'expérience Blum', but in face of acute political divisions failed to make good its victory at the polls, and fell back into a confusion which left it incapable of coping with the disaster of 1940. In the Scandinavian countries the moderate Socialists registered large successes in coping with the great slump, which fell much less heavily on them than on the rest of Western Europe. Finally, in Spain, the victory of the Republicans and Socialists was wiped out in blood by a civil war in which the Fascist powers gave large help to the revolutionary forces, while the democratic Western powers stood timorously by in a one-sided attitude of so-called 'non-intervention'.

The balance-sheet of world Socialism during this troubled period is not at all easy to draw up. On the one side are the sheer destruction of the German and Austrian working-class movements and the near-eclipse of working-class and Socialist action in most parts of South-Eastern Europe; the total eclipse of the Spanish movement after its heroic resistance in the civil war; the serious setback to the British movement in and after 1931; and the degeneration of Russian Communism into a system of personal tyranny unrestrained by any moral scruples — but nevertheless accompanied by vast economic achievements which laid the foundations for the still more remarkable technological and scientific progress of more recent years. Against these adversities have to be set the rapid rise of Trade Unionism in the United States, unaccompanied by any revival of Socialist influence; the emergence of as yet small, but significant, Socialist movements in India and in other economically underdeveloped countries;[1] the successes of moderate Socialist Governments in Scandinavia; the appearance of Socialism as a substantial force in Canada and the strengthening of Labour influences in Australia and New Zealand; some growth of Socialism — and also of Communism — in Latin America, most notably in Mexico; and, among the intellectuals in many countries, the development of passionate anti-Fascist sentiment as a counter to the rising influence of Fascism in other sections of the middle classes. On the whole, it seems evident that, up to 1939, the Socialist losses far outweighed the gains; but the gains were none the less real, and their effects were greatly reinforced by the conditions of war — at any rate from 1940 — as it became indispensable to mobilise popular opinion behind the war effort and as this involved, in the democratic countries at all events, taking Labour into partnership at the cost of greatly

[1] The chapters dealing with India, Palestine, and Arab Socialism were unfinished at the time of the author's death.

increasing both its practical influence and its social prestige.

In Europe, west of the Soviet Union, the 1930s were the great age of Fascism; and it is of the first importance for understanding this to form a correct estimate of what Fascism actually was. It is, in my opinion, grossly misleading to treat Fascism as the final throw of capitalism in decline, though Fascism of course received large help from capitalists in its rise to power, and in its measures for accomplishing the destruction of the working-class movements. Fascism was, I agree, the ally of capitalism in this struggle; but it was not the mere lackey of capitalist interests. Its growth was greatly influenced by the economic conditions of the time, and by the moods of frustration which economic adversity stirred up in the minds of the young; but it was, all the same, not fundamentally an economic movement, but rather the manifestation of aggressive nationalism appealing to the violent passions of the underman. To attempt to characterise it in purely economic terms is to miss the essential key to its driving force and to leave out of sight its most dangerous quality — its irrepressible drive towards war. Hitler would most likely never have come to power in Germany had there been no great depression to throw millions of Germans out of work and to impose very bad working conditions on those who were able to keep their jobs. But this does not mean that Hitler, or the movement he inspired, was exclusively, or even mainly, a product of economic conditions, even if these were the main cause of his rise to power. The Nazi movement was in its essence political rather than economic: it arose out of the thwarted feelings of a defeated Germany intent on national self-assertion and revenge. It used the German capitalists, rather than was used by them; and the Germany which it created was far less capitalistic than militaristic and driven on by a fanatical belief in the superiority of Germans to the rest of the human race. Its anti-Semitism and anti-Slavism were not at all manifestations of capitalist sentiments or attitudes: they arose out of much more primitive psychological sources. If Nazism was essentially unstable, as it doubtless was, its instability arose, not out of the contradictions of capitalism which it was unable to escape, but out of its inherent propensity to make war on its neighbours in order to demonstrate German mastery on a world scale.

The Communists, whose Marxism led them to interpret everything preponderantly in economic terms, were incapable of seeing Nazism as it really was. They promptly recognised it clearly enough as an enemy to be fought by every means in their power, and did their best to come to terms with anyone who might be induced to join hands with them in any sort of anti-Fascist 'United Front'. But the German Communists in particular showed an entire lack of capacity to understand what they were up against during the critical years when Nazism was rising towards power, and, as we saw, even collaborated with the Nazis against the Social Democrats at certain critical moments.[1] Working-class unity offered the only possible chance of successful resistance to Nazism during the closing years of the Weimar Republic; but the German Communists, accusing the Social Democrats as the betrayers of the German Revolution, were in far too bitter hostility to them for any sort of unity to be possible. In these circumstances the Communists managed to convince themselves that a Nazi victory would be nothing so terrible after all, because it would be of its very nature evanescent, and doomed to perish on account of the capitalist contradictions it would be unable to escape or transcend : so that, in effect, Nazism would be preparing the way for Communism against its will and interest. This notion was no doubt comforting at the time ; and it did indeed prove true that the victory of Nazism did not endure for more than about a dozen years. What brought it down, however, was not its entanglement in the contradictions of capitalism but its insane lust for power, which led it into aggressive war and caused it wantonly to extend the number of its enemies by attacking the Soviet Union as well as by provoking the United States to come to the rescue of the West European allies. It was true enough that Nazism was inherently unstable ; but the Communists were wholly wrong about the reasons for this, and could hardly have comforted themselves as they did had they rightly diagnosed the Nazi evil, and foreseen how much destruction and devastation its overthrow would involve — most of all for the peoples of the Soviet Union.

Let me then begin by stating, as clearly as I can, what I

[1] See Vol. IV, Part II, pp. 657 ff.

believe the real character of German Nazism to have been. It is usual to lump together, under the handy label of Fascism, a number of régimes of the 1930s which were in fact considerably different in nature — though I do not deny that they had also something in common. These include, besides Nazism, Italian Fascism, the Horthy régime in Hungary, the various dictatorships set up in the Balkans, the régime of the 'Marshals' in Poland after Pilsudski's death, Salazar's dictatorial rule in Portugal, and the Franco régime in Spain after the civil war. These régimes were all in spirit strongly nationalist, and they were all bitter enemies of Socialism and of the working-class movement. They all received capitalist support; but in no one of them was capitalism the main driving force. Arising in countries at widely different stages of economic development, they differed in their economic characteristics. Some were essentially conservative or reactionary in their economic policies, and relied largely on the support of feudal, aristocratic classes alarmed by the danger or revolution from below, but not necessarily of *proletarian* revolution, for in some of the countries affected the proletariat was far too underdeveloped to make a revolution of its own, and the main revolutionary force was that of the peasants, without whose active participation successful revolution simply could not occur. Such feudal aristocratic elements, which everywhere supported Fascism when it became active, were particularly prominent in Hungary, in Poland, and in Spain — and also, of course, in Eastern Germany and in Southern Italy. In these cases, as in some others, the Catholic Church was also a powerful agent on the anti-Socialist side. In others, the main driving force was by no means feudal or aristocratic: on the contrary it was mainly plebeian, drawing its strongest support from elements in the lower middle classes which bitterly resented the equalitarian ambitions of the working classes, and found themselves adversely affected by economic depression and shortage of superior jobs carrying social prestige. This lower-middle-class element was of great importance in both Germany and Italy; and its influence differed greatly from that of the conservative elements that rallied to Fascism; for it was concerned, not with the retention of an existing social order, but with the setting up of a new order that would present to

5

it the opportunities for power and advancement which the existing order denied. In practice, in both Italy and Germany, Fascism of this more radical and subversive type in the event allied itself with the aggressive forces of feudalism and capitalism, though not, in Germany, without a 'blood-bath' in which the most radical elements were forcibly destroyed. But, even when such alliances had been consummated, German Nazism did not become, in its essence, either feudal-aristocratic or capitalist : it remained fundamentally nationalist and militarist, and moved the masses who supported it chiefly by its appeals to their deeply rooted nationalist aggressiveness, rather than by any appeal to economic motives. Doubtless, such motives played a large part in the mental attitudes of many of its individual supporters, who saw in it the prospect of financial gain as well as of power. But the economic corruptions of Nazism ought not to blind us to its real nature, as resting on primitive drives towards cruelty and intolerance, which it contrived to make the allies of aggressive nationalist sentiment.

Before Hitler, Mussolini had built Italian Fascism round the cult of the nation, conceived as essentially an assertive power group, activated by a collective 'social egoism' in its dealings with the rest of the world, and inspired by a cult of 'violence' that exalted violence and cruelty into virtues when they were manifested in the cause of the nation so conceived of. In practice, however, though the Italian Fascists practised thuggery without scruple and denounced every sort of liberal humanism as despicable sentimental imbecility, they were much less thorough-going in their behaviour than the Nazis, and showed much less cruel bestiality in their treatment of their opponents. They did not stop short of murder, as the cases of Matteotti and of the Roselli brothers among others made clear ; but they did not resort to mass murder or, generally, to systematic torture. There were but few Jews in Italy ; and, partly no doubt for that reason, anti-semitism never played an important part in Italian Fascism, which was in its driving force nationalistic rather than racial ; whereas in Germany fanatical anti-semitism was a leading feature of the Nazi doctrine, and the exaltation of the Germans as the *Herrenvolk* was continually in the foreground of the Nazi appeal. Nazism was in fact a much viler movement than Italian Fascism, and

6

involved a much more far-going repudiation of the entire tradition of civilisation after the West European pattern, and therewith a much more positive evocation of the submerged amorality of the underman.

The two chief forms of Fascism differed also in the place they assigned to the 'leader'. Mussolini was 'Il Duce', and entitled as such to great power and reverence from his followers ; but he was never, to anything like the same extent as Hitler, the sole source of authority, even in theory. Italian Fascism combined in itself the notions of personal leadership and of the 'corporative State', in which great authority belonged, as of right, to the Fascist General Council as the representative agency of the Fascist Party, and some authority, even if but secondary, was recognised as belonging to the Corporations, through which the Fascists set out, for the most part unsuccessfully, to organise the main activities of their society, especially in the economic field. The principles on which authority was supposed to be shared between these three — Duce, Party, and the Corporations — was never clear ; but there was at any rate no such uncompromising insistence as in Nazi Germany on the derivation of all powers from the will of the inspired Führer. Mussolini had no doubt his *charisma* — to use Max Weber's well-known word ; but the charisma that attached to him fell a very long way short of Hitler's claim to embody in his own person the entire will and destiny of the German Volk. It may be said that in reality the Italian Corporations counted for very little, and indeed hardly existed in any full sense ; but even if they are left out of account, the distribution of powers and functions between the Duce and the Fascist Party was essentially different from that between the Führer and the Nazi Party in Germany. This difference no doubt arose largely out of a difference of national temperament between Italians and Germans : the Germans were much more ruthless and humourless in pushing their doctrine to the extreme point. They liquidated Röhm and got rid of the Strassers, who stood for a more collective view of the Party's functions than Hitler could tolerate ; whereas within the Italian movement such men as Bottai were able to keep their places and to continue to stand up in some degrees for the claims of corporative leadership. Nor was the expression of discontent ever suppressed in

Italy to the same extent as in Germany. I myself heard a local Fascist leader, at the height of the régime's power, tell an improvised open-air meeting that he was 'fed-up' with the responsibilities of office, and meant to resign and retire into private life. I do not know whether he actually retired, or what happened to him as a consequence of his speech; but I am sure that no such incident could possibly have occurred in Germany after the Nazis had established their rule. *Gleichschaltung* was practised to a substantial extent in Italy as well as in Germany; but it was far less complete, and it was much easier for individual Italians than for Germans to go on living their own lives undisturbed so long as they kept quiet, provided they had no political records that exposed them to persecution.

There was indeed always in Italian Fascism an element of play-acting that was markedly absent from Nazism. Mussolini's gibes at 'pluto-democracy' had always a rhetorical ring widely different from that of the denunciations of Goebbels or the anti-Jewish fulminations of Streicher. It may be held that this only shows the German Nazis to have been more deeply sincere in their horrible doctrines; and no doubt many of them were. But the difference is none the less marked. Both Italian Fascism and German Nazism made use of the more brutish and violent elements in the human make-up; but the Nazis went much the further in deliberately building their régime on a cult of sheer bestiality. Of course, many of those who rose to positions of authority within both régimes were either natural thugs or unscrupulous self-seekers with a lust for power, without much regard for the ends for which it was used. Persons of these types gravitated naturally to both, and found in either the means of satisfying their evil impulses. But side by side with the thugs and power-seekers there were in both movements genuine devotees; and within the limits set by compliance with the general aims of both movements, there did arise among such persons a kind of genuine comradeship in evil-doing that could find expression in personal sacrifice. This spirit, I think, was much stronger among Nazis than among Italian Fascists, and was an important source of strength to the Nazi régime, rendering it more potent and thorough in its abominable behaviour — for what is called 'human' can be evil as well as good.

What I feel certain of is that neither in Italian Fascism nor in Nazism was the main driving force either economic or mainly based on *class*-interest or sentiment. Both of course did contain these elements, and had as one of their chief features the rallying of the groups that laid claim to social and economic superiority against the equalitarian tendencies that found expression chiefly through the working-class movement, which both set out to destroy. But both Nazism and Italian Fascism did succeed in enrolling a substantial body of working-class support, which was not, I think, won mainly by the promises so freely made of rescue from unemployment and distress — though these undoubtedly counted for something, especially in the earlier stages of the movements' growth. The main body of working-class support was attracted to Nazism much more by its intransigent nationalism and racialism than by its economic appeal, or at any rate became consolidated in its support of Nazism chiefly for these non-economic reasons. Even if the capitalists and a large section of the middle classes saw in Nazism most of all a force capable of meeting and maintaining their social and economic superiority over the workers, this cannot explain why so many workers threw over Social Democracy or Communism and rallied lastingly to the Nazi cause. The Weimar Republic in its final years was not only depressed economically, but even more profoundly depressing to those who wanted to be able to assert themselves as active human beings, and felt Germany to be suffering under the degradation of the Versailles *Diktat*. This sense of degradation affected workers as well as persons from the 'superior' classes, and enabled the Nazis to win power in the name of the nation rather than of the classes economically hostile to Socialist levelling. I am, I repeat, not saying that the economic features were unimportant, but only that it is a gross error to regard them as all-important, or to interpret Nazism as simply the throes of capitalism in decline.

The situation was, I think, different in other countries which fell between the wars a prey to régimes that are commonly called 'Fascist'. In Hungary, for example, the Horthy régime, though it had features in common with Italian and German Fascism, owed clearly, in its essential driving force, much less to capitalistic influences than either, and had as its main

9

elements of support on the one hand the landowning aristocracy and its dependants, who largely manned the Civil Service, and on the other a powerful Magyar nationalism intent on restoring and maintaining Magyar superiority over the Slav elements that remained under, or might conceivably be again subjected to, Magyar rule. The economic elements were powerful in it, especially after Béla Kun's bid for power; but they were, in the main, aristocratic-feudal rather than capitalistic, as they were bound to be in view of the under-developed character of much of Hungarian industry and of the extent to which both industry and commerce were in non-Magyar hands. In Franco Spain, though capitalism was a serious factor in Catalonia and in a few other areas, it did not count for a great deal in the rest of the country; and the main driving force of the counter-revolution came from the Church and the higher cadres of the armed forces rather than from economic sources. In the Balkan countries, ambitious monarchs, surrounded chiefly by military counsellors, were primarily responsible for the destruction of the parliamentary régimes established after 1918; and the capitalists, who were relatively weak, were no more than their subordinate allies, apart from the sinister part that was sometimes played by foreign capitalist influences. In Poland, where Pilsudski began as a man of the left, and never came to terms with Dmowski and the nationalist right, the régime of the 'Marshals' after Pilsudski's death was the outcome of an accommodation of the military leaders with the landowners rather than of any really powerful or pervasive capitalist influences — though of course it received capitalist support in its warfare against the Socialists, the Trade Unions, and the left wing of the peasant movement. In not one of these countries is the rise of the movements called 'Fascist' capable of being understood in simple terms of economic conflict between the rich and the poor, or between the working classes and the rest of the nation, though in all it did involve a bitter struggle between the 'superior' classes and the organised working-class movement, which was almost annihilated in every country in which any of these régimes achieved power.

The main reason why it is plausible to explain Fascism, in all its varied manifestations, in terms of economic forces and of class-war is that, almost everywhere, the working-class movements constituted the main, if not the only, organised forces of opposition to the new régimes. The liberal-democratic oppositions, as far as they had been represented by bourgeois parties of the left and centre, everywhere showed themselves incapable of putting up any sustained fight against the new authoritarian forces, which simply swept them aside ; and even the Social Democratic parliamentary parties fared not much better. It was left to the Communists and to a small minority of left-wing Trade Unions, which came mainly under Communist control, to play the main part in such underground resistance movements as were able to continue in being under the Fascist régimes. Of the Social Democratic leaders a few, when they were given the chance, accommodated themselves to the very limited possibilities of constitutional opposition inside the Fascist States : the majority fled abroad and tried to maintain skeleton 'parties in exile', which speedily lost touch with their former supporters and were reduced to representing very little besides themselves.

The fact that, in one country after another, Fascism, whatever its basic character, made relentless war on the Socialists and on the working-class movement rendered it plausible to suggest that Fascism must be essentially a form of capitalism, with the main purpose of overthrowing its chief enemy, Socialism. The economic crisis of the 1930s was diagnosed, on the whole correctly, as a crisis of the capitalist world, from which the Soviet Union, with its socialised economy, was immune ; and the capitalists were seen as failing to resolve the crisis by purely economic counter-measures, and as resorting, in their dilemma, to violent political action, in the hope of getting a free hand by putting it out of the workers' power to oppose them. There was much talk of capitalism drawing near to its final crisis, in which it would break down past repair under the burden of its inherent contradictions — above all, its inability to find markets for the ever-increasing productivity which was a necessary consequence of technological advance. It was argued that Marx had been correct in seeing in the limitation on mass-consuming power the final cause of the recurring crises of capitalism ; for if the purchasing power of the masses was held down by capitalist exploitation, the consequent limitation on the total market needs must set limits to the profitability of investment, and thus lead to general depression and unemployment. The conclusion was drawn that the smashing of the working-class movement, which would enable the capitalists to exploit the workers even more, could bring no remedy, because by further menacing the consumers' market it would cause investment to fall off still more, and make the depression worse instead of better. Accordingly the capitalists, in resorting to Fascism, would really be digging their own graves, whatever their immediate success in destroying working-class power; for with it they would be destroying capitalism itself and sowing the seeds of world revolution, which would somehow come about as a consequence of the workers' increasing misery even if the working-class organisations were broken up and driven underground. The capitalists could not see this, because they were blind to the real causes of depression and hoped to remedy it by getting a free hand to deal with labour as they pleased. Therefore, it did not really matter if the Socialist Parties and the Trade Unions were broken up: indeed, it might be a positive advantage if constitutional Socialist Parties and reformist Trade Unions were deprived of their power to mislead and betray the workers, so as to leave the road open to the real revolutionaries, whose doctrine would enable them to build up, even under Fascist dictatorship, underground forces that would in due course put an end to a capitalism no longer capable of organising the productive powers.

If Fascism had been in fact simply a manifestation of capitalism at its last gasp, these hopes might have had some real foundation; for a capitalist dictatorship clearly aimed at increased exploitation of the workers and at depriving them of all means of collective resistance might indeed, in face of deepening depression from which it could find no way of escape, have led to a revolutionary situation by which a determined underground resistance would have been able to profit. But, in sheer factual terms, the diagnosis was utterly wrong. In Germany at any rate the Nazis were able to reduce unemployment to relatively modest dimensions and to expand production to a significant extent. It is true that this was done largely by public provision of emergency employment on a non-economic basis and, presently, by a maximum increase in spending on armaments — on 'guns' in preference to 'butter'. But, even if wages were low and the inherent contradictions of capitalism remained fundamentally unresolved, most workers were provided with jobs of a sort ; and, in face of this, underground agitation found itself quite unable to stir up mass revolt. The capitalists were able to exploit the workers unchecked by Trade Union resistance ; but they were also subjected to heavy demands from the State in the interests of intensive militarisation with a view to building up resources for aggressive war. At the same time the entire population, including the workers, was swept by intensive nationalistic and militaristic propaganda, which acted very powerfully upon it as all the resources of the State were mobilised under Nazi leadership, and as every latest psychological technique was enlisted in its service. These conditions were not at all what the capitalists wanted, at any rate after they had achieved the destruction of the working-class movement. They rendered capitalism, not the master, but the tolerated servant of militarism and of the Nazi gospel of violence and sadistic national assertion. The entire German economy, under Nazism, became a vast structure of military preparation : so that the fortunes of German capitalism became linked to the prospects of victory in war — victory, not primarily or essentially for the capitalists, but for the *Herrenvolk* led by the Nazi Party and its inspired lunatic Führer, whose ambitions knew no stopping-point short of conquest and subordination of the entire world.

The Communists were thus correct in deciding that the Fascist systems of the 1930s were inherently unstable, but quite wrong about the causes of their instability. What made them unstable was not their inability to employ the workers, but their leaders' determination to apply the resources of production primarily to war preparations and with a definite purpose of waging war on their neighbours. If Nazism had been merely capitalism seeking ways out of economic crisis and depression, it would not have preferred 'guns' to 'butter' : it would have sought the largest possible markets for the enlarged product of German industry. But the powers that were in the saddle in Nazi Germany were interested in capitalism only in so far as they could make use of it to serve their ends of nationalist aggression and would have turned on it promptly and decisively had it failed to fall in with their plans.

Moreover, in the capitalist countries which escaped Fascist domination the economic crisis of the 1930s did not prove to be the 'final crisis' of capitalism, as the Communists had hoped. In the United States, where its impact was greatest of all, President Roosevelt's New Deal did bring about a substantial, though incomplete, economic recovery, which was accompanied by a real change in the distribution of social power. American Labor Unionism, hitherto ineffective outside a narrow range of industries and generally low in social prestige, experienced a great renaissance as the Congress of Industrial Organisations successfully established its hold over the great mass-production industries, such as automobiles and steel, as the widespread 'company' Unions were liquidated, and as American employers perforce adapted themselves to the practices of collective bargaining. American industrial relations were essentially transformed within a few years; and it became a recognised practice that the workers should be allowed a substantial share in the fruits of technological progress. Under these altered conditions, American capitalism was reconstructed with remarkable success, on terms broadly acceptable to the main body of American workers: so that, while Labor Unionism grew steadily stronger and more influential, American Socialism almost completely disappeared. Capitalism recovered its power, but did so on condition of accepting the new status of the Unions and of recognising in practice an enlarged element of public intervention in economic affairs, including both a substantial growth of public social services and a measure of public responsibility for the maintenance of employment at an adequate level. Many American capitalists were very reluctant to accept these changes, and hankered after a return to the old conditions of *laisser-faire* and 'devil take the hindmost'; but their cries were for the most part ineffective in bringing about a revival of the old conditions of open class war. At the same time, there existed in the United States still mainly latent tendencies towards nationalistic intolerance similar to those which underlay the growth of Fascism in Europe; but these did not take Fascist forms in face of the basically more democratic character of the American 'way of life'. Instead, they came into the open later on in the form of McCarthyism and 'Hundred per cent Americanism', with their witch-hunts at the expense of any kind of progressivism that could be represented as disloyalty to the established régime. Most of this, however, developed seriously only well after the period I am now discussing : through the 1930s the main current in the United States appeared to be flowing in the direction of a more liberal, reformed capitalism readier to come to terms with working-class claims and to make concessions to any large groups that were getting obviously less than a 'square deal'.

Meanwhile, in Great Britain the impact of the world economic crisis had been much less extreme than in the United States ; and, in spite of the almost complete eclipse of the Labour Party in the General Election of 1931, the Trade Unions showed remarkable success in limiting wage-cuts despite their weakening after the General Strike of 1926. Depression was indeed very serious in certain areas — notably in the shipyards and in the coal and steel industries ; and recovery in these depressed areas remained slow and incomplete right up to the outbreak of war. Politically, the Labour Party slowly regained strength after its defeat, but was still much too weak to make an effective challenge at the election of 1935 : so that the Conservatives enjoyed an uninterrupted term of political power right up to the outbreak of war and during the opening year of 'phoney war'. Labour's recovery might have been more rapid had it not been caught up in a serious dilemma between its deeply rooted pacifism and its desire to play a part in collective resistance to Fascism as an international disturbing force. Its pacifism, reinforced by its deep suspicion of Conservative intentions, held it back from supporting rearmament under a Conservative Government ; whereas it became more and more evident that nothing short of massive armed power could possibly be effective in checking Nazi aggression. The ambiguity of the Labour attitude also came out plainly in connection with the Spanish Civil War, when, partly under pressure from the Blum Government in France, which was also weakened by the strength of French pacifist feeling, it supported an unreal policy of 'non-intervention' which in no sense held back the Fascist powers from intervening on the side of the rebels against the Spanish Republican Government.

The Labour dilemma was indeed very difficult to resolve.

Almost every month made it clearer that the Fascist powers — above all, Nazi Germany — were heading for war, and that nothing but an overwhelming show of force would avail to stop them. It remained, however, uncertain in what order Hitler would decide to attack his enemies ; and among British Conservatives there were many who hoped to the last that he might leave the West alone and direct his onslaught against the Soviet Union, the destruction of which they would have welcomed even at Hitler's hands. The Labour Party, even after it had accepted rearmament, continued to base its hopes of peace mainly on collective security through the League of Nations — which was in fact a broken reed. Having no power to determine, or even seriously to influence, the Government's policy, it had to stand by helpless, though protesting, at the time of Munich ; and when war actually broke out in the West in 1939 it remained impotent till after the collapse of France had driven Chamberlain from office and forced Winston Churchill, as the new Prime Minister, to call upon the Labour Party to take a leading part in a Government that needed to rally the whole nation behind it in the apparently desperate task of fighting on practically alone.

In France the depression came later than elsewhere, chiefly because Poincaré had stabilised the franc at a low level which left the French economy a good deal of elbow-room when currencies were tumbling right and left in and after 1931. Politically, however, the French had by no means recovered from their heavy loss of young manhood in the first world war ; and a large part of the French people reacted to the rise of Nazism in Germany with a mood of apprehension that made them, not gird up their loins for a renewed conflict, but prepare to come to almost any terms with the Germans in order to avoid war. The French working-class movement, unlike the British, had been disrupted by the quarrel between Communists and democratic Socialists, and the major part of the organised manual workers had gone over to Communism, leaving the Socialist Party a mere rump, backed largely by functionaries and other non-manual groups. This division, which extended to the Trade Unions, rendered the economic movement almost powerless ; and it also became plain that there was no prospect of any durable left-wing Government without Communist support. In these circumstances the United Front, which was rejected in Great Britain, won acceptance in France, but did so very much less for international than for domestic reasons. The *Front Populaire* led by Léon Blum was directed much less against Fascism than towards improving the condition of the French workers by progressive social legislation. It carried with it the reunion of the Trade Union forces in the *Confédération Générale du Travail*, which thereafter passed largely under Communist control. There followed the Matignon Agreements, which involved both fuller recognition of collective bargaining rights and increased State intervention in industrial disputes, and the introduction of the forty-hour week, which imposed a considerable strain on an economy by no means up to date in equipment or methods of production. The workers reaped, for the time being, real economic gains ; but the French balance of payments suffered. In this situation, the employing classes grew more and more restive ; and the right wing retorted upon the governing left with growing manifestations of Fascist or semi-Fascist violence. Blum felt too weak to give any help to the Spanish Republicans or to take a firm line with the Germans ; and his successor as Prime Minister, the Radical Daladier, was an equal partner with Chamberlain in the Munich surrender. The parliamentary régime was seriously shaken by the violence of the Cagoulards and of other Fascist groups : Pierre Laval and an influential group of politicians were insistent on the need for a deal with the Fascists ; and the whole country was at sixes and sevens and clearly in no mood likely to lead to success in war. French military strategy had rested, since the rise of Nazism, almost exclusively on a basis of stationary defence, with the Maginot line as its bastion. But when war came and the futility of reliance on this form of defence was quickly and disastrously exposed, France collapsed spiritually as well as militarily, and fell an easy prey to German occupation and to the despicable pretences of the Vichy régime, which tried to make Marshal Pétain into a father-figure to cover its shame, but succeeded only in bringing yet further shame on a defeated and crest-fallen people.

While Socialism was suffering utter eclipse in Germany and was experiencing serious setbacks in both Great Britain and France, the Scandinavian countries were offering a sharply contrasting spectacle of moderate Socialist success. Scandinavia as a whole got off lightly during the years of depression, partly because its main exports were of goods which remained throughout in high demand, and partly because its Governments for the most part showed great common sense in coping with such difficulties as did beset them. While most other countries living under capitalist régimes were attempting to combat economic adversity by deflationary measures which, temporarily at all events, made the situation worse, the Swedes especially showed the good sense to incur temporary budget deficits in order to combat unemployment, while guarding themselves against inflationary finance by providing for the redressing of the balance in later years. These prudent policies were adopted under Social Democratic Governments either backed by independent parliamentary majorities or sustained by coalition with sufficiently like-minded lesser parties. These Governments did not, indeed, attempt to make large advances in the socialisation of the means of production, which they were content to leave for the most part in capitalist hands. They embarked rather on extensive measures of social security and contented themselves with exerting an increasing regulative influence over capitalist behaviour. Aided by favourable economic conditions, they were in general reasonably successful, and were able to maintain themselves in power over long periods on a basis of popular support. They were undoubtedly helped by the fact that differences of wealth and income among the people were already substantially less than in the great capitalistic countries; for this nearer approach to equality lowered the temperature of political controversy and prevented the growth of Communism as a serious rival to Social Democracy. It became common in the 1930s to refer to Sweden as the supreme example of moderate Socialist success and also, economically, as a pioneer in the use of new techniques of State action for the maintenance of a high level of employment. On the whole, these laudations were well earned, even if much of the success was due largely to favourable circumstances rather than to any special Socialist genius in finding solutions for really intractable problems. The weakness inherent in Scandinavian Socialism was that it seemed bound, before very long, to come to an end of what could be done to improve working-class conditions by social legislation, and that it showed no sign of being ready to advance to the further stage of setting about the building of a fully Socialist economy. For the time being, however, sufficient unto the day was the benefit thereof ; and the Scandinavians — especially the Swedes — appeared to be furnishing a convincing example of the potentialities of evolutionary Socialism pursued with the sustained support of popular and, on the whole, well-satisfied bodies of parliamentary electors.

In Holland and Belgium, on the other hand, and also in Switzerland, the Socialists appeared to have reached a position of stalemate. After making considerable advances immediately after the first world war, the Socialist movements in these countries had settled down as the representatives of large bodies of minority opinion, but showed no sign of advancing towards the winning of majorities that would enable them to take the Government into their own hands, even possibly in coalition with other parties which they would need to treat as equal partners and not as subordinate allies. In both Holland and Belgium, the main obstacle to Socialist advance was the presence of confessional parties — in Belgium Catholic and in Holland both Catholic and Protestant — which were able to command substantial working-class support, but were in the last resort controlled not by their working-class adherents, but by conservative influences closely connected with the hierarchies of the Churches concerned. Trade Unions too were split in these countries between rival movements under Socialist and religious control ; and there appeared to be no way of uniting the working class either politically or economically, or, in the absence of such unity, of achieving parliamentary majorities.

In Spain, the 1930s saw the rise and fall of the Republic and the victory of the Fascists led by General Franco and the Falange. The Republic came into being as the successor to a dictatorship — that of Primo de Rivera — and gave place to another very much more severe and reactionary, after tearing itself to pieces by its internal dissensions. The Republican forces were at the beginning a most intractable coalition of diverse elements — from conservative Catholic constitutionalists, such as President Alcalá Zamora, through bourgeois liberals and anti-clerical radicals to a wide variety of Socialists, Syndicalists, Anarchists, and Communists — who held entirely irreconcilable views about the character of the new society they wanted to establish. Some were strong centralisers, some determined pluralists, and some out-and-out opponents of States in any form. Most, but not all, of the leaders were strongly anti-clerical, and involved themselves in a fight to the death against the inordinate privileges of the Catholic Church, which in Spain was utterly intolerant and monopolistic. Many of their supporters were natural rebels against any sort of authority — against Republican authority no less than against other forms. The mass strike had long been endemic in many parts of Spain, and the spontaneous peasant uprising in many others ; and the collapse of the dictatorship and the monarchy and the promise of a general 'new deal' afforded an evident opportunity for such manifestations on an unprecedented scale. There was in Spain no disciplined, closely knit party capable of riding the storm which accompanied the Republican Revolution ; and the groups that had joined forces to make it speedily fell asunder when it became necessary to decide how to act after their initial success. At first the disputing elements were, for the most part, able to come together in drawing up the new Republican Constitution of 1931, which set up a single-chamber legislature, the Cortes, elected by universal suffrage and secret ballot ; but even at this early stage the right-wing Republicans withdrew their support when the Church was attacked, and the anti-clerical Radicals soon joined them in opposition, while on the extreme left, Syndicalists and Anarchists, standing apart from the new State machine, gave no support to the successive Governments which attempted to ride the storm. An attempt was made to re-establish Republican unity through the Popular Front of 1935 ; and electorally this achieved signal success when in February 1936 the left wing won a clear majority in the Cortes over right and centre combined. By this time, however, no Government was able to exert any real authority. Strike followed strike in endless succession, and peasants, aggrieved at the lack of real progress under the Agrarian Law, which the centre had refused to operate with any zeal, more and more took matters into their own hands and seized the land without waiting for legal sanction. Meanwhile the right was making its preparations for counter-revolution; and, after its prospective leader, Sanjurgo, had been killed in an aeroplane crash on his way from Portugal, General Francisco Franco raised the standard of open revolt in Spanish Morocco in June 1936; and the civil war began.

In Europe, outside the countries discussed already, there is little to say about Socialism in the 1930s, for it hardly existed except on a small scale underground or among small groups of exiles who were more and more out of touch with the movements of opinion inside their countries; and neither the underground conspirators nor the exiles were in a position to make original contributions to Socialist thought — though that did not prevent them from becoming involved in bitter faction fights. In Yugoslavia, for example, after the royal-military *coup* of 1929, Socialism and Communism were both in effect persecuted and only underground activities were possible. The Social Democratic leaders, of whom Topalović was the best known, established themselves abroad, and most of the Communists also fled the country and attempted to direct the Party's work from Vienna. Even when Tito had taken over the leadership in 1937, the Yugoslav Communists could do little until the Axis occupation of the country during the second world war enabled them to put themselves at the head of a national resistance movement and thus prepared the way for the 'Liberation' of 1945.

Internationally, Socialism could make little impact during the 1930s. The only country in which it was strong was Palestine. In that country the Zionist movement was largely led by Socialists, and much of the economic development took Socialist forms, both in the collective agricultural settlements, the 'Kibbutzim', and in the Histadrut, the Trade Union organisation which ran a good deal of industry on co-operative lines. Elsewhere, the story was depressing. The Labour and Socialist International continued to meet in periodic Congresses and found plenty of occasions for protesting against the violent measures taken against Socialists in the States subject to Fascist or other forms of dictatorial government. But it was greatly weakened by the eclipse of Socialism in Germany and later in Austria, and was engaged in a continuous struggle with the Comintern, which had become more and more plainly an agency for the furtherance of Russian interests after Stalin had given up his hopes of World Revolution and gone over to the attempt to build 'Socialism in one country' on a foundation of intensive industrial planning and agricultural collectivisation. This shift did not of course mean that the Bolsheviks gave up their efforts to strengthen Communist Parties outside the Soviet Union; but it did mean that they gave less of their attention to fomenting revolution in the advanced capitalist countries and much more to embarrassing these countries by stimulating Communist activity in their colonial areas and dependencies and in countries subject to economic penetration by them — for example, India and other parts of Asia, and Latin America. In a number of these areas Communist Parties developed quite fast during the years of depression, which hit the less developed countries particularly hard by leading to a very sharp fall in the world prices of primary products, and thus seriously worsened their 'terms of trade' with the advanced countries. Democratic Socialism, as well as Communism, began under these conditions to strike roots in some under-developed countries in which it had hardly existed before as an organised movement — for example, in India, where its initial growth took place within the framework of the Congress Party as the main organ of the national struggle for independence. There were also small and tentative steps towards the establishment of Socialist movements in some of the Arab countries, notably Egypt; but such movements were still mainly among intellectuals, and had as yet little popular support. There was, however, a marked tendency for Communism to give greater attention to anti-imperialist tendencies outside Europe, and to do all it could to make things awkward for the imperialist powers, which were preoccupied with their domestic difficulties.

This is true especially of the earlier 'thirties. As the Nazi menace of world war became more insistent, the Russians were led gradually to change their immediate policy and to subordinate their activities directed against the great empire-ruling powers to the endeavour to build up, wherever possible, broadly based anti-Fascist movements in the shape of Popular Fronts. We shall see how they succeeded in this in France, re-unifying the Trade Union movement and giving their support to Léon Blum's left-wing Government — though they were soon led to attack it for its failure to come to the help of the Republicans in Spain. We shall see also how the movement for a Popular Front in Great Britain was abortive because of the Labour Party's entire refusal to respond to Communist blandishments, and how in Spain itself the Popular Front, after enabling the left to win an outstanding electoral victory in 1936, dissolved under the impact of rebellion and civil war. In inter-governmental affairs, the Soviet Union, with Maxim Litvinov as Foreign Commissar, did make for a while a real effort to come to terms with the Western powers for united resistance to Fascist aggression and to use the League of Nations as an instrument for this purpose; but this effort came to nothing in face of the policy of 'appeasement' followed by Chamberlain and Daladier and of the West's refusal to treat seriously the military talks at length arranged for between the Soviet and Western military commands. The outcome of these events was the sharp reversal of policy in the Nazi-Soviet Pact of 1939; but that extraordinary *volte-face* did not mean that the earlier attempts of the Russians to bring into being a common world front against Fascism were not genuine enough while they lasted, or that the entire blame for the Pact can be laid on the Russians. It is not really open to doubt that the attitude of the Western statesmen who went so far in 'appeasing' Hitler at Munich included a hope that he would turn his forces against the Russians rather than against the West, or that they were even prepared to encourage him in such a policy, which seemed to many of them the natural outcome of the Anti-Comintern Pact concluded between the Axis powers. The Nazi-Soviet Pact was no doubt a gross betrayal of the anti-Fascist faith which had been at the root of Communist world policy during the preceding years; but it was not without excuse in face of the attitude of the Western 'appeasers', hard morsel though it was for many Communists *in partibus infidelium* to swallow when it burst on them utterly unexpected and required them to eat their words or abandon their deeply rooted faith in the Soviet Union as the protagonist of the world Socialist cause. That most Western Communists did swallow the unappetising meal was due not only to the immensely strong hold the Soviet Union had over their loyalty, but also to well-justified suspicions of the intentions of the Western powers as long as the 'appeasers' remained at the helm of their States during the 'phoney' war of 1939–40. The fall of France and the evacuation of the British forces from Dunkirk rudely shook many of them up; and when, in 1941, Hitler tore up the Pact and launched his attack on the Soviet Union, they were happy to change sides again and to rally once more to the anti-Fascist crusade from which they had been rudely diverted less than two years earlier.

The second world war, however, was not, even after the Soviet Union had been forced into it, a war for Socialism. It was a struggle to the death against Fascist aggression, with the Western powers and the Soviet Union as reluctant and naturally mistrustful partners in resisting a common danger. While it lasted, the deeply rooted antagonism between the West and the Soviet Union was temporarily overshadowed by the imperative need for working together, but remained always in the background and was clearly destined to come to the front again as soon as the fighting ended.

To a limited extent, this situation existed in the 1930s, but it was then complicated — and the division of the world into two antagonistic *blocs* prevented — by the existence of Fascism as a major challenge to both Socialism and parliamentary government. Moreover, this challenge was then so direct and immediate as to distract attention away from the fundamental antagonism between Communism and parliamentary government, and to put some of the supporters of both these systems — though by no means all, or even enough — into a mind to join forces against it. Earlier, in the late 1920s and early 1930s, this antagonism had been much more apparent. During those years the Comintern, held firmly under Russian control, was instructed to follow the policy, throughout the world, of the 'United Front from below', or, to use the slogan that was everywhere brought into use, of 'Class against Class'. This meant in practice a continual attempt by Communists to attract the workers into a 'United Front' under Communist leadership and to draw them away from the Social Democratic leaders, who were denounced as lackeys and allies of the bourgeoisie and, increasingly, as 'Social Fascists'; for it became the tactics of Communism to deny any real difference between Social Democrats and Fascists and to accuse the Social Democrats of positive collaboration with the Fascists against the working class. Throughout the period of the Nazis mounting to power in Germany the Communists persisted in this attitude, rejecting all notion of common action with the Social Democrats against them.

Indeed, in all countries in which the parties of the Comintern were at all able to influence the course of events, the same broad policy was followed both while capitalism seemed prosperous and advancing and after it had plunged into the great crisis of the early 'thirties. Not until some time after the German working-class movement had been completely destroyed did the Comintern change its line by throwing over its 'Class against Class' slogan, and its policy of the 'United Front from below'. In Germany those leaders who advocated a change of policy before Stalin was ready for it — such as Remmele and Neumann — were driven out of the leadership, which was left in the hands of the ever-pliant Thaelmann; and there were similar purges in a number of other countries — in particular of Kilbom in Sweden and certain dissidents in the United States. Whatever excuse the policies of the Social Democratic right wing may have given them, the Communists undoubtedly followed, during the late 'twenties and early 'thirties, a disastrous policy that was largely responsible for Hitler's victory in Germany and for the weakening of working-class resistance throughout the world to the evil consequences of depression and to the rise of Fascist influence.

In the Soviet Union itself, it is clear that the coming to power of the Nazis in Germany and the evident unwillingness of the British and French Governments to do anything effective to check Nazi aggression in Europe had very serious effects on the development of the system of government and on the climate of Bolshevik opinion. It is beyond dispute that the great treason trials of the late 'thirties, in which so many Communist stalwarts fell victims to Stalin's absolutism, were closely linked to the fears inspired by the rise of Nazism and by the declaration of enmity to Communism by the Axis powers. It will always remain a moot point how far the degeneration of Communism in the 1930s was due to Stalin's personality, or how far Stalin was merely embodying a reaction which would have manifested itself in his absence under other leaders. It does, however, seem clear that Stalin's suspiciousness and lust for personal power were important factors influencing the methods actually employed in liquidating critics, or even potential critics, of the régime, and that, to that extent, what has been said since his death about the abuses of the 'cult of personality' has some real justification. It should not, however, be forgotten that intolerance and impatience of traditional moral restraints were from the first 'built-in' characteristics of Bolshevism, even in Lenin's day, or that they could find authority in many of Marx's own utterances, especially when he was writing frankly to his friend, Friedrich Engels. Stalin was by no means the inventor of these aspects of Communist behaviour, even if he did plenty to make their manifestations more and more extreme. Nor was the growth of economic inequality as a constituent of Soviet planning in the 1930s simply an outcome of Stalin's personal views. It is at least highly probable that Stakhanovism and the other economic incentives held out under the Five-Year Plans did achieve a more rapid advance in output than could have been achieved without them, and could on that account be held justifiable by anyone who regarded the success of the Plans as taking priority over everything else. Stalin's personal temperament doubtless made it easier for him to take this line, because it rendered him unaware of the values that were being sacrificed to the building up of Soviet power in face of a hostile world; but even those who had more appreciation of these values might take the view that they had to be sacrificed in the interest of sheer survival of the Soviet power. Stalin could not have behaved successfully, as he did, had his doings really and deeply shocked most of his colleagues in the Communist Party. All the evidence goes to show that they did not — perhaps because the full iniquity of his methods was not understood, but also perhaps even if much of it was. The conditions under which the collectivisation of agriculture was carried through left, indeed, no room for doubt about Communist ruthlessness and callousness in the matter of human suffering; and these qualities were plainly present, not only in Stalin, but also in most of the leaders of the Soviet Communist Party — and probably in most of its followers as well. That was hardly surprising, in view of the legacy of inhumanity which Communism had inherited from the Russian past—though it was terrible enough for all that. It is, however, difficult to believe that most of Stalin's collaborators were fully aware, or even conscious at all, of the extent to which the 'framing-up' of his opponents and the fabrication of evidence were being carried on in the treason trials, even if many of them must have known, or at least strongly suspected, that a great deal contained in the charges could not possibly be true. It was very hard for outsiders like myself to form any confident judgment on what was happening inside Russia in the 'thirties; and I doubt if it was much easier for the Russians themselves.

At all events, it seemed in the 'thirties to most Socialists — even to most who were strongly hostile to Communism — immensely important that the Russian Revolution should survive and the great adventure in Soviet planning succeed — the more so because there was so little to hearten us in events in the rest of the world, and so much to increase our fears in the almost unopposed advance of Fascism in Europe. However much Socialists were impelled to criticise both the Communist philosophy and its actual manifestations in the Soviet Union, most of them were not prepared to carry their criticism to the length of wishing to see the Soviet system overthrown by the forces that were actively ranged against it. Many who were deeply hostile to Communism nevertheless admired greatly the colossal achievements of the Soviet Union in laying the foundations of a highly advanced industrial economy, in providing for education on a scale unparalleled in any other country — or at all events in any still existing in almost primary poverty — and in developing social services at a highly advanced level. It was noted that these things had been done only at the expense of immediate consumption and had involved immense sufferings for the people; but many held that the sufferings were in the main an unavoidable condition of economic success, and that, when success had been achieved, compensation would speedily be given both in higher living standards and in greater personal freedom. In these circumstances there was a widespread disposition to turn a blind eye to the defects of what was felt to be an emerging Socialist economy of the highest promise; and the abuses were condoned, or simply ignored — much to the dismay of intransigent anti-Communists — especially exiles — who indefatigably denied that the Communists of the Soviet Union had any valid claim to rank as Socialists and were ready to make common cause with almost anyone who proclaimed his anti-Communism stridently enough. It was even less easy then than it is to-day to steer a reasonable course between out-and-out upholders of everything that was done in the Soviet Union and out-and-out enemies of Communism; but the scales were heavily weighted in the 'thirties on the side of the Soviet Union by the vehemence with which the Fascists denounced it, and most Socialists, at any rate on the left, felt a genuine admiration for its economic achievements.

Over and above this, a good many Socialists who were opposed to Communism felt some genuine admiration for the Communist Party and for the discipline which it exercised over its members. The devoted service given by Communists to their Party was contrasted with the laxity, or even indifference, with which the vast majority of Social Democrats treated the claims of their parties; and the difference was widely attributed to the fact that the Communists had a basic philosophy to guide and inspire their loyalty, whereas the Western Socialist Parties had no such bond of unity in a compelling common creed. This was not in fact quite true; for parliamentary Socialism had in reality its own philosophy, widely different from that of Communism and based rather on a continuation of the traditions of Western liberalism than on a denial of them. It was, however, true that Communism made immensely greater demands on its members than Social Democracy, and appeared, despite its fulminations against 'idealism', to be in practice much the more idealistic creed, and to inspire much greater practical devotion and readiness for personal sacrifice. In the countries in which the Communists were not in power, but were a disapproved-of or even a persecuted minority seeking to overturn the existing order, the profession of Communist faith did often involve serious personal sacrifices, which were willingly endured for the 'cause'; and in the Soviet Union itself, though doubtless Communism attracted many self-seekers and lovers of personal power, there was still a large body of sheer devotion on which the leaders could draw, and much genuine service was rendered out of sheer enthusiasm for the new society that men believed was being brought painfully to birth. Even if, by the 'thirties, the Communist Party in the Soviet Union had been vastly bureaucratised — as I feel sure it had — and had shed a great deal of its inner democracy under Stalin's manipulative régime, the need to build up the Soviet power for resistance to Fascism still seemed to many pre-eminent, and inspired genuine sentiments of willing acceptance of centralised party control.

Despite all the iniquities that were practised in the 'thirties by Stalin and his henchmen — despite the ruthlessness of agricultural collectivisation and the denial of the very elements of justice to the so-called *kulaks*, and despite the utter immorality of the processes by which Stalin 'framed-up' his opponents, real or imagined, despite the fantastic lengths to which denunciations of 'Trotskyism' were carried and Trotsky himself was pursued — despite all these things, I believe those who continued to rally to the defence of the Soviet Union against its enemies to have been essentially in the right. No doubt, Hitler and Stalin were alike in being totalitarian autocrats avid above all else for power and entirely unscrupulous about means. Nevertheless, there was between them the great difference that they sought power in pursuit of different ends — Hitler in pursuit of an aggressive nationalism bent on conquering the world in the interest of an allegedly superior race (an ambition only to be realised by victory in aggressive war), and Stalin in pursuit of a world-wide revolt of the exploited and repressed which ranged the Soviet Union basically on the right side in world affairs, despite all the malpractices involved in pursuing it. It will be objected to this view that in fact Stalin, in the 1930s, was pursuing not World Revolution but the national interests of the Soviet Union; and this is largely true. Nevertheless, the Soviet Union, with all its perversions, remained in the 'thirties a real bastion of Socialism against Fascism, and vastly to be preferred despite its evident backwardness in the amenities of civilised living. It was reasonable to expect that, if the Fascist threat to the Soviet Union's very existence could be removed and the need to sacrifice living standards for the sake of security ceased to be present, the severity of Soviet dictatorship would be gradually reduced and, under popular pressure, personal freedom gradually enlarged. This did not necessarily mean that in course of time the Soviet Union would go over to the institutions of liberal democracy as understood in the West; but it was reasonable to expect that the Russians would in due course work out for themselves a way of living less incompatible with Western conceptions than their existing form of one-party dictatorship. The Soviet State might no doubt take an uncomfortably long time to 'wither away', as had been promised; but surely it would begin to 'wither' when once the pressure upon it had been definitely relieved by the elimination of Fascism.

At all events, that was what I hoped and expected, in common with many other observers of world affairs during the troubled 'thirties; and I think it was a reasonable hope. Two decades later, I continue to entertain the same hope and believe there are some signs of its realisation in a perceptible relaxation of the control over expression of opinion, as well as in the giving of greater weight to the claims of consumers. No doubt, the Soviet leadership is still pretty tough, and intensely suspicious of the West; but has it not the right to be suspicious, in face of the record of American policy and of West European submission to American insistence? Having taken, almost by compulsion, a tough line, has the Soviet Union been offered any sufficient inducement to modify it in recent years? Surely not.

I wish, however, in this chapter to concern myself mainly with the 1930s rather than with the present day. What I am urging is that, in the 'thirties, it was right for Western Socialists, despite Stalin's evil-doings, to be on the side of the Soviet Union against its enemies, and to be ready to make common cause with it against Fascist aggression. Had this been done, and had Hitler been forced from the outset to fight a war on two fronts instead of one, the West would in all probability never have had to undergo the disaster of 1940, and the Nazi defeat would have been from the outset assured. As matters stood politically in the West in 1938–9, the left was too weak to insist on such common action even if it had been united in working for it — which it was not. There were divided Socialist counsels in Western Europe as well as in the Soviet Union, and the policy of 'appeasement' brought Western

Europe to the very brink of irreparable disaster before it was
fully given up and Great Britain, under new leadership, left to
fight on for a time almost alone — to be saved, in the event, by
two things, the entry of the United States into the war and
Hitler's insane onslaught on the Soviet Union. These two
things between them availed to destroy Nazism, but not to
achieve, save for that limited purpose, any accommodation
between the Soviet Union and the West: so that, nearly
twenty years later, the world remains a prey to 'cold war' and
is deterred from a new world war only by the prodigious pace
at which the power to destroy has outrun every other human
achievement and become a threat to the very survival of the
human race.

CHAPTER II

THE ECLIPSE OF SOCIALISM IN GERMANY

I N the fourth volume of this History, I attempted to delineate
the history of the Weimar Republic up to the really serious
onset of the world depression in 1931, and to describe the
continuous erosion of the democratic elements in Germany by
the growing predominance of the military commanders and the
rising tide of nationalist feeling. No doubt there was, from
1924 onwards, a rapid economic recovery, made possible by
large borrowings of capital, chiefly from the United States.
With the currency stabilised under the Dawes Plan and the
more fantastic Allied claims for reparations in practice given up,
Germany became for a few years an attractive field for the
investment of foreign capital ; and as long as capital flowed in
on a sufficient scale, the modified, but still quite unrealistic,
claims for reparations could be met, not out of any real surplus,
but out of the borrowed money. In reality the sums paid out
in reparations by the Germans were paid by American investors ;
and continued payment depended absolutely on the continued
in-flow of foreign funds. This, however, was not obvious while
the flow continued : the subscribers to the Dawes Loan and
to other loans to Germany duly received their interest and the
instalments of reparations due under the Dawes Plan were
paid. German production and exports expanded fast ; and
wages, very low at the outset, gradually rose under Trade
Union pressure. There were confident predictions that the
worst was over, and that Germany was on the high-road to
lasting economic recovery.

This situation continued until 1928, when the first signs
of real instability became evident. The Americans, in the
pursuit of a domestic boom of their own, began to find foreign
investment less attractive than speculation at home, and the
flow of American funds to Germany slackened off and presently
ceased almost entirely. By the end of 1928 a reverse current

had set in, as American institutions began actually to withdraw short-term funds lent to the Germans, in order to employ them in gaining speculative profits at home. The Germans, who had been using these short-term loans largely for the provision of longer-term credits to their trade customers in Europe, found themselves without the means of repaying the borrowed money at short notice, and made every possible effort to secure loans elsewhere to fill the gap. But other countries were also suffering from shortage of funds due to the export of money by their own financiers eager to share in the profits of the American boom ; and though Germany did secure substantial loans from Great Britain and elsewhere, the sums thus borrowed also became locked up and could not be paid back when the creditors began to press for repayment. Germany's immediate troubles thus arose, not out of a depression in the United States, but out of a speculative boom there which was raising security prices out of all relation to well-founded expectations of business earnings.

The German financial situation was already very precarious when, in the autumn of 1929, the American stock market boom came to an abrupt end, and a sharp fall in security prices set hosts of unwary speculators scrambling for liquid funds wherewith to meet their losses. The change from boom to depression in the United States, far from easing the difficulties of Germany or of other European countries, greatly increased them by leading to a veritable scramble to recall money invested abroad. For a while, in 1930, absolute crisis was stalled off ; and during the interval the terms for reparation payments were again revised at the Hague, and a further attempt was made to stabilise the German economy with the aid of the loan that formed part of the Young Plan. The Young terms, however, though they further scaled down the total sum to be exacted from the Germans, were still entirely unrealistic except on the assumption of continued expansion, at well-maintained prices, in the demand for German exports ; whereas this demand was clearly being seriously curtailed by the growing balance of payments difficulties of the purchasing countries. By the summer of 1931 the great world depression had fairly set in. The collapse of the Credit Anstalt in Austria had given the signal of impending disaster in European finances ; the British Labour Government was facing a financial crisis which drove it ignominiously from office in August; and the Americans themselves were gradually waking up to the magnitude of the economic disaster which faced so many of them as the penalty of the speculative excesses of the preceding years.

At the outset, the calamity fell most heavily of all on the Germans, because they had no reserves to fall back on and were faced with an accumulation of claims which it was utterly impossible for them to meet. Between 1924 and 1929 German industry had been rapidly reconstructed with new instruments of production that could produce at remarkably low costs as long as they were fully employed, but whose costs of production rose sharply when sales fell off. Moreover, the basis of German export industry was narrow, and depended mainly on a high level of demand for capital goods, especially steel, engineering, electrical, and chemical products; and these were for the most part goods that could be sold only by giving extended credits, and were in any case among the most exposed to constriction of demand in times of economic depression. The Germans found themselves faced with rapidly mounting unemployment as well as with a sheer inability to meet their foreign debts.

Attempts were made in these circumstances to tide over the German economy by a succession of temporary expedients. In the spring of 1931 the Hoover Moratorium suspended reparation payments for a year, but still required Germany to find the interest on the Dawes and Young loans. During the ensuing months a series of Standstill Agreements allowed a moratorium on repayments of Germany's short-term debts. But these arrangements, which had to be renewed when they expired a year later, were entirely inadequate to deal with the situation: nor did the Lausanne Agreement of 1932, which scaled down the Allies' claims to reparations to a fraction of what they had been even in 1930, and also allowed a complete moratorium on reparation payments for the next four years, go nearly to the root of the matter — though, by the time it was made, a great many people at length realised that payment of reparations was most unlikely ever to be resumed. Nothing that was done checked the sharp fall of German exports, or prevented unemployment inside Germany from assuming terrifying proportions, or the wages of those still in work from being drastically driven down.

These heavy economic blows, falling on a country which was already in a condition of great political instability, before long brought the Weimar Republic to an ignominious end and carried the Nazis to complete power. For a time, the reactionary Catholic politician, Brüning, attempted to ride the storm by drastic measures of deflation and restrictions on imports, which involved a rapid fall in German standards of living — a fall which the Social Democrats and the Trade Unions saw no way to resist. The political consequence of the Brüning régime was a rapid decline in the following of the parties of the centre — among whom the Social Democrats must be numbered — and a rapid rise in the support given to the extremists — Communists on one side and Nazis and Nationalists on the other. In the General Election of 1928 the Nazis had been able to return only 12 members to the Reichstag: in July 1932 they returned 230, and polled $13\frac{3}{4}$ million votes. True, in the swiftly ensuing election of November 1932 their poll fell to $11\frac{3}{4}$ million and their total of elected members to 196; and many at that time believed that Nazism had passed its zenith, and would speedily decline. But two months later, in February 1933, when Hitler had already become Chancellor despite the November setback, the Nazi poll rose to $17\frac{1}{4}$ million, and, with the Communists already driven out of the Reichstag, they had a clear majority in conjunction with their 52 Nationalist allies.

The coalition Government headed by the Social Democrats had fallen from office in March 1930, when the Social Democrats' partners in it demanded drastic curtailments of unemployment benefits and of the social services. The Brüning Government, which replaced it, lasted until June 1932, when it was dismissed in favour of a right-wing Nationalist Ministry headed by von Papen. Von Papen then stayed in office, becoming more and more unpopular, till December 1932, and was then replaced by von Schleicher, also a member of the old right wing, who made a brief attempt to conciliate the Trade Unions, but was driven out by President Hindenburg the following month, and replaced by Hitler, whom the President compelled to enter into coalition with the Nationalists and to accept von

Papen as Vice-Chancellor. In practice, however, the coalition was never real, and complete power fell at once into Nazi hands. Very soon, the Nationalist leader, Hugenberg, was forced to resign, and his Nationalist Party forcibly absorbed into the Nazi Party. Under the Nazis, the Social Democratic Party was completely destroyed, and the free Trade Union movement shared its fate, the workers being forcibly enrolled in a new 'Labour Front' under Nazi leadership and control. The Communist Party had already been banned and driven underground; and the bourgeois parties were also ruthlessly liquidated. The Nazis set out, with their policy of *Gleichschaltung*, to bring every influential organisation in German society under Nazi control, and to remove every possible point of focus for opposition. The Social Democratic leaders — those who were not caught and liquidated — fled abroad, and attempted to establish in Prague a headquarters for propaganda in Germany, but were unable to carry on to any effect. Thousands of Socialists and Trade Unionists and even of bourgeois liberals were killed or beaten up and confined in concentration camps, where they were treated with the utmost brutality. The Churches, both Protestant and Catholic, were also vehemently attacked, except where they made complete submission. All Germany passed speedily under a dictatorship much more brutal and complete than that of Fascist Italy.

Moreover, German Nazism was animated through and through by sentiments that rendered it prodigiously dangerous to the rest of the world. In its exaltation of sheer force and of the racial superiority of the German people it was quite unable to accept as a fact that the German armies had met with defeat in the field, and it resorted to the myth of the 'stab in the back', in which the military *débâcle* was explained away as the consequence of a betrayal of the soldiers by civilians who had either lost their nerve or been deliberate traitors to the German cause. Anyone who, in the hour of defeat, had accepted the Peace of Versailles, usually called the Versailles *Diktat*, or had subsequently accepted the policy of 'fulfilment' under the Dawes Plan, was denounced as a traitor; and the entire Weimar Republic was regarded as embodying this contemptible attitude of submission and as fundamentally contrary to the requirements of the German people for a régime embodying their sense of national superiority and self-assertion. Every suffering experienced by any loyal German, every obstacle found in the way of any such German's ability to achieve a satisfying way of life, every frustration, whatever its nature, was attributed to the machinations of evil men who had made themselves masters of German society and were using their power for its abasement or disruption. The jobless were told that their lack of the means to earn a decent living was due to the malpractices of the enemies of the people, who were feathering their own nests at its expense. Bankers were denounced for refusing credit in the name of pursuing monetary stability; shopkeepers and trade associations for conspiring to overcharge the consumers; and these onslaughts were reinforced by identifying the offenders with alien elements that had forced their way into key positions in the German economy — above all others, Jews, who were said to dominate the higher fields of finance and commerce and to be using their influence deliberately to ruin and degrade the honest, Nordic elements that truly constituted the German people. Quite often, these denunciations of the persons and groups holding power in the Weimar Republic had on the surface a strongly radical tone, which did in fact alarm many capitalists and many relatively comfortably placed members of the middle classes. But within this was contained a furious rancour against the working-class movement, which was denounced for its common pacifism and its devotion to forms of democratic parliament-arianism incompatible with the claims of militant nationalism and with devotion to the reassertion of German rights. Anti-semitism had deep roots in German society long before the Nazis converted it into a basic principle of action and made the possession of Jewish blood a sufficient reason for the denial of even the most elementary claims of common humanity.

The original programme of the Nazi Party, drawn up in 1920 mainly by the engineer, Gottfried Feder, opened, as the first of its Twenty-four Points, with a demand for 'the union of all Germans in a Pan-German State (*Grossdeutschland*), in accordance with the right of all peoples to self-determination'. It was not explained whether this *Grossdeutschland* was to include areas in which Germans formed only a minority of the population; but the proposal to unite *all* Germans seems to imply this, even if the reference to self-determination for all peoples seems to deny it. In practice, of course, the Nazis never troubled about the rights of anyone who was not a German. The second point, however, demanded no more than that the German people should have 'equal rights with those of other nations', and that the Treaties of Versailles and St. Germain should be abrogated. The third point demanded *Lebensraum* for the maintenance of the German people and for the settlement of its surplus population — thus reasserting Germany's colonial claims.

So far the programme was simply ultra-nationalist. It went on, in the fourth point, to lay down that only persons of German blood could be citizens of the German State, or could be regarded as fellow-countrymen, and to draw the significant explicit corollary that 'no Jew can be regarded as a fellow-countryman'. Thus, anti-semitism was proclaimed from the outset as an essential part of the Nazi creed, no other kind of non-German being singled out for mention. The programme then turned in more general terms to the relations between Germans and non-Germans in the proposed Pan-German society. Point Five laid down that non-Germans could live in this State only as aliens and subject to special alien laws. Point Six confined voting rights to citizens (*i.e.* Germans), and excluded all non-Germans from holding any public office, whether central, regional, or municipal. It also declared opposition to 'the democratising parliamentary administration whereby posts go by party favour without regard to character or capacity'.

Next came, in Point Seven, the demand that 'the States should undertake to ensure that every citizen has a fair chance of living decently and of ensuring his livelihood' — with the significant rider that 'if it proves impossible to provide sustenance for the whole population, aliens must be expelled from the State'. Point Eight went on to demand not only the entire prohibition of any further immigration of non-Germans, but also the expulsion of all aliens who had entered Germany since August 1914. Then came, in Point Nine, the demand that rights and duties shall be equal for all citizens, and, in Point Ten, the proclamation that work, mental or physical, is 'the first duty of every citizen', and that no citizen shall carry on any work that is deleterious to the community, but shall contribute to the benefit of all.

These ten Points form a kind of general preamble to the more particular demands that followed. The first of these, contained in Point Eleven, is sufficiently sweeping. It demanded categorically the abolition of all unearned incomes. Then came, in Point Twelve, a demand for the confiscation 'down to the last farthing' of all gains from war profiteering, coupled with the declaration that all personal gains resulting from the war must be regarded as treason to the nation. Point Thirteen demanded that the State should take over all trusts, and Point Fourteen that the State should share in the profits of all large industries. Point Fifteen called for very greatly increased State pensions for the aged.

Next came, in Point Sixteen, a demand for the 'creation and maintenance of a sound middle class', followed by an explicit demand that the large stores should be communalised and rented chiefly to small traders, and that in all contracts for public supplies preference should be given to small traders. Point Seventeen turned to agrarian reform, demanding the expropriation without compensation of any land needed for national purposes, the abolition of ground rents, and the prevention of all speculation in land. Point Eighteen was very general : it demanded 'relentless measures against all who work to the detriment of the public weal', and punishment of death for all 'traitors, usurers, profiteers, etc.', regardless of race or creed. Point Nineteen demanded the supersession of Roman Law, 'which serves a materialist ordering of the world', by German Common Law.

Point Twenty dealt with education and culture. It laid down that 'in order to make it possible for every capable and industrious German to obtain higher education and therewith the opportunity of rising to important posts, the State shall thoroughly organise the entire cultural system of the nation'. The curricula of all educational institutions were to be arranged 'in accordance with the requirements of practical life'. The 'conception of the State Idea' was to be inculcated in the schools from the very beginning. Specially talented children of poor parents were to be educated at the State's expense.

Next, Point Twenty-one laid on the State the duty of raising the nation's health standards by providing maternity welfare centres, by prohibiting child labour, by introducing compulsory games and gymnastics, and by the greatest possible encouragement of all associations concerned with the physical welfare of the young.

Next came, in Point Twenty-two, the demand that the professional army be abolished and replaced by a 'national army'. This was followed, in Point Twenty-three, by a series of demands dealing with the Press. Action was to be taken against all who used the Press to propagate and disseminate what they knew to be 'political lies'. All editors and journalists of newspapers published in German must be German citizens. Non-German newspapers could be published only with State authority and must not be in German. No non-German was to be allowed to have any financial interest in, or influence on, any German newspaper. Journals transgressing against the common weal were to be suppressed. Legal action was to be taken against 'any tendency in art or literature having a disruptive effect on the life of the people', and any organisation fostering such tendencies was to be dissolved.

Point Twenty-four dealt with religion. It demanded freedom for all religious creeds in the State, 'as far as they do not endanger its existence or offend against the moral or ethical sense of the Germanic race'. It then stated that the Nazi Party 'represents the standpoint of positive Christianity without binding itself to any particular confession', and went on to declare the Party's opposition to 'the Jewish materialist spirit both within and without' and to declare that lasting recovery of the nation could be achieved only from within, on the principle 'the Good of the State before the Good of the Individual'.

Finally, in order to bring about what had been demanded in all these Points, Point Twenty-five called for 'the creation of a strong central authority in the State, and for the unconditional control by the central political Parliament of the entire State and of all its organisations'. It then demanded the formation of professional committees and of committees representing the several estates of the realm, to ensure that the laws promulgated by the central authorities are carried out in the individual States of the Union. In the closing words of the Programme, the leaders of the Party undertook to promote its execution 'at all costs, if necessary, at the sacrifice of their lives'.

This programme, which Hitler six years later — in 1926 — declared unalterable — though it was in fact greatly altered when the Nazis came to power — has four outstanding characteristics. It is Pan-German, anti-semitic, authoritarian, and petit-bourgeois. Negatively, what is most notable in it is the absence of any reference to a 'Leader' as having any special place in either formulating it or carrying it into effect. It dates, in fact, from a period before Hitler had established himself as *the* Leader, and before the very conception of a single charismatic leader had come to be entertained. It was the collective product of a group, none of whom except Hitler was destined to play a major part in the full development of Nazism ; and the very manner of its drafting relates it clearly to the situation that existed in Germany during the years immediately after 1918 — years of extreme economic and social dislocation, or widespread unemployment, and of unstable currency and extravagant Allied demands for reparations which it was utterly beyond Germany's power to meet. At its very root was aggressive Pan-German nationalism ; but it was poles apart from the old-style aristocratic Nationalism of the former ruling class and, in its social and economic aspects, vehemently anti-capitalist as well as anti-Socialist. Its emphasis on the claims of the small shopkeeper — much more definite than its espousal of the cause of the peasants — brings out its essential petit-bourgeois character, and is clearly linked with its absolute anti-semitism by the fact of Jewish pre-eminence in commercial affairs. Finally, in its general outlook it is strongly Statist, centralising and authoritarian, and contains the foundations of the policy of *Gleichschaltung* which the Nazis set out to carry through when they came to power. It is Socialist, if at all, only in the sense of demanding the entire subordination of the individual to the claims of the State and in proclaiming the State's responsibility for ordering and planning the conduct of economic as well as of social and political affairs. Subject to this overriding principle it clearly contemplates the continuance of private enterprise as the main basis of economic action ;

but at the same time it declares war on trusts and large concentrations of capital — though it does not demand the breaking-up of large-scale industry, but only public participation in its profits. It is anti-landlord and requires the complete disappearance of all forms of unearned income; but it does not even declare specifically for the break-up of great estates, though it does for the abolition of ground-rents. Its aim is not to put back the system that had been overthrown in the Revolution of 1918, but to create a new Germany in which power would be in the hands of a German people inspired by an intense fervour of nationalism and a vehement aggressiveness against foreigners of all sorts — most of all against Jews, and next to them against other foreign settlers — chiefly Slavs — in territories claimed as falling within the boundaries of the 'Great German' State. Nazism, whatever may have been its later developments, assuredly did not begin as a last throw of capitalism against the rising tide of Socialism, but as an attempt of middle-class Nationalist elements to throw off the consequences of Germany's defeat in war and to rebuild the power of the German nation on the basis of a strongly centralised and authoritarian one-party State.

Nazism was, however, from the very outset the bitter antagonist of the Socialist and working-class movement. The Nazis hated Socialism and the Trade Unions associated with it for a variety of compelling reasons. One of these was that, in Nazi eyes, even the Majority Socialists were tainted with internationalism and pacifism and rejected the racialist ideas that were the most fundamental unifying force behind the Nazi movement. Not a few Jews held important positions in the Socialist movement; and it was easy to represent them as having much more influence in it than they actually possessed — even, indeed, as controlling it through a secret conspiracy inspired by the most sinister purposes.

Secondly, German Communism was definitely part of a movement which was under Slav inspiration and leadership and accepted orders from Moscow as the determinants of its policy. These orders were no doubt finally issued not by the Soviet Government or the Soviet Communist Party but by the Comintern, which was in form a supra-national representative of the working class throughout the world. This, however, would not have made it any more acceptable to the Nazis, whose gospel was aggressive German nationalism; and in practice, as everyone knew, the control of the Comintern was in the hands of the Russians and its policy settled in accordance with the interests of the Soviet Union. True, the German Communists and the Nazis had at times worked together in hostility to the Weimar Republic, and had been told to do so by the Comintern, which held the mistaken belief that the Nazis, in overthrowing the Republic, would unwittingly be preparing the way for the Communist Revolution. Such co-operation, however, could not affect the fundamentally irreconcilable opposition between Nazism and Communism; and the German Communists derived less than no profit from their readiness to join forces with the Nazis against the Weimar Republic. The Social Democrats were of course in a quite different position in this respect: they were deeply hostile to the Communists and were the foremost defenders of the Republic, even when it was governed by their declared enemies, such as Brüning and von Papen. But, in Hitler's eyes, they too were accursed Marxists, exponents of 'Jewish' materialism and enemies of the national spirit, and accordingly fit only to be rooted out equally with their Communist opponents. Their greatest sin was that they were levellers, opponents of the claims both of private property and of the legitimate personal ambitions of good militant Germans to rise to positions of social superiority by asserting their quality in the service of the national spirit. German Social Democracy, despite all its confusions in its attempts to defend the Weimar Republic, was in the Nazi view the party of poltroons and supporters of mediocrity against the natural self-assertiveness and self-reliance of the Nordic spirit, and was thus the greatest obstacle to national revival and to successful defiance of the forces that were holding Germany down. It could not, indeed, be pilloried equally with Communism as a movement under alien control; but it was no less marked out for destruction and, as far as possible, identified with Communism as no better than another exponent of the Marxian anti-national standpoint.

In dealing with the Trade Unions the Nazis felt it needful to be more circumspect, until political power passed definitely into their hands. While eager to build up a following among the industrial workers, the Nazis, throughout their years of struggle for power, stopped short of any attempt to set up Trade Unions of their own in rivalry with the predominantly Socialist 'Free' Trade Unions or with the smaller Christian Trade Unions chiefly associated with the Catholic Centre Party. In 1928 they had indeed established a body called N.S.B.O. (National Socialist Industrial Cell Organisation) to act as a recruiting agent for their party in the factories and work-places; and this body, reorganised in 1931 under the leadership of Reinhold Machow, soon had its cells in most factories and achieved a considerable membership, but was precluded from attempting to play any part in wage-bargaining, or from usurping other ordinary Trade Union functions. It acted solely as a political agency for enlisting working-class support for Nazism and for procuring recruits for the Nazis' private brownshirt army, the S.A. The Trade Unions were thus left to carry on their collective bargaining activities without the Nazis, as a party, taking sides — though this attitude led to considerable dissensions among the Nazi leaders. Gregor Strasser, in particular, who held high office in the Berlin area, and stood on the left wing of the Nazi movement in social and economic policy, wished the Party to take a definitely anti-capitalist line and would have liked it to make a definite bid for Trade Union support. Strasser also wished in the later months of 1932, when Nazi influence appeared to be rapidly waning after its great advance earlier in the year, to come to terms with General von Schleicher and the Trade Unions against the socially reactionary forces grouped behind von Papen, in the hope that such an alliance would enable the Nazis to win a sufficient share of power in a coalition under Schleicher as Chancellor to carry out a large part of their programme on anti-capitalist lines. But the outcome of Strasser's revolt was that early in December 1932 he was compelled to resign from all his offices in the Nazi Party in face of Hitler's determined opposition to his policy. This happened at a moment when Hitler, who was determined to win power only by constitutional means, was holding back the strong pressure of many of his supporters for the seizure of power by a forcible *coup d'état*, and was thought by many of them to be letting his chance slip. The Nazis, in July 1932, had won a resounding election victory that gave them 230 Reichstag seats out of a total of 607 — nearly two-fifths of the total; and there had been negotiations between Hitler and President Hindenburg in which the President had consented to take Hitler into the Government as Vice-Chancellor under von Papen — an offer which had been angrily and scornfully rejected. Von Papen had carried on as Chancellor, though he was in a hopeless minority in the new Reichstag, of which the Nazi, Hermann Göring, became President. Von Papen, faced with defeat in the Reichstag, used the President's authority to dissolve it; and new elections took place at the beginning of November. At these elections the Nazis lost more than two million votes, and fell from 230 seats to 197, whereas the Communists rose from 89 to 100 and the aristocratic Nationalists from 37 to 51. The Social Democrats fell from 133 to 121, and the Centre Party from 97 to 89. Thus the extreme Right and the extreme Left both gained at the expense both of the middle parties and of the Nazis. Moreover, during the ensuing weeks the Nazis lost still more heavily in the local elections for the State Diets, and appeared to be losing their influence at an increasing rate. These were the circumstances that led up to the fall of von Papen, who was hated by the Centre as well as by the Nazis, and to the elevation of General von Schleicher to the post of Chancellor, though he had no possibility of being able to govern the country unless he could secure some measure of both Nazi and Centre support. There followed a welter of intrigue. Gregor Strasser, who wished to come to terms with Schleicher, was utterly defeated inside the Nazi Party and driven out of all his offices. Schleicher, in his attempt to find a compromise way out of Germany's economic difficulties, antagonised Hindenburg and the Nationalists by proposing agrarian reforms involving some redistribution of the great estates of Eastern Germany; and Hindenburg refused his request for a further dissolution of the Reichstag, to be followed by a new election. The extreme Nationalists wanted the Reichstag to be dissolved, but no elections to be held — in other words, they wanted a *coup* that would set up a presidential dictatorship and do away with the Weimar Constitution. Hindenburg, deeply mistrustful of Hitler, wanted to bring von Papen back as Chancellor, but realised that there could be no sufficient basis for such a Government without Nazi support, and tried again to persuade Hitler to become Vice-Chancellor in a von Papen Cabinet in which he would be without effective power. Hitler stood out for the Chancellorship, but refused to make any attempt to seize power by force. Hindenburg, urging the need for a Ministry of 'Concentration', based on the support of a Reichstag majority, refused to accept Hitler as Chancellor in his capacity as Party leader. A complete impasse seemed to have been reached.

A way out was found when Hitler came to an agreement with the leaders of the Nationalist and Centre Parties and with von Papen that he should be made Chancellor and von Papen Vice-Chancellor in a Coalition Government in which the Nazis would be definitely in a minority. On these terms Hindenburg was induced to accept Hitler as Chancellor, stating definitely that he was appointing him, not as the leader of the Nazis, but as the representative of a concentration of national opinion. In doing this, both Hindenburg and the leaders of the other parties were under the most mistaken impression that they would be able to keep the Nazis under control and that Hitler himself was pledged not to use his office for party ends. The Nazi leader was indeed forced to accept von Papen as Prussian Prime Minister as well as Vice-Chancellor; but the Nazi, Frick, became Reich Minister of the Interior and Göring held the corresponding position in Prussia. The Nationalist Hugenberg held two Ministries — Trade and Agriculture — both in the Reich and in Prussia: the Conservative, Baron von Neurath, remained as Foreign Minister; and the other Cabinet posts were mostly given to friends and supporters of Hindenburg and von Papen. The old-style reactionaries were confident that they had outmanœuvred Hitler and consolidated their own power.

They were speedily undeceived. Göring, from his point of vantage at the Prussian Ministry of the Interior, immediately set to work to displace all high police officials who were not reliable from the Nazi standpoint, and to replace them with Party stalwarts. He also proceeded to supplement the police forces by mass enrolment of special constables, drawn mainly from the S.A. and S.S., and to issue a series of orders which were in effect incitements to police violence, including assurances that they would receive full support for the most ruthless measures against 'enemies of the State' and especially against Communists. 'Police officials who make use of firearms in the execution of their duty can count on every support regardless of the consequences of their action', declared Göring's order of February 17th, 1933. Thereafter, there was practically no limit to the violence that could be offered, not only to Communists, but also to Social Democrats and even to moderate bourgeois opponents of the Nazi creed. The police were given virtually unlimited power to break up and disperse meetings; and the Press was subjected to strict control which prevented more than the mildest criticisms of Nazi policy. Many people were killed, and very many more beaten up by S.S. or S.A. thugs, either enrolled as policemen or without hindrance from the police. The Communists attempted to call a general strike, which was easily and ruthlessly put down. Even Centre Party meetings were broken up after Hitler had rejected the Centre's demands for a measure of constitutional freedom.

To the accompaniment of this systematic campaign of violence an immense electoral effort was put forth in the hope of winning a majority in the new Reichstag to be chosen early in March. When the election was over, the Nazis had won 288 seats out of 647, and were thus considerably stronger than in the July of 1932 — their previous period of success — but still some way short of a clear majority. There were, however, 52 Nationalists; and the two Parties between them had a clear majority. The Social Democrats, despite the terrorism practised at their expense, were still able to return 120 members, as compared with 133 in July and 121 in November 1932, and the Communists 81, as compared with 89 and 100 at the two previous elections. The Centre Party had 73, as compared with 75 and 70 : all the remaining Parties had between them a mere 14 seats. The once powerful People's Party — Stresemann's — had shrunk to as few as two seats. Moreover, the Communists, despite their relative success in face of bitter persecution, were in effect shut out from all share in the new Parliament. Most of their representatives were speedily gaoled or in concentration camps set up under Göring's new dispensation ; and a substantial number of Social Democrats shared their fate. These exclusions gave the Nazis the clear majority the electors had denied them, and enabled them to ride roughshod over their nominal partners in the Government coalition. They proceeded to introduce into the Reichstag a Bill of Authorisation which in effect abrogated most of the Weimar Constitution and authorised the Government to make binding laws without the Reichstag's endorsement, thus in effect abolishing even the semblance of parliamentary government. This measure was duly passed by 441 votes against 94 votes of the Social Democrats — the Centre and the lesser Parties as well as the Nationalists voting with the Nazis in its support.

The Communist Party had been declared illegal in February, before the election was held, though voters were allowed, if they desired, to vote for its candidates at the March election. After its outlawing, what was left of it went underground, some of its leaders being arrested and put in concentration camps, while others fled abroad and a few remained to carry on their work as fugitives from Nazi justice. The Social Democrats, except those who were arrested or murdered, were allowed, as we saw, to take their seats in the new Reichstag; and the Party, though subject to violent persecution, kept its legal existence for a short time. It made, indeed, desperate efforts to accommodate itself to Nazi rule, in the hope of being able to preserve its property and organisation. Otto Wels, its leader, resigned his position in the Labour and Socialist International when that body strongly denounced the Nazi régime; and in April the Party elected a new Central Committee, excluding those of its leaders who had already escaped abroad. This half-surrender was of no avail. On May 10th Göring occupied the buildings and newspaper offices of the Party and confiscated its funds. In spite of this, the Social Democrats, a week later, appeared in the Reichstag and voted in favour of Hitler's declaration on foreign policy, only to be rewarded, the following month, by a decree of Frick's prohibiting all further activity by their Party, excluding its members from all parliaments and local government bodies, and finally closing all its premises and suppressing its newspapers and publishing offices. By that time many more of its leaders had fled abroad or been arrested, and Otto Wels and his supporters had set up a party headquarters in exile at Prague.

Speaking generally, the Nazis were able to establish their new order almost without resistance, so completely were the means of force in their hands, and so ruthlessly were they applied by the use both of legalised violence and of unlawful violence which went wholly unsuppressed. The Social Democrats showed at the outset some personal courage in attending the Reichstag and voting against the Authorisation Bill; but they made no attempt to oppose force with force and allowed their party 'army', the Reichsbanner, to be destroyed without any attempt to use it against the Nazi storm troops. No doubt, any such attempt would have been doomed to defeat, even if Communists and Social Democrats had sunk their differences and acted together in defence of the Republic — which neither party was at all disposed to do. The last moment at which such resistance would have stood even the smallest chance of success was when von Papen drove out the Social Democratic Government of Prussia in July 1932; and even then the prospect of victory would have been very small. The Reichsbanner, though fairly numerous, was almost without arms; and the Communists had shown themselves bitterly hostile to the Prussian Social Democrats, who, besides, lacked a majority in the Prussian Diet, and had stayed in office only because there was no majority capable of uniting against them. The S.A. — and still more the S.S. — were relatively well armed; and, apart from this, the well-armed Reichswehr and the Nationalist Stahlhelm would have taken the field against them. The Prussian Government of Otto Braun and Karl Severing would almost certainly have been routed had it attempted forcible resistance to von Papen instead of yielding under protest to a show of force. At that stage, however, resistance was still barely possible; whereas at any later stage the possibility of it had practically disappeared. Undoubtedly, one important factor in turning the scale against resistance to von Papen's *coup* had been the attitude of the Trade Unions, which, under the leadership of Theodor Leipart, threw their weight heavily on the side of submission and maintained their policy of abjectness in face of Hitler's and Göring's subsequent accession to power. This abject submission brought no advantage to the Trade Union leaders, who had hoped by it to save their funds and premises and to be allowed to maintain a shadow of organised existence. On May 1st, 1933, the Nazis converted the old Socialist May Day into a great Nazi festival under the auspices of their newly established Labour Front: the following day they seized every Trade Union building, arrested hundreds of Trade Union leaders, and transferred the members of the Unions bodily to the Labour Front. In this body, which was definitely subordinated to the Nazi Party under the control of Dr. Ley, who was also at the head of the party organisation, the members of the former rival 'Free', Christian, and other Trade Unions found themselves compulsorily amalgamated into fourteen 'Unions', each connected with a particular range of industries. Ley at first tried to give the 'Labour Front' a corporative character, by enrolling in it employers as well as workers; but this attempt failed. But, though the 'Front' purported to represent the workers, it had no real power to act on their behalf. On May 19th Hitler's Government appointed for each of the 13 regions into which it had divided Germany a Labour Trustee, chosen in consultation with the regional Gauleiter; and to these Trustees was given the authority to replace collective bargaining by deciding on wages and conditions of work. The function of the Labour Front was not to bargain about such matters or to defend the workers' special interests, but to mobilise the national manpower in the service of the Nazi State. Thus, the German Trade Union movement was liquidated completely with almost no resistance; and its leaders, Leipart and Grossmann, despite their submissions, were sent to concentration camps.

What part in these events, we must now ask, was played by the leaders of the German employing class? Some big employers — notably the steel magnate, Fritz Thyssen — had gone over to the Nazis a considerable time before the *coup* and had contributed heavily to the finances of the Nazi Party. Thyssen and those who took his line wanted to use the Nazis in the service of German capitalism in order to suppress and destroy both the Socialists and Communists and the Trade Unions, and hoped to be able to control Nazism and to use it as a reliable support for capitalist claims; and as the Nazi challenge to the Weimar Republic became more powerful and more violent an increasing number of capitalists went over to this point of view, and identified themselves with Nazism despite the unrepudiated anti-capitalist elements contained in the Nazi programme. Nevertheless, even when Hitler became Chancellor, this was not the predominant attitude among the leaders of the employing class, which was politically divided between adherents of the various bourgeois Parties — especially the Centre Party — and reactionary forms of Nationalism much more closely allied to Hugenberg's German Nationalists than to the Nazis. Hitler's accession to office as Chancellor gave the signal for a series of struggles for power inside the central representative agencies of German capitalism, including the National Association of German Industry, of which Krupp von Bohlen was President. Demands were made for Krupp's resignation, and the Association's managing director, Kestl, was actually driven to resign. Krupp, however, was able to keep his position; and in the main Dr. Otto Wagner, the Nazis' principal economic director, was heavily defeated in his attempt to bring the Association under party control. Wagner, in common with Dr. Ley, had wished to reconstitute the Association as an element, together with the Labour Front, in a Corporation including employees and workers; but the Association would have none of this. Instead it proclaimed itself to be the regional Corporation (*Reichstand*) without any participation by the workers; and largely under its influence Hitler abandoned his projects of corporative organisation. Wagner was displaced from office and replaced by Wilhelm Keppler, who was acceptable to the industrialists; and in June another whole-hearted supporter of capitalist interests was appointed as Minister of Trade. The other chief capitalist representative agencies in Germany were the Association for the Preservation of Economic Interests in the Rhineland and Westphalia — known as the 'Long-Name Union' — and the North-Western Employers' Association, chiefly active in the coal and steel districts. The first of these was headed by a Dr. Schlucher, formerly of the German People's Party, but latterly connected closely with Hugenberg's Nationalists. Schlucher was rapidly forced to resign and, after a short interval, was replaced by Thyssen, who became also President of the North-Western Association and was thus elevated to the highest position of influence in West German industry. Generally speaking, the Nazis did succeed in gaining control over the main organisations of German capitalism, but only on condition of accommodating their economic policies to fit in with capitalist interests and of throwing over their promises of a corporative organisation transcending class differences. On these terms most of the big employers were fully prepared to work with the new Nazi régime, especially when they saw how furiously the Nazi vendetta against the working-class movement was being pursued.

Not that the big employers had in reality much room for choice. As a consequence of the serious depression, a large part of German industry had passed under the control of the banks, which had themselves been driven to look for support from the State. Whoever controlled the State machine was therefore in a very powerful position for ensuring their compliance; and the Nazis were not the kind of persons who were likely to make less than full use of any opportunity of adding to their power. However, long before 1933 Hitler at any rate had lost interest in the anti-capitalist elements that had gone to the making of the Nazi programme. These elements had been useful in attracting recruits among the petit-bourgeois, who could be enticed by denunciations of the great commercial and industrial concerns. But as Nazism widened its appeal and became more and more the spokesman of extreme popular nationalism, its need to appeal to the petite-bourgeoisie against the richer elements grew less, and its crusade against the working-class movement impelled it into alliance with the big employers. Nevertheless, right up to 1933 many small traders and small employers, organised in a 'Fighting Association' of the Industrial Middle Classes, still looked confidently to the Nazis to carry through their programme of breaking up the big commercial combines and handing them over to the 'small man'. In March 1933 the Fighting Association, clearly under Nazi control, took the initiative in setting up a Reich Corporation of German Trade under Dr. von Rentelen; and this body also won control over the German Industrial and Trade Committee, the central union of the local Chambers of Commerce, of which also von Rentelen became President. These bodies, however, soon found themselves in sharp conflict with Dr. Ley, who wished to base the new corporative structure of the Nazi Reich on his Labour Front, rather than on the organisations of the petite-bourgeoisie. In the event, both contestants met with an equal defeat when Hitler, instead of giving his support to either, threw over the whole idea of the Corporate State and came down in effect on the side of the big capitalists against them both.

This, however, did not mean, as I have pointed out in my opening chapter, that Nazism became simply or mainly an instrument of German capitalism in its struggle against Socialism. In the resulting alliance between Nazism and capitalism the Nazis, rather than the capitalists, came out top dogs. German capitalism was enabled to escape from its pressing difficulties and to revive under Nazi rule, and in the main it gave strong support to Nazism during the ensuing years. It was, however, throughout the subordinate partner in the alliance, compelled to follow the Nazi lead in putting 'guns' before 'butter' and to give priority to the Nazi drive towards rearmament and war over its own economic advantage. The fact that this accommodation was well worth the capitalists' while because it both removed the threat of Socialism and gave the employers a massive advantage in dealing with the workers does not make it the less true that under the Third Reich the Nazis rather than the capitalists were in a position to call the tune and to subordinate German industry to their own nationalistic purposes.

It was less easy for the Nazis to come to terms with the big landowners, who were hostile to any measure designed to break up the great estates of Eastern Germany. In 1933 the Nazis had already behind them a new peasant movement, organised in the so-called Agrarian Political Apparatus of the Nazi Party under the leadership of R. Walther Darré, an Argentine-born social economist who had risen rapidly to influence in the Party and was noted chiefly for his insistence on the need to reduce real interest rates to 2 per cent — a measure opposed both by Hugenberg, who stood mainly for measures designed to increase agricultural prices, and by the leading financial experts of the Party, such as Schmidt and Hjalmar Schacht. Darré, with Hitler's support, set out to organise the German peasantry into a Reich Corporation of Food Producers and Consumers under his personal control and to enact laws preventing the sale of peasant land or the eviction of peasants for debt. The peasants, he announced, were the true foundation of national greatness and the promoters of the nation's spirit; and he hoped to be able to bring about large measures of peasant settlement on the large estates of Eastern Germany. This policy, however, brought him into sharp conflict with Hugenberg and also with President Hindenburg — both stout upholders of the landlords' rights; and he also failed to secure the support of Hitler, who declared that the problem of *Lebensraum* for the German people could not be solved by colonisation at home, but imperatively required the conquest of areas for settlement beyond the existing territories of the Reich — principally in Eastern Europe. Darré, in order to maintain his authority, was forced to abandon his demand for a reduction of interest to 2 per cent, and to go slow with his projects of land settlement in Eastern Germany. These consequences, however, did not profit Hugenberg or his Nationalist supporters. In June the Nazis launched a mass onslaught on the Nationalist Clubs and Circles throughout Germany, occupying their premises and making numerous arrests. Hugenberg made violent and fruitless protests in the Cabinet against these attacks and on June 27 resigned his office. Hitler retorted by dissolving the German Nationalist Party; and, a fortnight later, the Cabinet proclaimed a new decree-law, which declared the Nazi Party to be the sole political Party authorised to exist in Germany, and declared all other Parties to be dissolved.

Thus ended the uneasy coalition by which Germany had been nominally governed for the first six months of Hitler's Chancellorship. The sharing of power had never been real, though Hugenberg's presence in the Cabinet had served in certain respects — notably in connection with land reform — as a brake on Nazi intentions. The chief effect of Hugenberg's removal from office was to enable Hitler to consolidate his control over the Reichswehr and, in doing so, to reduce his dependence on the S.A., whose leader, Röhm, desired to press on with revolutionary violence in forms that were bound to antagonise both Nationalist and large elements of capitalist and bourgeois opinion. In August 1933 Göring, in Prussia, went so far as to disband the special constabulary, which had been drawn mainly from the ranks of the S.A. The stage was being set for the conflict which culminated in 1934 in Röhm's overthrow and death. Nazism, having won exclusive power, was already turning from a revolutionary movement directed against the existing order into a defender of the new order it had brought into being and, in repudiating many of its earlier subversive economic doctrines, was becoming the represser of those who were still set on acting in this spirit. This did not mean that Nazism was growing to be less a doctrine of violence, but only that the objects against which its violence was to be directed were becoming more clearly, and also more narrowly, defined. It did not at all relax its persecution of Jews or Communists or of Social Democrats or 'Free' Trade Unionists; but it did cease to direct its violence against capitalists who accepted the Nazi new order and against such Aryans as were prepared to work with it, or even tacitly to accept its rule.

The overthrow and killing of Röhm in the summer of 1934 brought with them the final destruction of the S.A. as a power capable of independent action, and therewith the final subjection of the Nazi left wing. Thereafter, at any rate, Hitler was openly a Nationalist rather than in any sense a National *Socialist* leader of the German people, and a firm upholder of capitalist enterprise against all who wished to assail it, whether in the interests of the common people or of the petit-bourgeois elements that had contributed so largely to his rise to power. As we have seen, the change in Nazism had begun and gone a long way much earlier. It had indeed begun well before Hitler became Chancellor, as soon as the Nazi Party began to receive large subventions from Thyssen and other leading capitalists; and it had become evident within a very few months of Hitler's acceptance of office, as soon as he settled down to his self-appointed tasks of rearmament and preparation for warlike aggression. For these purposes, he needed the support both of big business and of all nationalistic Germans who could be induced to accept him as 'Leader' — especially of those who held positions of influence in any movement that could be subjected to the process of *Gleichschaltung*. As soon as the possibility of resistance from the original Socialist and Trade Union movements had been removed, there remained no possible dangerous focusing point for opposition except in the Churches, with which the Nazis felt it needful to deal more circumspectly than with their other antagonists.

German Socialism, with its basis in Marxian theory, had been by tradition an anti-religious movement, hostile both to the mainly Lutheran Protestantism of the eastern parts of Germany and to the Roman Catholicism of the Rhine-Westphalian region and of Bavaria and other parts of the South. Under its influence, religion had no hold on a very large section of the working class, and the Socialist and 'Free' Trade Union leaders stood right outside confessional influences. The rival Christian Trade Unions, though open to Protestants, were mainly Catholic in leadership and attitude, but represented only a small minority of the Trade Union movement. Nazism, on the other hand, was from the beginning irreligious rather than anti-religious. Claiming to speak for all true Germans, it had to appeal to both Protestants and Catholics and to avoid as far as possible issues that were liable to divide them. Hitler was by upbringing a Catholic, and remained one at any rate in form, though he showed but little interest in religious matters. President Hindenburg, on the other hand, was a determined Protestant and a strong upholder of Protestant claims to pre-eminence and of the idea of Protestantism as standing for a Church closely allied with the State, at any rate in Prussia. The Protestant Churches in Germany were organised, not on a unitary basis for the whole country, but on a regional basis, each State within the Reich having its own Church closely linked to the State Government. They were thus in some degree associated with conceptions of feudalism and of State rights, though in practice some degree of pre-eminence attached to the Prussian Lutheran Church. Nazism, as a centralising movement resting on a strong insistence on the national unity of all Germans, thus came early into some degree of conflict with the regionalism of the German Protestants ; and the Nazi assertion of the absolute authority of the Reich Government involved a definite subordination of religious to political authority which ran counter to ecclesiastical claims to overriding moral authority over the faithful. Some Nazis were before long demanding that Christianity must be brought into line with the Nordic pretensions of the Nazi gospel by a definite acceptance of racialism as an article of faith ; and as

Nazi influence became more and more pervasive, there arose a movement of Nordic Protestantism which, in its more extreme forms, came near to an active rejection of Christian morality. The Lutheran pastor, Hassenfelder, became the leading exponent of a so-called 'German Christianity', and set to work to unify the control of the Lutheran Churches by removing the established leaders from office. Despite the tradition of Church subjection to State control, Hassenfelder's attack provoked widespread opposition; and Hitler removed him from office and appointed an East Prussian Reichswehr chaplain, Ludwig Müller, as head of the German Christians in his place. There followed, in May 1933, a formal three-day conference between Müller and a number of prominent Churchmen, in the course of which Müller conceded Church freedom from State tutelage; and upon this the Berlin Church authorities elected a noted orthodox theologian, Friedrich von Bohl-schwingh, as *Reichsbishop* — that is to say, as head of the German Lutheran Church. This was too much for Hitler, who rejected Bohlschwingh's nomination and instructed Göring, as head of the Prussian Government, to appoint a civil servant, by name Jäger, as Church Commissioner with supreme powers. Jäger thereupon deposed the established leaders of the Prussian Church and appointed Müller as leader of the German Evangelical Church Union. Bohlschwingh was driven out; and the Nazis occupied the Protestant Churches and ran up swastika flags over them. This challenge brought President Hindenburg into action. He sent for Hitler and demanded that the freedom of the Churches should be restored and the issues between the Nazis and the Church leaders settled by friendly negotiation. Hitler for the time being gave way. Müller's order that in future the Church authorities should be appointed by the Government was rescinded; and the so-called 'Aryan clause' confining member-ship to those of 'Aryan' race was dropped, except for the clergy. The independent control of creed and worship by the regional State Churches was reaffirmed; and Jäger was removed from his position as Commissioner. Provision was made for the re-election of the Church assemblies, which the Nazis had been subjecting to a process of *Gleichschaltung* designed to bring them completely under Nazi control. Hitler was able to report to the President that his orders had been complied with, and that agreement had been reached between the Churches and the State.

So far, the Nazis appeared to have met with a signal defeat, but they lost no time in reasserting their claims. The elections for the new Church Assemblies were carried on under conditions of widespread intimidation, and resulted in sweeping victories for the German Christians, especially in Prussia. Müller was thereupon elected as State Bishop of the dominant Prussian State Church, and a little later, in September 1933, was chosen as *Reichsbishop* by a National Synod at Wittenberg. These measures caused strong protests from the orthodox. Two thousand pastors signed the 'Marburg' manifesto of protest, and the Bonn theologian, Karl Barth, published his famous pamphlet, *I Say NO*, in opposition. But the protests were ineffective; and Hindenburg did not intervene further. Nevertheless, the recalcitrant Churchmen had gained something; for the German Christians, warned by the crisis, did refrain from carrying *Gleichschaltung* to extremes, and their opponents were able to keep a small degree of power to sustain their attitude of protest.

Meanwhile, the Nazis had been endeavouring to come to terms with the Catholic Church. Before Hitler's advent to power, the Catholic bishops in Germany had made several formal pronouncements against Nazism; but in face of the Nazis' political victory they made haste to modify their attitude. In March 1933 the bishops declared that, without revoking their condemnation of particular religious and moral heresies advanced by the Nazis, 'the episcopacy believes itself to be justified in regarding its former general prohibitions and warnings as no longer necessary', and thus took a long step towards accepting the Nazi régime. The Catholic Church did, however, continue to dissociate itself from the extreme racial doctrines of Nazism and to protest against the violent excesses practised by the S.A. The Nazis, for their part, caused the dissolution of the Catholic Centre Party and of its counterpart, the Bavarian People's Party, as well as of the Christian Trade Unions; but Hitler also sent von Papen to Rome to negotiate for a Concordat with the Vatican, and in July agreement was reached, and a Concordat signed. Under its terms, freedom of creed and public worship was conceded to the German Catholics, and the independence of Church management was guaranteed ; but in return the Papacy agreed to forbid priests and monks to take any part in political affairs and also to consult the civil authorities in all appointments of bishops or archbishops and to authorise every bishop to swear an oath of loyalty both to the particular State in which his diocese lay and to the Reich and its government. These were large concessions ; and though the Catholics were able to secure the maintenance of their existing participation in educational activities and a substantial toleration of Catholic social and religious associations, the victory on the whole rested clearly with the Nazis and showed the unwillingness of the Papacy to take any effective stand against the pretensions of the Nazi régime.

Protestants and Catholics alike were at any rate able to secure from the Nazis a measure of tolerated activity provided they accepted the general supremacy of the new order in Germany. For the unfortunate Jews no similar possibility existed ; and they were from the first exposed not only to crippling legal disabilities but also to severe personal maltreatment and violence. It was impracticable immediately to drive out all the numerous Jews practising in the main professions, such as medicine and the law ; but the Nazis did not hide their intention of Aryanising these and other professions as rapidly as they could, and almost from the first the number of Jews allowed to remain in practice was drastically restricted. Nor was it practicable to close at once all Jewish shops, or to exclude all Jews from participation in wholesale trade or commerce ; but after a one-day complete boycott of all Jewish traders had been enforced by violent means, though the absolute boycott was discontinued, insults and violence continued to be widely used to discourage dealing with Jewish firms, and Jews continued to go in constant danger of personal violence and economic ruin. There was, indeed, in 1933 no approach to the sheer horror of Nazi anti-semitism in its subsequent manifestations during the second world war ; but what took place even in 1933 was bad enough to ensure strong international protest and to send a steady stream of German Jews who were able to escape into exile. Many had hoped that the Nazis, having won political power, would discard much of their anti-semitic violence together with their anti-capitalist radicalism; but the trend was all the other way. Racialism proved to be a much deeper and stronger constituent of the Nazi attitude than the social radicalism it had made use of in its quest for power, and the anti-semitic fervour grew stronger and more bitter with each further step along the road of persecution. At first the wealthier Jews fared considerably better than the poorer; but before long the Nazi Government turned its weapons against Jewish property owners as well as against the more helpless poor Jews. Even then, not a few wealthy Jews were allowed to escape abroad at the cost of leaving most of their property behind; and only after the outbreak of war did the Nazis embark on their campaign designed to achieve the sheer extermination of German Jewry. But almost from the beginning Nazism, when it had achieved power, went a long way beyond the policy laid down in its original programme, which had allowed the Jews the means of earning a living while depriving them of all political rights.

The extinction of Socialism in Germany was a far more serious blow to Socialism as a world movement than its extinction in Italy by the Fascist power had been, not only because Germany was a much more powerful country, able to exert far more influence on the course of world affairs, but also because Germany had been the home of the most strongly organised Socialist Party and the principal fountain-head of Social Democratic doctrine in the West. The impact of the German collapse on the rest of the world was no doubt lessened by the evident failure of the German Revolution of 1918 to establish a viable new order in place of the disrupted Hohenzollern régime, and by the evident decline of the S.P.D. over the ensuing years. German Social Democracy had fallen a very long way from its predominant position of the period before 1914 many years before its entire destruction by the Nazis, not only because it had become sharply divided into contending Communist and Social Democratic factions, but also because both these factions had given clear indication of their incompetence in coping with the fundamental problems of Germany under the Weimar Republic. The Communists had discredited themselves by their manifest failure to understand the real nature of the danger from the Nazis, and by their readiness, on occasion, even to join hands with the Nazis in opposition to the Social Democrats; while the S.P.D., in its attempts to 'save the Republic', had repeatedly given way to the forces of reaction and had allowed its own position to be disastrously undermined by repeated compromises and concessions. These tendencies had been clearly manifest even before the onset of the great depression had laid the country prostrate economically and had enabled the Nazis to rally behind them the vast and heterogeneous mass of discontent and disillusionment that finally carried them to power. In retrospect, it was easy to see, after the collapse, that successful resistance to the Nazis had been quite beyond the power of the German working-class movement in the conditions of 1933. Nevertheless, it came as a severe shock to Socialists in other countries that the once-mighty German Socialists should have allowed their movement to be annihilated without attempting to strike even a single blow in its defence.

With Germany as well as Italy put completely out of action for any sort of Socialism, the effective force of world Socialism was shut in within very narrow limits. The Labour and Socialist International, from 1933 onwards, was in effect little more than a loose federation of the British and French Parties with those of certain small States of Western Europe; and of these Parties the French had lost to the Communists the status of principal working-class Party, and the British had recently met with overwhelming defeat in the General Election of 1931. Social Democracy had been almost wholly eclipsed in Eastern Europe, and wholly eclipsed in the Soviet Union; and outside Europe it had almost disappeared in the United States and had failed to strike deep roots in any part of the American continent. Nor had Socialist Parties any effective existence in any country of Asia or Africa; and in Australasia, though Labour was powerful as a political force, there was very little Socialism in its make-up, and no disposition to make common cause with the Socialism of Western Europe. Even very considerable Socialist progress in Scandinavia and the prominence of Socialist elements in the Spanish Republican movement were scant compensation for the shrinking up of Social Democracy which the Nazi victory in Germany brought clearly into relief.

Nor was Communism in much better case. The Comintern was in effect entirely dominated by the Russians, and had met with what appeared to be utter defeat in China. Of all the Communist Parties outside the Soviet Union only the French Party was of any real importance, and its power to affect the course of events in France seemed to be almost nil. The underground Communist Parties of Eastern Europe and the embryonic Parties in Latin America were still of little account; and in the United States the tiny warring factions of Communists counted for no more than the weak and discredited Socialist Party. There was, of course, nothing new in Socialism being only a weak minority movement in most parts of the world outside Western Europe; but hitherto, however weak it was, it had appeared to be advancing and and gaining new adherents, whereas by 1933 it seemed to be almost everywhere losing ground. Even in Austria, where the Socialists had put up their most manful fight against reaction, it was being steadily driven back, and was faced with a new and desperately formidable threat by the triumph of Nazism in Germany.

The world-wide setback to the Socialist cause was of course favourable to the survival of capitalism; but I must repeat that capitalism was not the principal agent in bringing about the setback. Indeed, never in its history had the prestige of the capitalist system throughout the world been so low as it was in 1933. This was the case most of all in the United States, where the responsibility for the deep depression was placed squarely on the shoulders of American big business, and social radicalism, though not Socialism, made unprecedentedly rapid advances under stress of widespread bankruptcies and mass unemployment. In Great Britain, no doubt, the rout of the Labour Government in 1931 carried with it the victory of the capitalist forces; but even there the depression lowered capitalist prestige. Finally, in Germany, although Hitler shed the apparent economic radicalism of Nazism in its earlier phases and made German capitalism his ally in destroying the working-class movement, the essential victory went not to the capitalists but to the racialist nationalism which plunged the country into an essentially militarist struggle for world power — a struggle in which capitalism was the gainer only at the price of subordinating its profit-making ambitions to the overriding claims of racialist aggression. In short, the Fascism of the 1930s, in which German Nazism played throughout the leading rôle, was definitely not the 'last throw' of capitalism in decline or the realisation of capitalist dominance in the shaping of national and international policies, but the expression of deeply rooted nationalist and racialist instincts raised to boiling-point by economic adversity, but manifesting themselves predominantly in drives in which economic motives played only a secondary, albeit an important, part.

CHAPTER III

GREAT BRITAIN IN THE 1930s

W HEN the British Labour Party went down to utter defeat in the General Election of 1931, the main cause was that for the first time in its history it had to face a nation-wide coalition of its opponents against it. There were in most constituencies straight fights between a Labour and a Coalition candidate, all three wings of the Liberals being for once united in opposition to it. There was also a substantial desertion of voters drawn from the middle-class groups which had rallied to the Labour Party in 1929. In all, the Labour poll fell by two million, whereas the Tory poll rose by more than three million. The Liberals — including all groups — lost nearly three million votes : the votes for MacDonald's 'National Labour' followers, for Sir Oswald Mosley's New Party, and for the twenty-six Communists were very small. The total poll was a million less than it had been in 1929.

In terms of seats won, the losses were much more devastating. Official Labour M.P.s fell from 259 in 1929 to a mere handful of 46 in 1931 ; but in addition there were six Independents, three elected under I.L.P. auspices and three others, two of whom were in fact closely associated with the I.L.P. 'National Labour' won 13 seats, with Coalition support : the New Party, with only 24 candidates as against the 400 they had promised to put in the field, and the Communists, both failed to win even a single seat. Of the 46 elected under Labour Party auspices, a full half — 23 — were miners' candidates, and another 9 official candidates of their Trade Unions. Only 13 M.P.s, some of whom were Trade Unionists, survived as nominees of Divisional Labour Parties ; and the Co-operative Party was reduced to a single representative. 45 Labour seats were lost in Greater London, 39 in Lancashire and Cheshire,

34 in Scotland, and 33 in Yorkshire. Wales did relatively well, with only 10 losses out of 25. The election of 1931 left the Labour Party without a single seat in the south of England, outside Greater London, and with only one, that of Sir Stafford Cripps, in the West. Only one Labour Cabinet Minister — Lansbury — held his seat: his chief lieutenants in the new House of Commons were Attlee and Cripps. Henderson, Clynes, Dalton, Greenwood, Morrison, Shinwell, Susan Lawrence, Ellen Wilkinson, and Margaret Bondfield were among the defeated. For the I.L.P. Maxton and Kirkwood got back, but Jowett was among the casualties. Webb and Noel-Buxton had already gone to the House of Lords.

The surviving Labour Party was thus very weak in numbers, and its ranks were still further depleted, only a few months after the election, by the secession of the I.L.P. As already mentioned in an earlier volume,[1] the I.L.P. had begun, quite early on in the life of the Labour Government, to quarrel with the Party over policy and party discipline, and had before long reached the point at which the I.L.P. Members of Parliament were refusing to conform to party instructions and were in fact developing a sectional 'discipline' of their own, a situation which was intolerable to the Labour Party leaders. After the election, Maxton's leadership accentuated these tendencies, and in 1932 the inevitable break occurred, and the I.L.P. disaffiliated; a minority, however, was unwilling to sever connections and sought some way of remaining within the Labour fold.

The weakness of the Labour Party in debating strength paralleled its weakness in numbers. Henderson was re-elected Leader, though he had no parliamentary seat and was for the most part out of England, presiding over the Disarmament Conference, which was already beginning to stagger towards its dismal end. In his absence Lansbury became Chairman of the Parliamentary Group, with Attlee as Vice-Chairman. Henderson returned to the Commons in September 1933; but he had already, a year earlier, resigned the leadership, which devolved upon Lansbury.

In general, the immediate effect of the defeat of 1931 was to impel the Labour Party leftwards. It was widely believed

[1] Volume IV, Chapter XXI.

that the fall of the Labour Government had in the last resort been due to a 'bankers' ramp' inspired by Montagu Norman, Governor of the Bank of England, and there was an expressed determination that Labour must not again be caught in the same way. At the same time, however, or at least as soon as the immediate shock of the disaster had worn off a little, 'post-mortem' discussions were held in which the view was expressed that its causes lay further back, in the absence of any clearly defined policy and programme for the second Labour Government, and that if ever Labour returned to office, with or without a clear majority, it must not be without such a programme. One of these discussions led to the formation of the New Fabian Research Bureau described later in this chapter.

There was general agreement that the Bank of England ought to be nationalised and put firmly under Treasury control, and that the Labour Party should start upon the formulation of a new programme which would commit it to definite Socialist action, comprising public ownership of the fuel and power industries, including coal and electricity, and of the essential transport services; and to present to Conference reports thereon. When the first two of these reports were presented to the Leicester Conference of 1932, the swing to the left was manifest. The Report on Banking and Finance, while urging the nationalisation of the Bank of England, stopped short of proposing to nationalise also the joint-stock banks, although public ownership of these was regarded by many Socialists as a necessary basis for effective economic planning. An amendment to nationalise them was carried by a narrow majority against the platform; the result was hailed as a victory for the newly formed Socialist League. The second controversial issue related to Trade Union representation on the boards of nationalised industries and services. The official report proposed boards consisting entirely of Government nominees, and this was strongly criticised; as, however, the Trades Union Congress had not yet made up its mind either way, the issue was shelved for the time being by referring it for further discussion between the two bodies.

Meanwhile, there were clear signs of mounting unrest in the country, especially in the Depressed Areas and in the large towns suffering heavily from the unemployment which continued to rise after the formation of the National Government. A new Hunger March, largely led by Communists, was organised in 1932, and met with widespread Labour support; and there was great anger over the cuts in benefit and in the social services imposed by the Government. Marches and protests, such as the 'Black Coffin' demonstrations organised by Wal Hannington, when unemployed workers laid themselves down end to end across the road in Oxford Street at rush-hour and carried a dummy coffin with a legend saying 'He Was Refused Winter Relief', continued sporadically for the next couple of years. These manifestations, however, were bedevilled by the running quarrel between the Trade Unions and the Right on the one hand and the Communists and the Labour Left on the other. In 1933 the T.U.C. at length made some attempt to enrol the unemployed in an official movement under the auspices of those local Trades Councils which were prepared to accept its leadership; but the attempt was half-hearted, and met with little success against the Communist-dominated National Unemployed Workers' Committee Movement, which was firmly established in the main industrial centres.

The Leicester Conference had been on the whole a victory for the Left. But the victory was fleeting, for the Labour Party itself was still largely led, outside Parliament, by men who had been closely connected with the fallen Government, who, before its fall, had been prepared to go a long way in making concessions to its foes; and it was not long before they were back in control of the Party. The political opposition, though active and vocal, was in fact not strong; after 1932 it consisted, apart from the Communists, mainly of the Socialist League and the disaffiliated I.L.P.

The Socialist League was itself the outcome of an amalgamation of sorts. Towards the end of 1930, when, as the world depression gathered force and the Labour Government seemed to have little idea of coping with it, a group of Socialists, on the initiative of myself and my wife, C. M. Lloyd of the *New Statesman*, H. L. Beales, G. R. Mitchison, W. R. Blair of the Co-operative Wholesale Society, and some others, began to meet at Easton Lodge in Essex, the country house of the

Countess of Warwick whom Robert Blatchford had converted in her youth to ardent Socialism, and organised in the new year a new Society for Socialist Inquiry and Propaganda, based on individual membership. Its nickname of 'Loyal Grousers' indicated what it conceived to be its relationship with the Labour Party; it acquired Ernest Bevin for Chairman, and Attlee, Cripps, and others as members, and embarked upon a programme of lectures and pamphlets. It recruited its early membership from many sources, the most energetic being a group of ex-University Socialists such as Hugh Gaitskell, a good few of whom subsequently held office in the third Labour Government.

Shortly afterwards, as already mentioned, there was formed, largely out of the same elements, a body called the New Fabian Research Bureau which, since the Fabian Society itself had fallen into stagnation, intended to devote itself to 'purposeful' research of the kind pursued by the Fabian Society in its prime. The name 'New Fabian' was deliberately chosen to emphasise the continuity of tradition, with the consent of the Fabian Executive and the active encouragement of Henderson, Hugh Dalton, Leonard Woolf, the international and colonial expert, W. A. Robson of the London School of Economics, and the Webbs; and a comprehensive programme of research in three sections, international, political, and economic, was drawn up by Woolf, Robson, and myself.

My original idea had been that N.F.R.B. and S.S.I.P. should be interdependent, the former doing the research while the latter popularised the results; but this plan never came into real effect, for in the summer of 1932 the minority of the I.L.P., led by E. F. Wise, which had refused to follow Maxton into the wilderness, approached S.S.I.P. with proposals for an amalgamation, with Wise as chairman of the new body. After long discussion this was accepted by a majority, a decision which I felt was unwise, though at the time I acquiesced in it, and S.S.I.P. terminated its brief existence. The most serious result was the resignation of Bevin in a mood of great resentment which affected thereafter his attitude towards intellectuals in the Socialist movement. The new body took the name 'Socialist League' in direct reminiscence of William Morris; Wise died a year after the amalgamation, his place as Chairman being taken by Stafford Cripps. I had resigned in the spring of 1933, feeling that the political line which the League, under Wise's leadership, was taking was certain to bring it into direct and unfruitful collision with the official Labour Party.

The New Fabian Research Bureau, as a separate organisation, was unaffected, and continued to carry on with its own research programme. Very small at first, it continued, with John Parker (elected to Parliament in 1935) as its General Secretary and myself as Honorary Secretary, through the 'thirties and grew in membership and reputation until on the eve of war it joined forces with the rump of the Fabian Society. The name 'Fabian Society', with its fifty-year-old history, was retained, as were the local Fabian Societies — then reduced to a handful, but rising to over a hundred during the war years — and the affiliation to the Labour Party ; and a new rule (taken over from N.F.R.B.) was added to its constitution, which laid down that no policy should be put forward, either in publication or resolution, in the name of the Fabian Society, but only in the names of the individuals or group which prepared it. This 'self-denying ordinance' was of great importance ; it both removed any risk of the Fabian Society setting itself up as a rival or opposition inside the Labour Party and enabled Socialists of widely differing opinions to associate and work within it. The fruit of this association, and of the long years of steady research work, can be seen not only in the lists of pamphlets, tracts, books, and reports brought out first by N.F.R.B. and later, after the war began, by the Fabian Society, but in the numbers of Fabians returned to Parliament in 1945. Over half the Labour Cabinet were Fabians. Very different, as we shall see, was the history of the Socialist League.

In the Labour Party Henderson, though nominally its Secretary, played little part after 1931, owing partly to ill-health and partly to preoccupation with the Disarmament Conference. For this reason Lansbury remained Leader in the Commons, though he too fell seriously ill at the end of 1933, and did not resume his place until the autumn of the following year, Attlee meantime holding the fort with the assistance of Arthur Greenwood, who had got back in a by-election. Henderson died in 1935, a few weeks after the

Brighton Conference, which he had been too ill to attend, had elected the Acting Secretary, J. S. Middleton, to succeed him, on the strict understanding that he should not stand for Parliament. There is little doubt that this interregnum in the leadership, both in Parliament and outside, made for added confusion in a situation already gloomy.

For the events described above had taken place against a background of deep depression. Unemployment had been very severe in 1932 and 1933 — above all in the shipbuilding and heavy engineering centres and in the coalfields — and the National Government had no idea how to deal with it. The general tariff to which it resorted under its 'doctor's mandate' could naturally do nothing to help the export trades, which were the worst sufferers. For those who were able to keep their jobs, or to find new ones, the effects of the depression were mitigated by the sharp fall which it brought about in the prices of primary products, including foodstuffs; and in these circumstances a rift opened between the workers in the depressed areas and industries and those who were better off. This prevented united action from developing as it would otherwise have done, but helped those Trade Unions whose members were less affected to maintain their position, while preventing them from rallying solidly to the support of the unemployed. The Government, in addition to the cuts which it made in unemployment benefit in 1931, set up before the end of that year a Royal Commission to investigate and report upon the whole question of unemployment insurance and other forms of relief; and from the Commission's deliberations emerged the Unemployment Insurance Act of 1934. This, in effect, divided the unemployed into three categories — those whose needs could be met by contributory insurance, those who, having exhausted their insurance claims, were in need of further assistance from national funds, and those who either were not eligible under these heads or had exhausted their limited claims under both, and were eligible only for Public Assistance on a local basis, under the Poor Law and subject to its disabilities and to varying conditions from place to place according to the attitude of the local Public Assistance Committees. To administer the second of these forms of aid the Act set up a National Unemployment Assistance Board, with instructions to work out its own scale of relief. The Board issued its proposed scale in December 1934, the cuts of 1931 having been restored earlier in that year as recovery from the great depression set in. When the new scales were published, it speedily became plain that under them many unemployed workers would get less than they had been getting under the arrangements previously in force. Widespread agitation followed, and the U.A.B. was compelled to withdraw its proposed scale and to think again. The result, in 1936, was a new scale, under which the hated Means Test, which had been at the root of the trouble, was considerably modified. These changes took the edge off the unemployed agitation, which was thereafter concerned more with demands for Government action to help the depressed areas than with claims for improved treatment of the unemployed. Hunger Marches from these areas were again organised in 1936–7, chiefly under Communist leadership; but in face of the improvement in industrial conditions they attracted much less public attention. Indeed, by this time the centre of interest had shifted mainly from home to international affairs — above all, to the anti-Fascist struggle in connection with the Italian aggression in Abyssinia and the civil war in Spain.

This shift of interest was natural. In 1933 the Nazis won power in Germany, and destroyed the German working-class movement. By the end of that year the worst of the world depression was over, and Roosevelt had set out on his drastic recovery measures which go by the name of the 'New Deal'. The prices of primary foodstuffs and materials were showing signs of recovery, and the limitations of tariff policy in a country so dependent on foreign trade as Great Britain were being more widely appreciated. 1934 was definitely a year of economic recovery, and in Great Britain at least of diminishing economic and political tension. In the spring, as we saw, the 1931 cuts in social benefits were restored. The Labour Party, at the March elections, won in 1934 for the first time a clear majority on the London County Council, in which it has held power ever since.

As against these favourable trends there were some highly unfavourable developments overseas. In Austria came the civil war of February, in which Dollfuss's Christian Socials overthrew the Austrian Socialists and established his fragile dictatorship — only for Dollfuss to be assassinated in July and replaced by Schuschnigg, who attempted to do a deal with Mussolini in the hope of protecting Austria against Hitler. In the Far East the Japanese installed a puppet emperor at the head of the puppet-state, Manchukuo, and proceeded in April to repudiate the Nine-Power Treaty regulating intervention in China. In May dictatorship was installed by a *coup de main* in Bulgaria, and in June came Hitler's 'blood-bath' at the expense of Röhm and Otto Strasser. Three months later, on Hindenburg's death, Hitler became President of Germany and gained a completely free hand in German affairs.

Meantime, in France, the breaking of the Stavisky scandal had brought down the French Government and replaced it by a more reactionary Ministry under Doumergue. This led, in July 1934, to a decision of the French Communists and Socialists to form a United Front and in October to the reunion of the French Trade Unions in the C.G.T. Before this latter event, the United Front had spread in September from France to Spain, where it was followed in October by a big general strike movement — the prelude to civil war. In November, Roosevelt's Democrats won the Congressional Elections in the United States; in December Kirov was assassinated in mysterious circumstances in Leningrad, and, in the Far East, Japan denounced the Washington Naval Treaty.

This year, 1934, was thus one of Fascist advance abroad and of growing menace in the Far East, but also of anti-Fascist concentration in France and Spain. In Great Britain the Communists and the I.L.P. naturally seized their chance to press for a similar United Front, but were met by a sharp refusal from the Labour Party, which declared the only true United Front to be that of itself, the Trades Union Congress, and the Co-operative Union, already joined together in the National Council of Labour, and, reaffirming its hostility to any kind of dictatorship, reasserted its faith in 'Democratic Government, with a free electoral system and an active and efficient parliamentary machine for reaching effective decisions, after reasonable opportunities for discussion and criticism'. At the Party Conference that year, the Labour Party Executive brought forward, as well as a number of additional Policy

Reports on special issues, a new draft general policy statement, designed to replace *Socialism and the Nation* and entitled *For Socialism and Peace*. To this the Socialist League put forward no fewer than 75 amendments, traversing the entire policy advocated by the Executive ; and by thus challenging the whole, practically ensured that it would not succeed in amending the draft programme in any particular point, by rousing the will of the rest of the Conference to defend it. In taking up this line, I feel sure the Socialist League made a big mistake. It had been founded, after all, by those left-wingers who wanted to go on working inside the Labour Party rather than to break away from it ; but to challenge the entire policy of the Executive and at the same time to accept a United Front with the Communists in face of the Executive's hostility was pretty certain to make its position inside the Party untenable, whereas enough sympathy existed for some of its proposals to have had a reasonable prospect of success had they stood by themselves, instead of forming part of a comprehensive challenge. *For Socialism and Peace* was in fact by no means a reactionary document, but rather a considerable advance on its predecessor as a statement of Socialist objectives. It began by laying down five general principles which would guide the Party in defining its objectives. The first of these five committed the Party to seek peace by removing the root causes of international disputes, by consultation and arbitration, by renouncing war as an instrument of national policy, by disarmament, and by co-operation through the League of Nations and with States not yet members of the League.[1] The second principle laid down the object of securing for every member of the community a satisfactory standard of life, with equal opportunity for men and women alike. The third provided for converting industry from a haphazard struggle for private gain to a planned national economy aimed and carried on for the service of the community. The fourth dealt with the democratic expansion of education, health, and other social services. Finally, the fifth dealt with taxation, which was to be so adjusted as to make due provision for the maintenance and improvement of the national apparatus of industry (*i.e.* for investment), and for

---

[1] The Soviet Union joined the League in September 1934, after the Statement had been drafted.

the surplus created by social effort to be applied for the good of all.

The Socialist League began by challenging these principles, not because it disagreed with them, but as not being explicit enough to constitute any precise commitment for an incoming Government. This they were not meant to do, the entire Statement being conceived in terms of long-run objectives rather than as a programme for a Government in power. It did indeed include a number of specific proposals; but it was left deliberately unclear how many of these would rank in the current programme of a Labour Government during its initial term of office. In its concluding section it was definitely parliamentary and constitutional, while announcing itself as pledged to the abolition of the House of Lords and promising to proceed to abolition should the Lords obstruct the carrying out of its programme, and also announcing the urgent need for House of Commons procedural reforms — which were also dealt with in a Special Report submitted to the 1934 Party Conference. What the Socialist League objected to was, first, the absence of a definite immediate programme, and secondly the unequivocal commitment to constitutional methods, irrespective of any action that might be taken by Labour's opponents to defeat its measures. The League wanted an indisputable commitment to 'a decisive advance within five years towards a Socialist Britain', including a decisive change in 'the whole basis of production and distribution so that productive power may be used to satisfy the needs of the people in accordance with a planned economy'. Sir Stafford Cripps moved its amendment on these lines. Dalton, for the Executive, asked for withdrawal of the amendment, and promised a shorter statement embodying Labour's immediate programme. The League refused to withdraw, and was beaten by more than ten to one, after Herbert Morrison had attacked what he held to be the Communist motive underlying the amendment. Nevertheless, the League persisted, and went down to similar defeats with a number of other amendments. Finally, *For Socialism and Peace* was adopted almost unaltered by the Conference. With it went a special Statement on *War and Peace*, put forward under the auspices of the National Council of Labour. This dealt with a proposed system of collective security through the League of Nations and the I.L.O. It argued for the internationalisation of civil aviation, and for bringing the Soviet Union into the League, while advancing step by step in agreement with the United States. It advocated individual resistance to service in any war undertaken in violation of League principles; but it rejected the General Strike against war as inappropriate in face of the destruction of the German and Italian Labour movements, limiting its commitments to the policy, already approved, of convening a special Trades Union Congress to decide what action to take in face of a danger of war. This Statement too was challenged by the Socialist League, which regarded the League of Nations as bound up inseparably with the Treaty of Versailles and as incapable of doing more than uphold the *status quo*. Its amendment demanded the closest relations with the Soviet Union, and called on the workers everywhere to resist war by every means in their power, including a General Strike. On this issue too the Socialist League was voted down; but 673,000 votes to 1,519,000 were cast against the Statement as a whole by the combined left and pacifist groups.

In these affairs the Socialist League represented an intense reaction to the disaster of 1931, not sufficient to drive it out of the Labour Party with the I.L.P., but strong enough to range it in sharp opposition to the constitutionalism and the League-mindedness of the Labour Party leadership. At Leicester in 1932 this mood had been widespread enough to allow it to carry the resolution calling for the nationalisation of the joint stock banks with the Miners' and the Railwaymen's support. But by 1934 a good deal of this leftward reaction had been dissipated, and the leadership of the Party was even more firmly in the hands of men who had been prominent in the Labour Government and had been associated with its policy of compromise up to the final rupture with MacDonald. This was not prevented by the fact that most of the old leaders — among them Morrison and Dalton — were out of the House of Commons; for they were all the better able to devote their energies to resuscitating the Party and to imbuing it with a better thought out programme than it had possessed in 1929, or in 1931. The lessons of 1931, as they were read by such old stalwarts as Morrison, Dalton, and Pethick Lawrence, were not that Labour should abandon its policy of gradualist constitutionalism, but that it should be better prepared with a practicable programme for the next Labour Government to carry out. They were in search of that clear majority in Parliament to the lack of which in 1929–31 they attributed most of their troubles, and they did not anticipate that the bourgeois Parties would readily throw over constitutionalism in order to obstruct them, or believe they would get a majority if they came forward with a challenge to parliamentarism. The Socialist League, on the other hand, attributed the Labour Party's downfall to the readiness of its opponents to resort to any expedient in order to defeat it, felt sure that this policy would be repeated in the event of a Labour victory at the polls, and believed that an attitude of forthright challenge would secure stronger support than one of compromise. There was thus a sharp conflict of views between the Left and the Right, with the Trade Union block vote, after 1932, cast in favour of the right wing against the semi-revolutionary proposals of the left.

Soon after the Labour Party Conference of 1934 the Labour Party issued a series of special Reports dealing with the Depressed Areas, calling for action to clear out the great stagnant pools of unemployment that continued to exist in them despite the general recovery. The Government issued a Special Areas Bill setting up Commissions to help these areas, but endowing them with very limited powers, which the Parliamentary Labour Party sought vainly to get enlarged. The U.A.B. issued its draft regulations in December; and the general protest which they provoked reunited the local Unemployment Committees behind a new crusade, which was widely supported by Trades Councils and Trade Union branches. The T.U.C., through the National Council of Labour, joined in the protests, but refused to recognise the Communist-led National Unemployed Workers' Movement; and the Labour Party rejected several applications for affiliation from the Communist Party and the I.L.P. The Communist Party, in February 1935, adopted and published its own policy, under the challenging title *For Soviet Britain*. Lloyd George also came forward again with a programme of his own, under the slogan *Organising Prosperity*, drafted without prior consultation with the other Liberal groups. He wanted a Supreme Economic Council, directed by a small inner Cabinet, to carry through a large programme of development of the major industries, still mainly under private ownership, but with financial assistance from the State where needed; and he offered to collaborate with the National Government in carrying this programme into effect. But nothing came of this. Instead, in June 1935 the Tories at length jettisoned Ramsay MacDonald, and reconstructed the Government as a purely Tory administration, under Stanley Baldwin as leader.

In Great Britain, issues of international politics, as well as of home affairs, sharply divided the Socialists. The Labour Party, as we saw, came out in favour of an all-out policy of collective security under the League of Nations; but this did not afford any clear guidance to the attitude to be adopted towards rearmament. Right up to and including the Peace Ballot campaign of 1934–5, the Labour Party continued to talk in terms of disarmament, despite the manifest failure of the Disarmament Conference to make any progress and also despite the manifest flouting of the disarmament provisions of the Versailles Treaty by the Nazis. In 1935, however, the centre of attention was Italy, where Mussolini was making open preparation for war on Abyssinia. At the Stresa Conference in June 1935, called on account of Germany's reintroduction of military conscription, no mention was made of Abyssinia, though Laval had made a pact with Mussolini five months earlier. The British Trades Union Congress pledged its support for measures to restrain the Italian Government; but Mussolini, undeterred by the threat of League sanctions, proceeded to bomb his way into Abyssinia. In face of this, economic sanctions of a sort were actually applied by the League in October; but they were half-hearted, and did not prevent the dispatch of oil for use by the Italian forces in the invasion.

In November 1935 came the General Election, in which Baldwin, much influenced by the Peace Ballot, strove to appear as the champion of a League policy of collective security, and was able to get his majority renewed. Labour of course gained seats, returning 154 members as against the mere 46 of 1931, but 134 fewer than in 1929. In the new Parliament, candidates sponsored by national Trade Unions were still in a majority, but most of the leaders defeated in 1931 regained their seats. MacDonald, defeated by Shinwell at Seaham, was re-elected for the Scottish Universities later in 1935, but died the following year. Of the Cabinet seceders of 1931, only Thomas remained until he resigned in 1936, as the outcome of a Budget leakage scandal. The Independent Liberals, by this time out of the Government, fought 161 seats, but won only 21 as against the 33 won by the National Liberals with Tory support. The Tories had thus still a comfortable majority; and when the election was over they came forward with a programme of rearmament which they had not ventured to put before the electors. The Labour Party, which had hitherto, despite its opposition to Fascism, voted against increased expenditure on armaments, had now to make up its mind whether to support or to oppose the Government programme: it could no longer sit on the fence by keeping its support of armaments within the limits imposed by adding up all the national forces potentially available against an aggressor, and refusing to contemplate the possible need for unilateral British action. The decision, however, was not easy, in view of the suspicion that the Government wanted increased forces, not for the purpose of making the League more effective, but rather as a basis for coming to terms that would leave the aggressors free to turn their forces against the Soviet Union.

While Mussolini pursued his aggression in Abyssinia undeterred by the League, Hitler continued with his attempts to reassure the West that he was not threatening its security and honestly desired peace with it, while pursuing his campaign to protect Western Europe from Bolshevism. Meanwhile, at the 1935 Labour Party Conference, Lansbury had been driven from the leadership after an unbridled attack on his pacifism by Ernest Bevin; and Attlee had replaced him as Leader. Lansbury was indeed much loved by the left wing; but his pacifism had alienated the anti-Fascists among them without propitiating his right-wing opponents, and he was no longer in a position to give the leadership that was required. The discreditable Hoare-Laval Agreement of December 1935, which proposed to leave Italy in possession of most of her

conquests, aroused so much popular indignation that it had to
be repudiated; but the dishonour of British foreign policy
was unamended. In March 1936 Hitler marched into the
Rhineland, breaking the Locarno Treaties and provoking a
fresh European crisis; and in June the Spanish Civil War
began with General Franco's rebellion in North Africa. This
at once raised the question of the Spanish Republican Government's right to buy arms and receive aid from abroad; and the
Fascist States promptly began to give large-scale aid to the
rebels. The Western Allies tried to counter this by means of
a 'Non-Intervention Pact', to which the Fascist States adhered
without any intention of observing it. The *Front Populaire*
Government of Léon Blum, which had come to office in France,
was not prepared to take action without full British support,
in face of the strength of French pacifist feeling and of
the powerful influences which favoured coming to terms with
the Germans; and the British Government was hostile to the
Spanish Republicans. The Fascist States were thus able to
flout the Non-Intervention Pact with impunity, whereas the
Soviet Union was too far away to bring more than very limited
help to the Republicans, who nevertheless fell increasingly
under its influence.

This was the situation the Labour Party Conference had
to face when it met at Edinburgh in October 1936. The
Executive secured in the early days of the Conference a resolution supporting non-intervention, but insisting on its observance
by all parties; but the Spanish fraternal delegates were able
to make such sensational revelations of the breaches of the
Pact by the Fascists that the Conference changed its mind,
sent Attlee and Greenwood on a mission of protest to the
Government, and, on their return, carried a new resolution
much more helpful to the Republican side. Already in May
the National Council of Labour had issued a manifesto,
Socialism and the Defence of Peace, in which it declared that
'Labour must be prepared to accept the consequences of its
policy', and that 'a movement which supports the League
system cannot desert it in a crisis'. The emphasis was still
put on League action, and opposition was expressed to unilateral rearmament; but it had clearly shifted from unqualified
opposition to qualified support of the policy of rearmament,

while still leaving to the Parliamentary Labour Party the task of deciding when to vote for or against the Government's actual proposals. The Labour Party was in fact in a dilemma between its decision to organise opposition to the Fascists and its fear that armaments in the hands of the Tory Government would be used, not to uphold collective security, but against it.

In this dilemma, Cripps and the Socialist League, as well as the I.L.P., took up a definite line in refusing to support rearmament as long as the Tories remained in power, whereas the majority of the Party went over by stages to the policy of voting for heavier armaments despite their mistrust of the Government. The Edinburgh Conference voted in favour of an ambiguous resolution by a majority of more than two to one ; but the real decision was taken by the Parliamentary Party. Meanwhile, on the issue raised by the Spanish Civil War, the leadership's attitude remained ambiguous and in effect confined to trying to make the Non-Intervention Pact work. A delegation from France, headed by Jean Longuet, came to London in November 1936 to ask whether the British would back France in breaking off the Pact in order to intervene on the Republican side ; but it got only a dusty answer in face of fears that intervention might lead to war. Nor was the Soviet Union prepared for all-out intervention unless it could be assured of French and British support. The Civil War therefore dragged on, with increasing intervention on the Fascist side, and went more and more against the Republicans, though Madrid managed to hold out until early in 1939, when the end of the fighting was followed by an orgy of reprisals, and by the total suppression of the Spanish working-class movement, which lived on only in exile — chiefly in Mexico and France.

In July 1937 the National Council of Labour issued a new manifesto, *International Policy and Defence*, which came to be regarded as making a definite concession to the policy of rearmament, even by a Tory Government. It recognised that the League of Nations 'for the time being has been rendered ineffective', and, while standing for its restoration and for collective security in principle, insisted that a Labour Government, if returned to power in the existing world situation, would need to be able not only to defend the country, but also

to play its part in collective security and to meet any intimidation by the Fascist powers, and would be unable to renounce
the policy of rearmament until it had been able to change the
world situation for the better. This policy, though strongly
attacked by Aneurin Bevan, then fast coming to the front as a
leading figure of the Left, was endorsed by nearly 10 to 1 at
the Bournemouth Party Conference. Before this, the Japanese
had launched their full-scale attack on North China and at
Shanghai; and the Conference also passed a resolution calling
for action, in conjunction with the United States, to bring the
Japanese aggression to a halt by financial and economic
pressure. The National Council of Labour called meanwhile
for a boycott of Japan; but, though a League Conference met
in Brussels in November to consider the matter, nothing
effective could be agreed on. Actually, while the meeting was
in progress, Germany, Italy, and Japan signed an Anti-Comintern Pact, and renewed their attempt to secure Western support
for their designs against the Soviet Union. In this atmosphere
1937 ended, and the year of Munich began.

At the beginning of the Czechoslovak crisis there had been
not a few even in the Labour Party who saw some force in the
Sudeten claims, and hoped that the Czechs would be able to
meet them without sheer surrender. But the negotiations
during the summer convinced most of them that Hitler would
be content with nothing short of the destruction of Czechoslovakia's power to resist any further demands he might put
forward later; and well before the Munich discussions opinion
had swung round almost solidly in favour of supporting the
Czechs at any cost. There were attempts to establish a common
front of the British and French Labour and Socialist movements; but the French, rent by their internal divisions and
conscious of their weakness, held back. For technical reasons
of a change in the date, there was no Labour Party Conference
in 1938; but the National Council of Labour prepared and
submitted to the T.U.C. in September a Statement, *Labour
and the International Situation: On the Brink of War*, in which
it declared the Nazi demands to be such as no Government
had any right to recommend the Czechs to accept, and said
that 'the time has come for a positive and unmistakable lead
for collective defence against aggression and to safeguard

peace'. 'The British Government', it added, 'must leave no doubt in the mind of the German Government that they will unite with the French and Soviet Governments to resist any attack upon Czechoslovakia.' This, of course, was written well before the later stages of the crisis, and could be interpreted as leaving the decision conditional on the participation of France and the Soviet Union. With the latter there had been no prior consultation and no attempt at concerted military planning; but it is clear that the Soviet Government, not feeling strong enough to intervene alone, was waiting on the decisions of Great Britain and France, and stood ready to intervene if they came in too.

Well before Munich, the final equivocation had disappeared from the Labour pronouncements in Great Britain, and it had been made clear that British Labour, by a vast majority, stood for defending Czechoslovakia, with only a small group of absolute pacifists still opposing. There had been, however, many acrimonious internal disputes before this near-unanimity was arrived at — particularly over the question whether the Labour Party should continue to stand alone, preparing for a General Election in which it could make a bid for a clear majority of its own, or should seek allies for an immediate anti-Fascist crusade, either within the working-class movement, by accepting the overtures of the Communist Party, the I.L.P., and the Socialist League for an united working-class front, or by going further than this, and calling for the collaboration of all anti-Fascists in some sort of Popular Front, largely modelled on those created in France and Spain. To both these campaigns the Labour Party Executive, supported by the Party Conference, offered unqualified opposition, urging that all men and women of goodwill should rally to it as the only viable agent of an alternative policy, and questioning that any sort of United or Popular Front would secure wider, or even as wide, electoral backing as the Labour Party standing alone for a coherent policy.

As we saw, the Socialist League, challenging the party leadership chiefly on matters of internal policy, had been sharply defeated at successive Party Conferences; but from 1936 onwards the dispute was confined mainly to the field of international affairs, especially after the Civil War had broken

82

out in Spain. In May 1936 the publisher, Victor Gollancz, aided by H. J. Laski and John Strachey, launched the Left Book Club, which through its local groups and its regular circulation of books of left-wing appeal, chiefly on international affairs, soon began to exert a widespread influence, especially among the younger members of the Labour movement and among the intelligentsia.

Of the two theorists of the Left Book Club, the younger, John Strachey (b. 1901), had come to the fore originally as an advocate of monetary reform, and as a Labour M.P. had supported Oswald Mosley, whose New Party he joined at its inception, though he left it almost immediately. In 1931 he lost his parliamentary seat, and his political attitude moved further and further to the left. His speeches and writings had a very strong appeal to the young; in particular his *The Coming Struggle for Power* (1932), with its concentration upon issues of class and power, made him one of the most effective apostles of the United Front against Fascism.

From the standpoint of Socialist thought, however, much the most important of the Left Book Club's sponsors was Harold J. Laski (1893–1950), who was Professor of Political Theory at the London School of Economics and also from 1937 a member (elected by the local Labour Parties) of the Labour Party Executive, on which he was generally the leader of a dissident minority. He was no Communist, despite his willingness to work with Communists; the Executive, indeed, with considerable adroitness often put him up as its spokesman at Party Conferences against resolutions emanating from Communist sources, in which capacity he made very effective speeches. He had been well known as a writer from the time of publication of his first book, an academic treatise on political theory (*The Problem of Sovereignty*, 1917), and had made for himself a reputation in the United States as well as in Britain, serving for some years as a university teacher in Harvard, Yale, and other American universities — where, upon one occasion, he got into serious trouble by giving open support to workers on strike. He had also played an active part in the women's suffrage movement and was a leader-writer on Lansbury's *Daily Herald* before the first world war. In the 'twenties he was especially active in the Fabian Society, and in 1926 succeeded to Graham Wallas's chair at the School of Economics. Beginning as, on the whole, a moderate Socialist, he moved steadily leftward after attaining his professorship, and became increasingly active in the Labour Party. In his capacity as teacher and lecturer he had a great influence over his students, over whom he took infinite trouble ; and as these included a large number from overseas, from both British dependencies and foreign countries, his influence extended all over the world, particularly during the depression years. In 1925 he had published his well-known *Grammar of Politics*, and in 1927 his Home University Library volume on *Communism*, which marked his emergence as a left-wing thinker. Thereafter his books on current politics became increasingly propagandist and subject to Karl Marx's influence, though there always remained in them a strong streak of Utilitarianism uninvolved with his adherence to Marxian concepts. He also wrote a good deal in critical descriptive vein about the United States of America, based partly upon personal experience and partly on contacts with his many American friends and disciples. As the leading figure in the Left Book Club he came to play, naturally, a prominent part in the movements for a United, or a Popular, Front ; but though he was an ally of the Communists in these campaigns, he remained a sharp critic of Communist tactics, and retained his position in the Labour Party and on its Executive when his closest collaborators, Cripps and Aneurin Bevan, were expelled from the Party.

Much of the Left Book Club's success, in the 'thirties, was due to the ardent support of the Communists and near-Communists, who not only provided the material for many of its publications, but eagerly formed circles for the dissemination of its books and its monthly journal. But Victor Gollancz, its founder, like many others, had no stomach to swallow the Nazi-Soviet Pact, and as Communist support failed, the Club, in spite of a temporary rally when Hitler's invasion of Russia brought Communists and other Socialists together again, gradually faded away.

At about the same time as the foundation of the Club, *Reynolds News*, the Sunday journal which, after a long history as a Radical organ, had passed into the ownership of the Co-operative movement, came out with propaganda for a popular crusade against the Government in the anti-Fascist cause. Meanwhile, the Labour Party Executive was engaged chiefly in a campaign against the Labour League of Youth, which as a semi-independent body was claiming a right to criticise the party leadership, and with the elaboration of an Immediate Programme to supplement *For Socialism and Peace* by setting out more exactly what an incoming Labour Government, with a parliamentary majority behind it, would set out to do during its first term of office. *Labour's Immediate Programme* actually appeared in May 1937, and was ratified by the Party Conference in October. It had little to say on questions of foreign policy, but pledged the Party to nationalise the Bank of England (but not the joint stock banks), the coal industry, the major transport undertakings, except shipping, and the supply of gas and electricity. It also proposed measures for easier land acquisition for public purposes, but not for general land nationalisation, and for the reorganisation of British agriculture and of food supply, holidays with pay for all employed workers, a standard working week of 40 hours, with some exceptions, and higher wages, to be sought in co-operation with the Trade Unions and the I.L.O. Improved social security measures, including pensions for the aged, were also promised, together with an improved Health Service and the abolition of the Means Test. On foreign affairs it only reaffirmed the League policy of collective security, including the internationalisation of Air Forces, and pledged itself to the maintenance of adequate armed forces 'to defend our country and to fulfil our obligations as a member of the British Commonwealth and of the League of Nations', and to establish a Ministry of Defence. This was a substantial programme, not far short of what the Labour Government of 1945 was actually to put into effect. But the General Election for which it was designed did not happen ; and it gave no guidance for dealing with the immediate problems of Labour in opposition.

Before the *Immediate Programme* was issued, the Communist Party, the I.L.P., and the Socialist League had published their *Unity Manifesto* of January 1937, signed, among others, by Cripps and Laski, as well as by Jack Tanner of the Amalgamated Engineering Union, Arthur Horner of the Mineworkers, Maxton, Jowett, Pollitt, and Tom Mann. The *Manifesto* differed from Labour Party pronouncements chiefly in its militant tone and in the stress it laid on the struggle against imperialism in India and the colonies, and also in its insistence on not waiting for a General Election, but embarking on the struggle at once, especially on the home front and by means of a clear Pact with France and the Soviet Union for the defence of peace. The Labour Party Executive promptly responded to the *Unity Manifesto* by expelling the Socialist League from affiliation and declaring membership of it to be incompatible with membership of the Labour Party. These decisions confronted the League with a serious choice; for many of its members were most reluctant to suffer expulsion from the Labour Party. The League met the situation by dissolving itself, and thus leaving its individual members still in the Labour Party, unless they were individually expelled. But the Party Executive, in a further manifesto, issued during May, called on its members to refrain from any joint activities with the Communist Party or the I.L.P. and to concentrate on the Party's own proposals — that is, on *Labour's Immediate Programme*, which had just been issued.

The Socialist League having been dissolved, the Unity Campaign was reduced to the Communists and the I.L.P., with some Leaguers still participating as individuals. Side by side with it, these latter formed a Committee of Party Members Sympathetic to Unity, which in its turn was promptly banned by the Labour Party Executive. The Executive also banned all the resolutions in favour of unity sent in for the Annual Conference by affiliated bodies, on the plea that the issue had been dealt with already and could not, under the Standing Orders, be debated again for three years. This left reference back of the Executive's Report as the only way of challenging the decision open to the former Leaguers; and when the Conference met in October Cripps duly moved this on their behalf, urging that the Executive's ban on the Unity Committee of party members was wholly unconstitutional. He was seconded by Laski, and answered by Clynes and by Herbert Morrison, who said that the Executive had been, up to that point, very tolerant and had no desire to enforce uniformity by collective discipline, but would be forced to do so if the rebels persisted. Morrison pleaded with the rebels, having had their fling, to 'drop it' and remain in the Party as 'good comrades'. Then came the voting, first directly over the expulsion of the Socialist League and then over the question of the United Front; and in both cases the reference back was defeated by very large majorities, against minorities of between 300,000 and 400,000. The 1937 Conference, however, did amend the Party Constitution, both by giving two additional members on the Executive to the local Labour Parties and by providing that, in future, these should choose their own members, instead of having them elected by the Conference as a whole. The first of these changes, however, went through by a fairly narrow majority — 1,408,000 against 1,134,000, whereas the second was approved by nearly three to one. The date of future Conferences was also shifted from October to Whitsuntide, in order to avoid following so rapidly on the annual Trades Union Congress. This accounts for there being no Labour Party Conference in 1938, at the time of the Munich surrender.

These events made an end of the United Front, though propaganda for it continued. Its place was largely taken, in 1937–8, by the Popular Front as an attempt to promote a general rally of anti-Fascists, including those in the Liberal Party and perhaps even a few dissident Conservatives. This move, strongly backed by *Reynolds News* and its editor, S. R. Elliott, in the form of an United Peace Alliance, secured the endorsement of the Co-operative Party, only to be rejected in June 1938 by the Co-operative Congress, which held final jurisdiction in Co-operative affairs. The Popular Front movement was never able to organise itself successfully on a national scale; but it took shape in a number of local movements, and succeeded, in November 1938, in getting the left-wing Liberal, Vernon Bartlett, elected as M.P. for Bridgwater, in a straight fight with a Tory for a Tory seat. He took his seat as an 'Independent Progressive'. The advocates of the United Front were still opposing rearmament while Chamberlain remained in power, whereas the Popular Frontists favoured it, insisting that a Government of the Left would be helpless to resist the dictators unless it was adequately armed.

Bartlett's victory at Bridgwater and other Popular Front candidatures came after the Munich crisis, and largely as a response to it, Cripps, who remained a member of the Labour Party Executive, now attempted to take the lead in it. He circulated to the Executive a memorandum advocating the creation of a Popular Front open to every Opposition group, and demanded an Executive meeting to consider his proposals. This was held, and they were rejected by 17 votes to 3 ; but Cripps, not accepting defeat, then circulated his memorandum widely, under the auspices of an *ad hoc* National Petition Committee. The Party Executive demanded that he should publicly withdraw his memorandum, and that he should reaffirm his loyalty to the Party Constitution. Cripps refused, and the Executive thereupon expelled him from the Party and, when the campaign continued in spite of its ban, proceeded to further expulsions, including Sir Charles Trevelyan and Aneurin Bevan. Cripps announced his intention of appealing to the Party Conference against his expulsion, but was told that, being no longer a member, he was not entitled to be heard. This raised such a clamour that the Executive drew back, and agreed to leave it to the delegates to decide whether he should be heard or not. When the Conference met, at Whitsuntide, a small majority voted for hearing Cripps ; but he alienated a good deal of sympathy by making a legalistic speech defending his right to act as he had done instead of emphasising his real differences on policy, and the attempt to refer back the Executive's Report was defeated by a vote of five to one, just over 400,000 votes being cast on Cripps's side.

This was, in effect, the end of the Popular Front movement. By this time, the Spanish Civil War had ended with the fall of Madrid in March 1939, the Germans had marched into Prague and annihilated the Czechoslovak State, and the Italians had seized Albania. Neville Chamberlain, in March, had changed his tune by giving his extraordinary guarantee to Poland and other States of Eastern Europe — extraordinary in the sense that, after the fall of Czechoslovakia, Great Britain was without means of coming to their help and because it was given without any consultation with the Soviet Union. Negotiations in Moscow did indeed drag on through May ; but by that time it is clear that the Soviet Union had given up all hope of coming to satisfactory terms with the West. Maxim Litvinov, who had made every possible effort to invigorate the League system, was driven from office ; and Stalin began to turn his attention to the idea of a pact with the Nazis which would preserve the Soviet Union while leaving Hitler a free hand in the West, and would allow the Nazis and the Soviet Union to partition Poland between them.

Immediately, the Nazi-Soviet Pact presented the Western Communists with a very awkward problem. For years they had been trumpeting the cause of Anti-Fascism and calling on Governments and peoples for active resistance to it. Now they had suddenly either to eat their words or face expulsion from the Communist fold. A very few chose the second course ; but most of the leaders were so committed to holding the Soviet Union right on all occasions as to prefer the first. In Great Britain Harry Pollitt first published a pamphlet calling for support for an anti-Fascist war and, when disowned and driven from his position as Secretary of the Communist Party, bowed to party discipline and ate his words. A fair number of rank-and-file Communists, however, left the Party ; and the mortality was much greater among the fellow-travelling intellectuals, who were mostly anti-Fascists first, and sympathisers with Communism a long way second. The defections would have been much heavier had it not speedily become apparent that the 'Western democracies' were pulling their punches instead of making an all-out effort to defeat Hitler. 1939–40 was the period of the 'phoney war', which ended only when France had been knocked out and Great Britain was left to choose between fighting on virtually alone and accepting the defeat which not a few regarded as inevitable.

The British people chose to fight. Chamberlain was driven from office, though he still enjoyed the support of a majority of the Conservatives. Winston Churchill replaced him at the head of a Coalition in which the Labour Party found itself in main charge of the 'home front' and, through Ernest Bevin as Minister of Labour and National Service, of the mobilisation of national man-power as well. Churchill indeed put his veto on the raising of controversial political and industrial issues, even rejecting Labour's drive to get rid of, or at least to modify, the Trade Unions Act of 1927, passed as a Tory reprisal after the General Strike. But this did not upset, or seriously shake, the alliance. As long as the war lasted, Churchill, keeping its conduct and the final voice in international affairs in his own hands, left most home matters to the Labour Ministers, who were not ill content with the division of power. They knew at any rate that they could trust Churchill not to give way to Hitler; and that was what they, like most of their followers, cared about most of all.

During the war the Labour Party offered no electoral challenge to the Conservatives; but from 1941 onwards it was actively engaged in bringing its programme up to date. The process was begun with a general policy statement, *The Old World and the New Society*, issued in 1942 and approved in general terms in a resolution moved by H. J. Laski at the Conference that year. This statement, like its predecessors from *Labour and the New Social Order* to *For Socialism and Peace*, was not designed as an election programme and did not indicate precisely what a Labour Government would set out to do if it were returned to power. It was rather a general statement of long-term objectives, vigorously drafted and definitely Socialist in tone. It opened with an assertion of the need for complete victory over the Fascist dictators and for a remodelling of world forces against aggression that the people of the defeated countries would have to respect and accept. It traced both appeasement and Fascist dictatorship to the evils of an unplanned capitalist society and demanded 'planned production for community consumption' as the essential condition of freedom. It called for the maintenance of war controls during the period of post-war transition, and for full employment and orderly marketing under public ownership and control. Its four main emphases were on full employment, on rebuilding Britain to standards worthy of its citizens, on greatly expanded social services, and on education for a democratic community. On these issues it limited itself mainly to generalities, taking for granted the details worked out in earlier policy statements on particular points. It gave much more space than any previous general statement to international affairs, marking out for Great Britain a rôle of democratic leadership in post-war Europe. In relation to India it was somewhat equivocal, declaring for self-government but not for independence; and in relation to colonial areas it also stopped short of promising independence outright, though it denounced all forms of colour bar and declared for trusteeship as the basis of colonial government. Finally, it emphasised the need for arriving, before the war ended, at a clear understanding with both the United States and the Soviet Union, apparently without realising how difficult such a double understanding would prove to be. In general it was a forthright and even a stirring document, though it had serious weaknesses and omissions.

The omissions were to some extent made good in the long series of special Reports drawn up by the Labour Party's Reconstruction Committee during the ensuing years. These owed a good deal to the steady work, begun well before the war, of the N.F.R.B. and the reconstructed Fabian Society, to which reference has already been made. The close tie between the Party and the Society ensured that not merely were the reports and pamphlets published by the latter studied by members of the Committee and its sub-committees, but that active Fabians were among those members, carrying on the Society's traditional rôle of advice, criticism, and drafting. By 1944 the Committee had produced some fourteen Reports, each covering a special field of policy in considerable detail and, together with the similar Reports drawn up and approved before the war, forming, at any rate in home affairs, a fully adequate foundation for an incoming Labour Government. Coverage of international problems was much less thorough; and there was nothing at all dealing comprehensively with foreign trade, though it was clear that highly intractable problems were bound to arise in this field. There was, however, fully enough for the Executive to select from when it came to drafting a shorter programme of immediate action. This appeared early in April 1945, under the title *Let Us Face the Future*, and became in effect the Labour Party's election manifesto for that year. *Let Us Face the Future*, though it began and ended with rather general paragraphs about international aspirations, had to do mainly with home affairs. 'The nation', it said, 'wants food, work and homes'; and it proceeded to lay down how the Labour Party would set about providing these things. A Labour Government, it promised, would ensure full employment and high production 'through good wages, social services and insurance, and taxation bearing less heavily on the lower income groups'. It would control rents and prices, and also the location of industry, and would plan investment through a National Investment Board. It would make an end of Depressed Areas, and nationalise the Bank of England and 'harmonise' the operation of other banks with public needs. It would socialise the fuel and power industries, inland transport, and iron and steel, and would prohibit restrictive trade practices and bring monopolies under public control. It would put houses before mansions and necessaries before luxuries over the whole field of production, plan agriculture for higher food production of quality products, and maintain the new services developed during the war, including civic restaurants and canteens and cheap milk for mothers and children. It would hold food prices steady against inflationary forces. It would set up a Ministry of Housing and Planning — this is one of the few things in its programme that the Labour Government failed to carry into effect — provide a National Health Service, open to all, and introduce comprehensive legislation on Social Insurance. It would enact 'wider and speedier powers of land acquisition for public purposes, with fair compensation subject to a charge for "betterment"'. It would carry the Butler Education Act, already enacted, into full effect.

This was direct and specific enough, but on international affairs nothing specific was promised except the formation of an international organisation to keep the peace, based on the continued collaboration of Great Britain, the Soviet Union, and the United States, in association with France, China, and other countries which had contributed to the common victory. Nothing was said about relations with other Labour and Socialist movements, or about the problems of democracy in post-war Europe or in the rest of the world. Doubtless, it was difficult to be precise about such matters ; but the lightness with which they were treated, or passed over altogether, was ominous. The plain truth is that the Labour Party emerged from the war without a clearly thought-out foreign policy, and was speedily to suffer in consequence when power was placed in its hands. Few, however, realised this at the time of the 1945 election, in relation to which *Let Us Face the Future* was a very telling pronouncement.

CHAPTER IV

FRENCH SOCIALISM IN THE 1930s

THE depression of the 'thirties struck France later than other countries, mainly because Poincaré's stabilisation of the franc in 1928 had been at a rate low enough to give French exports a considerable advantage in world markets. As against this, French exports were largely luxury goods, and therefore specially affected by the fall in demand, and France also depended largely on tourist traffic, which was also seriously curtailed. Nevertheless, for a time the low exchange rate of the franc gave France some respite, though, even apart from the world depression, French finances were in considerable confusion, and there was much social discontent.

The election of 1928 had brought victory to Poincaré and the parties of the so-called Centre — that is, of the more conservative Republicans. After Poincaré's resignation, a succession of short-lived governments, some Radical, but mostly of the Centre and Right, held office under Briand, Tardieu, Steeg, Chautemps, and Pierre Laval, who was in office when the next elections were held in 1932. They resulted in a victory of the Left, including the Radicals, who were in fact sharply divided between a left wing under Daladier and a right wing in which Caillaux and Malvy were leading figures. For the Socialists Léon Blum had declared before the election their readiness to take office if they emerged as the largest party. But this did not happen, though they returned 129 strong to the new Chamber of Deputies, as against 157 Radicals and a mere 14 Communists, the latter having decided to fight the elections in isolation, on their slogan of 'Class against Class', and having accordingly gone down to defeat in the second ballot, in which Socialists and Radicals had for the most part acted together against the Right. These two parties, however, failed to agree on a common programme in terms on which the Socialists were prepared to enter the Government;

and the Radicals took office without Socialist participation except that of Paul-Boncour, who broke away from his Party to become Minister of War and presently Prime Minister, when Herriot resigned on failing to induce the Chamber to agree to continue war debt payments to the United States, after reparations from Germany had been finally written off at the Lausanne Conference.

Paul-Boncour and his successor Chéron did not stay long in office. They were succeeded by Daladier, who made renewed offers to the Socialists to enter the Government, but again failed to come to terms with them. The Socialists were, however, sharply divided among themselves, a substantial minority, especially among the deputies, holding that it was necessary to revive the *Cartel des Gauches* in order to combat the rising tide of Fascism in the country and to defend the Republic against its enemies. Prominent among the upholders of this view were the old leader of the Socialist right wing, Pierre Renaudel, the mayor of Bordeaux, Adrian Marquet, and the apostle of a planned economy, Marcel Déat, from the Auvergne. These advocates of Republican unity, however, failed to convince the majority of the Party, the more so because Daladier had included in his measures to combat the budget deficit a proposal to cut the salaries of the Civil Servants, who formed one of the strongest elements in the Socialist Party. The dissidents, none the less, persisted in their attitude and issued a manifesto, which was followed by their exclusion from the Party. They thereupon formed a Party of their own, the Neo-Socialists, which took away about 20,000 of the 130,000 members of the old Party.

During this period, in 1933, following Hitler's *coup* in Germany, but more clearly modelled on Italian than on German Fascism, the anti-Republican movement in France was rapidly assuming menacing proportions outside Parliament, at any rate in Paris. At its head were above all two organisa-tions — the *Camelots du Roi* inspired by the Royalist *Action Française*, led by Charles Maurras and Léon Daudet, and the *Croix de Feu*, originally an ex-soldiers' organisation, led by Colonel de la Rocque. Both these bodies, and also a number of others, such as the *Jeunesses Patriotes*, engaged in riotous demonstrations and disturbances in which it was alleged that the police to some extent connived. Fuel was added to the flames by the exposure of Serge Alexandre Stavisky, a swindler who had been under charges as early as 1927, but had never been brought to trial until the affair of the fraudulent bond issue at Bayeux was brought to light in December 1933. Stavisky, who committed suicide after the exposure, was alleged to have received protection in high political quarters, including a Radical Minister, Dalinier. In Parliament, the Right pressed for a full enquiry into the scandal, which Chautemps, then still in office as Prime Minister, refused. Public agitation then grew furious, and Chautemps resigned, giving place to a new Ministry under Daladier, who added to the disturbance by dismissing from office the Paris Prefect of Police, Jean Chiappe, a lively Corsican of extreme right-wing views, on whose dismissal the Socialists insisted as a condition of supporting the Daladier Government.

The Government, with Socialist aid, was sure of its parliamentary majority ; but such a majority was no longer enough to protect it against the violence of the Fascist leagues. On February 6th, 1934, when Daladier was making his official statement on behalf of the Government to the Chamber of Deputies, huge crowds assembled just across the river, on the right bank, and attempted to cross and capture the Chamber. They were repulsed, but with difficulty, and considerable damage was done. The greatest damage, however, was to the Republic's prestige. Daladier resigned, and Doumergue, a former President of the Republic, took his place at the head of a so-called Government of 'National Union'. In effect, the right wing was back in office.

Hot on the heels of the right-wing disorder of February 6th came a wave of strikes, short demonstration strikes, but none the less remarkable and successful. The French workers were at this time divided into rival Trade Union movements — where they were organised at all, which the majority were not — the old C.G.T., independent but in practice allied to the Socialists, and the C.G.T. Unitaire, run by the Communists in subordination to the Communist Party. But the events of February 6th and the strike movement led to a movement for reunion between the contending factions, which was finally consummated in January 1936 and was accompanied by a sensational rise in membership to about five million by the end of that year. There was a parallel movement for political collaboration between the Socialist and Communist Parties. Moscow had been led at length to change its line by the events in Germany, and the French Communist Party, which had been vehemently denouncing the Socialists during 1933 for their support of Radical Governments, followed the Comintern's new lead and began to call loudly for unity, not only with the Socialists but with anyone who was prepared to rally to the anti-Fascist cause. A small Party, called at first Socialist Communist and later the Party of Proletarian Unity, which had broken away from the Communists in 1923 and had subsequently joined forces with other dissident groups, had been trying for some years to bring the rival working-class Parties together, but had achieved no results. The leader of this third group was Paul Louis, the historian of French Socialism; but it was never strong enough to return more than a handful of deputies, even in the decisive election of 1936. The events of February 1934, however, induced the Socialist Party to accept the overtures of the Communists for a United Front; and at its Boulogne Congress the Socialist Party laid down a programme in terms of which it was prepared to join an anti-Fascist Popular Front, including both Communists and Radicals. This programme included the dissolution by law of the Fascist leagues, the nationalisation of banking and insurance, and of the great industries subject to monopoly control, the reduction of the standard working week to forty hours, the general recognition of collective bargaining rights, and the establishment of government control over the prices of wheat and meat, as well as a progressive tax on capital and other radical reforms.

Meanwhile, to the Stavisky scandal had succeeded, on February 21st, 1934, the discovery of the murdered body of Albert Prince, a high legal official concerned in the investigations. The murderers were never discovered; but it was widely put about that Prince had been killed, and vital papers stolen from him, in order to prevent disclosures of facts which would have incriminated high political personages. There was no proof of this, but it was widely believed at the time. Special Commissions, set up by Doumergue to investigate the

Stavisky affair in its political bearings, uncovered a certain amount of corruption, implicating a number of deputies and a section of the press, but exonerating the high figures against whom charges had been made. Doumergue, for his part, came forward with proposals designed to increase the powers of the Prime Minister and the Cabinet at the expense of the Chamber of Deputies. He proposed that deputies should give up to the Cabinet the right to advance projects involving expenditure, and that the President, on the advice of the Prime Minister, should be empowered to dissolve Parliament without needing the consent of the Senate, the powerful Second Chamber in which the Radicals and their immediate allies held a comfortable majority.

Doumergue's proposals were too much for the Radicals in his Government of 'National Union' to swallow; and in November 1934 his Ministry was forced to resign. He was replaced by the Centrist, Pierre-Étienne Flandin, whose mission it was to keep the Fascist leagues in order and to defend the franc, which had remained tied to gold since Great Britain went off the gold standard in 1931. This latter was a problem of growing difficulty as the effects of the world depression gradually overtook France, and enforced an increasingly deflationary policy. Food prices especially sank very low in the world market; and the French found that it was one thing to fix by law a minimum price for wheat, and quite another to secure its observance by farmers whose grain remained unsold at the official price. To complicate the situation, already complex enough, there arose a widespread movement of peasant discontent, led by the Conservative politician, Dorgères, while in the towns de la Rocque's *Croix de Feu*, aided by the *Camelots du Roi* and the other Fascist leagues, kept up an unending tumult. Stavisky was soon almost forgotten; but there developed a loud clamour about the overweening powers of the great banks and especially of the privately owned Bank of France, which was regarded as a tool of the 'two hundred families' said to dominate the economic affairs of the Republic and to be responsible for the deflationary policy of successive Governments which did their bidding. At the same time there was a very strong public sentiment against further devaluation of the franc, which

Poincaré had stabilised at one-fifth of its pre-war gold value as recently as 1928. The French, as a nation of small savers, did not wish to see their savings robbed a second time of their value. They wanted, in fact, inconsistent things — high prices for farmers, a low cost of living, and a maintenance of the franc at its 1928 value. And the deputies were by no means prepared to cover the deficit in the public finances by accepting higher taxation. The Government could not make both ends meet except by borrowing, which put it into the hands of its creditors and brought it into conflict with the Bank of France, which favoured retrenchment and deflation as the alternative remedy. Flandin in his turn resigned, unable to cope with the situation; he was succeeded by the one-time Socialist, Pierre Laval, by now definitely an ally of the right wing, who bowed to the Bank of France and instituted a thoroughgoing policy of deflation.

The formation of the Laval Ministry gave the signal for further outbreaks of Fascist violence, and Dorgères' Peasant Front launched a tax-strike against the Government. The Left called loudly for a dissolution of the Fascist leagues, towards which the Government was accused of undue complaisance. Laval, faced with the defection of the Radicals, whom he needed for his majority, promised action against the leagues. A Bill was passed making para-military organisations unlawful and empowering the Government to dissolve them and to make incitement to murder or violence a punishable crime. To a great extent, the new law was effective. The wings of the *Croix de Feu* were clipped, and it ceased to be more than an electioneering agency of the right wing. The danger of a Fascist *coup d'état* was at an end, if it had ever really existed. But Laval's political position was hardly less precarious on that account; for he was still faced by the mounting clamour against deflation and the Bank of France, and the international situation was becoming rapidly more dangerous. Laval's main idea, at this stage, was to keep Germany and Italy apart by placating the Italians, who, apart from their Abyssinian designs, were strongly opposed to Hitler's ambitions in Austria. In July 1934 an attempted Nazi *coup* in Austria had failed, though it had resulted in the murder of the Austrian dictator, Dollfuss. Laval set out to win Italy over to the side of France, and that meant giving the Italians a free hand in Abyssinia. For the time being, he appeared to succeed. Visiting Rome in January 1935, Laval negotiated terms with Mussolini on a number of outstanding issues, which in effect included letting him have his way in the Abyssinian conflict. In this he believed he could feel sure of British support; for, in face of the League's failure to intervene against Japan in Manchuria, he rated very low the prospect of League action against the Italians, especially as the British had opposed Abyssinia's entry into the League of Nations and had negotiated with Italy in 1925 about their respective spheres of influence in that country. But in Great Britain, which had been seriously upset over the Manchurian failure, 1935 was the year of the Peace Ballot and of the General Election in which the Labour Party was making its bid to remedy the disaster of 1931; and the British Government could not afford to throw over the League Covenant until the elections were safely behind it. The British Foreign Secretary, Sir Samuel Hoare, appeared as an advocate of sanctions against Italy; and France, it appeared, had to choose between going on with its policy of *rapprochement* with Italy and securing continued British support. But the British Government, though it invoked League sanctions against Italy, was content with mild measures that did not seriously hamper the invasion of Abyssinia and made no attempt to cut off Italian supplies of oil — a measure which would have been at once effective, and would have meant that Mussolini must either withdraw and admit defeat, or go to war with the League powers and throw himself wholly into the camp of Germany. More-over, in December the British Foreign Secretary visited Paris and negotiated with Laval the Hoare-Laval Plan, under which Italy was to be allowed to annex a considerable part of Abyssinia and to obtain economic rights over the rest of the country. This plan, published in Paris immediately after the Conserva-tives had won the General Election, created such an outcry in Great Britain that Hoare was forced to resign, and Eden took his place as Foreign Secretary. Mild sanctions were continued; but they did not stop Mussolini from completing his conquest of Abyssinia in defiance of them, while the preoccupation of France and Great Britain with Italian affairs gave Hitler his opportunity to march into the demilitarised Rhineland in

March 1936, thus finally tearing up the Treaty of Versailles and confronting the French with German forces immediately on their frontier.

Hitler's march into the Rhineland was, indeed, a decisive step on the road to world war. In combination with the weakness of League policy towards Italy it forced the Italians into alliance with Germany and involved the breakdown of the structure of French alliances in Europe. Hitler followed up his re-militarisation of the Rhineland by putting forward a Peace Plan which was in effect an attempt to separate Britain from France and to ensure the isolation of both from the Soviet Union. The Locarno powers replied with a counter-plan, which Hitler rejected, announcing that he would make counter-proposals after holding a plebiscite in Germany — as he duly did, securing of course an overwhelming vote in his support. He then put forward a revised 'Peace Plan', to much the same effect as the first, but with greater emphasis on the revision Germany would expect in existing treaties if she agreed to join the League of Nations as an equal partner. The British did not reject Hitler's plan outright, but called for further explanations, while the French responded with a far-reaching plan of their own. In July 1936 the British Government invited France, Belgium, Italy, and Germany to a London Conference to consider the German plan; but nothing came of their initiative, and Italy moved more and more into the orbit of Germany, especially as Hitler signed in July 1936 an agreement with Austria guaranteeing not to interfere in its internal affairs on the understanding that it would regard itself as a German State — an agreement he had no more intention of keeping than any other of his promises to keep the peace.

By this time a new danger had appeared in Western Europe with the outbreak of civil war in Spain. In July 1936, General Franco raised the standard of revolt in Spanish Morocco and there were military risings against the Republican Government in many parts of Spain. The Spanish Government sought to buy abroad arms to replace those which the insurgents had seized, and the rebels on their side sought assistance from the Fascist powers, which showed every readiness to afford it. France and Great Britain, however, shrank back at the danger of European war arising out of the Spanish conflict, and prepared to negotiate with Italy and Germany — and also with the Soviet Union — a so-called Non-Intervention Pact under which they withheld all help from the Republican Government, whereas the Fascist powers paid almost no attention to their promises and sent both men and arms to Franco's help in defiance of the Pact.

In France, meanwhile, the situation had been dramatically changed by the formation of the People's Front of Socialists, Communists, and Radicals and by its thorough victory at the General Election of April–May 1936. On July 14th, 1935, the advent of the new alliance of the French Left had been fore-shadowed by immense demonstrations, in which the Communists, following the new Moscow line, ardently joined. This was followed by formal negotiations for common action; and on January 11th, 1936, the Parties of the Left published the agreed programme of their *Rassemblement Populaire*. This included still more stringent laws against the Fascist leagues, laws compelling newspapers to disclose the source of their finances, a national unemployment fund, the reduction of working hours without wage reductions, a revaluation of agri-cultural prices without a rise in the cost of living — the middle-man being assumed to be responsible for the gap between wholesale and retail prices — and a reform of the tax system to prevent evasion by the wealthy classes.

With this agreed programme the Parties of the Left entered the General Election. That they would win it was almost a foregone conclusion; but the nature of their victory meant a big change in the distribution of power, even though the Left, which had won the previous election in 1932, could gain only about 30 additional seats. What was significant was that, whereas the Radicals lost almost as many as the Left as a whole gained, the Communists, now aided by the electoral pact, polled twice as many votes as in 1932, and actually won 72 seats as against a mere 12. The Socialists, with two million votes and 146 seats, also gained, but much less spectacularly. They became, however, the largest Party, and it fell to their leader, Léon Blum, to form the new Government, which the Communists agreed to support, though they refused to join it. Blum accordingly formed a Government made up of Socialist and Radical Ministers, and set to work to implement, not Socialism, to which the Radicals were bitterly opposed, but the agreed programme on which the election had been fought. A minority of the Socialists, headed by Marceau Pivert and Zyromski and backed by the Seine Federation of the Party, were opposed to these compromises with the bourgeoisie, but they were swept aside.

The advent of the Blum Government, just as civil war was breaking out in Spain, was saluted in France by a great outbreak of strikes, in which unorganised as well as organised workers took part. In one area after another, the strikers occupied the factories, so as to prevent the employers from using blacklegs to break the strikes ; but they made no attempt, such as the Italian strikers had made in 1920, to carry on production. They simply sat tight, and defied the police to dislodge them until their terms — shorter hours, higher wages, and complete rights of collective bargaining — were duly recognised. Blum, for his part, refused to take any action to turn them out, knowing the strength of the popular feeling. He summoned the employers to his office at the Hôtel Matignon and induced them to sign the Matignon Agreements, under which they agreed to raise wages and to concede full bargaining rights, the details being left to be adjusted by specialised agreements for each industry or establishment. He also went ahead with the enactment of legislation for the forty-hour week and for holidays with pay. The employers, terrified by the strikes and by the strength of popular feeling, felt themselves in no position to resist. They gave way, although French industry, with much of its equipment out of date and with costs already high, was ill-placed to bear the new burdens imposed on it. The Left had won a famous victory, even more industrially than politically ; and workers came rushing into the Trade Unions.

The Matignon Agreements and the forty-hour week were real working-class victories ; and so, for the moment, were the wage increases of 12–15 per cent which the employers were compelled to grant and the public works policy which the Government set on foot to provide additional employment. But troubles soon began over the detailed implementation of the agreements, as the employers regained their nerve, and

prices soon began to rise obstinately in face of government
prohibition until the wage-advances were more than cancelled
by the higher costs of living. Moreover, the Government was
still in acute financial difficulties, being forced to keep the franc
at the existing parity as long as it possibly could. The peasants
were indeed conciliated by the creation of an Office du Blé
empowered to stabilise the price of wheat by becoming sole
purchaser of the peasants' crop; but this too cost money and
added to the Government's financial difficulties. The Blum
Government did indeed effectively nationalise the Bank of
France by abolishing its Council of Regents and taking the
appointment of the Governor into its own hands; but this
did not give it any escape from its financial troubles. At length
in 1936, despite its promises, it was driven to devalue the franc
by fixing a new and lower rate of exchange after securing
promises from Great Britain and the United States not to
follow suit; but it did not venture to go far enough to give it a
respite for long. In less than a year after the Popular Front
had taken office, Blum was announcing the need for a 'pause'
to consolidate the gains already made — gains that were in fact
already slipping away; and it became evident to his supporters
as well as to his enemies that the Government was actually
in full retreat. By June 1937 Blum was driven to appeal to
Parliament for plenary powers for his Government, after the
two financial experts he had appointed to advise him in the
hope of placating the investing classes had resigned. France's
great gold reserve had been slipping away fast, and much gold
had been hoarded by speculators both at home and abroad.
The Senate, which had been from the first highly critical of
the Government's policy and had accepted it only because of
the strength of popular opinion, now saw its chance and rejected
Blum's demand for special powers. Blum thereupon resigned,
and the first Popular Front Government came to an end in
June 1937. Its place was taken by a second, under the Radical,
Chautemps, in which Blum agreed to serve; but the impetus
of 1936 was over, and no fresh advance was to be expected
from such as Chautemps.

Blum, while he remained in office, had clung to the policy
of non-intervention in Spain, despite strong Communist
protests, both because he had to follow the British lead and

because the alternative seemed to involve the risk of European war, which he was set on avoiding at almost any cost. The peasants, he was constantly being told, would not fight for Spain; and, for that matter, neither would a large part of the whole population. The French right wing was in favour of Franco — not only the French Fascists, but also many of the Catholics, though by no means all; and the bourgeoisie for the most part cared nothing for the Spanish conflict. There were wild stories of atrocities by Spanish Republicans — and some true ones too — as well as about the atrocities of the Spanish Right and its Moorish mercenaries; but above all else there was a wish for peace, almost at any price. Pacifism was very strong in the Socialist Party, in which the preservation of peace was an article of traditional policy, often backed by invoking the great name of Jaurès, whom Blum ardently admired. It was against Blum's nature to be a war leader, and against the grain of the Socialist Party to accept the need for war save in the very last resort, if at all.

Probably Blum was not at all sorry to escape from the post of Prime Minister in June 1937, when it was already evident, not only that the Fascist powers were not observing the Non-Intervention Agreement, but also that before long Hitler would be advancing fresh demands endangering peace. Chautemps was a politician well used to being at the head of ephemeral, do-nothing Governments which fell as soon as stronger men were available to replace them, and was unlikely to do anything very dreadful while in office. What he, or rather his Finance Minister, Georges Bonnet, reluctantly did was again to devalue the franc, which was this time left to float at about 130 to the pound sterling; and then to drive the Socialists out of his Government and form a purely Radical Ministry at the beginning of 1938. Less than three months later Chautemps resigned: so that when Hitler marched into Austria and annexed that country, France, in a state of political crisis, had no Government at all. Presently, a second Blum Ministry replaced that of Chautemps; but by that time the mischief was done, and Austria incorporated in the German Reich with no more than ineffective protests from London. In Great Britain, Anthony Eden had resigned from the office of Foreign Secretary in February 1938, in protest against Neville Chamberlain's policy of 'appeasement'; and Lord Halifax had taken his place. It was already evident that Hitler had fresh demands in contemplation, and that Czechoslovakia was likely to be the next victim of his attentions. Czechoslovakia was France's almost only remaining ally, and the Blum Government gave several assurances that France would honour its pledges to come to its aid in case of need. But by April the Blum Government had fallen from office and a new coalition Ministry of Radicals and Socialists had been formed under Daladier. In May 1938 Great Britain and France were jointly urging on the Czechs the need to make large concessions in the cause of peace. The Runciman Mission to Czechoslovakia followed in July and it became plain that the Czechs were in serious danger of being abandoned by their Western allies. The Soviet Union promised to go to their aid if France and Great Britain did the same; but in both Western countries 'appeasement' definitely had the upper hand.

So matters went on until the Munich Conference at the end of September 1938, at which Chamberlain and Daladier finally made their ignominious surrender of Czechoslovakia to Hitler. By this time, the Popular Front in France was dead indeed, though its parliamentary majority remained intact and a Radical Government in office. The French could argue that the only course open to them had been to follow the British line, and that first the Runciman Mission and then Chamberlain's visits to Berchtesgaden and Godesberg in September had shown unmistakably what that would be well before the Munich meeting. This was indeed true enough, given the situation as it existed in 1938. The question is whether the French could have done more to prevent that situation from coming into being by trying to collaborate more closely with the Soviet Union after the signing of the Franco-Soviet Pact of 1935 and in view of the Soviet Union's membership of the League during the ensuing years. Doubtless they could have done much more; but it is not irrelevant to observe that in the interval the Soviet Union, as well as France, had been passing through a great internal crisis following on the murder of S. M. Kirov in December 1934. The Franco-Soviet Pact would have had plenty of inveterate enemies in France in any case; but they were strongly reinforced by doubts about the trustworthiness of the Soviet armed forces and of their leaders with whom negotiations would need to be conducted. Litvinov, at the Soviet Foreign Office, was undoubtedly doing his utmost to bring the Soviet Union into closer collaboration with the League in a policy of resistance to Fascist aggression ; but it was doubtful how far his authority extended and what line Stalin was disposed to take. The Comintern and, under its direction, the Communist Parties of the West had undoubtedly altered their policy. The slogan of 'Class against Class' had been given up, and instead of it there had been a concentration on efforts to attract into anti-Fascist People's Fronts anyone who could be induced to take part in them. The French Communist Party in particular had gone over to a patriotic policy of an extreme sort, appealing not only to the Catholic Trade Unions as well as to the Socialists, but also to the middle classes, who, it was announced, could save themselves by alliance with the proletariat, if they would only unite with it against the 'two hundred families' and the whole gang of exploiting monopolists and middlemen who were battening on them as well as on the workers. Indeed, the French Communists were out-shouting the Socialists with their cries for the broadest possible anti-Fascist alliance. For, whereas, in dealing with the Socialists, the Communists found it hard to get away from interpreting the 'United Front' as meaning a single, highly disciplined Party and movement under their own centralised control — which involved the sheer absorption of the Socialist Party—in dealing with non-working-class political allies they put forward no such pretensions and felt free to advocate a limited co-operation that would leave such allies free, at any rate for the time being, to follow their own line.

Thus, the unity negotiations between Socialists and Communists that went on intermittently, to the accompaniment of much mutual recrimination, during these years were conducted largely at cross-purposes. The Communists wanted the Socialist Party to amalgamate with them, confident that they would be able, with their concentrated energy and determination, to establish their control over a united Party ; whereas the Socialists, who rejected the whole notion of 'democratic centralism' and party dictatorship but understood the strength of popular feeling in favour of united action, favoured a form of collaboration between the two Parties that would leave both of them intact. There was much disputation over the question whether organisational unity or common immediate action ought to come first; and this was really a dispute between amalgamationists and advocates of temporary federal collaboration. There was never really any chance that the Socialist Party would agree either to merge itself in the Communist Party or to unite with it in a single Party which would expose it to Communist penetration, as had happened as a consequence of the fusion between the C.G.T. and the C.G.T.U. in the industrial field. But something had to be done to ensure united anti-Fascist action; and the Communists, while they continued to press for complete unification of the working-class forces, were prepared, in default of it, to go even further than the Socialists in pressing for a broad Popular Front open to all who could be induced to join.

The antagonism between the rival Internationals to which the two French Parties adhered also helped to frustrate the negotiations for unity when they were resumed after the creation of the Popular Front. The Socialists accused the Communists of trying to push the claims of the Comintern and to insist on obedience to its dictates, while the Communists demanded from the Socialists guarantees of their acceptance of a duty to rally to the defence of the Soviet Union. The Socialists were annoyed with the Communists for refusing to take office in the first Blum Government, whereas the Communists, pledged to support the Government but remaining outside it, were able to claim the credit of its achievements while free to criticise its shortcomings. There was no love lost between Maurice Thorez, the Communist leader, and Paul Faure, who took the leading part in the negotiations on the Socialist side. Relations improved during the early months of the first Blum Government, but deteriorated rapidly when it ran into difficulties and when Blum first called for a 'pause' and then began to beat a retreat.

The Blum Government was, indeed, evidently pushed by the march of events after its assumption of office a good deal further than it would have been likely to go of itself. The great wave of stay-in strikes that immediately greeted its appearance forced it to give effect at once to the forty-hour week and to compel the employers to sign the Matignon Agreements, whereas it would undoubtedly have preferred to adopt a more elastic structure of working hours and to confine wage-advances within narrower limits ; for it must have been well aware that French industry could ill bear the burdens imposed on it, especially by the general reduction of working hours, and that there would be immense complications both over the introduction of the new working week and over the detailed application of the provisions for collective bargaining as a statutory right. The Communists, on the other hand, were troubled by no hesitations about such matters. Their aim was to exact the maximum concessions at once ; for they were well aware that the employers, if allowed time, would recover from their panic and would offer increasing resistance to the workers' claims. The Communists had not been mainly responsible for bringing about the strikes, which were in the main a spontaneous outburst of popular feeling ; but they were in the best position for taking advantage of them, and for pressing the Government to make the largest possible concessions. France in fact passed quite suddenly into a new structure of industrial relations for which it was entirely unprepared. Trade Unionism had been very weak during the period of its division into two or three rival and contending movements, and collective bargaining had occupied only a small part of the field. Suddenly it became almost universal, and countless employers who had never dealt with a Trade Union had to do so for the first time. For the moment, they had to put up with this, and to concede the forty-hour week and paid holidays as well. But they did not like it at all, and as soon as they began to recover from their panic, the first thought of many of them was to get their own back. They had, indeed, real grievances — a heavy addition to their costs of production without any respite for adapting themselves to it. Especially were the small employers indignant at what had been thrust upon them as the outcome of negotiations between the Government, the Trade Unions, and the bigger firms organised in the Grand Confederation of French Production, without any consultation with themselves. As an outcome of the strikes, Trade Unions greatly extended their influence, and *comités d'entreprise*, which they dominated, were set up in most substantial establishments. But there remained numerous small firms in which no organisation existed; and the application of the Matignon Agreements to such concerns was a source of much difficulty from the outset.

The considerable wage-concessions granted in response to the strikes were before long eroded by the rise in prices, which the Government was unable to control effectively. The workers then found themselves no better off in real wages than before, or even worse off, though they still enjoyed the advantages of paid holidays and of the shortened working week. At first, they poured out into the countryside to enjoy their vacations; but before long, in face of the rising prices, many of them were looking for second jobs to eke out their wages, and the Trade Unions had to take action to check this tendency in view of the shortage of jobs. At first, as we saw, the Government attempted to embark on an ambitious scheme of public works in order to provide additional employment; but it was very short of money, and the reserves of gold were melting away rapidly as they were either exported or secreted in private hoards. Vincent Auriol, Blum's Minister of Finance, had promised to maintain the franc's value; but, when he came to borrow, he was compelled to offer a loan repayable at a fixed gold value, and, when he had to devalue the franc after all, his attempts to secure the profit on hoarded gold for the State broke down and the hoarders had to be allowed to keep it for themselves. The Senate, which as we saw had given way at the outset in face of popular feeling, was only biding its time to clip the Government's wings; and by refusing Blum the special powers for which he asked — and which it subsequently allowed to the Radical Chautemps — brought the Blum Government down. It was in fact impossible for the Popular Front to carry out its promises, or to meet the demands of the workers, without large structural changes in the whole economy, on which the Radicals were by no means agreed; for the Radical Party, though it had its left wing, was in the main a very conservative Party — the most deeply attached of all to economic *laisser-faire* and the firmest upholder of private enterprise. Its following was mainly among the lower bourgeoisie and a section of the peasants; and it by no means relished the concessions made at the outset to the urban working classes. It did not go back on its alliance with the Socialists in any formal way; but it was determined to go no further than it was positively driven in the economic field. The Radicals stood for *laïcité*, and were staunch opponents of the claims of the Catholic Church; but they did not at all like a situation which forced them to side with the workers against the smaller as well as the big employers.

The *expérience Blum* was thus doomed to frustration from the very first, because it was an attempt at contradictory things — at attacking the great financiers and monopolists, but not the general run of small employers, and at the same time at satisfying the demands of the working class. It had also to satisfy the peasants, who had been very restive for some time. But to find a way of increasing agricultural prices without at the same time allowing the cost of living to rise was beyond its power. The Office du Blé and the other institutions designed to help the peasant did help him, but damaged the consuming public at the same time. Yet the Popular Front could not escape from these contradictions because it had promised to come to the assistance of the common man without attacking the capital-earning classes, except the very rich; but short of such an attack its attempted reforms were bound to put the economy in still greater jeopardy.

What was in truth wrong with the French economy, that it could so ill bear even the most moderate productive reforms? It suffered, in the first place, from a chronic instability in its public finances, due in part to a very large amount of tax evasion, especially by the richer classes and the peasants, and partly to a reluctance of the Chamber of Deputies to impose the necessary taxes to make ends meet. There had been a comfortable interval following Poincaré's stabilisation of the franc in 1928; but by the time the world depression fell on the French the advantages of this had been exhausted, and the budget deficits were back again. Moreover, France had now to cope with economic as well as financial adversities. Capital owners, instead of investing their money in bringing the means of production up to date, preferred speculation while the going seemed good and hoarding, at home or abroad, when times were bad; and savers clung to the gold value of the franc when it had come to be overvalued after the devaluation in Great Britain and the United States. Savers had over four-fifths of the nominal value of their francs swept away by Poincaré's devaluation; and they did not want the same thing to happen again. The Blum Government was caught between the conflicting wishes of its friends, the wage-earners, and the claims of the consumers, whom it also wished to be friends with, for lower, or at least not rising, prices. There was, however, no way of satisfying both, especially for a Government which needed to borrow, and had therefore to placate those who had money to lend. The Government clung to the fixed franc as long as it could, at the cost of seeing its resources melt away; and when it was driven to devaluation, it acted half-heartedly, not venturing to devalue enough to allow itself elbow-room. In other nations, the results of the Blum experiment were watched with deep interest. Inevitably, it was compared with Roosevelt's revolutionary New Deal. But the French situation differed widely from the American, in that the causes of depression had come upon it mainly from outside, and could not be dealt with by purely domestic measures — at any rate, not by those on which the Popular Front could agree. In less than a year the Popular Front was in full retreat, unable to undo the forty-hour week, but also unable to prevent its wage-concessions being cancelled by rising prices and its public works programme from being brought to a halt by lack of the means of paying for it.

What, then, was to be done? The Front had a clear majority in the Chamber of Deputies, and its members were by no means minded to give back to the Right the power they had won in the election of 1936; for the French Right was bitterly reactionary and hostile to the Republic. The Fascist leagues, even when they had been dissolved by law, continued their activity under new names. De la Rocque's *Croix de Feu* refused to convert itself into a political Party or to put up candidates for election in 1936; but it remained as a large and impressive organisation of forces hostile to the entire conception of political democracy and a potential, if no longer an actual, danger to the Republican régime. There had to be a Government nominally representing the victors of 1936; and when Blum's partners had become unstable, the only possibility left was a Government under Radical leadership, with the Socialists either in it or supporting it from outside — for without the voting support of both in the Chamber no Government could survive. Both alternatives were tried: Blum served under Chautemps, and then Chautemps carried on without Blum; but the Socialists continued to uphold the Government by their votes, even when they did not agree with it — for otherwise there could have been no Government able to command a parliamentary majority. But the Popular Front, though in form it remained in existence, had lost its spirit even before Blum resigned in 1937. Its basis of unity was negative: it knew what it was against, but not what it was for. To carry on the spirit of 1936 a new movement of enthusiasm outside Parliament was indispensable as a driving force; but the measures taken under this outside pressure could not be made effective within the framework of the existing order. The Blum Government, while the pressure lasted, bit off much more than it could chew when the pressure was relaxed; and its successors under Radical leadership had no policy except to hold on somehow and hope for the best.

This was the position in home affairs. Internationally the picture was even more difficult. The Popular Front had been formed with a mandate to combat Fascism both at home and abroad, but also to preserve the peace. But, in face of the attitudes of both Mussolini and Hitler, it was impracticable to keep the peace except by repeated surrenders to one Fascist claim after another.

Moreover, throughout these critical years there was the running ulcer of the civil war in Spain. It was most unfortunate for the Blum Government that the opening of their struggle coincided with the Popular Front's accession to power. For the Spanish War roused very strong passions on both sides. For the Fascist powers and for their sympathisers, it was another blow at the pretensions of democracy and an opportunity to extend Fascist rule, not merely to another country, but to one which would complete the encirclement of France and expose the French to the danger of a war on three fronts. To many Catholics it was a war of the Church for the restoration of its privileges, which the Republicans had taken away, and which was in dire peril of further indignities.

As against this, it was for many Radicals, as well as Socialists, a battle for *laïcité* — for the secular State against the priests, and for Republicanism against Monarchy. For Socialists and Communists alike, it was a war of the working class against its bourgeois and feudal enemies, a war of Left against Right in which a Front Populaire was ranged against a combination of reactionary forces. For Fascists it was part of the struggle against 'materialism' and for the assertion of the national spirit; whereas for the Communists it was the direct opposite. At the outset, it seemed a matter of course that, in accordance with international law, the Republican Government should enjoy full freedom to buy arms for its defence; but it was speedily realised that if arms were not supplied to the Government, even with full payment, nothing could stop the Fascist powers from assisting General Franco, despite his status as a rebel, and that, if help were freely given to both sides, there was danger of the war spreading until the great powers were fighting one another directly on Spanish soil. It was also feared that, in a free-for-all, the Fascist powers would throw themselves much the more intensively into the struggle, as Mussolini was threatening to do from the first.

In France, as well as in Britain, stories of atrocities were from the first invidiously disseminated in the newspapers, most of them putting the main emphasis on those of the Republicans, and particularly on those directed against the Church. Though Franco was undoubtedly a rebel, using his Moorish troops against a Christian people, most members of the upper and upper middle classes were on his side, and were very ready to believe atrocity stories directed against the illiterate barbarians who were held to form the backbone of the Republic. In these circumstances, it was hard to resist those who urged that, even if Franco could not be given open backing, steps should be taken to isolate the conflict and to prevent outside interference that might lead to an extension of it. Thus was born the notion of a Non-Intervention Pact, which would prevent the Fascist powers from helping Franco at the same time as it left the Republican Government to fend for itself. The assumption — or at any rate the ostensible assumption — was that the Fascist powers would actually observe such a Pact if they could be induced to sign it; and on this assumption the

French and British were prepared to deny the Spanish Government its undoubted legal right to buy arms for its defence. The Soviet Union, preoccupied with its great Treason Trials, also agreed to participate, with the precaution of declaring that it would observe non-intervention to the extent to which others observed it, and no further. On these understandings the Pact of Non-Intervention was signed by the five leading powers chiefly concerned. As might have been expected, its sole effect on the Fascist countries was, not to prevent their intervention, but to make it take as far as possible forms in which its existence could be denied.

In both France and Great Britain the Spanish Republicans' chief friends were the Communists, who throughout the struggle protested against the farce of Non-Intervention and called for a general rally of the Left to the cause of the Republic. In this they had the support of the main body of intellectuals and of student youth in both countries ; and the Spanish struggle became the rallying point for anti-Fascists of almost any sort, except orthodox Social Democrats, who saw in it the principal means by which the Communists were able to seduce recruits and therefore remained lukewarm where they did not positively oppose the *ad hoc* movements set up for Spanish relief and recruitment of volunteers to fight in Spain. For the French, of course, the Spanish issue was much nearer and more compelling than for the British ; for Spain was on France's frontier, and France could ill afford a further enemy among her neighbours. But even in Great Britain the intellectual and emotive aspects of the Spanish struggle had a deep influence which survives even to-day in the minds of many who were young and impressionable then.

In Spain, fully as much as in Austria or Czechoslovakia, the policy of 'appeasement' betrayed the anti-Fascist cause, partly because of want of sympathy with the Republicans, but much more because of a readiness to give up almost anything in the hope of avoiding war — or perhaps of persuading Hitler to turn his forces loose on Russia rather than on the West. It is a disgraceful story, for any Socialist who was guilty of connivance in it ; but it has to be recognised that it was extremely difficult for the French to take any action in which they could not depend on full British support, and that the main responsibility rests accordingly, not on the British Socialists — even if they must take some share in the blame — but on the Chamberlain Government.

So much for events in Spain, which are discussed more fully in a separate chapter. We must now ask what was happening during the 'thirties in France in respect of Socialist thinking. The answer, I fear, must be, very little; for in the continual bickerings between Socialists and Communists almost nothing that was new emerged. As in other countries, the Communist Party suffered repeated splits, sometimes expelling a recalcitrant group and sometimes experiencing a secession. These processes of alternation had been going on throughout the 1920s, ever since the French Communist Party had taken over the apparatus of the old Socialist Party; and the French Communists had been almost continuously at loggerheads with the Comintern, which claimed the right not only to settle their policy for them from Moscow, but also to decide over their heads who was to be expelled or demoted and who to be appointed to positions of party authority. Again and again, at the cost of repeated secessions and expulsions, the French Party had bowed to the Comintern's orders, only to find that the new leadership pleased Moscow no better than the old, and to undergo a further round of Comintern discipline.

What was astonishing in these circumstances was that, though the turnover of membership and the fluctuation in numbers was very great, the French Communist Party always managed before long to enlist new recruits to replace those who left. It shed in turn its Syndicalists, who were guilty of the sins of federalism and syndical autonomism, its Trotskyists, the Doriotists, and a number of other groups; but though it was never able, until 1936, to return more than a small group of members to the Chamber of Deputies — partly because it stood aloof from electoral arrangements with other Parties — it was able to remain as a lively and energetic body of militants and to reap a large reward for its participation in the Popular Front of 1936. Many of the seceders from it before long rejoined the Socialist Party, and others were able to hold together for a considerable number of years in a Socialist-Communist Party of their own.[1] But through all vicissitudes

[1] See Vol. IV, Part II, p. 485.

the Party held together as a powerful, mainly proletarian group, with its main strength in Greater Paris and the old Guesdist Nord, but with factory-based cells in many of the larger industrial establishments throughout France.

In the Communist Party Maurice Thorez soon emerged as the outstanding leader. He had been a miner and was the descendant of miners in the Socialist stronghold of the Nord and had gone to work in the mines at twelve years of age. Faithfully following the lead of Moscow through all its changes, he avoided the successive purges and remained at the head of the Party — as he does to-day, at least in a formal sense.

Thorez is not a political thinker of any note. He is a working-class militant who grew up in one of France's strongest Socialist regions and fell heir to the traditions of Jules Guesde, the devout follower of Social Democratic Marxism and admirer of German Social Democracy. The Guesdists of the Nord for the most part went into the Communist Party at the Tours Congress of 1920, and remained faithful to it through all its subsequent vicissitudes. Thorez, too young to have experienced Guesde's direct influence, started his adult life as a fully fledged Communist and was marked out for leadership by his capacity as a speaker and by his working-class origin; for Moscow insisted strongly that the French Party should be led by workmen and not by intellectuals, of whom in France it had deep suspicions as fomenters of indiscipline and as undue lovers of personal liberty.

Meanwhile the Socialist Party, as reconstituted after the split with the support of most of the Socialist deputies, though not of the rank and file members of the old Party, recovered gradually from their defeat at Tours, but were never able to recover their old position as *the* working-class Party. They were, indeed, sharply divided among themselves and, like the Communists, experienced a number of splits and secessions. The main issue inside the Socialist ranks was that of the degree of collaboration to be practised with bourgeois Parties of the Left — mainly with the Radicals — both in elections and in the Chamber. Up to the time of the Popular Front the great majority of party members opposed actual participation in a bourgeois Government; but, short of this, many favoured both electoral alliances, especially at the second ballot when it was in force, and support from outside for bourgeois Governments of the Left.

Thus, the Socialists, in the 1930s, were mainly engaged in adapting themselves to changing conditions, and had little energy to spare for fundamental questions of Socialism. With the Communists following faithfully the changing lines dictated to them from Moscow, rather than attempting to think out policies for themselves, there was little major Socialist thinking unless one counts the Neo-Socialists, who speedily made their way right out of the Socialist movement, some of them to stop short at the stage of economic planning, but others, such as Déat, to pass over to the French Right and to become in due course supporters of Vichy after the fall of France in 1940. Some former Communists underwent a similar evolution — notably Doriot, who had taken a leading part in the unity negotiations of 1933, but was excluded from the Communist Party the following year, and founded his *Parti Populaire Français* in 1936. He subsequently became a most virulent Fascist, and his P.P.F. took over many of the more violent members of the *Croix de Feu*, as well as other thugs and hooligans of many sorts. In 1944 he fled to Germany, where he was killed the same year — it is said, by an Allied bomb. Déat, on the other hand, survived until 1955, having fled from France to Germany on the liberation and become a member of the Sigmaringen 'Government' there. After the war he found religion and retired to a monastery in Italy, where he lived unmolested till his death. Above all else a planner in his early years, he became under Vichy a strong anti-Socialist Fascist of the Fascist left wing, rather in the manner of Otto Strasser in respect of social policy. Another 'Neo', Marquet of Bordeaux, became Pétain's first Minister of the Interior in 1940, and was a close friend of Pierre Laval. Of these three, Doriot was by far the most disreputable, and Déat the cleverest. All had passed a long way out of the working-class movement by the later 'thirties.

Among the orthodox leaders of the Socialist Party there was no notable Socialist thinker. Blum was a fervent disciple of Jaurès. He made some contributions to French thought about governmental and administrative organisation, and was able to carry out some of his ideas in reorganising the government departments while he was Prime Minister; but this was hardly a distinctive contribution to Socialist thought. Blum was a highly cultured Jewish intellectual, and deeply devoted to the Socialist cause; but he was neither a strong nor a great man. More eminent as a Socialist thinker was the classical scholar, Alexandre Bracke, whose real name was Desrousseaux (1861–1955), who was the best-known French Marxist scholar as well as the editor of Herodotus and Sophocles. He too had a deep admiration for Jaurès, in whose steps he followed; but he can hardly be said to have been an original Socialist thinker. Marx's grandson, Jean Longuet, leader of the French minority during the first world war, died in 1938, but had been out of the picture long before that. He too was never a significant theorist. Pierre Renaudel, his great rival who ended up by seceding with the Neos, had died well before him, in 1934. Younger men, such as Jules Moch and André Philip, who were to be important after 1944, had hardly made their mark in the 1930s. All in all, the French contribution to Socialist thinking during the pre-war decade was practically nothing.

CHAPTER V

THE CIVIL WAR IN SPAIN

IN Spain the dictator, Primo de Rivera, resigned in January 1930. His successor, General Damaso Berenguer, held office for a year, and then gave place to Admiral Aznar, who fixed municipal elections for April 1931, to be followed by a General Election. The results of the municipal elections were never fully announced; but they went heavily in favour of the Republican Parties, which had entered in August 1930 into the Pact of San Sebastián. In December of that year there had been a Republican rising, which had been suppressed by force, and the leaders tried for high treason and convicted, but immediately set free. After the big cities had all elected Republican candidates in spite of the use of the corruption habitually used in Spanish elections, the Republican Committee, headed by Niceto Alcalá Zamora, a Catholic Conservative who had quarrelled with the authorities, demanded the King's abdication in face of the overwhelming national feeling. Alfonso XIII refused to abdicate, but agreed to suspend the exercise of his powers and to leave Spain 'in order to abstain from any course which might plunge my compatriots into a fratricidal civil war'. The Republicans were left masters of the country, and arranged for the election of a Constituent Cortes to decide on its future government. The election, held in June 1931, resulted in a heavy majority for the Republican Parties, but their majority of 315 out of a total of 466 deputies was a very mixed body of Conservatives, Liberals, Radicals of various types, and Catalonian and other autonomists standing for provincial self-government, with only a sprinkling of Socialists of the right and left wings. The Anarchists and their supporters were advised to abstain from voting, but probably a good many of them voted all the same. They were, however, of course without representation in the Cortes.

At the outset of the Republic the great outstanding issues were broadly three — land reform, the diminution of the excessive authority in the hands of the Church, and the claims of Catalonia and the Basques for a wide measure of regional autonomy within a federal Spanish State. The most urgent of these was the question of the Church, on which the Prime Minister, Alcalá Zamora, differed sharply from most of his colleagues, with the result that he and the Conservative Republican, Miguel Maura, resigned from the Government in October, after many physical attacks had been made on churches and the Government had decided on measures against the Catholic Church. The Government was reconstituted under Manuel Azaña, the leader of the Republican left wing; but in December the right-wing Radicals, headed by Alexander Lerroux, followed the Conservatives into opposition to the new Government's social policy. Meanwhile, the Cortes had been drafting the new Republican Constitution, which was a thoroughgoing expression of parliamentary democracy, coupled with a forthright attack on the privileges of the Catholic Church. Under its religious clauses, which provoked Alcalá Zamora's resignation, the Church was disestablished and the payment of clergy from public funds discontinued. Religious orders exacting obedience to an authority 'other than the legitimate authority of the State' were to be dissolved, and their property confiscated, other religious orders were to be registered, and the property they might hold restricted to their legitimate needs; and all religious orders were forbidden to engage in industry or commerce, or in education. This was a blow especially at the Jesuit order, which possessed immense property and was widely engaged in commercial undertakings, and, more generally, at the Church control over education, which was well nigh complete.

The secular clauses of the new Constitution provided for a single-chamber legislature, elected by universal suffrage and secret ballot for not more than four years — women, as well as men, having the right to vote and sit as members — great innovations in a profoundly backward country, for which the Republicans were to pay dearly in the election of 1933. But at the outset the swing to the left was strong. The new Azaña Government, having shed the Conservatives and right-wing

Radicals, had a marked leftward tendency, but still within the limits of bourgeois and petit-bourgeois Radicalism, with very few Socialists in its ranks, or even in the Cortes. The President under the new Constitution was to be chosen by an electoral college made up of the Cortes together with an equal number of persons specially elected; and this college chose Alcalá Zamora as President, for, despite his differences with the Government and the Cortes over religious issues, he was deemed to be a good Republican and his name to carry wide prestige both at home and abroad.

The Cortes, having enacted the Constitution, proceeded to deal with the three big issues. During its first year it enacted an Agrarian Law (1932) for the expropriation, with compensation, of some of the vast, and mainly uncultivated, estates of the great nobles, and for their distribution to land-hungry peasants. This Act also set up an Institute of Agrarian Reform representing both employers and land workers, to carry out the projected changes in land tenure and distribution. The Cortes also enacted a Catalonian Statute of Autonomy, under which it restored to the Catalonian Generalidad the powers which had been taken away from it under the dictatorship — powers to control police services, education, and various other services — and made Catalan and Castilian co-official languages in the Catalonian region.

From these measures the Government passed in the following year to legislation giving effect to the religious clauses of the Constitution, which had been so far little more than declaratory. The Law of Religious Confessions and Congregations forbade all teaching by members of religious orders after the end of the year, and thus struck a direct blow at the religious schools, though the Government was by no means ready with enough secular schools and teachers to replace them and to cope with the vast mass of illiteracy that existed, especially in the rural areas. The President, whom the Constitution left no option but to sign the law, deferred his signature till the last possible day. Meanwhile, in April, municipal elections had gone heavily against the Government, many Conservatives and enemies of the Republic being elected; and at the General Election later in the year the Left Republican Parties did very badly, being reduced to 99 seats in the new Cortes, as compared with 207 for the right-wing Parties and 167 for the Centre — that is, for the Republican right wing. Azaña fell from office, and was replaced by a series of short-lived Ministries under Lerroux and other Centrist leaders, who not only called a halt to further left-wing legislation but also did their best to avoid implementing the laws already passed.

Such was the parliamentary situation from 1931 to 1933 and from 1933 onwards. But in Spain what took place in Parliament was only a small part of what actually occurred. There was no tradition of parliamentary government, in any real sense, and no disposition to obey the Cortes under the new conditions any more than under the old. The forces which had driven out the King and set up the Republic were not parliamentary : they had their roots in mass-discontent and found expression in widespread popular movements, especially among workers and peasants. Spain, except for a large part of Catalonia and a small part of the Basque area round Bilbao, was mainly a deeply impoverished agricultural country dominated by vast estates belonging to the great nobles or to the Church and for the most part cultivated by the most primitive methods, if at all. Huge tracts lay waste because the owners refused either to till them or to allow the landless peasants to do so ; and other areas, such as Galicia, were occupied by exiguous peasant holdings on which the crowded inhabitants could barely live. There were a few relatively prosperous areas in the Basque provinces or in river valleys in the east — round Valencia, for example ; and in Catalonia the *rabassaires*, who held the lands they cultivated under a semi-feudal tenure, sharing the crops with their landlords, had become strongly organised under Francisco Layret and his successor Luis Calvet in alliance with the Esquerra, the Catalonian left-wing bourgeois Party led first by Colonel Francisco Macia and after his death by Luis Companys ; whereas in many other areas, especially Andalusia, the rural proletariat was largely under Anarchist or semi-Anarchist influence and was accustomed to break out from time to time into savage local revolts, easily suppressed because each area acted in isolation from the rest.

In the towns and wherever industries, large or small, were found, there were Trade Unions ; but these were divided into a number of separate and rival movements. Much the most numerous of these was the C.N.T. — the *Confederación Nacional de Trabajo* — which was largely under Anarchist influence and leadership and was strongest in Catalonia, where it greatly outnumbered its rivals. The C.N.T. held aloof from party politics and favoured a form of libertarian Communism utterly different from the centralising Communism of the Communist Party. Its leaders, whether out-and-out Anarchists or not, were at one in opposing the State and advocating the reconstitution of society on a basis of free local Communes, loosely federated, but so as to leave the fundamental authority in the hands of the free localities. In fact, the C.N.T. was divided internally between Anarchists and Syndicalists — the latter looking much to the French C.G.T.'s great days for their model, whereas the Anarchists followed after the ideas of Bakunin and Malatesta and were in closer touch, up to the Fascist victory, with Italian than with French ideas. The C.N.T. in 1931 was large, and largely formless because of its repudiation of centralised authority. In the early years after the Russian Revolution of 1917 it had sympathised with the Comintern and the R.I.L.U., but had since been repelled by Communist insistence on centralised discipline and subordination of Trade Unions to the Party. Its best known leader was Ángel Pestaña, and after its break with the Communists it remained very definitely on the left, as the advocate of revolutionary Trade Unionism, though Pestaña and a section of it so far departed from its anti-political principles as to set up within it a sort of Syndicalist Party. In practice it threw itself as a whole into the cause of the Revolution.

Whereas the C.N.T. was predominant among the workers in Catalonia and was powerful in some other areas, Madrid was the stronghold of the chief rival Trade Union movement, the U.G.T. — *Unión General de Trabajadores* — which was closely associated with the Socialist Party. Its leader was Francisco Largo Caballero, who had accepted advisory office under Primo de Rivera, but moved rapidly leftwards after the Revolution and, for a time, acted closely with the Communists after the outbreak of Franco's rebellion. The U.G.T. was a much more disciplined organisation than the C.N.T., of which it stood for the most part distinctly to the right, often refusing to join in the general strikes which were a familiar weapon of the Spanish workers, though it sometimes collaborated in them with the C.N.T. In addition to Madrid, the U.G.T. was the main force in Bilbao and among the Asturias miners, who formed its left wing; but it had little strength in Catalonia — almost none in Barcelona — though it had a considerable following among the miners in the south of Spain and was able to recruit a great body of new members after the Revolution, even in parts of Catalonia not under C.N.T. control. On its right wing was Julian Besteiro, who became its President. Such following as it had in Catalonia consisted mainly not of manual workers, but of employees in the public services and other non-manual employees.

Outside both these bodies were numerous unattached Unions, ranging from the Esquerra's *rabassaires* in Catalonia to so-called 'Free' Unions which were really strike-breaking organisations of thugs set up by employers and, after the Revolution, to a small group of Communist Unions called the *Confederación General de Trabajadores Unitarios* — C.G.T.U. — which subsequently amalgamated with the U.G.T., though some of its sections broke away and joined the C.N.T. instead in areas in which the latter held a predominant place. There were also Unions which held aloof from politics altogether; and there were, or came to be, a few associated with other political working-class Parties — such as P.O.U.M. But the main body of organised workers was throughout divided between the Socialist U.G.T. and the Anarcho-Syndicalist C.N.T., and no united movement was possible except when they could act together.

In 1931, among working-class political parties, the Socialist Party easily held the leading place. The Communists were few and unimportant, and had split into a number of groups, Leninist, Stalinist, Trotskyist, and others; but they had little influence. The Socialist Party, with its main centre in Madrid, stood on the whole for centralisation, though it had to make concessions to Catalonian, Basque, and other autonomist claims. It was the old Marxist Party of its founder Pablo Iglesias, who had spent his life in fighting the Anarchists and their libertarian Communism and had died at a ripe age in 1925, leaving Largo Caballero in Madrid and the Asturian

Indalecio Prieto as the outstanding leaders. Between these two no love was lost; Largo Caballero was at the head of the U.G.T., but at Bilbao Prieto was in command over its local section. The third working-class Party of some importance — the P.O.U.M., the Workers' Party for Marxist Unification — did not come into being until 1935, when it resulted from a fusion between Joachim Maurin's Workers' and Peasants' Bloc and Andrés Nin's Communist Left. Thereafter, its main strength was in Catalonia, as was that of the P.S.U.C. — the United Socialist Party of Catalonia — also formed in 1935 by a fusion between the main bodies of Socialists and Communists in the region.

The Spanish Socialist Party had a traditional quarrel with the Anarchists going right back to the days of the First International. The main Anarchist organisation, F.A.I. — the Iberian Anarchist Federation — was not formally constituted until 1927, and remained an illegal body until the outbreak of the rebellion in 1936. Prior to 1927 the Spanish Anarchists had worked individually or in small groups, and largely in connection with the C.N.T., in which they exerted a great influence, though the 'pure' Anarchists among them were suspicious of its Syndicalist tendencies and, still more, of any sign of its willingness to ally itself with any political Party. The Anarchists, as a group, were not primarily bomb-throwers, though some of them did throw bombs at times. They were an exceptionally high-minded group of libertarian theorists, who believed in the innate capacity of the masses, and were acutely hostile, not only to 'God and the State', Bakunin's twin bugbears, but also to every kind of bureaucracy or centralisation — even to any sort of paid official, or, at all events, to any who received more than a workman's wage — and to any form of authoritarian organisation possessed of coercive power. This attitude ranged them in sharp opposition to the Socialist Party and to its ally, the U.G.T., as well as to all the bourgeois Parties and, of course, to the Communists — who became important only with the outbreak of the Civil War.

We find, then, in 1931 an extremely confused and confusing situation. The Republic was set up not by Socialists or Communists, but formally by a wide coalition of Conservatives, Liberals, Radicals of many sorts and actually by the shapeless, but formidable popular movement. The King's deep unpopularity gave it at the outset the support of a large part of the Army, including General Sanjurgo, who was soon to rise in arms against it. The working-class part in it was played mainly, not in parliamentary politics, but in great waves of strikes which the new Government would not have dared to repress even if it had wished; and the rural workers joined in with great protest riots accompanied in some cases by actual seizures of land. These manifestations came partly from workers in large-scale industry in Catalonia, in Bilbao, and among the miners; but they came also from a host of small-scale enterprises of artisan industry and from many service occupations — waiters, hairdressers, clerks, and the like. Their leadership was mostly local, and on the whole spontaneous, with the Trade Unions following, rather than leading, the popular movement. The C.N.T. was indeed largely controlled by the Anarchists; and the C.N.T. Unions threw themselves energetically into the struggle; but the U.G.T. Unions also, despite their close connection with the Socialist Party, were led into the fray by the common impulse, which extended far beyond the ranks of the rival Trade Union federations. These profited by it in enrolling new members at a great rate and were driven much closer together in pressing their common claims; and the politicians, whether they liked it or not, had to give way to them and recognise them as representatives of popular forces far beyond their parliamentary strength.

It was one of the Republic's great difficulties that the political forces it had put into office did not correspond to the popular feeling. Azaña was indeed a thoroughgoing Radical of strong left-wing sympathies; but he had no clearly-thought-out economic policy or attitude to the working-class movement. He was happy enough in attacking the Church and the religious orders and in carrying through the Catalonian Autonomy Statute, but considerably less at home in dealing with the great landowners and still less in coping with industrial demands. His position was made the more difficult in that his coming to power coincided in time with the great world depression, which hit the Spanish balance of payments, and was speedily followed by Hitler's conquest of power in Germany. Large concessions which the Spanish economy could, it appeared, ill afford had to be made at a most inconvenient time ; and the new Government had no policy for adapting the economy to them. In these circumstances it was bound to lose a great deal of its initial popularity. The spontaneous attacks on religion, the church-burnings that occurred in many areas, alienated many Catholics who had taken initially the side of the Republic ; and the recurrent strikes were unpopular with many of its bourgeois supporters. First Alcalá Zamora and then Lerroux and his Radicals had passed into opposition to the Government before the end of 1931 ; and the enfranchisement of women, whatever its long-run effects, was likely to react in the immediate future on the Church's side.

Moreover, both land distribution and the reform of education on secular foundations were very complex matters, in which success could not be rapid, at any rate if it was to be achieved by constitutional means. Teachers had to be trained, and schools built ; and it was an immense task either to settle the landless peasants on the great estates or to improve the conditions of those who already occupied some land — usually too little to live on save in dire poverty — as tenants or owners. Matters could advance more rapidly when the peasants were able to seize the land without waiting for legal sanction ; and such seizures took place sporadically in a number of areas. Church schools too were seized, and new schools were opened, without waiting for the Government to seize or provide them ; but no such action could provide the large number of new teachers who were needed.

Already in August 1932 the Republic had to face its first right-wing military revolt. General Sanjurgo rose against it in Seville, but was promptly suppressed with very little fighting and received no support from the main bodies of the Republic's enemies. His *coup* was premature and ill-planned : after it he was sentenced to death, but reprieved after two million persons had signed a petition calling for mercy. The Republicans constituted an armed police force, the *Guardias de Asalto*, to defend the Republic ; but in other respects matters went on as before. The old Civil Guard remained in being, but was not to be relied upon, and largely continued its accustomed methods of brutality in dealing with the people.

Then came the elections of 1933 and the sharp defeat of

the left Republican Parties. For the next two years one Government after another went as far as it dared to undo the achievements of the previous two years without absolutely making an end of the Republic. Gil Robles organised his combination of right-wing Parties, the Ceda (*Confederación Española de Derechas Autónomas*) and José Antonio Primo de Rivera, son of the late dictator, his *Falange Española* with its militant auxiliary, the *Juntas Ofensivas Nacional-Sindicalistas*. Calvo Sotelo's *Renovación Española*, definitely monarchist, modelled themselves largely on Italian Fascism. All these and many other right-wing bodies were in full cry against the left wing and also against the so-called 'Centrist' Governments which had replaced Azaña after the elections. They wished to drive these Governments further and further to the right, and presently to replace them; but they understood that their time had not yet come.

The Republic staggered along under increasing difficulties. In the autumn of 1934 rebellions broke out in Catalonia and the Asturias. The signal was given by the fall of the Samper Ministry and the formation of a new Lerroux Ministry including right-wing Ministers from Gil Robles's Ceda. In Catalonia an exceedingly confusing situation existed, with Companys's Generalidad engaged in a bitter dispute with the Madrid Government, Madrid's troops in Barcelona, the Esquerra itself divided between Doncas's Separatists of Estat Català and the followers of Companys, a Workers' Alliance of Socialists, Communists, and Trade Unions arrayed against Doncas, and the F.A.I. Anarchists under persecution both by Doncas and by the Generalidad's own police. In this state of affairs there developed an insurrectionary movement, in the midst of which Companys, under pressure from Doncas, proclaimed 'The Catalonian State within the Spanish Federal Republic' — a slogan which pleased nobody and brought on him the full weight of the military from the castle of Montjuich, the workers vainly calling, but too late, for arms to enable them to resist. Against only sporadic and ill-armed opposition, the soldiers occupied the principal buildings, and Companys was forced to surrender. The Generalidad was deprived of its powers, and Catalonia passed back under the reactionary rule of Madrid's new right-wing Ministry.

The Catalonian revolt was tragi-comedy : what happened in Asturias was sheer tragedy. The Asturias miners were the most solidly organised section of the Spanish proletariat and, in 1934, almost the only section in which the Communists yet held a strong position and were closely allied to other groups and Parties. Under a sequence of local Workers' Alliances, of varying political complexion but co-ordinated by a regional Alliance in Oviedo, the Asturias workers rose in revolt against the Government and occupied Oviedo and other towns. At once large military forces were concentrated against them ; and they were desperately short of arms and still more of ammunition. Inexorably the government forces closed in and overcame their dispersed resistance, suppressing the revolt with an extreme brutality which deeply shocked those who got to hear about it. Thousands of victims were killed, and thousands more sent to concentration camps where they were brutally ill-treated. There had, no doubt, been atrocities on their side before their defeat ; but the reprisals were on an infinitely larger scale.

After the Catalonian and Asturias rebellions, arrests of Republican leaders spread far and wide. Azaña and Companys were both arrested and put on trial as rebels. The right wing seemed to be triumphant over its enemies of the left ; but it was still unable to govern without the support of the centrist Parties, which held the balance of power in the Cortes, but were equally unable to maintain themselves without the support of Gil Robles and the extreme Right. In fact, what took place after the events of 1934 was a rapid swing back of popular opinion towards the Left, together with a determination of the Left to make an effort to sink its internal quarrels in order to regain the control of the Cortes which it had lost in 1933. Round Azaña — as the popular man of the Left — the Popular Front began to form in readiness for the General Election of 1936.

Into the *Frente Popolar* formed to fight the elections entered Socialists and Communists, the bourgeois Republicans of the Left, the Catalonian and Basque autonomists, the Trade Unionists of the U.G.T., and many smaller groups. The anti-political C.N.T. did not join the Front, but for the first time issued no instruction to its members to abstain from voting ;

and even the Anarchists of F.A.I. were quite largely drawn into the movement. When the elections were held, in February 1936, the Left Parties won a resounding victory. With 256 seats they had a majority of 39 over the Right and Centre combined. The Right had 165 seats, and the Parties of the Centre a mere 52, as against the 167 of 1933. The Left was thus in a position, constitutionally, to carry through whatever legislation it thought fit; but the real forces released by its victory were much more outside the Cortes than inside it. Inside, the new majority used its power to depose Alcalá Zamora from his position as President of the Republic; and in May 1936 Azaña was elected in his stead. Cesares Quiroga became Prime Minister, but could do little to influence the course of events. Again, as in 1931, there were strikes and troubles almost everywhere, accompanied by a recurrent outburst of church-burning and attacks on the religious orders, which had largely re-established themselves during the two years of reaction. There were also widespread seizures of land by the peasants, and a general breakdown of the forces of law and order. Many murders were committed on both sides, among them that of Calvo Sotelo, the Monarchist Fascist leader who was the bitterest and most formidable of the Republic's enemies.

This was the position when, in July 1936, General Franco in Spanish Morocco raised the standard of armed revolt and set out to invade Spain with the aid of the Spanish Foreign Legion and an army of Moors. He had some difficulty in transporting his forces from Africa, as the navy had for the most part stood by the Republic — though the killing of most of the officers left it unable to attempt much on the Republican side. But there were military risings in many parts of Spain, though by no means everywhere; and Franco managed to transport his forces to Cadiz, partly by air. In both Madrid and Barcelona, however, military risings failed when the soldiers refused to follow the officers and fraternised with the people.

It is no part of my plan to tell over again the oft-told tale of the Spanish Civil War in its military aspects. My concern here is solely with its political aspects. At the outset there was some disposition on the Republican side to underestimate the seriousness of the danger, especially when Madrid, Barcelona, and Valencia had all been successfully held against attempted military rebellion. But before long the seriousness of the rebellion was fully appreciated, especially after the fall of Toledo in September 1936 and the advance of rebel armies almost to Madrid in the closing months of that year. Málaga too was taken during the winter of 1936–7, and then in the summer of 1937 the rebels made themselves masters of the Basque country, including Bilbao, and of Santander. The following year, advancing eastwards, the rebels penetrated into Catalonia and, by reaching the Mediterranean, bisected Republican Spain. Meanwhile, Madrid was under siege, and the Government retreated to Valencia. The Republicans made a determined stand on the Ebro from July to November 1938, but were forced to evacuate Catalonia in February 1939. The following month, the fall of Madrid after its long and heroic resistance brought the Civil War to an end. Franco's victory was at length complete. Azaña had resigned from his office as President after the evacuation of Catalonia : Negrín, the last Republican Prime Minister, escaped into exile.

On the outbreak of the rebellion in July 1936 Quiroga resigned office as Prime Minister and a new Government was formed under the moderate Republican, Martínez Barrio, with the purpose of rallying moderate support to the Republican cause. But the Cortes refused to accept Barrio, and Azaña was forced to accept José Giral as Prime Minister in a Cabinet by no means mainly Socialist, but considerably further to the left than Barrio. Constitutionalists — or rather those whom it suited for the time to pose as such — asserted that this destroyed the Government's constitutional foundations, because the Constitution gave the President the sole right to nominate the Prime Minister ; but, as Azaña continued as President, the contention seems to lose its force. Azaña was, however, from this time mainly a figurehead, the reality of power resting with the successive Cabinets — or with the masses, whose puppets they virtually were. In any case, Giral's period of office was short : in September he was replaced by Largo Caballero, the leader of the Socialist Party and of the U.G.T. Largo Caballero stood at this time on the left of the Socialist Party, favouring alliance with the Communists, who had been steadily increasing their strength since help had begun to arrive from the Soviet Union. When the siege of Madrid began the Government moved its headquarters to Valencia and tried to strengthen itself by broadening its basis to include representatives of the Syndicalists, who had given up for the time being their anti-political attitude in face of the needs of war. This was a great concession on the part of the C.N.T. leaders; but many even of the Anarchists realised the need to rally all available forces to the Republic's defence.

But, despite the apparent union of the working-class forces behind Caballero's Government, there were still great divisions in the working-class ranks. In the early months of the Civil War effective power had fallen mainly into the hands of local Workers' Committees, either mainly under Anarchist control or consisting of representatives of all the local workers' organisations; and the army was made up mostly of workers' militia units largely identified with a particular Party or Trade Union. The Republic needed to create a new army, adequately trained and disciplined; but the various bodies which had militia forces under their control were very reluctant to give them up, despite their evident military inefficiency, or to accept the need for a regular corps of officers in place of the elected leaders of the various groups. Both the provision of arms and the training of a disciplined army were problems of special difficulty. Under international law, the Spanish Government had every right to buy arms abroad for the suppression of an internal rising, and in the case of France its right to do this was also safeguarded by treaty. France, moreover, had a left-wing Government — that of the Popular Front — which could be expected to be wholeheartedly on the Spanish Government's side. None the less, the right to buy and import arms was refused to the Spanish Republicans, and after a time volunteers from France and Great Britain were forbidden to go to Spain to join the International Brigade. We must now enquire how this remarkable situation was brought about.

The explanation, of course, is to be found in the condition of European politics when the rebellion occurred. Italy had just won the war in Abyssinia, and League sanctions against Italy were being called off. Negotiations were well advanced for a working 'axis' between Berlin and Rome. In France, the Blum Government had just come to power and was deeply preoccupied with its home affairs. In Great Britain the Tories, having won the 1935 General Election, were firmly seated in power, and the Labour Party had virtually given up its opposition to rearmament. In relation to Spain there was no doubt from the first about the Fascist countries' support for the rebels, who had been closely in touch with both Germany and Italy before the rising. France was afraid of a war on its frontiers in which Germany and Italy would be certain to intervene on the Fascist side, while the Soviet Union, by now converted to the policy of Popular Fronts against Fascism, did its best to help the Republican Government. Was not the best policy to try to prevent all this by negotiating a general agreement to leave the Spaniards to fight the struggle out among themselves, without help from abroad from either side ? There was something to be said for such a policy, if it were really practicable and would be carried out by the Fascist powers.

As a first step, Blum appealed to the British Government, which declared itself highly favourable. The Soviet Union also agreed, on condition that other countries did the same and that the pact was generally observed. Italy and Germany also nominally agreed, and lesser countries readily followed the example of the leading powers. Twenty-seven countries signed the Pact, including France, Great Britain, Germany, Italy, and the Soviet Union, and also Spain's totalitarian neighbour, Portugal. They all signed ; but whereas France and Great Britain generally observed the Pact and enforced it on their subjects, German and Italian intervention continued almost unchecked. Only Italy sent large conscript armies to fight on Spanish soil on the side of the rebels ; but the Germans poured in munitions and technical aid and supplied war planes which were of inestimable value to the rebel armies ; and both countries helped Franco to blockade the Republican ports, though he had almost no navy of his own, and engaged in piracy on the high seas against vessels carrying arms or supplies to Republican Spain. On the other side, the Soviet Union, when it saw how little the Pact was being observed by the Fascist powers, helped the Republicans with supplies as far as it could, but never on a scale nearly big enough to offset the doings of the Fascist powers.

Under these circumstances the defeat of the Republicans

was inevitable in the long run, however bravely they fought. For a time they were helped to stave it off by the International Brigade, which fought fiercely in defence of Madrid and suffered very heavy casualties. The International Brigade was made up of contingents from many countries, including France and Great Britain; but the nucleus of it came from exiled Socialists and Communists from countries which the Fascists had already overrun, notably Germany and Italy. There were also Russians, not only from the Communist Party, but also from groups which had quarrelled with it and had become Stalin's most venomous critics. For the Soviet Union, which had recently published the draft of Stalin's new Constitution, was engaged at the time of the Spanish rising in the deep internal troubles aroused by the great treason trials and was in a ferment which the official Communists were doing their utmost to play down.

Non-intervention was from the first a farce, and almost everyone knew it to be so. But the French and British clung to it as part of their common policy of 'appeasing' the dictators, in the hope either of staving off war or of turning it to the East instead of the West; and the Spanish Republicans were the sufferers. For a time it appeared that Largo Caballero's Government had achieved a wide basis of union among the Republican forces; but behind the façade of unity each section went on playing for its own hand and, in especial, there was no effective co-ordination of the various local war fronts. The continuing disunity played into the hands of the Communists — by now a rapidly rising force and firmly ranged against all who sought to press on with social revolution before the war was won. The Communists had, indeed, become definitely a right-wing influence in Spanish affairs.

In Russia itself, the Revolution had passed into its definitely Stalinist stage of rigid insistence on absolute conformity to official party policy, and of violent denunciation of all who were suspect of any deviation from the party line. A practice had grown up of denouncing nearly all such deviationists as 'Trotskyists', whether they had in fact any sympathy with the exiled Trotsky or not. In relation to Spain this meant that the official Communists were very sharply hostile to Communist dissidents, whether Spaniards or foreigners who had come to

Spain to take part in the defence of the Republic. It also ranged them in very strong opposition to the 'libertarians' of the C.N.T. and the F.A.I., and to all groups which were in favour of pressing on with revolutionary changes to the prejudice, as they held, of an united war effort. All over Spain, when employers were either killed or fled from their businesses in large numbers, the workers had taken over the abandoned factories and the peasants occupied the lands deserted by their owners. These things had been done very differently from place to place and from factory to factory. In many cases, especially in Catalonia, the workers had simply taken over the factories, elected committees to run them, and continued to produce as before, largely at unaltered wage-rates. In a number of rural areas the peasants had established their own free Communes, abolishing money and endeavouring to obtain what they required from outside by barter. In other areas factories or vacated land had been taken over by the municipal or other local authorities, and production had been continued under their auspices. The Communists now took up a strong stand against such factories as had passed under 'workers' control', chiefly by workers organised in the C.N.T., even using their influence to prevent such factories from getting supplies of materials in order to compel them to place themselves under official control. In Catalonia, the principal factory area, where the manual workers mostly belonged to the C.N.T. and Anarchist influence was strong among the factory workers, there ensued a bitter struggle between the Communists and the C.N.T., or rather between the latter and the United Socialist Party of Catalonia, in which Socialists and Communists had amalgamated into a single body, which the Communists had succeeded in prevailing to adhere to the Comintern. There were by this time many Russians in Republican Spain, not as soldiers but as experts of various sorts and as organisers on the political front. The Soviet Union did not send contingents to fight in Spain ; but as the main supplier of munitions for the Republic — munitions for which the Spaniards had to pay — its agents obtained great and growing influence over Republican policy. Whole-hearted supporters of a Popular Front, including the bourgeois Republican Parties as well as the Socialists, they at first supported

Largo Caballero's Government, even when the Syndicalists had joined it; but before long they passed into opposition to it and demanded a Government that would establish fully unified control and make an end of the large autonomy still enjoyed by the Workers' Committees and the separate parties and groups within the common front. On this issue they found it much easier to come to terms with the bourgeois Republicans and the right wing of the Socialist Party than with the left-wing Socialists or the C.N.T., with whom Largo Caballero was trying to work in amity. In particular, they were determined to drive out of the Government the representatives of the C.N.T. who had joined it and to prevent such dissident Communists and left-wing Socialists as were organised in P.O.U.M. from obtaining a footing in it. They were also very careful not to allow the arms sent in by the Russians to be distributed to any of the groups to which they took objection : so that the Aragon front, which depended for supplies on Catalonia, was starved of arms as long as the C.N.T. remained the dominant group there. The Russians had to contend with a good deal of xenophobic feeling among the Spanish workers, despite the outstanding service rendered by the International Brigade in the defence of Madrid; but in spite of this they made rapid headway. The Government, faced with immediate defeat if Russian supplies were cut off, could by no means afford to quarrel with them, or to say them nay; and they had on their side an ever-increasing number of the younger Spaniards in the areas held by the Republicans. The Anarchists and the C.N.T., meanwhile, were steadily losing ground as the Communists and the right-wing Socialists grew in strength. Even the U.G.T., though its leaders remained loyal to Largo Caballero, went over in part to their side.

In October 1936 the Cortes passed the Statute giving autonomy to the three Basque provinces. The Basque Nationalists, though ardent Catholics, had stood by the Republic against the rebels; and this was their reward. The rebels, however, were around them in León and Castile and in Navarre, the Carlist stronghold; and in the summer of 1937 the Basque area was overcome. Bilbao fell to the rebels in June, Santander in August, and Gijon in October. This would have involved a fresh offensive against Madrid had not a Republican offensive, launched by the reorganised Republican army, captured Teruel, in Aragon, in December 1937. The re-taking of Teruel by the rebels in February 1938 was the opening of the offensive which enabled the rebels to invade Catalonia and cut Republican Spain into two parts, isolating Barcelona from Madrid and from Valencia, except by sea.

But well before this happened Largo Caballero, accused of taking too much power into his own hands and at the same time of doing too little to establish unity of administration and authority, had fallen from office and been replaced by the ex-professor, Juan Negrín, with the support of the Communists as the foremost advocates of unity and centralisation. In May 1937, while the rebel attack on the Basque country was at its height, the Republican cause was seriously damaged by a renewed internal struggle in Barcelona.

What the Barcelona conflict was directly about it is nearly impossible to say — so complex were the issues, and so confused. As we saw, the predominant element in the local Trade Union movement was the C.N.T., which had close connections with F.A.I. But the rival U.G.T. Trade Unions had also enrolled a large membership, and were linked up with the United Socialist Party of Catalonia. This combined Party, the P.S.U.C., was represented in the Generalidad Provincial Government, with the Esquerra and its *rabassaires* and other groups, including the C.N.T. Outside the Government stood F.A.I. and the Marxist Revolutionary P.O.U.M., headed by Andrés Nin, and also a body called the Friends of Durruti — after the Anarchist leader Buenaventure Durruti, who had recently been killed, or murdered, at the front, whence he had been issuing appeals for anti-Fascist unity. The C.N.T., though represented in the Government, was in fact divided between Government and Opposition. The P.O.U.M. was demanding representation in the Catalonian Government, from which it had been kept out by the P.S.U.C., as standing for no coherent force. It was in fact an advocate of working-class solidarity without the bourgeois left and of workers' control in the factories, and had a minority following in the C.N.T.

Who began the Barcelona fighting it is hardly possible to say. There were widespread rumours that the F.A.I. had

planned a *coup* and were trying to seize the city; but the
F.A.I. and C.N.T. leaders denied this, and issued successive
appeals for peace. The beginning seems to have been a wrangle
at the Telephone Building between Generalidad Police and
Workers' delegates holding the building; but out of this
unintelligible incident there developed several days of confused
street fighting between the Generalidad's forces and a mob of
C.N.T. and P.O.U.M. fighters. This became so serious that
troops had to be recalled from the front and non-Catalonian
police and military sent from the Government at Valencia
before it died out when the C.N.T. insistently recalled its
members to work. There followed the arrest of the P.O.U.M.
leaders, including Nin — who was murdered in prison — and
the reconstruction of the Generalidad in such a way as to
strengthen the control of the P.S.U.C. and the U.G.T. and of
the C.N.T. elements which had opposed the rising.

The Barcelona affair was fatal to the Largo Caballero
Government in Valencia, which found itself faced with a
series of demands by the Communist Party for unified central
direction of the war effort under a Ministry effectively representing all working-class and Popular Front Parties, but removing the separate control of each over its own forces in favour
of a really unified organisation. Largo Caballero, after seeming
to accept the demands, came forward with a plan for a Ministry
under himself based mainly on the U.G.T. and C.N.T., to
the exclusion of the political Parties, as providing the best
basis for unity. The U.G.T. Executive and the main body of
C.N.T. leaders supported him; but the Parties vehemently
objected, and he resigned. The C.N.T. Ministers also withdrew, and a new Government was constituted under Negrín
to carry through this task of unification. Its leading Ministers
included Giral, a follower of Azaña, at the Foreign Office, and
Prieto, the rival leader of the Socialists, in charge of military
reorganisation. There were in all three Socialists, two Communists, two Left Radicals, a Basque Nationalist, and a
Catalonian from the Esquerra — a bare Socialist-Communist
majority in an essentially Popular Front Ministry, which took
its task seriously, did as the Communists demanded, and
proceeded rapidly to reorganise affairs on a basis of unified and
strongly centralised control. But it was too late for snatching

victory out of defeat, especially as the Germans chose the occasion to intensify their intervention by the naval bombardment of Almería on May 31st.

What was really at issue in the Barcelona fighting of May 1937? Amid many confused disputes, one question at issue was undoubtedly that of 'workers' control'. In the celebrated Catalonian Decree of Collectivisation and Workers' Control, issued in October 1936 and supplemented by the Order of the following month, it was laid down that industry should be divided into two classes — collectivised and private. In the former, responsibility for management was in the hands of the workers, represented by an Enterprise Council; in the latter, of the owner or manager, subject to the approval of a Workers' Control Committee. All enterprises employing over 100 workers, and all enterprises whose owners abandoned them or were declared rebels, were collectivised, and other establishments could be if three-fifths of their workers so desired. Enterprise Councils were elected for two years by all the workers in general assembly, and were re-eligible. They were responsible both to the workers and to the Industrial Councils set up under the Decree. They were generally responsible for both production and welfare services. Each elected a Director to execute its functions, and each included a Government inspector to ensure its compliance with the law. Similar Workers' Control Committees were elected in non-collectivised undertakings. The General Industrial Councils consisted of four Enterprise Council representatives, eight representatives of the Trade Unions (C.N.T. and U.G.T.), and four technicians appointed by the Government. It was their task to draw up plans for the various industries, and their decisions were binding on the Enterprise Councils.

This was the formal law; but it hardly corresponded to the reality. In fact, as we saw, enterprises had been collectivised or let alone after no uniform pattern, but variously, according to the different attitudes and policies of the workers concerned, or of the Parties or Trade Unions they belonged to. At one end of the scale were Syndicalists or Co-operators who had simply taken establishments under their control: at the other, establishments owned and controlled by the Government with some degree of Trade Union participation. F.A.I.

in December declared for complete socialisation, in order to prevent irregularity from arising from the appropriation of surpluses by the workers in particular establishments; but neither it nor the Generalidad was in a position to impose a common pattern. The C.N.T. favoured the Decree as a means to bring order out of the chaos, whereas the U.G.T. criticised it for its ambiguity on the financial side, and for its inefficiency, arguing that not the best men for organising production, but the best-known demagogues, got elected to the Committees. In effect, the Decree was a compromise between Syndicalists, who wanted workers' control and objected to bureaucratic centralisation, and the Communists and right-wing Socialists, who cared nothing for workers' control but were set on preventing it from degenerating into corporative profit-making on a factory co-operative basis. In this contest the P.O.U.M., like the F.A.I., took the Syndicalist side, but was of course no less opposed than the U.G.T. and the Communists to co-operative profit-seeking. Many held equal wages for all to be the ideal; but few advocated it as immediately possible. The opponents of profit-seeking wanted all profits to be handed over to a Central Industrial Bank for use in helping industries unable to meet their costs or in need of money for investment; but the financial implications of the Decree were left dangerously vague.

In practice, however, both in Catalonia and elsewhere, the exigencies of the war led towards the centralisation of industrial control in the Government's hands, and away from establishment control by the workers. In Catalonia, after May 1937, workers' control was largely superseded by one-man management under government responsibility in the war factories; and the Communists and their allies got their way at the expense of the C.N.T. and the Syndicalists. The Anarchists were not very directly involved; for many of them were almost as much opposed to the coercion of individuals by Factory Committees as by the State. But their influence too waned under the new order of centralised discipline and subordination of everything to the needs of war.

Throughout the complex struggles of the years after the Republican electoral victory of 1936 there was bitter warfare on the ideological front. As always in Spanish politics, the battle was carried on less between right and left wings as such than between centralisers on the one hand and libertarians on the other. Thus, the Communists, who became an increasing force as the war proceeded, were ranged with the Socialist centre and right wing under Prieto on the side of unification of control against the Syndicalists of the C.N.T. and against P.O.U.M., who regarded themselves as standing on the left with a mission to carry the Revolution on to a fully proletarian stage. Largo Caballero, who had been regarded as standing on the left wing of the Socialist Party against Prieto, and had shown himself ready to collaborate with the C.N.T., and with the unification of the Socialist and Communist Youth Movements, found himself dethroned when he stood out against measures of general unification that threatened to undermine his personal influence. The F.A.I., theoretically on the extreme left, but animated by a high idealism that knew not how to compromise, found itself, in the name of unity, rallying to the defence of centralised control against fissiparous tendencies, and lost half its influence over the C.N.T. The bourgeois Left Radicals, the followers of Azaña and Barrio, had no relevant theoretical contribution to make, but rallied to the thesis of unification in the interests of war efficiency. So for the most part did the Esquerra, against its Catalonian separatist faction, ensconced in the ranks of Estat Català led by Doncas. The P.O.U.M., no doubt, had pretensions to be the 'true' left, as advocating the immediate advance from the Popular Front to the Workers' Republic, resting on purely proletarian foundations; but, far from uniting the workers, it only divided them further. It had, moreover, hardly any strength outside Catalonia, where it was bitterly at odds with almost everyone else. Its most effective leader, Joachim Maurin, had been cut off and imprisoned in rebel territory in Galicia, whither he had gone on a visit before the outbreak: he was never heard of again. His second-in-command, Nin, was much less effective as a leader and, as we saw, was arrested and murdered in prison after the Barcelona rising of May 1937.

Among the Socialists the outstanding figures were Largo Caballero, secretary of the U.G.T., until his fall, and Indalecio Prieto, the Asturian who sat in the Cortes for Bilbao, and was the leading figure among the Basque Socialists. Prieto was by nature and instinct a Centrist, if not a right-winger; but his organising capacity and his faith in centralisation made him an ally of the Communists in the struggle against Largo Caballero, with whom he hardly ever agreed. He was a forceful personality, as well as a considerable orator, but always moderate in his general outlook. By origin a clerk, he had managed to identify himself with the hard-headed workers of Bilbao, and to establish a strong position despite his alleged bourgeois origin and the debt of gratitude he owed to the great Basque industrialist, Horacio Echevarrieta. Of other Socialist leaders, Julian Besteiro, President of the U.G.T., was very definitely a moderate; Luis Araquistain, the leading theorist of the Party, went out of office with Largo Caballero; Álvarez del Vayo was a specialist on foreign affairs, much abroad in Paris during the Civil War; and finally Juan Negrín was a university medical professor, called in to head the Cabinet when Largo Caballero was driven out. He had been Minister of Finance in the Largo Caballero Ministry, and was something of an expert on economic questions. Among the Communists, leading figures were Juan Hernández, Minister of Education in the Negrín Cabinet, and Vicente Uriba, Minister of Agriculture, together with the C.P. leader, José Díaz. Germinal de Souza was Secretary of F.A.I. and Manrico Vásquez of the C.N.T. Juan Comorera led the Unified Catalonian Socialist Party and Juan Casanovas the Estat Català, nominally attached to the Esquerra led by Luis Companys.

The Communists were accused of dominating the Republican Government to an ever-increasing extent, and in a sense this was true. Not only was the Soviet Union, after the breakdown of non-intervention, the only Government to which the Republicans could look for help or sympathy, except distant Mexico: in addition, the demands of the civil war required centralisation of the Republican forces and the overriding of the independent authority claimed by a medley of contending groups; and centralisation, with rigid discipline, was the essential policy of the Communist Party under Stalin. The official Communists found nothing to stand in the way of such centralisation, and much to recommend it; for their mission, under the Comintern's new policy of Popular Fronts, was to establish a united anti-Fascist league with as many participants as possible, and under its aegis to fight for the defeat of Fascism, and for nothing else. It went right against their policy to complicate the issue by fighting for Socialism at the cost of lessening anti-Fascist unity or hampering the war effort; they were thoroughly assured that Socialism — and Communism too — would follow a Fascist defeat, whereas nothing at all could be achieved without overcoming Fascism. So they had no wish to press their own claims against the other Parties of the Popular Front further than was needed for the establishment of unity in action. First win the war, they said, and then we will see about other things; but to divide the people till the war was won was to be guilty of criminal sectarianism, however worthy the objects of those guilty of it might be. Some of the objects of the sectarians were, however, in their view, by no means worthy. The Communists had no use for workers' control in the factories, which they regarded as a petit-bourgeois illusion of liberty. Nor did they have any use for the idealistic individual libertarianism of the F.A.I., which they regarded as contrary to class-discipline and class-unity. They could coalesce with Azaña's Left Radicals or with the Socialist right wing much more easily than with the Syndicalists or the P.O.U.M. The latter were indeed their greatest enemies because they were continually denouncing the bureaucratic degeneration of the Soviet Union under Stalin and because they harboured Communist dissidents who had broken away from the Stalinists and passed into bitter opposition.

As for the Socialists, their greatest concentration of strength had always been in Madrid; and Madrid and the provinces were to a great extent natural enemies. Madrid was usually for as much centralisation as it dared to advocate, in the same way as Catalonia was naturally for as much autonomy as it deemed to be practicable — and sometimes for more — when Estat Català was allowed its head. The Esquerra was at any rate a federalist Party, not quite desiring to break away from the rest of Spain and set up an independent State of Catalonia, but demanding full internal self-government with a very loose federal unity, and including a considerable section that went all the way towards full independence. Companys, its leader, when it came to the point, accepted Spanish Government help to put down the Barcelona insurgents; and the main body of the Catalonian Republicans accepted his lead. But Barcelona, though it became the final capital of the Republican Government, was never at ease with Madrid, which it suspected through all of sinister centralising designs; and even after the defeat of the extreme Federalists and Separatists in 1937 the tension continued.

As for the Basque country, it is surprising at first sight that the Basque Nationalists, as well as the Socialists, threw in their lot with the Republic, even in return for promises of Basque autonomy, which were duly fulfilled by Prieto despite his general support of a centralised system. Partly their decision was due to the proximity of the Carlist Navarrese, who sided with the rebels, and to the traditional hostility between Navarre and the Basque provinces. Partly, it was due to the strength of Socialism in Bilbao and to the influence of the neighbouring Asturias, still a left-wing stronghold despite the bitter repression of the left after the rebellion of 1934. But the Basque provinces had hardly got their statute of autonomy from the Republic when they were overrun by the rebels and put out of the fighting.

The Spanish Civil War, when it began in 1936, was essentially a war between Spaniards, or at least between Republican Spaniards and Spanish rebels aided by Moors and by the Spanish Foreign Legion. But as it went on it became more and more an international war fought on Spanish soil and on the seas round Spain by Fascists and anti-Fascists from many countries. First the Italians and then the Germans poured in munitions and in Italy's case whole armies — on the rebel side; and the Soviet Union retaliated by supplying munitions, but not fighting men. Men came, however, from many countries to join the International Brigade — from Italy and Germany, from France and Great Britain, and indeed from almost every country. The International Brigade was, for a time, almost the sole effective fighting force on the Republican side — till, at long last, the training of an unified Republican army was taken in hand too late to be of decisive effect. The International Brigade played the leading part in the critical defence of Madrid, and distinguished itself by its heroic conduct in face of shortage of necessary supplies, despite the great efforts made to send it help by the anti-Fascists, or at any rate by sections of them, in France and Great Britain. It was a notable achievement of the Popular Front as an international movement; but it was bedevilled in Great Britain by the main body of the Labour movement's rejection of Popular Front strategy, and in France by the Popular Front's own adherence to the Non-Intervention Pact and continuance in one-sided observance of it long after its non-observance by the Fascists had been admitted.

In the circumstances that existed in Great Britain, Spanish aid became the cry mainly of the British Communists and of such left-wingers as rallied to their aid, with the official Trade Union movement and the Labour Party standing aloof and disapproving, less on account of Spain, than of their fears of becoming entangled with the Communists. After the fall of the Blum Government a very similar situation existed in France, with the Communists virtually out of what remained of the *Front Populaire* and in increasing opposition to the Governments which were trying to undo its work. Thus the Popular Front in Spain stood alone in maintaining a Government supported by Radicals, Socialists, and Communists acting in continued close alliance right to the end. That was partly because the extreme reactionariness of most of the Spanish Parties, including Lerroux's right-wing Radicals, left the Radical Left with no choice; but it was also partly because the Communists and Socialists were determined not to quarrel with their bourgeois allies, and so weaken their appeal both abroad and at home. If the Communists gained an increasing control over Spanish affairs, this was perhaps less because of the dependence of the Republicans on Russian supplies or of any desire on the part of the Spanish Communists to run the show than because their policy best fitted the needs of the situation as it became more and more desperate in view of the sectarian attitudes of the rival groups. This is not to say that the Communists behaved rightly in Spain, and their opponents wrongly; for it is undoubted that the Communists pushed their antagonism to Syndicalists and to those they called 'Trotskyists' to absurd extremes, and that they were remarkably brutal and domineering in their methods. Moreover, before the war ended the Soviet Union had almost ceased to send supplies, and the Communist influence had shown clear signs of being on the wane.

It has often been said that Spaniards, because of their intense individualism and particularism, are incapable of the united effort needed to consolidate a Revolution. Their capacity to make one has been shown repeatedly; but it is one thing to overthrow an unpopular Government, and quite another to replace it by a viable alternative régime. The Spaniards easily overthrew Alfonso XIII in 1931, and at once set about the constructive tasks which lay before them. But at the outset their new Government could govern the country hardly more than that which it had replaced; and countless separate groups and factions took authority into their own hands and had to be placated by the Government giving way to them. Nevertheless, in two years the Azaña Government had gone a considerable way, at the cost of shedding a considerable section of its initial support and of suffering a heavy defeat in 1933. Then followed the two years of so-called Centrist Governments, undoing as much of their predecessor's work as they dared and providing an opportunity for the extreme Right to reorganise its forces in Gil Robles's Ceda and, outside the Cortes, in definitely Fascist organisations much further to the right and openly inciting their followers to violence. Into this situation came the Popular Front's electoral victory at the beginning of 1936, followed by a display of left-wing violence vying with that of the Fascists and, after only a few months, by the appeal to civil war.

So far, the left wing had been united against the Ceda and the Fascists; but it was less easy to say *for* what it was united. It was indeed rather a series of pressure groups, each pressing for its own objectives, than a constructively united movement. It was fairly easy for the politicians to come verbally to terms about Catalonian or Basque autonomy, or even about the rôle of the Trade Unions — though none of these was really simple. It was much more difficult for the Government to induce its supporters to trust one another, or to pool any of the sources of power they could get under their own command. Each Party and group had its own militia formations and the factions it controlled, as well as its independent factional organisations

146

jealous of all interference; and the Government attempted to work by enlisting the aid of the rival groups without knocking their heads together. Such a structure rendered it absolutely impossible to build up a Republican army capable of meeting the Fascists on equal terms in open battle, or to achieve a proper co-ordination of supplies, which each faction was apt to seize for its own use. Thus, even if the Syndicalists and the P.O.U.M. were right to be suspicious of Stalinist centralisation, to oppose it in the circumstances of the civil war was to invite defeat. There was, in effect, no alternative to it; and though one may sympathise with many of P.O.U.M.'s aspirations, to attempt to achieve them in the war situation of 1937 was, at the least, exceedingly silly and showed an incapacity for realistic analysis which can only be condemned. It was in fact condemned by the majority of Spanish Republicans, who saw the need to concentrate all efforts on the war and to postpone ideological disputes until they had won it. But this conversion to common sense came altogether too late.

To agree with the Communists on this crucial issue is not to deny that they were awkward bedfellows for other Republicans — even for those who agreed with them on this issue. For it is a characteristic of Communists to defend the Soviet Union through thick and thin, and never to admit there can be anything amiss with it or with its policies; and such defences were particularly difficult when the great Treason Trials were on in the Soviet Union — when Kamenev and Zinoviev and other former Bolshevik leaders were being sentenced to death, and when charges of the highest gravity were being levelled against the best-known generals of the Soviet army. The Spanish Communists, like others of their ilk, were doubtless self-righteous and contemptuous of everybody else. None the less, in the circumstances, their main policy was undoubtedly correct.

As for Largo Caballero, his fault was not that of being wrong, but of lacking the force to implement what he knew to be right. He was essentially a Trade Union leader, who had as his instrument the U.G.T., but saw the need for accommodation between it and the C.N.T., which far outnumbered it in Catalonia and the South, though far behind it in Madrid and the North. He wanted the U.G.T. and the C.N.T. to work

closely together, and was prepared to make considerable concessions in order to achieve this — indeed, so many as to
defeat the purpose of unity which he had in mind. As a
Socialist, he tended to favour centralisation, and seemed at
first to be on the right wing against the left-wing C.N.T.
Thus he moved steadily leftwards and appeared as the leader
of the Socialist left against Prieto and Besteiro. He became
Prime Minister as a left-winger, but failed in that office because
he was unwilling to coerce the left-wing extremists who sought
to maintain their sectional claims. Finally he was driven from
office at the head of a predominantly Socialist-Syndicalist
Government by Socialists well to the right of him who saw
eye to eye with the Communists on the overriding issue of
unified control. It must be remembered too that he was
oldish and tired — 67 in 1937, when he was driven from
office.

The Spanish struggle, for all its incoherence, became
symbolic of the fight against Fascism for many of the young
people of the late 'thirties. Faced with the deadly rot of
'appeasement' in France and Great Britain, they threw themselves generously into the Spanish cause. Many lost their
lives fighting in Madrid as members of the International
Brigade. Some, such as George Orwell and some of the
British I.L.P. leaders, were sorely disillusioned by the events in
Catalonia, and sided with the P.O.U.M. against the Communists
in the conflict there. But most of the foreign sympathisers
were not in a mood to criticise : they simply backed the
Spaniards who were in arms against Fascism, while France
and Great Britain were shilly-shallying before the Fascist
danger, or even half in sympathy with Hitler and Mussolini as
enemies of the Left. Spain became the chief focus for youth's
generous idealism ; and those who passed through the experience as young men and women will not forget it lightly. In
Great Britain, these were the great days of Victor Gollancz's
Left Book Club and of Harold Laski and John Strachey as the
co-editors of the Left Books. Even if they failed to carry the
main body of the Trade Unions and the Labour Party with
them, they played their part in preparing Socialist opinion for
the war that broke out amid the collapse of 'appeasement'
in 1939 ; and, unlike the Communists, the rest of them did not

change sides with the signing of the Nazi-Soviet Pact, but continued steadily on their anti-Fascist line through the disasters of 1940, until the Communists came back to them after Hitler's assault on the Soviet Union in 1941. British and French Labour both failed, indeed, to give the Spanish Republicans the support that was their due; but the British Left has cause to congratulate itself that, in this at least, it did what it could.

CHAPTER VI

THE ECLIPSE OF AUSTRIAN SOCIALISM

THE 1930s were a period of eclipse for the Austrian Socialist movement, incomplete though far-reaching under Dollfuss and Schuschnigg, and virtually complete after the Nazi invasion and annexation of the country in 1938. Indeed, as we saw in the preceding volume of this study, the retreat of the Socialists had set in at least as soon as 1927. In that year, the violence of the Heimwehr's irregular forces, tolerated and positively encouraged by the Government of that sinister ecclesiastic, Dr. Seipel, had reached a new height; and a jury had acquitted certain Heimwehr members charged, on incontrovertible evidence, with the murders committed during the affray at Schattendorf, in the Burgenland. The acquittal had roused very strong feelings among the workers; and huge bodies of demonstrators had marched on the Inner City of Vienna and, opposed by the police, had set fire to the Palace of Justice. The demonstration had been unexpected, and had not been arranged by the Socialist or Trade Union leaders: so that the working-class para-military force, the Schutzbund, had not been called out to help in preserving order. The vast crowd had been for the most part unarmed; but the outnumbered police, rallying their forces after the first surprise, had resorted to strong measures to disperse it, and in the indiscriminate shooting which followed, 85 demonstrators, or mere onlookers, had been killed, and more than a thousand wounded. The effect of this manœuvre had been to arouse the workers to still greater indignation. The Chancellor, Seipel, was openly favourable to the Heimwehr, whose leaders were continually issuing open threats to destroy the democratic Republic by an armed rising; and Seipel, though biding his time, made no secret of his determination to sweep the democratic constitution away. The Socialists were firmly entrenched in control of Vienna and were powerful in other industrial towns; but they had very little following in the country districts and seemed condemned to remain permanently in a minority in the national Parliament against the combined forces of their chief rival, the Christian Social Party, its allies the Heimwehr and the Agrarian League, and the Pan-German Nationalists. The Christian Social Party included elements that were prepared to work under the parliamentary system, but was passing more and more under the domination of Seipel, who was an open enemy of democracy and had announced his intention of destroying the Socialists and remodelling Austrian institutions after a new pattern in which the authority of the Church would be effectively restored.

The Socialists, after the massacre of July 1927, had to consider seriously what action to take. Their leaders could not do nothing: the feeling among their followers was much too strong. The question was whether a point had been reached at which they in their turn should appeal to force by resorting to civil war. This, however, they were very reluctant to do, if there were any way short of surrender by which it could be avoided. In the early days of the Republic, when the Socialists had been in power and their opponents in head-long retreat, they had made great efforts to create a new army loyal to the Republican Constitution, and had for a time been successful. But they had been outside the Federal Government since 1920, though they remained in control of Vienna, which had the rôle of a self-governing State within the Federation; and after their fall from power the Federal Governments controlled by the Christian Socials had largely undone their work in this respect, replacing the officers they had appointed by others on whose support they could rely. The Socialists felt fairly sure that the army, as it was in 1927, would take sides with Seipel against any attempted rising; and the Republican Schutzbund, though large in numbers, was ill-armed and unused to fighting, whereas the Heimwehr irregulars were better armed, as well as far more ruthless. In these circumstances the likelihood of defeat if the Socialists attempted a rising in arms was high; and the leaders looked hard for an alternative that would show a will to act strong enough to prevent a section of their followers from taking matters into their own hands. The solution they adopted was that of calling a general strike, to which there was a massive response. But clearly a general strike could not last for long. Either it must compel Seipel's Government to resign, or it must turn into a revolutionary movement, or it must fail. Seipel, well understanding this, and probably confident that the Socialists would not resort to an armed rising, simply allowed the strike to take its course, refusing all concessions; and the strikers presently returned to work with nothing achieved. Seipel, a man of strong nerve and great determination, was able to strengthen his hold over the Christian Social Party and to continue his close collaboration with the Heimwehr leaders; and the Socialist Party began upon the policy of restraint and attempted compromise that was to end in its destruction, as an overt power, in the fighting of 1934.

There was yet another reason why the Socialists deemed it best in 1927 to accept a very serious setback rather than resort to arms. This was the very difficult international position of Austria, even before the onset of the world depression and the advent of the Nazis to power in Germany. The Austrian Republic was not economically a viable society: it had to seek help from, and to accept economic control by, the League of Nations. The Socialists were well aware that a resort to arms on their part would meet with strong disapproval from the League Powers, and that, even if they won the civil war, they would be faced with extreme difficulties in feeding the population afterwards. The Austrian reactionaries had become thoroughly accustomed to unmeasured denunciations of the Austrian Socialists as Marxists who were set on leading the country into subjection to a Communist régime; and so much of this mud had stuck in the minds of foreign statesmen as to make it certain that an Austrian Socialist régime would meet with their strong opposition, especially if it emerged from civil war.

In fact, of course, the Austrian Socialists were by no means Communists, or supporters of Communism, which had failed to win more than insignificant support among the Austrian workers. The Austrian Communist Party had never been strong enough to win even a single parliamentary seat, or to cause any significant rupture in the solid ranks of Austrian Social Democracy. The Social Democratic Party had its right and left wings; and its left wing, led by Otto Bauer, was on the whole the more powerful in shaping its programme. It was, however, sheerly fantastic to regard either Bauer or Deutsch as crypto-Communists. As we saw, the Austrian Party had been a strong supporter of the 'Two-and-a-Half' International, which had its headquarters at Vienna. It had refused to endorse the declarations of the rival Second International that democracy, in the sense of the achievement of a parliamentary majority, was to be regarded as in all circumstances the indispensable prerequisite of the advance to Socialism, and had insisted that there might be, at any rate in certain countries, conditions which would justify proletarian dictatorship as the sole way left open for Socialists to follow. It had favoured, against both the Second International and the Comintern, a single International including both Social Democrats and Communists, and had maintained its unsuccessful struggle for this unity as long as there was the smallest hope of success. But the Austrian Socialists had used their brief tenure of power to establish in Austria not a Soviet system but a completely democratic parliamentary Republic, no doubt in the hope that they would be able to win a majority in it, but also because that was what they, quite genuinely and sincerely, thought to be right. In this they had acted as a united Party, with the support of their left wing as well as of the right. They had, to be sure, insisted that within the Republic, constituted despite its limited size and population as a federal State, Vienna, their stronghold, should be accorded the status of a constituent federal unit, with large powers of self-government in social and industrial affairs; and they had realised that the possibility of holding a Socialist majority in the country as a whole was bound to depend on their success in gaining some amount of support among the peasants. But in the early years of the new Republic this hope had not seemed unreasonable. There were elements in the Christian Social Party with its large peasant membership which both accepted parliamentary democracy in principle and were prepared in practice to collaborate with the Socialists in running the country on that basis; and the Socialists hoped that the peasant policy which Otto Bauer drafted for them would win an appreciable number of converts. They still entertained these hopes in 1927, though by then both the Christian Social Party, under Seipel's influence, and the Peasant League had become much more reactionary and more favourable to the anti-democratic claims of the Catholic Church. In addition to these political Parties they had to face the growing challenge of the Heimwehr, led in the main by members of the old aristocracy and by ex-officers of the imperial army; and the Heimwehr from the first had proclaimed itself the enemy of the democratic system, which it openly threatened to overturn by armed force. There had been constant clashes, of growing violence, between Heimwehr units and working-class bodies; and these clashes became much more menacing when the Heimwehr took to organising marches and demonstrations in towns in which the Socialists were the predominant Party, and when the Government refused to ban such marches or to protect the working-class areas against acts of violence arising out of them.

The Heimwehr, despite its repeated declarations of intention to destroy the democratic Republic by force, never actually ventured an armed rising. It was probably deterred in part by its inferiority in numbers and by the lack of solid Christian Social support, and in part by the feeling that the army of the Republic — even after it had been largely purged of Socialist leadership — would obey orders to put it down if it took the plunge. But after 1927, as before, the Heimwehr was allowed to keep its arms and to procure fresh ones, whereas the Socialist Schutzbund was exposed to constant raids and searches for arms, which were confiscated in considerable quantities by the police. Despite these raids, considerable supplies of arms remained hidden in Socialist possession; but the increasing raids seriously hampered the Schutzbund in building up fresh stores. Seipel worked throughout in close collusion with Starhemberg and the other Heimwehr leaders, using them as means to convert the Christian Socials and Agrarians to fuller support of his counter-revolutionary policy.

Seipel, at this stage, was attempting not to overthrow the democratic Republic by armed force, but to bring about a revision of the constitution that would remove the democratic elements from it and substitute what he professed to regard as 'true' democracy. In particular, he wanted a great extension of the powers of the President, who hitherto had been mainly a figurehead, so as to enable him to become the supreme ruler of the country, with the sole right to appoint or dismiss Ministers, and with the power to govern by decree in the absence of Parliament. Seipel also favoured a revision of the voting system to give representation not to numerical majorities, but to special groups and interests on the lines of Vogelsang's projects of a corporative State in which the claims of the Church would receive large recognition. Between these ideas and the Socialist adherence to parliamentary democracy there was no possible bridge; but both Seipel and, still more, his successors in office were continually negotiating with some of the Socialists for a compromise which would involve some sacrifices by the Socialists in the name of national unity. Danneberg, the Secretary of the Socialist Party and a leading member of its right wing, was usually the chief participant in these negotiations, which were usually carried on in private, but never with any prospect of lasting success.

Seipel remained in office as Chancellor for only a year and a half after the events of 1927. He then resigned, and was succeeded by a somewhat less unaccommodating member of the Christian Social Party, but continued to direct policy from behind the scenes. Projects for the amendment of the consti-tution were again brought forward, and again the Socialists were invited to 'compromise'. On this occasion, in 1929, they actually did so, to a certain extent. One of Seipel's proposals had been that the President of the Republic, instead of being chosen by Parliament, should be directly elected by the whole people. This the Socialists now agreed to accept, on condition that the change should not apply to the next election — which was in fact the last — but only subsequently. All the other major changes were dropped, because it was impossible constitutionally to amend the constitution except by a two-thirds majority of Parliament — which was impossible without the Socialists.

The Socialists thus came well out of the crisis of 1929; but further troubles were soon to come. In 1929 Schober, the police president of Vienna, who had been largely responsible for the shootings of 1927, became Chancellor and negotiated the compromise with the Socialists on the question of constitu-tional reform. Having done this, Schober went on to negotiate a Customs Union with Germany, which was promptly vetoed by the French. The *Anschluss* — full unity with the German Reich — had been part of the Socialist programme ever since 1919, but had been specifically forbidden in the treaty of peace, which had required Austria to remain independent. The contacts between the German and Austrian Socialist movements were nevertheless very close — Kautsky himself and Rudolf Hilferding were both by origin Austrian — and in the new Austria almost the entire population was German by speech and cultural sentiment. Germany at this time was still the country of the Weimar Republic, and Nazism, though gaining ground, was still only an opposition movement: so that Customs Union, or *Anschluss*, still seemed possible on a basis of democratic parliamentarism, which would, it seemed, be strengthened in Austria if it entered into the Reich as a constituent State, or Land. But in face of the French veto, backed up by the other Powers which had signed the Austrian Treaty, nothing could be done.

Soon after this, Schober's Government broke down over a quarrel between it and the Heimwehr, which had been trying to oust the Socialists from control of the railwaymen, and had demanded the appointment of a railway general manager who would join with them in the campaign. Schober refused to make the proposed appointment, on account of certain episodes in the past of the person proposed; and he was therefore driven from office and replaced by his Vice-Chancellor, Karl Vaugoin, who was a strong supporter of the Heimwehr. Schober thereupon attempted to form a middle group between the Catholics and the Socialists, based on the smaller Parties, and enlisted enough support to deprive Vaugoin of his majority in Parliament, despite the fact that Seipel himself presently agreed to join his Ministry as Foreign Minister, and that two Heimwehr leaders, including Starhemberg, were given office in it. The Government was unwilling to face elections, in which it had no prospect of success against Schober as well as the Socialists; but the latter threatened to resort to arms if an attempt were made to govern without Parliament. The Government was compelled to hold an election, from which it emerged without a majority. The Heimwehr, fighting as a separate

Party, was able to win only 8 seats, and so exposed their weakness. The Vaugoin Government resigned, and was replaced by a more moderate Christian Social Ministry; but the Christian Social Party, which had suffered heavy electoral losses, was by this time in a state of disintegration. It had still a large amount of peasant support; but its leaders, including Seipel, had become so compromised by alliances with the Heimwehr as to leave it in a hopelessly ambiguous position, while Schober, who had pledged himself not to pursue constitutional reform except by constitutional means, commanded enough support to present an absolute obstacle to Seipel's aim — which was, above all else, the destruction of the Socialists as a means of restoring the power of the Church.

Seipel, recognising the impasse and infuriated with Schober, then took the step of offering to enter into a coalition Government with the Socialists, whom he was pledged to destroy. Seipel himself was to be Chancellor, and Bauer Vice-Chancellor, in such a Government. No such coalition, however, was even remotely possible; and the Socialists at once rejected the offer. That was in the spring of 1931; and the immediate occasion of the offer was the collapse of the Credit Anstalt, the great Austrian bank controlled by the Rothschilds, which had been plunged into difficulties by being forced to take over the reactionary Boden Credit Anstalt, which had collapsed some time previously. The fall of the Credit Anstalt, which had repercussions far beyond Austria, marked the really serious onset of the world economic depression. In good and bad times alike Austria, ever since 1918, had suffered from permanent heavy unemployment, as a consequence of the loss of former markets in the Succession States of the Austro-Hungarian Empire. Almost the first act of the Socialists after the establishment of the Republic had been to provide a system of social and industrial legislation which included public maintenance of the unemployed; and Vienna had made use of its considerable legislative powers to supplement national provision in various ways, especially by the control of rents and the building of subsidised housing for working-class tenants. These measures of social security, which enjoyed some support from the more advanced elements in the Christian Social

Party, the anti-Socialist majority had been unable to undo, though it had done its best to make things difficult financially for Vienna. But the economic blow that fell on Austria in 1931 and continued almost unabated for several years was of altogether unprecedented severity, and seriously weakened the bargaining power of the Trade Unions, though it did nothing to shake their hold on the industrial workers over most of the country. Only one big industrial concern, the Alpine Montan-Gesellschaft, was able to take advantage of the opportunity to break up the Socialist Trade Unions among its employees and to reorganise them in 'company' Unions attached to the Heimwehr. This company was subsequently bought by German capitalists, who, when Hitler came to power in 1933, transferred these 'company' Unions to Nazi leadership and thus gave the Austrian Nazis their first substantial working-class following.

Seipel's aim in offering a coalition to the Socialists was to implicate them, in the name of national unity, in drastic measures for coping with the economic crisis — wage-cuts, especially for public employees, who included the railwaymen, cuts in social service benefits, especially for the unemployed, and so on. If the Socialists had agreed to participate in carrying through such a programme, they would have inevitably been accused of betraying the workers, and would have lost much popular support. But they had no opportunity to carry out any alternative programme of their own, even if they had had one ; for any attempt to form a Socialist minority Government would at once have rallied all the other Parties to enforce its defeat. What happened was that a sequence of weak Christian Social Ministries held office without a majority, and that in the process Austrian democracy melted steadily away.

From this point, however, a new factor began to become of pressing import in Austrian politics — the rapid rise of Nazism as a current of popular opinion. In the regional and municipal elections held over most of Austria in April 1932 the Nazis, not yet in power in Germany, made a sudden appearance as a powerful force in Austrian politics. Their great gains were made at the expense, not of the Socialists, who held their own, but of the Christian Socials, who in Vienna lost nearly half their seats to the Nazis, and a section of the

Heimwehr transferred its allegiance from Austrian to German Fascism. From that point there were two bitterly hostile forms of Fascism struggling for power in Austria, equally determined to overthrow the democratic Republic, but pledged, the one to maintain Austrian independence under a reactionary régime dominated by representatives of the old imperial army, the landowning classes, and the bankers and financiers of Vienna, and the other to the *Anschluss* with Germany, which in January 1933 passed under Nazi control. Against these two were ranged the Socialists, who had always supported the *Anschluss*, but began to feel quite differently about it when it came to mean the submergence of Austria in a Nazi Germany, instead of a self-governing membership of the Weimar Republic. Doubtfully placed among the conflicting forces was what remained of the Christian Social Party, which under Seipel had become the ally of the Heimwehr, but which was made up largely of peasants who had no clear view on national politics, except a systematically instilled horror of the Socialists, who, they were told, were Bolsheviks determined to take away their land.

At this point, in 1932, Seipel, the arch-antagonist of the Socialists, died, and the Christian Socials had to find a new leader to replace him. Seipel, in or out of office, had been unquestionably Austria's strong man for many years, following a tortuous policy of intrigue which had only two clear objectives — the utter destruction of the Socialist Party and the democratic régime foisted by it on the Austrian State, and the resurrection of the power and influence, in politics and in the entire national life, of the Roman Catholic Church. Both these objectives were fully endorsed by the man who succeeded him, Dr. Engelbert Dollfuss, who became Chancellor and managed to get together a Ministry with a majority of a single vote in Parliament, so that it was quite unable to enact seriously controversial legislation. The Catholics, in order to secure this basic majority, had to rely on the support of the handful of Heimwehr M.P.s. But the support of the Heimwehr in the country was already being seriously eroded by the advance of Austrian Nazism; and outside Parliament the alliance with what was left of it, under Starhemberg and Major Fey, probably antagonised more supporters than it secured. Dollfuss, however, as a devoted son of the Catholic Church and a bitter enemy of democracy, took up with enthusiasm Seipel's plans for constitutional revision, while slanting them more openly than Seipel had ever done, towards a definitely clerical version of Fascism based on a structure of 'estates' in place of parliamentary representation. Dollfuss was the illegitimate son of a peasant, and, having been financially helped on account of his intellectual promise, had found his way to Vienna University. Unwilling to become a priest, he had found a career as an official in Catholic organisations and had soon become secretary to the Chamber of Agriculture in Lower Austria and a recognised Christian Social expert on peasant questions. He had been at first in the more democratic wing of the peasant movement, but had gone over to the right, mainly under Seipel's influence, and had become a thoroughgoing exponent of authoritarian ideas. He was not, perhaps, by instinct a dictator, though he came to be one for a time ; but he loved power and was determined to carry on the struggle against the Socialists by every means at his command.

Dollfuss had not been long in office when the opportunity unexpectedly offered itself to get rid of the Austrian Parliament once for all. His Government, at its wits' end for money in face of the economic crisis, decided to pay the railwaymen, who were State employees, their wages in three instalments, instead of at the beginning of the month. The railwaymen called a two hours' strike by way of formal protest ; and the Government seized the chance to proceed to wholesale dismissals of active Trade Unionists. The matter being carried to Parliament, the Government was defeated by one vote, but it was subsequently discovered that one of the Socialists had voted not with his own voting paper, but by mistake with that of his next-door neighbour. A great dispute then arose on the question whether the vote was valid or not ; and in the course of the ensuing clamour, the Socialist Speaker, Karl Renner, resigned his office, and was followed by his Catholic colleague — the first Vice-President. The second Vice-President, a Nationalist, saw his chance, and resigned too, leaving no one who was entitled by the terms of the constitution to call the Chamber together. The Government, glad to find an escape from the parliamentary impasse, upheld the view that the

Chamber could not be re-convened, but that, as it had not been dissolved or adjourned, it remained nominally in being.

This curious situation arose on March 4th, 1933, a few days after the Reichstag Fire in Berlin and the day before Hitler won his resounding majority in the German General Election. The trouble on the railways had already become involved with the Hirtenberg arms affair, which the railway-men had played the leading part in bringing to light. This was the case of an arms factory at Hirtenberg, which was shown to be producing rifles for export to Hungary, in violation of the peace treaties and contrary to the official policy of the Austrian Government. It then came to light that most of the weapons in question had not been manufactured in Hirtenberg, but had been imported from Italy and were intended to be sent to Hungary, not for Hungarian use, but for transference to Croatian rebels who were planning a rising against Yugo-slavia. The Italians, on very bad terms with the Yugoslavs, had sent them to be reconditioned in Hirtenberg on their way to Croatia ; and Mussolini was annoyed at the disclosure and was from that moment determined to give all possible help in destroying the Austrian Socialists, who would have perhaps thought twice about bringing the affair to light had they known in advance what it involved.

Renner's resignation, given in the heat of the moment, was undoubtedly a bad tactical error ; for he did not foresee that the two Vice-Presidents of the Chamber would, by following his example, create a constitutional impasse in which Parliament would no longer be allowed to function at all. The effect, indeed, was to convert Dollfuss from the Chancellor of a formally democratic Republic into a dictator. He became a dictator much less because he so desired than because he could see no alternative. There were now not two but three main forces in Austria contending for political power — the Socialists, who held their strength but were making no advance, Dollfuss's Christian Social-Heimwehr alliance, which was losing ground heavily, and the Nazis, who had already absorbed most of the old Nationalists, or Pan-Germans, and a part of the Heimwehr, and were gaining at a great rate all over the country. No one of these three groups could gain a majority under any parlia-mentary system ; but it was also out of the question for any two of them to combine against the third. Between Dollfuss and the Socialists the gap was far too wide ; and, besides, alliance with the Socialists would have meant uniting Italy and Germany in hostility to continued Austrian independence. Alliance with the Nazis, who were set on abolishing Austria altogether as an independent State, was no more possible from the moment of Hitler's victory in Germany. There remained only a Christian Social dictatorship, though it had been shown that the Christian Socials and the Heimwehr together commanded less than a third of the Republic's voting strength.

Dollfuss's dictatorship depended entirely on Germany and Italy being disunited in their Austrian policy, as they in fact were. Hitler had long expressed his intention of absorbing Austria into the new Pan-German Reich, whereas Mussolini had no wish to see German forces in command of the Brenner Pass, with direct access to Italy. Dollfuss accordingly relied on Italian support for his peculiar brand of Catholic Fascism, which differed radically from both Nazism and Italian Fascism in that it did not rest on the support of a mass-party. There was nothing in it even remotely analogous to the rôle of Party or of Führer or Duce in Germany and Italy. Instead, there was a harking back to Vogelsang's ideas of a Christian State resting on a foundation of 'estates' (*Stände*), but with the difference that, whereas Vogelsang had advanced his ideas as means of preventing the development of large-scale industry and finance, his successor had an important part of his backing among the big industrialists and bankers, as well as among the surviving aristocrats of the old imperial régime. The system which Seipel and Dollfuss advocated was indeed radically unfitted to the needs of a modern society, in which the Church had completely lost its hold on the industrial workers and on a considerable section of the peasantry, and the *Stände* into which it was proposed to reorganise the occupied population, irrespective of class barriers, could have no reality. Dollfuss realised clearly enough that he could not hope to realise his 'estate' structure unless he could somehow break entirely the power of the Trade Unions, which were the backbone of the Socialist Party ; and he accordingly set out to use every means in his power of attacking them. He had, however, to fight a continuous battle on two fronts — against the Nazis as well as the Socialists ; and he was well aware that the Christian Social Party was by no means solidly behind him, but included a Catholic Trade Union movement he would need also to overthrow, as well as many peasant politicians who were by no means whole-heartedly in support of his alliance with the Heimwehr.

By this time the Heimwehr, having become a government party, was a nuisance mainly to the Socialists — though it had its affrays with the Nazis too. Dollfuss made considerable efforts to placate the Nazis, especially by strong measures directed against the Socialists, but presently became convinced of the futility of attempting to come to terms with a Party completely committed to the *Anschluss* and to the acceptance of Hitler as 'Leader'. The Nazis, indeed, responded to Dollfuss's overtures with a campaign of bomb-throwing and violence, which compelled him to take repressive measures against them. His main attack, however, continued to be directed at the Socialists and to the seizure of the considerable quantities of arms that still remained in the hands of the Schutzbund despite the searches and seizures already made. These searches were now intensified, and culminated in the seizure of the Socialist Party's headquarters in Linz in February 1934. The Linz Socialists determined to fight without waiting for permission from the party centre in Vienna ; and from Linz the rising spread to other areas, but by no means to the whole country. In Vienna the central party committee, on getting the news, decided by a majority of one vote to call a general strike, which was by no means a hopeful step in view of the prevailing heavy unemployment. A part of the Vienna Schutzbund took to arms, but only a part. The strike was a complete failure. The section of the Schutzbund that took part in the rising fought a losing battle for four days, but stood no chance when the Government brought artillery into the field against them. Severe damage was done to the Karl Marx Hof and other big blocks of workers' flats built by the Vienna municipality ; and much heroism was shown by those who fought. They had, however, no chance at all ; and Major Fey, who directed the operations against them, began shooting those who had been taken prisoner, including at least one severely wounded man. After seven rebels had been hanged out of hand, this practice was brought to an end following serious protests from foreign powers.

Though most of the Socialists had taken no part in the rising, the entire Socialist Party and the Trade Unions were held to blame. The Party was dissolved, and its offices seized; and the Socialist Trade Unions suffered the same fate. The principal leaders, except those of the extreme right wing, were driven underground or into exile. Otto Bauer escaped to Czechoslovakia, and settled down at Brno, from which centre he tried to continue his propaganda. Deutsch, the Schutzbund leader, also escaped abroad. But the dissolution of the Party and of the Trade Unions by no means extinguished either. The Party found new leaders who carried on its propaganda underground, and continued to hold the allegiance of the main body of industrial workers against both Dollfuss and the Nazis; and the Christian Social Trade Unions, which were allowed to survive temporarily pending their absorption in a new inclusive organisation under government control, became a point of focus for former members of the Socialist Trade Unions and engaged in bona fide bargaining about immediate questions of wages and conditions of employment. Out of this situation arose the so-called 'Unified Union' or *Einheitsgewerkschaft*, which, though based originally on the Catholic Unions, became more and more a general labour organisation subject to increasing Socialist pressure.

More serious for the Socialists was the displacement of the Vienna city administration, which was taken away from the elected Council, in which the Socialists had a large majority, and handed over to a Commissioner, who gave immediate orders that municipal house-building was to cease. In certain respects attempts were made to win favour from the Viennese workers, especially by appointing a progressive Christian Social, Dr. Ernst Winter, as Vice-Mayor. But Winter, though his personal views were fairly advanced, in the Lueger tradition, in respect of the social services, had little power to act and was soon displaced.

For the next few months after the rising Dollfuss, egged on by the Heimwehr leaders, pursued his vendetta against the Socialists, though some of his Ministers and supporters showed no zeal for his more extreme measures. Among his critics were Dr. Schmitz, the new Mayor of Vienna, Dr. Winter, and his Minister of Justice, Dr. von Schuschnigg, who favoured a milder policy. Then came in July 1934 the attempted Nazi *coup d'état*. Armed bands of Nazis seized the Chancellery and the wireless station ; and it was announced from the latter that Dollfuss had resigned and that Rintelen, a leading Nazi supporter, had taken his place. In the Chancellery the conspirators found and captured Dollfuss, who was mortally wounded by one of them, and held in custody without recourse to either a priest or a doctor. But meanwhile government forces had surrounded the Chancellery, and there was no sign of any widespread rising in support of the Nazis. Major Fey, who professed to be held captive, negotiated terms of surrender, and the Chancellery was given up. But by this time Dollfuss was dead. It is a disputed point whether Fey promised the conspirators a safe-conduct if they surrendered. They affirmed, and he denied, this ; but in any case no such promise was kept. A few leading Nazis were hanged ; but there were no mass reprisals. In addition to the attempted *coup* in Vienna, there were Nazi risings in Carinthia and Styria ; which were suppressed after heavy fighting. Many of the insurgents retreated across the frontier into Yugoslavia, which was already Germany's close ally.

One reason for the failure of the Nazi *coup* was that the armed forces of the Government stood firm against the Nazis, and that they had in Vienna very little popular support. Another reason, probably more effective in limiting the spread of the revolt, was that Mussolini moved two Italian divisions to the frontier at the Brenner Pass. Hitler had built up an Austrian Legion composed of Nazi refugees from Austria, and this body was moved to near the Austrian frontier in readiness to cross. But Hitler, when he learnt of the Italian troop movement, had second thoughts. German rearmament was still at an early stage, and he was strongly advised not to risk an embroilment with Italy that might bring on an immediate European War. He accordingly sent the Austrian Legion back to East Prussia, leaving the Austrian Nazis to their fate.

The death of Dollfuss led to a substantial modification of Austrian government policy. His successor, von Schuschnigg, was a lesser Tyrolean nobleman, a very devout Christian, a man of fairly enlightened views on peasant problems, and in his personal tastes something of a highbrow. He had nothing in common with such toughs as Starhemberg and Fey, or with the general outlook of the Heimwehr; and, though he was of course anti-Socialist, he felt no zest to persecute and annihilate those who preached a Socialist creed. Therefore, though he continued Dollfuss's dictatorship — having in effect no alternative — he made it much milder and made no attempt to stop the revival of Trade Unions through the *Einheitsgewerkschaft*. Schuschnigg was in fact an old-fashioned gentlemanly exponent of the old Austria, in its least reactionary form; and what he sought above all from 1934 onwards was a quiet life. He soon dismissed from his Government first Major Fey and then Prince Starhemberg, without provoking any serious trouble. In effect, he recognised that the Heimwehr as well as the Nazis had lost much of its appeal, and that what reasonable men now wanted was above all else to be left alone. There was, however, in the Austria of 1934 no moderate class of aristocrats to provide a basis for such a Government as Schuschnigg would have liked to see. He could just hold on as the head of a small, independent Christian State as long as his two most dangerous neighbours, Germany and Italy, did not see eye to eye — or rather as long as Mussolini was prepared to protect him against Hitler. But as soon as the two big dictators came to terms, Austria's collapse as an independent State was sheerly inevitable whenever Hitler made up his mind to act.

At this stage, in 1934–5, the French were making the utmost effort to keep Nazi Germany and Fascist Italy apart, and even to include Italy in an anti-Nazi Front based mainly on France and Great Britain. For this it was necessary to appease the Italians by allowing them to make war on Abyssinia and annex it, wholly or in part, as a field for Italian colonists. But an attack on Abyssinia would be a direct and open breach of the League of Nations Covenant, especially as Abyssinia had been accepted as a member of the League. This did not deter Laval, who considered condoning Italian aggression as well worth while in order to secure Italy's support against the Germans. But the Hoare-Laval Pact, between the British and French Foreign Secretaries, caused such an outburst of protest in Great Britain that Sir Samuel Hoare (later Lord

Templewood) was forced to resign, and the League had to consider applying 'sanctions' against the Italians for invading Abyssinia. After much wrangling, certain sanctions were applied; but the League Powers carefully avoided applying the one sanction that would have been immediately effective — an embargo on the supply of oil to the Italian armed forces. This sanction was held back because Mussolini openly declared that he would regard it as in effect a declaration of war.

Though the League shilly-shallied about sanctions, its half-hearted intervention in the Abyssinian War sufficed to throw Italy into the arms of Nazi Germany, and provided the basis for the 'Rome-Berlin' Axis and for the Anti-Comintern Pact. Italy, which had been subsidising the Heimwehr, withdrew its help; and it became apparent that Hitler could destroy the Austrian Republic when he pleased. He waited, in fact, until March 1938. By that time German rearmament had advanced much further, and it had already become plain that France and Great Britain were most reluctant to take any action to stop Nazi aggression that involved any risk of war. Hitler was already working up his venomous campaign against Czechoslovakia, with which Austria had been for some time on very friendly terms. It was in fact only a question which country the Nazis would attack first — Austria or Czechoslovakia — and Hitler decided to polish off the Austrians first, now that Italian protection had been definitely withdrawn. Schuschnigg could see well enough what was coming to his country, though he could not know in advance when precisely the attack would be made. Then, in February 1938, Hitler summoned Schuschnigg to Berchtesgaden, and ordered him to make the Austrian Nazi, von Seiss-Inquardt, Home Secretary, showing him the orders to the German troops to march into Austria unless Schuschnigg obeyed, which he was forced to do. Schuschnigg then returned to Vienna, and considered whether anything could be done to save the country. It was clearly out of the question for him to resist the Nazis with his own resources; and the only remaining sources of potential resistance were the Heimwehr and the banned and dispersed working-class movement. The Heimwehr, with which Schuschnigg had quarrelled, was clearly a broken reed; and the sole remaining hope lay in an accommodation with the workers. There were discussions with the factory delegates; and a few days before the end a large working-class conference was held with government consent and pledged itself to the defence of Austria. Thus in the final resort the Catholics, who had been endeavouring for so long to wipe out the working-class movement, were driven to come to terms with it as the only force capable of organising large-scale resistance. Schuschnigg, however, acted only half-heartedly and, in appealing to the workers, made no promises that his Government would fight to the end if they would help it. During the final days of Austrian independence the streets of Vienna were filled with cheering Socialist demonstrators. Schuschnigg determined to take a plebiscite for and against independence, and this decision probably precipitated the *coup*. On March 11th, 1938, the Nazis marched in, and the same evening Schuschnigg resigned without any attempt at resistance. He was sure that there was no chance, when Hitler, defying the advice of his generals, gave the order to march. In this he was clearly correct; for the workers had by this time only a very limited supply of arms and were clearly incapable of standing up to an attack by regular forces.

Thus the Austrian Republic came to an end in 1938, to be reconstituted only at the end of the second world war, under conditions of joint occupation that compelled the Socialists to enter a coalition Government, and to remain partners in it right up to the present time, when Austria, now evacuated by the occupying forces, has accepted a rôle of neutrality in the European struggle. But party alignments are very different to-day from what they were in the 1930s. The violent anti-democracy of Seipel and of the Heimwehr has disappeared: the Socialists, recognising their inability to gain an independent majority, have settled down to live with a Christian Social Party that is no longer bent on destroying parliamentary democracy, but readily accepts it as, in the circumstances, the only practicable system. The Socialists, who, as we saw, were never the revolutionaries their opponents made them out to be, but had always a strong constitutional right wing headed by such men as Renner and Danneberg, have gone over in a body to constitutionalism: the attempt to find an Austro-Marxism half-way between left and right has been given up. The Austrian Party is to-day a Party of social reform, as largely it always was ; but it has ceased to rest on any distinctive theoretical basis. Some of its old leaders — Friedrich Adler among them — are still alive but no longer active, and of younger men active before 1934, and still active to-day, one may mention Oscar Pollak of the *Arbeiterzeitung* and Julius Braunthal, who has recently retired from the secretaryship of of the Socialist International. For the most part, however, the old leaders are dead ; and new men, a good deal less theoretically minded, have come up in their place. Austro-Marxism, so long a term of opprobrium among Austrian anti-Socialists and also among Communists who denounced it as resting on philosophical foundations of Kantian Idealism or of Machian empirio-criticism, has passed away entirely as a living doctrine, appropriate to present-day conditions. The Austrian Socialists, however, have given more than once clear demonstration of their resistance and staying power, and not least during the years of oppression by the Nazis which began in 1938. They were always, I think, somewhat double-minded, and intensely reluctant to believe that the occasion had come when armed resistance was the only policy that offered a chance of success — the more reluctant because the chance of success was never more than poor. But, whereas the great German Socialist movement allowed itself to be struck down in 1933 without striking a single blow, the Austrian Socialists — or at least a substantial section of them — did resist in arms in 1934, and were widely felt, despite their defeat and the very partial character of their rising, to have saved the honour of Socialism in almost its darkest hour.

CHAPTER VII

SCANDINAVIA AND FINLAND

THE period between the two world wars was that in which Scandinavian Social Democracy won high acclaim, both among moderate Socialists and among the more moderate types of anti-Socialists, for its successful following of a 'middle road' between Socialism and Capitalism. What this meant in fact was that the Social Democrats in the three main Scandinavian countries — Denmark, Sweden, and Norway — after using the opportunity created by the war to secure the introduction of universal suffrage — including votes for women — and the institution of democratic reforms in political structure, went on to make these changes a foundation for far-reaching measures of social security and progressive tax and other reforms : so that the Trade Unions, which had greatly increased their membership and influence, were well placed for successful collective bargaining. Not a great deal had been actually accomplished in the way of social reforms by the end of the 1920s ; for throughout the 'twenties the Social Democrats were still in a minority position in their several Parliaments — though, in spite of this, they had formed several short-lived Social Democratic Governments. Paradoxically, the Socialists' main successes were accomplished during the disastrous world slump that set in during 1931, and to the accompaniment of the Nazi triumph in Germany at the beginning of 1933.

How did this happen, not in one country alone, but to some extent in all three — though most of all in Sweden, where Social Democratic Governments, or Governments based mainly on the Social Democratic Party, held office continuously, with only one very brief interruption, from 1932 up to the outbreak of war in 1939 ? Undoubtedly one reason was that Sweden was in a much more favourable economic position than most of her neighbours. Though unemployment rose sharply in Sweden and caused a very strong demand for measures to help hose out of work, there was nothing at all approaching the devastation that was caused in many other countries. Indeed exports were relatively well maintained; for they consisted largely of wood pulp and paper, which remained in relatively good demand, and of other forest products, together with the very high quality iron produced in the north of the country; and for this the rearmament programmes of the 1930s provided, above all in Germany, an almost inexhaustible outlet, despite the difficulty of getting payment from the Germans. Swedish imports consisted mainly of raw or semi-finished materials for use in industry; for Sweden was only a small importer of either foodstuffs or finished industrial products, which were manufactured at home in great variety. There was indeed in the earlier phases of the world depression a sharp fall in Swedish trade with Germany, due mainly to German balance of payments difficulties. But with the rise of Nazism this trend was reversed by the high German demand for iron ore, iron, and steel products which Sweden was able to supply. The Swedes thus got off lightly during the depression, and were the better able to take measures for combating it because Sweden had both high gold reserves and a very favourable balance of payments position, and was thus able to spend money on public works for the provision of employment without being driven into difficulties over its balance of payments. The Swedish Socialist Government was in fact able to give a clear demonstration of the effectiveness of public works policy as a means of action against unemployment at a time when other Governments, less favourably placed, were protesting their helplessness in this respect, or even, as in the case of Great Britain, denying that it could be effective, on the manifestly untrue pretext that any addition to employment provided by public agencies would simply be cancelled by an equal fall in privately provided employment, leaving the total situation no better than before. It may be a moot point whether the Swedes would have been able to act as they did had their balance of payments been less favourable and their exports harder hit by the depression than they actually were; but the credit is none the less due to them for having been the first to regard economic crises not as 'acts of God', which action by the State could do nothing to better, but rather as opportunities for action. Mr. Ernst Wigforss, their Finance Minister, was largely responsible for the policy they followed; and great credit is due to him as a pioneer in what has now become the orthodox way of government action in maintaining the level of employment instead of seeking a deflationary outlet.

Apart from this, the main achievements of the Swedish Socialist Governments were in the field of social security. Sweden was already a country in which rich men were few, and absolute poverty was relatively rare, except in the far north. Urban standards of living were high; and a large part of the rural population consisted of small, but fairly prosperous, farmers, who had to a large extent common interests with the industrial workers. Farm labourers, who were worse off, were not very numerous. There was a large middle class of professional workers and traders, raised only a little way in standards of living above the skilled workers, and largely organised with them in the powerful and pervasive consumers' Co-operative movement, which, under the masterful leadership of Albin Johannsen, had declared war on monopolists who attempted to exploit the consumers, and had entered into direct competition with them in both wholesale and retail trade and production, especially in the fields of electric bulb manufacture and in the making of cash registers, but also over a much wider field. This consumers' Co-operative movement maintained strict political neutrality, and was in no way linked up officially with the Socialist Party. But Socialist households usually belonged to it; and the informal links between the two movements were very close. *Kooperativa Forbundet,* known as 'K.F.', which served the Co-operative both as a wholesale trading and producing agency and as a central policy-making and propagandist body, was strongly entrenched in all the towns, and also penetrated into the rural areas. But the farmers had their own separate Co-operative organisations, especially for the marketing of milk and other quality foodstuffs; and these worked, as a rule, in sufficient harmony with K.F.

The Socialists, when they came to office, showed little zeal for nationalisation. There was already a considerable sector of public enterprise, including, besides the railways, the iron mines, a substantial number of public forests and forestry works, and over two-thirds of the supply of electricity based on water-power for public consumption, or well over one-half if concerns generating power for their own use are included in the total. Any attempt to nationalise the land would have met with formidable opposition from the farmers, small as well as big; and the strong position of the Co-operative movement practically ruled out any extension of state activity in the sphere of either wholesale or retail trade. Nor was there any strong pressure for nationalisation among the industrial workers, who, strongly organised in a powerfully centralised Trade Union organisation, were able to bargain on terms of equality with their employers. By the 1930s the great Swedish General Strike of 1908 had largely passed out of memory, and there was a long record of peaceful negotiation over wages and conditions of work. By no means all were satisfied with the results: the centralised Trade Union leadership was accused of following an unduly accommodating policy and thus of betraying the workers' interests. But by the 1930s left-wing Unionism was on the wane, though still of some importance among the forestry workers: in industry generally the central body, L.O. or Lands Organisation, held almost undisputed control.

Swedish Governments, long before the coming to power of the Social Democratic Party, had been much concerned with social security. Insurance for liability to Workers' Compensation has been compulsory on employers since 1901; compulsory sickness and old-age insurance for all came in in 1913; and since the first world war the activity of the State in the social service field had been almost continuously extended. In Sweden, however, the State usually acts not alone but in conjunction with local authorities and voluntary agencies; and few of the services provided in the 1930s were absolutely free to the recipients, who were usually called on to bear a part of the cost — though in many cases the part so borne was small. Moreover, a good many of the services provided are on a voluntary basis, limited to those who subscribe towards them of their own will, usually through some society which may be either wholly or partly under public control, or entirely independent of the State — at any rate apart from receiving subsidies from it. Thus, though compulsory Health Insurance was proposed in 1919, no Act introducing it was carried, and Health Insurance was managed by a number of registered sickness benefit societies sponsored by the State Pensions Board and receiving subsidies from the State. By the end of the 'thirties, upwards of a million persons belonged to such societies, out of a total population of all ages of little more than 6½ million. In 1931 the scheme was re-cast to provide for two kinds of society, one local and one central, each insured person belonging to a society of each type. The local society was made responsible for medical aid, hospital treatment, and sickness benefit for a limited period, after which the central society was to take over with medical benefit of unlimited duration and hospital treatment, where needed, for two or three years. Charges were, however, made to cover part of the cost of medical treatment, and deductions from the amount of sickness benefit could be made, within limits, to meet these charges. Unlike sickness insurance, insurance against invalidity and old age had been compulsory ever since 1913, and these services were administered by and through local Pensions Committees co-ordinated by a Royal Pensions Board attached to the Ministry of Social Affairs. Annual contributions in 1937 ranged from 6s. to 20s., and consisted of 1 per cent of the contributor's income up to this maximum. The pension, payable at 67 or on total incapacity, was 70s. plus 10 per cent of the member's total contribution per annum. Supplementary pensions were also paid to persons whose total incomes were below certain levels. The State and the municipality between them met the extra cost of this supplementary payment. There was also a special pension scheme — known as the 'Personal Pensions Scheme' — under which non-manual employees contributed to a Fund, managed by representatives of a wide variety of interests subject to State supervision. This scheme, which started in 1915, was reconstructed in 1929.

Swedish unemployment insurance was on a voluntary basis, through state-subsidised Benefit Societies formed by the Trade Unions. In the middle 'thirties it covered only about 100,000 persons. The main provision for unemployment took the form of relief works largely under the auspices of local authorities; and the persons employed on such works were paid at rates well below those of unskilled workers employed in a regular way. Since 1924 a State Unemployment Commission had been responsible for public works policy under the Ministry of Social Affairs. The works undertaken, which had to be highly labour-intensive, and were in practice mainly on the roads, were of three kinds — those in the hands of the State directly, those carried out by local authorities with State financial aid, and those financed entirely by local authorities. Pecuniary relief was granted only where work could not be provided. This system worked tolerably as long as unemployment was not severe, and in the 1920s roughly a third of the registered unemployed were set to relief work, whereas only about 10 per cent, or less, received pecuniary relief. But with the onset of the depression the proportion employed fell off sharply, whereas the numbers receiving pecuniary relief rose very fast. This was the situation when, in 1932, the Social Democratic Party polled over 40 per cent of the votes cast for the Second Chamber at the General Election and were able to form a Government, though not with a clear majority over all other Parties. This election occurred in the midst of the world depression, and was fought largely on the measures to be taken in dealing with it. The Social Democrats shared the objection of the other Parties to giving pecuniary relief save in the last resort; but they also objected to the system of relief work at less than Trade Union rates and demanded instead a 'public works policy' under which employment would be provided under standard rates and conditions, the cost being met, as far as necessary, by borrowing. This meant repudiating the orthodox view that the Budget should be balanced year by year and putting in its place the notion of a budget deficit in bad years to be made good by a surplus in years of prosperity. Not having a clear majority in Parliament, the Social Democrats were not able to carry out their policy in full; but they were able to institute an active policy of public works, for which labour was engaged under standard rates and conditions, and also to raise the standards of pay on relief work to the full unskilled rates. The Budget was unbalanced; but provision was made for making good the deficit in subsequent years by special taxes, and this was actually done. Thus Sweden, from 1933 onwards, met the depression not by monetary deflation, but by making good the decline in private investment by increasing investment in public enterprise and thus maintaining the level of employment until the exceptional conditions of depression came to an end. As we saw, this could be done the more easily because Swedish exports were well maintained despite the depression and the balance of payments was in a healthy state ; but great credit attaches to the Social Democratic Party and to Wigforss, its Finance Minister, for their success in guiding Sweden through the depression with less adverse effect than was felt by other countries which attempted to meet it by the orthodox deflationary methods. The Swedish Socialists had the advantage of having worked out their policy completely in advance, so that they knew precisely what they were doing and did not need to improvise the methods from hand to mouth ; and their success was a sufficient answer to their critics. They did replace in subsequent years the money they had raised by loan to meet the crisis, insisting on maintaining taxation at a level that allowed this to be done. They did not, however, allow public investment to fall back to its earlier level as private investment recovered, as they wished permanently to extend the range of public investment in nationally desirable projects. They contented themselves with trying to keep total investment, public and private, at a level that could be sustained without further borrowing for capital expenditure in good years.

The effect of this policy was that the need for pecuniary relief of the unemployed was greatly reduced and also that relief works, as distinct from public works properly so called, were reduced to secondary importance. In addition, the level of taxation was kept high, instead of being reduced with the passing of the depression, in order to provide funds for improved social services, especially in the reform of pensions in 1937.

The Social Democratic Government of 1932 and the following years was a minority Government enjoying the support of the Agrarian Party. After the General Election of 1936, at which the Social Democrats increased their strength, polling about 46 per cent of all the votes cast, the Socialist Prime Minister, Per Albin Hansson, formed a new Government including Agrarians as well as Socialists, and thus commanding a clear majority. The change to a coalition had, however, no notable effect on policy; and the new Government proceeded to legislate for better pensions, unemployment insurance, paid holidays, and a number of other social reforms, but made no attempt to advance towards Socialism by any measures directed against private enterprise. When the world war broke out in 1939 the Government was reconstructed as a national Coalition with the Socialist leader, Hansson, as Prime Minister. Sweden had declared well before 1939 its intention to remain neutral, but had taken a number of steps to put its defences in order in face of the rising tension. When war came, Sweden did preserve its neutrality, but was compelled to make considerable concessions to Germany, especially after the German invasion of Norway and Denmark. In the General Election of 1940 the Social Democrats further improved their position, securing a clear majority of all the votes cast and an absolute parliamentary majority; and when the war ended a purely Social Democratic Government was again formed under Hansson, Tage Erlander succeeding him as Prime Minister on his death in 1946. Hansson had held office practically continuously from 1932 to 1946, at the head of either Socialist or Coalition Cabinets. In his early days a leader in the Socialist Youth Movement, he had become a highly respected and popular figure as the successor of Branting, and had been chosen as Party Leader in 1928. Unassuming and forthright, he had known well how to hold the Party together and had collaborated well with Ernst Wigforss in carrying through the anti-crisis policy of 1932, and in the subsequent measures of social reform. He was indeed just the leader to suit the Swedish Socialists, with their programmes of advanced social reform measures and of representing the general body of poor and middle consumers rather than the proletariat in any exclusive or class-war sense.

Swedish Socialism, as it existed in the 1930s — and indeed as it exists to-day — is essentially reformist and uninspired by any emotion of class-antagonism. The structure of Swedish society leads naturally to an alliance between small farmers and industrial workers and also to a considerable community of outlook between the skilled workers and the lower grades of the professions, which are not much separated from them in standards of living. There have, indeed, been bitter industrial conflicts in Sweden, notably at the time of the General Strike of 1908, when the closely co-ordinated Trade Union movement came into head-on conflict with the central body of employers, and underwent serious defeat. But since then, except on very rare occasions, Trade Unions and employers have found out how to co-exist on favourable terms and to adjust wages and conditions by closely co-ordinated processes of collective bargaining. The great strength of the Co-operative movement, with its political neutrality and its general concern for consuming interests, greatly affects Socialist policy; for the Socialists can by no means afford to quarrel with the Co-operatives, which for the most part favour their measures of social reform, but feel no enthusiasm for socialisation. The Social Democrats are in theory a Marxist Party; but there is little sign of this in their attitude to economic problems, and they show neither wish nor intention to proceed to any general attack on capitalism as a system. Their attitude is indeed a reflection of an actual social situation which most of them feel to be not unsatisfactory in its general features, though capable of further amendment by particular reforms. They had secured by the early 'twenties the electoral support of one-third of the total number voting in elections under universal suffrage, established in 1919, and by 1924 had increased their share of the total vote to 40 per cent, at or above which it thereafter remained, except for one temporary setback in 1928, when it fell to 38 per cent. But only once, in 1940, have they polled an absolute majority over all other parties, falling back thereafter to about 46 per cent at each successive General Election. To the left of the official Party there have been always dissident groups; but these have never been large enough to challenge its influence in any fundamental way. If Socialism meant no more than the Welfare State accompanied by a considerable degree of economic planning, Swedish Social Democracy could well be regarded as the model Socialist Party; and many do indeed so regard it. Nor is it easy to see how it could with advantage have acted otherwise, in essentials, than it in fact did. The Swedish working-class standard of living is one of the highest in Europe; and in the absence of any large class of really rich persons there is no economic incentive to radical social change.

DENMARK

Denmark, where too the social structure is broadly democratic and the standard of living high, shared in its Socialism of the 1930s many common characteristics with that of Sweden. From its formation in 1920 Denmark was governed by a coalition of Socialists and Liberals right up to the German invasion of 1940, under the Socialist, Th. Stauning, as Prime Minister; and this Government followed a largely similar policy of social welfare legislation.   In Denmark, as in Sweden, after the establishment of universal suffrage the Social Democrats found it a relatively simple matter to attract more than one-third of the total votes, and by 1935 had increased their share to 46 per cent.   They were never, however, able to win an outright majority over all other Parties and remained in coalition with the Radicals, who in the main agreed with them in matters of social policy.   Denmark was unlike Sweden in that Co-operation, while very strong in both, was in Denmark strongest of all as a farmers' movement, though consumers' Co-operation also was strongly entrenched, especially in the towns.   It was, however, like Sweden in having a high standard of living; and it had a stronger Radical tradition in the countryside: so that the alliance between Social Democrats and Radicals corresponded to a real community of sentiment as well as of interest. The Danish Socialists, like the Swedes, were in theory a Marxist Party; but in practice they were very little affected by the Marxist theories they had taken over.   Strongly pacifist in outlook, they had gone to the extreme in unilateral disarmament during the 1930s; and, when Hitler broke the neutrality pact he had made with them only the previous year and invaded Denmark in 1940, they were in no position to resist and allowed the Germans to occupy Denmark without fighting.   But before they were overrun they had carried through an extensive programme of social reform.   The most important single measure was the co-ordinating social insurance law carried by the Socialist Minister of Social Affairs, K. K. Steincke, in 1933.   This brought the numerous separate Acts already in being under unified control by a public board for each area, and also considerably extended the scope of public provision.   Further laws followed, including one for holidays with pay, enacted in 1938. Steps were also taken for the improvement of industrial relations under conciliatory collective bargaining. The system of public conciliation in industrial disputes, originally started in 1910, was extended in 1934, and has been largely successful in preventing stoppages of work when collective agreements expire and need to be renewed.

In countries such as Denmark and Sweden, though there is little scope for really reactionary Parties, and the Parties of the Left are almost sure of a combined majority as long as they are able to work together, it has become clear how difficult it is for the Socialists, however much they may adapt their policies in order to secure a wide measure of popular support, to win over a clear majority of all the voters to support of the Socialist Party. Sweden has achieved this only once, in 1940, whereafter it was lost again, though not by a great deal; but it seems as if constitutional democratic Socialism can arrive fairly easily at a proportion of voting strength which makes it difficult, or even impossible, to create any stable Government on a basis of anti-Socialist coalition, but also leaves the Socialist Party unable to carry on the Government without support from at least one bourgeois Party, such as the Agrarians in Sweden or the Radicals in Denmark. This, I think, is less because the marginal voters object to anything the Socialists have on their actual programmes, and intend to do in the immediate future, than because of an unwillingness to be associated with their longer-run, Socialist objectives, or with the name of Socialism. Farmers in particular are not easily drawn into a Socialist Party, even if it declares its intention of leaving the land in private ownership and of protecting agriculture against the perils of fluctuating world prices. Large farmers, no doubt, are usually opposed to Socialist policies, as well as to remoter Socialist objectives; but even the small farmers, who favour social legislation, are not easily drawn into the Socialist camp, even when the Parties which they control are prepared to act in alliance with the Socialists against the reactionary Parties. Thus, there emerges in such countries, where the industrial proletariat and the small farmers are each strong, but neither strong enough to govern alone, the kind of democratic policy which concentrates on the consolidation of the 'Welfare State' and on the use of progressive taxation as a means of redistributing incomes and of preventing great disparities of wealth, to the exclusion of any attempt to do away with profit-seeking private enterprise or to transfer ownership of industries and services to the public except where nationalisation, or some alternative form of public control — for example, by Co-operative enterprise — seems to be called for on account of special defects of monopoly or inefficiency, or to arise naturally as incidental to public planning for the prevention of unemployment. But even extensions of public ownership advocated on these grounds are apt to be postponed or set aside as likely to antagonise marginal support; and in proportion as such States make themselves into 'Welfare States' with a comprehensive provision of public social services, it becomes harder for their Socialist Parties to devise further programmes of reform along the same lines. The same difficulty may indeed confront other 'Welfare States' when their most far-reaching and spectacular social reforms have been carried into effect; but it tends to come sooner where the limits of practicable action are set by the need for industrial workers and farmers to act together.

NORWAY

Norway has in many respects a very different Labour movement history from either Sweden or Denmark. We saw in the previous volume how, under the influence of Martin Tranmael, the Norwegian Labour Party first entered the Third International in 1919 and then quickly seceded from it rather than agree to accept its marching orders from Moscow. Neither Tranmael nor most of his followers were indeed ever Communists, as Moscow understood the term. At the time when they joined the Comintern, that body was appealing for support not only from Communists, but also explicitly from Industrial Unionists and left-wingers of any kind, in the hope and expectation that, if they could be induced to join, they would subsequently accept the leadership the Communists meant to impose upon all. We saw that the affiliation to Moscow led to a split and to the formation by the critics of an independent right-wing Social Democratic Party, which reunited with the majority after the link with Moscow had been broken. As against this, the breaking of the bond led to the formation of a minority

Communist Party, directly loyal to the Comintern, but with no considerable following. In these circumstances the Norwegian Labour Party remained aloof from the revived Second International and from its successor, the Labour and Socialist International. The dissident Social Democrats indeed joined the last of these; but the affiliation lapsed when they rejoined the Norwegian Labour Party in 1927; and the combined body held aloof from the L.S.I. until 1938, when it at last joined. In 1927 the united Party polled nearly 37 per cent of the votes cast at the General Election, and came back to Parliament as the largest Party, but still a long way short of an absolute majority. Called upon to form a Government under their leader Christian Hornsrud, they agreed to do so; but, instead of trying to find the basis for a majority in compromise, declared their intention of proceeding at once with a thoroughgoing Socialist programme, and were driven within a few days into resignation by the storm of opposition their announcement aroused. In spite of this and of a small setback which followed at the General Election of 1930, when the Socialist votes fell to 31 per cent, they came back in 1933, at the nadir of the world depression, with a 40 per cent vote as the largest party and again agreed to form a Government, this time under a new leader, Johan Nygaardsvold, who was still in office when the Germans invaded Norway in 1940, and then became Prime Minister in a coalition Government which presently left the country and established itself in London till it was able to return in 1945. Nygaardsvold then left office, and was succeeded as Prime Minister by the former Secretary of the Labour Party, Einar Gerhardsen, who had returned from a German concentration camp after the Nazi collapse.

Before Nygaardsvold took office in 1934, the Norwegian Labour Party had drawn up a special Crisis Programme, of which the first point was the maintenance of full employment. By the time the Labour Government took office, the worst of the world crisis was already over, and it had become easier to find resources for an ambitious programme of social legislation. This followed much the same lines as in Sweden and Denmark, but with a larger part of the administration in the hands of local bodies and a good deal more difference from place to place. The Government, having no independent majority, depended on the support of one or more of the bourgeois Parties, and was in fact supported throughout the period up to 1940, either by the Agrarians, the Party of the large and middle farmers, or by the Liberals, who had a good record of social legislation of their own, or by both, with only the Conservatives in consistent opposition.

Throughout the 1920s Norway had been an area of almost continuous industrial unrest, with many strikes fought out with considerable bitterness by employers' associations and Trade Unions. But in 1934 this constant bickering was brought to an end by the conclusion of a general agreement between the two sides, providing for regular collective bargaining and peaceable settlement of differences; and this agreement worked on the whole smoothly during the remaining years of the decade, inducing a considerable change in the attitudes of both sides and greatly facilitating the work of the Labour Government in the field of social legislation. Norway became, in effect, almost as tranquil as Sweden or Denmark; and the left-wing theories which had been so influential in the 1920s steadily lost ground, though Tranmael remained active as journalist and propagandist and retained much of his influence.

FINLAND

During the 1930s Finland by no means shared in the tranquillity of the three Scandinavian States. After the resignation of the Tanner Social Democratic minority Government in 1927 came the rise of the formidable Lapps, or Lapuan movement, directed specifically against Marxism and addicted to methods of violence which at times recalled the evil days of the Civil War. After the Civil War the Finnish Communist Party had remained a proscribed organisation, though its adherents tried to operate through legal cover Parties in opposition to the Social Democrats, and also to infiltrate into the Trade Unions, which they were largely successful in bringing under Communist control. The Tanner Government had been successful in securing the release of those still under detention for offences committed during the Civil War, but had not been able to enact any considerable body of social legislation. The anti-Socialist Cabinet which replaced it showed no zeal in suppressing the Lapuans, or even in keeping their excesses within bounds; and matters went from bad to worse till in 1932 an attempted Lapuan *coup d'état* was followed by the legal suppression of the movement. During the years of the world depression there were bitter industrial struggles. The old Trade Union movement, which had come under Communist control, was broken up; and a new Trade Union Federation, founded in 1930, gradually built up its strength during the following years. The Social Democrats, who had lost some ground to the Communists, did well at the General Election of 1933, winning 12 seats and increasing their total representation in the Parliament to 78; and they also prospered at the following election in 1936. After the presidential election of 1937 they entered, together with the Agrarians, into the coalition Cabinet of A. K. Cojander. This Government remained in office in 1939, when the European war broke out. The Finns, who had entered in 1932 into a non-aggression pact for twelve years with the Soviet Union, declared their neutrality; but the Soviet Union demanded from them territorial concessions designed chiefly to protect Leningrad against a German attack, and, on the Finns' refusal to give way, invaded Finland with forces which before long proved over-whelming. The Western Allies, in order to go to Finland's help, tried to induce the Swedes to allow Allied forces to cross through Sweden into Finland; but the Swedes, determined to keep out of the war, refused permission, and the Allies were unable to bring effective help. The Finns, therefore, had to accept defeat, and the war ended early in 1940 with the Finnish surrender of the parts of Karelia claimed by the Russians and of Viborg and Hango. During the war the Russians recognised and attempted to establish a puppet Communist Government headed by the old Communist leader, Otto Kuusinen; but this attempt was abandoned when peace was restored. The Finns, however, with bitter feelings towards the Russians and cut off from effective contacts with the West, found themselves under strong pressure to come to terms with Nazi Germany and, in 1941, allowed the Germans to use their territory as the basis for an attack on the Soviet Union. The Finnish forces were able to retake all the territory ceded in 1940 and to penetrate deeply into the Soviet area. The Germans tried to induce Marshal Mannerheim, who had resumed the national leadership, to advance upon Leningrad; but he refused and kept his troops near to the old frontier of the years before 1939. When the war turned against the Germans, the Russian forces again advanced and recaptured Viborg, and the Finns were compelled to ask for a renewed armistice, which was concluded in 1944. Under this Finland again ceded the disputed territory in Karelia, Viborg and Porkkala (instead of Hango) and agreed to pay very heavy reparations, amounting to about 10 per cent of the national income, over a period of six years. After the war the Socialists again fell into serious dissensions, and their leader, Vaino Tanner, was for a time driven out on a charge of being 'responsible for the war' and having sided with the Germans against the Soviet Union. He retained his place at the head of the Co-operative Movement and was subsequently called back to power by the Social Democrats, who maintained an attitude of strong hostility to the Communists and their supporters. These quarrels, however, fall a long way beyond the scope of this history, which is intended to stop short with the outbreak of war in 1939.

ICELAND

Finally, Iceland, where the Social Democratic Party was formed in 1916 and has been represented in the Althing (Parliament) since 1921. It was led by Ján Baldvinsson until his death in 1928, and thereafter by Stefán Jóhr Stefensson until 1952, and until 1940 was directed by a common Executive with the Trade Unions, which then set up a centre of their own. In 1930 a section broke away to form a Communist Party, which did not secure much support; but in 1938 there was a much more serious split, in the course of which the left wing, including many of the Trade Union leaders, joined with the Communists to form the Socialist United People's Party as the representative of an anti-Fascist United Front. This new Party formed the sole Opposition when, in 1939, the Social Democrats entered into a Coalition with the Conservatives and Progressives on the outbreak of war. In the General Election of 1942 the S.U.P.P. polled more votes than the Social Democrats and elected 10 members to the Althing out of a total of 52; but at the Election of 1946 the two Socialist Parties were nearly equal, the Social Democrats electing 9 members and the S.U.P.P. again 10. Before the split, in 1934, the Social Democrats had polled over 20 per cent of the votes cast; whereas in 1942 they polled hardly more than 14 per cent, recovering to nearly 18 per cent in 1946, and then falling off again to about 16 per cent. The two Socialist Parties had thus between them round about one-third of the total number of votes in the early 'thirties. Both professed to be Marxist; but the one interpreted its Marxism in terms of Social Democracy and the other immediately in terms of the united struggle against Fascism under proletarian leadership.

CHAPTER VIII

BELGIUM, HOLLAND, AND SWITZERLAND

BELGIUM is one of those countries in Western Europe in which the Socialists were, during the 1930s, in the position of being the largest Party in Parliament, but fell short of winning an absolute majority, so that they could form a Government only in alliance with either the Christian Socials or the Liberals, or could constitute a powerful opposition when these two were united against them. In practice, the Belgian Labour Party alternated between opposition and participation in Governments of National Union. During the 1920s, from 1925 to 1929, they were the largest party and took part in a Government of National Union with the Christian Socials, and later with others as well, but in the election of 1929 they lost ground and returned to opposition. The world crisis hit Belgium hard, and led to a further Government of National Union in which Vandervelde, de Man, Spaak, and Arthur Wauters took part. In all there were between 1919 and 1940 no less than 19 Belgian Cabinets, of which 9 represented all the Parties, 7 Catholics and Liberals, and 2 Catholics and Socialists. The Liberals, who were always the weakest of the three Parties, were strongly anti-Socialist, whereas the Catholics included a left wing, based largely on the Christian Trade Unions, which was in sympathy with many parts of the Labour programme, originally adopted at the Congress of 1894 and reaffirmed by the Congress of 1923.

In 1938, when Vandervelde at length died, after leading the Labour Party for a long time, he was succeeded as President of the Party by Henri de Man, who had come forward earlier in the 1930s with his *Plan du Travail*, which was adopted both by the Labour Party and by the Trades Union Congress. In this *Plan* de Man set out from an attempt to revise the predominantly Marxian doctrine of the Party by propounding a plan for the immediate realisation of a mixed economy of

Socialism and capitalism — the former covering credit and banking, public services and monopolist industries, and the latter other industries, which were to be left under private ownership but brought under publicly planned control and co-ordination. De Man stressed the fact that under modern conditions the proletariat, properly so called, could not be expected to comprise a majority of the entire population : he therefore proposed to appeal for support, not only to the proletariat, but also to other sections which could be rallied against the financiers and monopolists who dominated the scene under existing conditions. The *Plan du Travail*, which was essentially an anti-crisis document designed to achieve recovery from the prevailing depression, aroused considerable interest outside as well as within Belgium. Originally put forward and adopted by the Belgian Labour Party in 1933, it was the principal theme of an International Conference held at Pontigny in France the following year, and was translated into English and published by the Fabian Society in 1935. It was still the adopted immediate programme of the Belgian Labour Party up to 1940, and had formed during the intervening years the basis of an attempt by that party to come to an accommodation with the left wing of the Catholic Party, led by van Zeeland, though in 1936 a General Strike launched by the Party and the Trade Unions forced the Government to pass a law providing for the forty-hour week. But when the Germans overran Belgium in 1940 de Man, believing them to have won the war, dissolved the Party and remained in Belgium as the King's adviser under the Nazis, and thus lost his influence with the Belgian Socialists, most of whose leaders fled to England during the war years, to return and reconstitute the Party, as the Belgian Socialist Party, in 1945, readopting the 1894 Declaration of Principles without any change. The Belgians thus returned to their older policy of complete independence of other Parties, and were once more in the position of commanding less than a clear majority of the electorate, renewing their conflict with the Catholic Social Party for predominance, with the Liberals still maintaining their position as a third Party holding the balance of power.

During the later 'thirties, this three-party distribution had been in some measure broken in upon by the rise of the Rexistes under Degrelle and of a Flemish National Movement. Both these new groupings took a Fascist direction and collaborated with the Germans during the years of occupation from 1940 to 1944. They thus lost most of their following, and were no longer of importance in the post-war period. The Communists, who had been relatively unimportant in the 1930s, were able to return 23 members (with 14 seats gained) at the General Election of 1946, which gave the Catholics 92 seats, the Socialists 69, and the Liberals 16 as compared with 73 Catholics, 70 Socialists, and 34 Liberals in 1919. In the 1930s Belgium lagged behind other countries — especially Scandinavia — in the provision of social services and in standards of living; but considerable improvements took place after the war. Women did not vote until the election of 1949, when as a consequence the Socialist poll declined to less than 30 per cent of the total, only to recover to upwards of 35 per cent the following year. In 1954 it was nearly 39, and in 1958 declined to a little over 37 per cent.

De Man's *Plan du Travail*, whether one agrees with it or not, was undoubtedly a major contribution to the re-thinking of Socialist doctrine in the 1930s. Drawn up under the influence of the great depression and in the spirit of parliamentary democracy, it was an attempt to find a way out of the economic crisis and to get the unemployed back to work by resisting negative policies of deflation and by driving a wedge between the class of financiers and monopolists and the main body of the middle classes, including the smaller employers, so as to unite the latter with the Socialists in a common campaign against the greater capitalists. On the basis of this alliance, the structure of banking and credit was to be brought under full public ownership and control, which was to be extended also to those industries and services which were under capitalist monopoly control. Other industries were to be left in private ownership, and were to be managed by their owners subject to such control and co-ordination under public auspices as might appear to be needed in the public interest in each particular case. De Man, who was a very intelligent person, with wide experience in the U.S.A. and Germany as well as in Belgium, did not believe that the collapse of capitalism was impending or the proletarian Revolution at hand: nor did he believe that, even under universal suffrage, the proletariat could expect before long to constitute a majority of the entire electorate, so as to bring Socialism about by peaceful means. He did believe, on the other hand, that the world economic crisis could be coped with successfully by employing the correct methods, country by country, and that for this purpose it was indispensable for the Socialists to find allies. In Belgium he thought these were to be found mainly by attracting the left wing of the Catholic Party, which included many Catholic Trade Unionists, into alliance with the Socialists ; but he felt that this could be successfully accomplished only by a Socialist agreement to leave the lesser industries and enterprises in private hands, subject to control only to the extent needed to bring about co-ordinated planning and to the extent of the dependence of all enterprises on a thoroughly socialised credit system. The emphasis of the *Plan* was throughout on the key rôle of credit in the national economy and on the need for an expansionist credit policy such as the State only could provide. Even where industries and services were to be taken into public hands, he stressed the importance of avoiding bureaucratic methods of control and therefore proposed that public services should be put into the hands of largely autonomous corporations, which would manage them on behalf of the whole community. The emphasis of the *Plan* was put on the importance of control as against ownership, and it was considered that the compliance of most enterprises with public requirements could be ensured by control, even without public ownership.

De Man did not succeed in his main objective of winning extensive middle-class support for the Belgian Labour Party or of splitting or winning over the Catholic Party or its Trade Union section. Indeed, during the rest of the 1930s, the prospects of an independent Socialist majority became even less in face of the rise of the Rexiste and Flemish National Movements, though these were more of a threat to the Catholics than to the Socialists. Meanwhile, internationally, the *Plan du Travail* exerted a substantial influence in other countries which were similarly affected by the economic depression and saw little or no prospect of winning Socialist majorities of their own. This applied especially to the Dutch and Swiss Socialist Parties, which each prepared anti-crisis Plans or Programmes largely modelled on de Man's, though less explicit in their acceptance of mixed economies as affording the best hope of economic recovery. In France, de Man's ideas appealed especially to the Neo-Socialists who grouped themselves round Déat, Marquet, and Renaudel, and presently broke away from the Socialist Party as a right-wing deviationist group, but failed to take with them more than a small proportion of its adherents, most of whom preferred to seek an United Front with the Communists and ranged themselves in due course behind *l'expérience Blum*. De Man himself was certainly never a Nazi, but as we have seen he allowed himself in 1940, under the belief that the Nazis had won the war, to become so deeply involved with the occupiers of his country and so estranged from his old party associates as to forfeit all his influence and to be unable to return to his own country when it was liberated. In his later writings after the war he attempted to exonerate himself from the charge of collaboration and wrote interestingly about the challenge to civilisation represented by the growth of mass-production and the subordination of personality which it involved. But little notice was taken of these later writings, because of the personal discredit into which he had fallen during the war; and he was still an exile in Switzerland when he perished in a motor accident in 1953.

HOLLAND

In Holland, nothing much happened to the Social Democratic Party during the 1930s, during which it commanded less than a quarter of the total votes cast at General Elections. At the Election of 1937 it won 23 seats out of 100. After the German occupation it was reconstituted by amalgamation with various other groups as the Dutch Labour Party in an attempt to rally to it all types of progressive opinion and was able to win 29 seats at the post-war election. Already, in the 1930s, it had considerably modified its policy in an attempt to enlist the support of non-proletarian elements and to seek an escape from the economic crisis; but, faced with both Catholic and Protestant opposition, it made little headway. The division on confessional lines extended to the Trade Unions as well as the Party, there being both separate Catholic and Protestant

Trade Union movements. An attempt was made to unite them after the Liberation of 1944–5; but it failed, though arrangements for co-operation between them and the Socialist and independent Trade Unions were arrived at, and lasted until 1954, when the Catholics brought them to an end.

Dutch Socialism, as we saw,[1] has always been predominantly a very moderate movement. There have been several breakaways from the main party on the left, including that led by Edo Fimmen in 1932 — which he was subsequently forced to leave in order to keep his position in the Trade Union movement as head of the powerful International Transport Workers' Federation. But these left-wing secessions had little effect on the main body of the Party, which after Troelstra's death in 1930 continued on its unambitious and on the whole uneventful way, attending more to immediate issues of social reform than to matters of Socialist principle, but unable in face of its minority status to exert any great influence even in its chosen field. The Socialist Trade Unions were no doubt, during the 1930s, the largest of the four factions into which Dutch Trade Unionism was divided; but they did not represent a clear majority of the organised workers, and neither they nor the Social Democratic Party were in a position to speak confidently on behalf of an united working class.

SWITZERLAND

We saw, in the previous volume,[2] how the Swiss Socialists, after a decision to join the Comintern and a revision of their programme to incorporate approving references to the Soviet system and the dictatorship of the proletariat, changed their line and returned to their allegiance to democratic Socialism, after a break in the course of which their dissident left wing seceded to join the Swiss Communist Party, which never obtained the allegiance of more than a small and dwindling section of the Swiss working class. The Social Democratic Party in the 1930s commanded under 30 per cent of the total votes cast at successive General Elections. In 1935, much affected by the rise of Nazism in Germany, it drastically revised its programme, declaring its support of national defence and of

---

[1] See Vol. IV, p. 512 ff.   [2] See Vol. IV, p. 509 f.

the credits needed for that purpose and deleting the sections of its programme dealing with the Soviet system and with dictatorship. It also limited its immediate ambitions to the institution of a planned economy and the nationalisation of industries controlled by capitalist monopolies, while declaring for an advanced programme of social security. In 1943 it further revised its programme, and sent its first Socialist Minister to join the National Government, in which it remained until 1953, when it seceded in protest against the Government's reactionary tendencies. In 1955 it obtained 28 per cent of the votes cast and demanded that two seats should be allotted to it in the National Government, but, on the refusal of this demand by the bourgeois parties, decided to remain in opposition.

During the depression of the 1930s the Swiss Socialists were among the parties which formulated special anti-crisis programmes, calling for a national effort to combat unemployment and introduce a planned economy. Though the Swiss Socialist Party line was vehemently anti-Fascist, it rejected all overtures to form a common front against Fascism with the Communists, preferring to ally itself with anti-Fascist groups further to the right, such as the Young Peasants and the organisations of white-collar workers. After becoming a member of the Vienna Union, it rallied to the Labour and Socialist International in 1923.

General

These three Socialist Parties have thus dissimilar histories, but with a largely similar outcome, in that all three ended by breaking with their left wings, which for the most part then joined the Communist Party — only for many of them to break with it later. All three put forward emergency plans at the time of the world economic crisis, and made, in doing so, an attempt to appeal to other social groups besides the proletariat. In the Swiss case the Socialist Plan was subsequently submitted to a referendum, but only 43 per cent of those voting were in its favour. In no case were these overtures successful in giving the Socialist Parties the majorities they hoped for, or in seriously undermining the appeal of their bourgeois rivals. All three emerged temporarily stronger from the trials of the second world war, during which two of the countries fell under Fascist occupation. But there was some tendency to fall back afterwards to a position in which, even if they remained the strongest single parties in their respective countries, there seemed little prospect of their becoming absolute majorities, or being able to form Governments of their own, independent of other parties' support. They were no doubt able, within this situation, to win substantial advances in the field of social legislation and in increased recognition of collective bargaining rights, but not to attempt any far-reaching reconstruction of the Social-economic system. Even in the matter of the Welfare State they lagged considerably behind the achievement of the Scandinavian Socialists, as they did in respect of the proportion of votes they were able to attract to their support. This was in two cases due mainly to the sustained strength of the confessional Parties, especially the Catholics, and in the third — that of Switzerland — to the greater size and solidarity of the middle classes, as well as to the strength of the Catholics, who in 1943 elected 43 members to the Federal Parliament, as compared with the 47 of the Radical Democrats and the 56 of the Social Democrats, who were thus yet again the largest Party, but still a long way short of a majority.

CHAPTER IX

EASTERN EUROPE

IN Eastern Europe the 1930s were a period of mainly underground struggle and increasing repression. One country after another established some sort of dictatorship under reactionary auspices; and what remained of the Socialist movement was driven for the most part underground. In general these conditions favoured the left wing, and especially the Communists, who were much better at underground activity than the Social Democrats, who for the most part either accepted a very limited toleration extended to them by the reactionary régimes or transferred their headquarters abroad and ceased to have any widespread following in their own countries. Of all the countries of Eastern Europe Czechoslovakia alone escaped right-wing dictatorship up to 1938, only to be then overrun by the Nazis and to have its democratic institutions destroyed. Elsewhere, conditions of more or less thoroughgoing dictatorship were established at various dates, where they did not already exist. Some of these dictatorships presented increasingly a Fascist character, chiefly under German influence, basing themselves on mass-movements of reactionary nationalism and anti-semitism, whereas in other cases they were never really Fascist, but depended on an alliance between the old aristocracy and the rising capitalist class, as in Hungary and, to a large extent, in Poland.

The countries of Eastern Europe were still, in the 1930s, all predominantly agrarian; but they can be divided into those in which land ownership was distributed widely among small peasant cultivators and those in which the large estates still remained for the most part undivided in the hands of the great landlords. In the Balkan countries small peasant holdings for the most part predominated, as in Bulgaria and Serbia, or had been largely established after 1918, as in Rumania. In Hungary and in Poland, on the other hand, the great estates were still dominant, land distribution having either ceased altogether, as in Hungary, or been slowed down to a snail's pace, as in Poland. In Bulgaria the agrarian interest, organised on a mass basis by Stambolisky, had been crushed in the struggles of 1923 and was not able to raise its head again effectively, though it remained as a mass-movement underground.

The economies of Eastern Europe were very badly hit by the world depression, which reacted most seriously of all on agricultural prices and also hit the high-cost industries which were in process of establishing themselves. The reactionary Governments did little to help the poorer peasants in their distress ; and even the Co-operative movements which they did little to encourage were of benefit mainly to the wealthier peasants. In general, agricultural productivity did not advance in face of the sheer inability of most peasants to apply improved methods : it was even to some extent damaged when the bigger estates were broken up. The Balkan countries especially suffered from severe rural over-population relatively to their standards of productive efficiency, even though their populations were small in comparison with those of Western Europe. Output of wheat per hectare of land under cultivation was hardly more than one-third of Denmark's, and there were far more persons living on the land than could be employed on it regularly to good purpose. Industry, though it had been developing quite rapidly up to the depression, did not provide enough jobs to make any substantial impression on the over-population of the rural areas. Moreover, the smaller peasants and the landless rural workers remained for the most part unorganised ; and the Trade Unions and Socialist Parties, when they were suffered to exist at all except underground, were in most cases firmly prevented from organising or recruiting in the villages and existed only in the towns, without much or indeed in most cases any hold except on the urban craft workers, among whom they could not, in many instances, be wholly put down. The Peasant Parties, which in the early 1920s had shown marked bureaucratic tendencies, were either crowded out or became increasingly reactionary as their leadership was infiltrated by other classes. Most of them had been led from the outset mainly by intellectuals, rather than by actual peasants ; and, as the various countries passed under one form or another of dictatorial rule, their reality as peasant movements was more and more eroded. In the 'thirties, over Eastern Europe as a whole, more than two-thirds of the peasants were smallholders whose land was inadequate to support their families : so that some members of their households had to seek employment on the larger holdings or in the towns. This situation could have been remedied only by long-term measures of technical education, rural credit open to the poorer peasants, road and railway construction, and planned industrialisation. But Governments were utterly disinclined to pursue such measures ; and for industrialisation at any rate the conditions of the 1930s were highly unfavourable owing to the disappearance of foreign investment and the reluctance of native capitalists to incur the risks of investment for the narrow home markets provided by the greatly impoverished populations. Instead of attempting to foster either agricultural or industrial advance, the Governments accordingly resorted to more and more repressive measures, treating every demand for rural or industrial reform as a form of Bolshevism and persecuting even those Co-operative Societies which attempted to cater for the needs of the poorer peasants.

In Czechoslovakia, by far the most highly industrialised of the countries of Eastern Europe, where less than half the total population depended directly on the land for a living, parliamentary government maintained itself until the Germans destroyed the Czechoslovak State in 1938–9. But throughout the 'thirties the working class remained sharply divided into Communist and Social Democratic factions, which were never strong enough to assume the government after the split of 1920. The Agrarian Party, either alone or in coalition, therefore stayed at the head of the Government throughout this period. The Social Democrats had been badly defeated by the Communists immediately after the split, but had thereafter gained in relative strength, though never enough to regain their earlier ascendancy. The Czech Agrarian Party was mainly at the outset a party of relatively well-to-do peasants ; but it was largely converted by the 1930s into the party of the Czech capitalist classes, replacing Kramář's National Democratic Party, which was unduly conservative in social matters. The Czech Socialists, meanwhile, alternated between entering primarily Agrarian Ministries and opposing them, but were not in a position to influence national policy to any great extent in face of the division of the working-class forces into rival parties. In the Slovak part of the Czechoslovak State the peasants were much poorer and more backward than in Bohemia or Moravia, and were much more under the influence of the Catholic Church. In the main they supported the Slovak People's Party, led by a priest, Father Hlinka, which tended strongly towards Fascism. Meanwhile the Czechoslovak Communists, after a period of sharp internal conflict and repeated dissensions with the Comintern during the 1920s, settled down under Comintern leadership, but never became strong enough effectively to challenge the Agrarian leadership of the country. They were of course liquidated for the time being when the Nazis took over control in 1938–9; but the leaders took refuge in Russia, whence they returned with the Russian forces at the end of the second world war. They had been accompanied in their exile by much of the Social Democratic leadership, including Zdanek Fierlinger, who then became Prime Minister in a coalition Government under Russian control and remained at the head of affairs until the Communist *coup* of 1948.

Meanwhile in Poland Pilsudski had seized power much earlier by the presidential *coup* of 1926, towards which the Socialists took up, at the outset, an undecided attitude. Subsequently they rallied in opposition to him and in 1928 elected 65 members to the Sejm, only to lose most of them in the elections of 1930, when they fell to 23 in face of the terroristic conditions under which the elections were then conducted. In 1933, still in face of terrorism, they succeeded in electing 41 members; but many of their leaders were arrested and imprisoned under charges of threatening to overthrow the Government by force. The Communists meanwhile were outlawed, but succeeded in electing a few members as representatives of their legal front, the Workers' and Peasants' Party. Two years later, in 1935, the Sejm was dissolved and elections were held under a new law which proscribed all opposition Parties. Thereafter, the Socialists continued their opposition outside the Sejm, but were able to achieve little until the country was occupied by the Germans and Russians in 1939. They then took an active part in the resistance movement during the war, especially in Warsaw ; and many thousands of Socialist militants met with death by execution at Nazi hands. The Russians, meantime, executed in 1942 two Socialist leaders, Henry Ehrlich and Viktor Alter, who had played active parts in the resistance movement, and also liquidated the leadership of the Polish Communists who had sought refuge in the Soviet Union. They then re-formed the Polish Communist Party under new leaders who were more prepared to obey their orders, and were able to install this new Party in power when the Nazis were driven out.

Meanwhile, in Hungary, the Socialist Party remained powerless and ineffective after the defeat of 1919. The Horthy dictatorship which was then established was never really Fascist, in that it did not rest on the support of any mass-movement animated by a Fascist ideology, but was rather a dictatorship of the old governing class inspired strongly by nationalist and anti-democratic ideas. It thus allowed a moderate Social Democratic Party a barely tolerated existence, provided it did not attempt to carry its propaganda into the rural areas. Nor did it wholly suppress the Trade Unions of the urban workers. The Socialist movement was, however, almost wholly ineffective : in 1939 it was able to elect only five members out of 323 to the Lower Chamber of the Hungarian Parliament. The Communists, who were outlawed, maintained their agitation despite the repression, but many of their leaders suffered long terms of imprisonment. Among these was Mathias Rakosi, who had taken part in Béla Kun's short-lived Communist Government of 1919. Returning from Russia to Hungary in 1924, he was captured and remained in prison for the next sixteen years, till he was exchanged in 1940 to become thereafter one of the leaders of the new Communist Hungary set up by the Russian forces after the second world war.

In the Balkan countries dictatorships were installed at various dates. In Rumania, where the Communist Party had been suppressed as early as 1924, the Social Democrats maintained a barely tolerated existence which they continued even after the establishment of King Carol's dictatorship in 1938. Thereafter, they underwent liquidation at the hands of the Nazis, who in 1940 forced King Carol to abdicate and installed the Fascist Iron Guard in power, only to allow General Antonescu to displace them the following year, after they had plainly demonstrated their incompetence as well as their ferocity. Carol's dictatorship, while it lasted, had all the trappings of a Fascist movement, but lacked a mass-following and showed itself quite consistent with the suppression of the Iron Guard, whose leaders he arrested in 1938 and caused to be shot, 'while attempting to escape', later in the same year.

In Yugoslavia, where the Social Democrats had been suppressed as early as 1921 and were thereafter consistently persecuted along with the Communists, Social Democracy had ceased to be an effective force well before the 1930s, and the main body of the workers followed rather the underground leadership of the Communist Party, which went through many changes of leadership and direction before it was reorganised in 1937 under the leadership of Josip Broz Tito, who helped it to recover much of its popularity during the next two years and became the head and forefront of Yugoslav resistance to the Germans during the war.

At the time of the Communist Party's suppression in 1921, its best known leader had been Simon Marković, who was a strong critic of nationalism and opposed the demands for national autonomy for the different groups in Yugoslavia as bourgeois and of no concern to Communists — an attitude for which he was taken to task by the Comintern in 1922. Thereafter for some years there was an acute faction fight inside the Yugoslav Communist Party, which had removed its head-quarters and leadership out of the country and held successive conferences abroad. In 1926 Stalin, through the Comintern, launched a strong attack on the Yugoslav Communists for their attitude on the national question, and the Party thereupon altered its tone and made a declaration in support of national self-determination ; but the faction fights continued. From 1926 to 1928 there were many strikes against worsening conditions among the Yugoslav workers ; but these did not mend matters, as they were ruthlessly suppressed, and the leaders in exile had increasingly lost touch with the workers inside the country. In 1928 the Comintern addressed an Open Letter to all members of the Yugoslav Party, concerning its fractionalist tendencies ; and the Party at its Dresden Conference that year threw out the leaders of both right and left wings and chose a new leader in Djuric Djaković, who was killed by the police the following year. From 1929 to 1931, following the establishment of the royal dictatorship, there was a police terror, in which many Communists were killed; and the remaining leaders, headed by Ratko Martinović, again fled abroad, whence they incited armed risings inside Yugoslavia, which were bloodily put down and resulted in the almost complete disintegration of the Party for the time being. It began to revive in 1932, when a new temporary leadership was installed by the Comintern under Milan Gorkić, Martinović and his group being removed from office. By the following year, Communist cells and even regional organisations were being recreated inside the country; and in 1934 the Communist Party was strong enough to hold a full Conference inside Yugoslavia, which confirmed Gorkić's leadership. But in 1936 Gorkić, who was accused of entering into too close relations with the left bourgeoisie, quarrelled with the majority of the Party's Central Committee. The same year, the organisational leadership was transferred to the Party inside Yugoslavia, while the political leadership was still left in the hands of Gorkić abroad; but in 1937 Gorkić was displaced from his post as leader, and the entire control of the Party was re-established on Yugoslav soil, with Tito emerging as the principal leader. There followed a rapid liquidation of the so-called fractionalist elements, including those who were denounced as Trotskyists or Anarchists, and Tito rapidly established his ascendancy over a new monolithic party, following the Comintern line of endeavouring to rally support for a common anti-Fascist Front under the leadership of the Communist Party, which gained greatly in strength as German pressure on Yugoslavia increased. The Yugoslav Communists sent a contingent to fight in the Spanish Civil War and declared their willingness in 1938 to send volunteers to fight on behalf of the Czechs at the time of the Munich crisis. During these years the Yugoslav Communists undoubtedly succeeded in establishing their ascendancy as the main opposition force in the country. In the 1938 election the Working People's Party in Croatia, set up in 1937, allied itself with the Croatian Democratic Coalition against the Government, though this policy was condemned by most of the Yugoslav Communists, who would have preferred that it should put up candidates of its own. In general, the Communists were weaker in Croatia than in other parts of the country, except Macedonia, where the local leader, Sarlo, was expelled in 1941 for refusing to join Tito's Partisans in armed resistance to the Fascist invaders and their supporters at home.

Tito's assumption of the leadership in 1937 was indeed the outcome of a reassertion by the Communists inside Yugoslavia of their right to determine policy after the previous leaders had unsuccessfully attempted to impose their leadership from headquarters in exile. In Croatia the Peasant Party, originally radical in policy and ready for alliance with the urban workers, passed more and more, after Stefan Radić's murder in 1928, into the hands of Croatian business men and middle-class intellectuals. Maček, its new leader, was a lawyer; and the Party developed a pro-Fascist right wing opposed to its radical left, while the centre attempted to hold a precarious balance between them as the principal exponent of Croatian nationalism against Serb centralisation of the Yugoslav kingdom. The left wing, on the other hand, under Professor Dragoljab Jovanonić, stood for a radical policy of social reform and sought for an alliance with the Serbian peasants, for the most part in vain.

In Bulgaria the moderate wing of the Agrarians, led by Gidev, joined the Liberal coalition under Malinov in 1931. But with the coming of the dictatorship in 1934 all Parties were banned and driven underground. The Communists, however, were able to maintain their underground organisation, especially in the towns, and to gain much public sympathy for the Popular Front policy. Thus, in Bulgaria as well as in Yugoslavia, there was in 1939 a potentially strong Communist Party making itself ready for the assumption of power, whereas Social Democracy, except for small Parties in exile, had practically ceased to exist as an organised force.

In Greece, the Communist Party, growing up mainly in the industrial centres — Piraeus, Salonika, and Kavalla — during the 1930s, held for a time a key position between the almost equally divided Republican and Royalist groups, though it was of course much smaller than either. In the Parliament of 1935 it held 15 seats. Alleged fears of Communism served as an excuse for the Metaxas dictatorship of 1936, under which the Party suffered severe repression, but was able to maintain its hold on the organised workers and to keep some support among intellectuals — the more so because of the failure of the bourgeois Parties and of the dictatorship even to attempt to solve the pressing social problems of the country.

Thus, in the 1930s, Social Democracy was all but extinct except in Czechoslovakia, where it was regaining some of the ground lost earlier to the Communists, and to some extent in Poland, where it was still putting up some resistance outside Parliament to the dictatorship. Communism, on the other hand, though everywhere proscribed, continued to command considerable support, and was actually gaining ground, despite its suppression, during the years immediately before the outbreak of war, at any rate in the Balkan countries, in all of which it was traditionally stronger than the Social Democrats who, in several instances, had compromised themselves badly with the organisers of dictatorial *coups*. In three countries only — Poland, Hungary, and Rumania — anti-semitism had become a leading issue ; it was of course fostered by the Germans to the best of their power and took an important part in the building up of local Fascist movements — especially those shaped after the German model. For in Italy the small numbers of the indigenous Jewish population prevented anti-semitism from playing a major part, whereas in Poland, Hungary, and Rumania anti-semitism had traditional roots and was fanned into flame by the general depression which hit these countries in common with others in the years after 1930. The depression indeed, by cutting off supplies of foreign capital as well as by reducing agricultural prices to a very low level, must be held mainly accountable for the wholesale resort to dictatorship and for the heavy persecution of working-class Parties and Trade Unions ; for semi-starvation bred a mass of discontent which made it impossible for bourgeois Governments to retain their power by constitutional means and invited recourse to armed force by the possessing classes.

There grew up a fashion during the later 'thirties especially of dubbing all the reactionary Governments which held power in the countries of Eastern Europe Fascists, whereas in fact some of them were much more in the nature of old-fashioned oligarchical dictatorships unsupported by any mass-movement such as Hitler was able to rally behind him in Germany, or even Mussolini in Italy. As we saw, the real Fascists of Rumania — the Iron Guard — were not raised to power until after Carol's abdication enforced by the Germans in 1940, and were not then left in power for long before they were replaced by the less severe military dictatorship of General Antonescu. Nor can the Polish or Hungarian dictatorships be properly regarded as Fascist in any strict sense, lacking as they were in any specifically Fascist ideology. They were, however, quite definitely anti-democratic and as hostile to Socialism and Communism as they could possibly be, and as prone to see Communism lurking behind every attempt of the workers to organise for their own protection. They had also a violent anti-semitism in common with the Fascists, because they were faced by considerable Jewish populations competing with them for a livelihood and, at any rate in the case of the traders, doing so with a large measure of success. Jews, moreover, held a considerable position among the industrial workers and in the Socialist and Communist leaderships and it was all too easy to accuse the Jews of being mainly responsible for the stirring up of unrest.

Conditions such as these were notably unfavourable to constructive Socialist thought. The Socialist and Communist movements were alike preoccupied chiefly with the day-to-day struggle for sheer survival. There were nevertheless a few thinkers who were prominent among Marxian scholars — notably George Lucacz in Hungary and C. Dobrogeanu-Gherea (or Katz, d. 1920) in Rumania — the latter the ideological founder of Rumanian, as Blagoev was of Bulgarian, Socialism. But it was hardly in the nature of things that new Socialist thought should emerge during the 1930s, when Social Democrats were chiefly concerned with defining their attitudes to dictators and when Communist Parties were compelled to live for the most part a clandestine existence under continued police repression. This did not indeed prevent the Communists from being torn by bitter faction fights arising mainly out of their relations to the Comintern and its changing policies ; but nothing novel emerged from these struggles, which had mainly to do with the international policy of Communism rather than with its internal policy in each country. The Comintern's shift to the Popular Front policy in the middle 'thirties undoubtedly benefited the Communist Parties of Eastern Europe, which were able, by following it while it lasted, to build up a wider basis of national opposition support in the various countries and were still reaping the benefit of this policy when war broke out in 1939. Most of them were taken aback by the Nazi-Soviet Pact of 1939; but German behaviour on the invasion and occupation of their countries gave them back the leadership which some of them had temporarily lost; and the resistance struggles of the war years prepared them for the seizing of power, under Russian armed auspices except in Yugoslavia, in 1944-5. They then settled down under their Popular Front Governments, dominated by the Communists, and were able to force the relatively weak Social Democratic Parties into amalgamation with them or into submergence when they refused. Thus, the Rumanian Socialist Party was finally liquidated in 1948, after a convention had agreed to amalgamation with the Communist Party and the leaders who rejected this had been driven into exile. The Yugoslav Social Democrats were similarly liquidated or driven into exile, after giving their support to Mikhailović rather than to Tito during the resistance. The Czechs, under Fierlinger, were impelled into the arms of the Communist Party; and the Poles maintained only a statutory Social Democratic Party in exile, while the Bulgarians carried on the traditions of Blagoev and his 'Narrows', and the Bulgarian Social Democrats, after taking part jointly with the Agrarians in the General Election of 1946, were ruthlessly liquidated after all their leaders and M.P.s had been arrested and condemned to prison or to concentration camps. One of their leaders, Kristin Pastochov, was killed in prison, and another, Zvety Ivanov, died in a concentration camp. The survivors escaped abroad and later set up a party headquarters in exile in New York. All political Parties had been suppressed after the *coup d'état* of Kimon Georgiev in 1934, and free Trade Unions had also been abolished in favour of a new movement under State control. But political activity had continued underground, and the Social Democrats had promptly summoned their own Congress in 1944, on the fall of the dictatorship and had entered the coalition Ministry which at first took over control, their leading representative in it being Dimitrov Neickov as Minister of National Economy, who remained in the Government when the Social Democrats mostly seceded from it in 1945, and subsequently joined the Communist Party.

CHAPTER X

THE UNITED STATES — CANADA — LATIN AMERICA

IN the United States of America the 1930s was the decade, not of Socialism, but of the great depression and of President Roosevelt's 'New Deal', which put an end to 'company' Unionism and brought into being an immensely strengthened Trade Union movement with a new social attitude and a place in public recognition which American Labour had never possessed before. If Socialism could be identified with State intervention in economic affairs, or even with really big advances in the direction of the Welfare State, the 'thirties would have to be regarded as a decade of unprecedented socialistic advance ; but they were also a period during which the organised Socialist movement in the United States not merely continued to decline but almost ceased to exist. By 1938 the American Socialist Party had shrunk to a membership of less than 7,000, as against 23,000 in 1934 ; and a year later it was very nearly extinct. Nor did the American Communists, though they made much more noise, command any considerable body of working-class support, their following being chiefly among intellectuals, whom they showed much skill in enrolling in a wide variety of 'front' organisations in the names of anti-Fascism and the campaign against War. The Trade Unions which in 1935 joined forces to form the Committee for Industrial Organisation and presently broke away from the American Federation of Labor and became the Congress of Industrial Organisations, succeeded for the first time in enrolling the main body of workers in the mass-production industries — steel, automobiles, oil, and the rest ; and this new Unionism stood for a policy essentially different from that of the American Federation of Labor and much more closely akin to that of the Labour movements of Western Europe. But, whereas in Europe the Trade Unions were for the most part closely allied, or even organisationally linked, to the Socialist political Parties, the C.I.O. had no such links and, instead of attempting to set up an independent Labour or Socialist Party, was drawn in more and more, through its Committee for Political Organisation, to throw its weight on the side of Roosevelt and the Democrats in support of the New Deal. While both Socialists and Communists were busily denouncing the New Deal as a conspiracy to set the disintegrating capitalist system back on its feet — which was indeed one of its aspects — more and more Socialists who were also active Trade Unionists found themselves forced to choose between the claims of their Trade Unions for energetic support of New Deal policies through the C.I.O. and forms of 'third party' Socialist agitation which offered no prospect of success and endangered the gains made through co-operation with the New Dealers. Such men as Walter Reuther, confronted with this choice, resigned from the Socialist Party. Its leader, Norman Thomas, who had polled 900,000 votes as its presidential candidate in 1932, could poll only 107,000 when he stood again in 1936.

The world depression of the early 'thirties hit the United States more catastrophically than any other country. The first manifest warning of what was in store had been the stock market collapse of 1929 ; but there were few who realised the fundamental unsoundness of the prevailing boom and many who confidently prophesied speedy recovery and resumed advance. There was in fact a brief rallying after the first crisis ; but before long the downward slide was resumed with much greater intensity, and a scramble for 'liquidity' set in. Production and employment by 1932 were almost halved : wage earnings fell catastrophically, and bank after bank closed its doors. By the time President Roosevelt took office in the early spring of 1933 the entire economic system lay in ruins, and the prestige of American business had been utterly shattered. The State had clearly to take drastic action to retrieve the situation ; but what was it to do ? The entire tradition of the American economy rested on confidence in the ability of business men to manage their own affairs and on a denial that the State bore any responsibility for maintaining the level of employment. Only a handful of economic heretics advocated any form of economic planning or realised that there was any connection between State action and the levels of demand for goods and services. Almost no one had contemplated a situation in which lack of business confidence would reduce investment to a mere trickle and throw out of work millions of persons for whom no provision of social services existed. It does not appear that the new President himself had any clear idea of what needed to be done, beyond the recognition that he was imperatively called on to come somehow to the relief of a nation in deep distress. The expedients to which he resorted were improvisations designed to cope with the dire emergency: they had behind them no clearly-thought-out remedy based on a real understanding of the situation. Indeed, some of them, such as the reduction in the gold value of the dollar, made no sense in view of America's international economic position. Two things, however, were clearly needed; and both were done. It was necessary that there should be, in one way or another, a vast outpouring of public money to swell the level of total demand; and it was necessary to put a stop to the drastic wage-cuts which were only making the position worse.

At the time of the collapse a large part of American industry was still refusing to recognise any rights of collective bargaining on the part of the workers it employed. In certain industries the Unions grouped in the American Federation of Labor were firmly established and had won the right to bargain collectively. But the A.F. of L. had succeeded in organising only a minority of the labour force, made up mainly of skilled workers, and had entirely failed to organise effectively the great mass-production industries, which were either without any organisation at all or were dominated by 'company' Unions under the control of the employers, who used them as means of keeping real Trade Unionism at bay. By the Industrial Recovery Act — which was subsequently ruled to be unconstitutional by the Supreme Court, but only when it had done its work — the New Deal set up a structure which brought the process of industrial wage- and price-cutting to an abrupt end; and under the Industrial Relations Act the workers got the legal right to form and join Trade Unions free from the employers' control and to enforce negotiation on the employers. The entire structure of 'company' Unions and of the so-called 'Open Shop' collapsed;

and for the first time in their history the American working classes as a whole were set free to create their own Trade Unions and to organise without fear of the State and the law being invoked to suppress them in the name of liberty.

This was an enormous gain, by which the Trade Unions were quick to profit. The advantage accrued to the Unions attached to the A.F. of L. as well as to those which grew up under the aegis of the newly established C.I.O. The A.F. of L., which had only 2·3 million members in 1933, rose to 3·7 million in 1938, when the C.I.O. had about $3\frac{1}{2}$ million and there were another million or so belonging to the Railroad Brotherhoods and other unattached Unions. Moreover, Trade Unionism, branded hitherto as in some way 'un-American', acquired under the New Deal a recognised status it had never enjoyed before. This was felt to be still precarious ; for, as the capitalist class got over its fright and conditions came back to something nearer pre-crisis normality, many employers denounced in downright terms the very measures by which they had been relieved and began to seek means of returning to their old anti-Trade Union attitudes. By that time, however, the Unions had entrenched themselves too strongly to be driven back easily, and most of the big manufacturers found it preferable to come to terms with them rather than run the risks of an all-out industrial conflict. The capitalist class was still in the late 'thirties acutely conscious of its lost prestige and aware of its dependence on the State to sustain its position, greatly though it still disliked the hand that fed it.

The Socialists were, in a sense, quite correct in saying that the effect of President Roosevelt's New Deal had been to give American capitalism a new lease of life. Indeed, what else could Roosevelt have set out to do, in the absence of any acceptable alternative basis for the structure of society ? Widespread though social discontent had been during the depression, there had been no effective challenge to capitalism and almost no advocacy of any other way of organising the nation's economic affairs. The Trade Unions — the C.I.O. as well as the A.F. of L. — advocated, not a change in the basis of the economic system, but only higher wages and better conditions under it, coupled with a greater degree of social security, which they sought partly indeed from the State, but also increasingly by the negotiation industrially of 'fringe benefits' enlarging the scope of collective bargaining. There had been during the depression an immense proliferation of projects of social betterment — plans for pensions, projects of Co-operative community living, and many others — but most of these notions faded away as the economy recovered from the worst of the depression and most, though not all, workers were again able to find jobs. Such movements as Upton Sinclair's E.P.I.C. — End Poverty in California — of 1933 had aroused for a short time a very large popular response; but this had speedily faded away as the New Deal produced its effects. The new America of the late 'thirties was in some vital respects very different from the old; but it was no less capitalistic, even if its capitalism had been made more responsible and more respectful of public opinion.

At the onset of the depression, American Socialism, in common with other movements of discontent, made temporary gains. The American Socialist Party, which had fallen to between 7000 and 8000 members in 1928, rose to 15,000 in 1932 and to 23,000 in 1934, but then fell back again rapidly after the split of 1936. Its outstanding leader, Morris Hillquit, died in 1933, and there was no one left in the Party's 'Old Guard' to take his place. After his removal, the A.S.P. became more than ever an arena for faction fights between insignificant groups. Hillquit, of some reputation as a Marxist scholar, was a New York Jewish lawyer with a strong local following. Bitterly attacked by the Communists, he was, despite what they said of him, a left-wing Socialist of advanced views, as far removed from the Socialist right wing of parliamentarian democrats as from the Communists themselves; but he had enough prestige and influence to hold the Party together. When he died the old leadership — or what was left of it — soon lost control. In 1934 the extreme left captured the A.S.P. machine, ousting Algernon Lee of the Rand School and other old stalwarts, till in 1936 matters came to a definite split and the right wing finally broke away. In that year the A.S.P. and the Communists actually entered into negotiations for joint action; but these broke down, mainly because the C.P. line changed to one of support for Roosevelt, to whom the A.S.P. was still strongly opposed. During the same year the A.S.P. underwent the experience of being joined *en bloc* by the American Trotskyists, who, headed by James P. Cannon and Max Schachtman, had been expelled from the C.P. in 1928 and had since maintained their existence as a separate small Party. This fusion was short-lived; after ten months of unhappy co-existence the Trotskyists were expelled from the A.S.P. in 1937 and resumed their existence as a Party on their own. Thereafter, Norman Thomas was almost the only figure of any eminence left to the A.S.P.; and his policy was almost exclusively that of keeping the United States out of war at all costs : so that in the years immediately before 1941 the A.S.P. was in effect more an isolationist-pacifist than in any constructive sense a Socialist Party. But in effect it did not matter what line the A.S.P. took up. It had lost all influence.

The Communists, on their side, showed at any rate much more activity. As we saw, during the 1920s they had been through split after split, each group of dissidents forming a new splinter Party at bitter enmity with the official Party recognised by the Comintern. Some of these splinter Parties had for a time some local importance; and some carried on to the 1930s — for example, John Kerache's Proletarian Party at Detroit, whose leaders played a part of some importance in creating the Automobile Workers' Union. But most of them speedily disappeared or shrank up to almost nothing, though J. P. Cannon's Trotskyists were able to maintain themselves on a small scale as a nuisance group, and the so-called Communist Opposition, headed by Jay Lovestone and Benjamin Gitlow, who were expelled from the C.P. in 1929, lasted on until 1940, whereafter Lovestone and Gitlow passed definitely into the Anti-Communist ranks, Lovestone becoming eventually, in 1947, Secretary of a Free Trade Union Committee set up by the A.F. of L. During the 1920s the Communist Party had been divided into rival factions, headed by W. Z. Foster and Earl Browder on the one side and on the other by Charles Ruthenberg, on whose behalf the Comintern had intervened in 1925, when he was threatened with exclusion. But Ruthenberg had died in 1927, and in the following year Cannon and his Trotskyist following had been expelled. Then, in 1929, came the expulsion of Lovestone and Gitlow and the reorganisation of the American Communist Party under direct instructions from Moscow. W. Z. Foster, who had hoped to be made General Secretary of the Party, was passed over in favour of his follower, Earl Browder, who thereafter retained the position until he was cast out from it in 1945 ; and from 1929 onwards the American Communist Party obediently followed every shift in policy dictated from Moscow. For the next few years this committed it to the policy of the 'United Front from below' — which meant treating the Socialists as the principal enemies of the workers and trying to break up their organisation by winning the rank and file away from the leaders. This policy lasted through the depression and the Nazi victory in Germany, and was not ended until it was replaced in the summer of 1935 by the utterly different policy of the Popular Front, organised by Dimitrov as the new Secretary of the Comintern. The American Communist Party promptly changed front and set to work to bring about a rallying of the American people to an anti-Fascist crusade based on the widest possible support. The change of line did not however improve relations with the Socialists ; for it led the C.P. into collaboration with the C.I.O. and thus indirectly into support of Roosevelt and the Democratic Party, to whom the Socialists remained strongly opposed. The Communists infiltrated into a number of the C.I.O. Unions and succeeded in capturing a few of them before the C.I.O. leaders recognised the nature of the challenge and turned upon their erstwhile allies and drove them out. Then, in 1939, the party line changed again abruptly on the signature of the Nazi-Soviet Pact, only to be reversed yet again when Hitler launched his attack on the Soviet Union in 1941.

In terms of American politics, all these shifts of policy meant very little ; for all the sects of Socialists and Communists, taken together, were too weak to have any real influence on the course of events. As far as the working classes counted in American politics they did so through the C.I.O. and the A.F. of L. and not through either the Socialist or the Communist sects ; and the C.I.O., as we saw, was concerned rather with consolidating the gains made under the New Deal and building up its strength as a collective bargaining agency than with any more distant objectives. The C.I.O.'s Political Action Committee set to work most effectively to mobilise the Trade Union vote for President Roosevelt in 1936, and turned aside correspondingly from all coquetting with attempts to form a third party in Federal politics — though this did not prevent the creation in New York of a separate American Labor Party, formed in 1936, which was able for a time to exert a considerable influence in local politics. In 1937–8 the Trotskyists secured wide publicity for the two reports published by an independent Commission, over which John Dewey presided, set up to make an impartial investigation of the charges made against Trotsky by the Communists; but this success in the realm of publicity, though it helped to discredit Stalin and the Comintern in American opinion, had no other connection with the course of political events. The great social developments in the United States during the middle and later 'thirties simply passed the Socialists by: neither Socialists nor Communists had any effective share in them. Nevertheless, under the impact of the depression and the New Deal, American society passed during these years through a revolution in class relations which, though it left the general economic structure mainly unchanged in form, fundamentally altered its working to the advantage of the working classes and achieved, not the overthrow of capitalism — to which no real alternative existed — but its transformation from a ruthless system of exploitation by unregulated economic power into one in which the notion of social responsibility had achieved a remarkable, if reluctant, recognition. The social problems of America were not solved, and have not been solved to-day; but a far more tolerable pattern of social relations was established and seemed likely to endure at least as long as the country could avoid a recurrence of the disasters of 1929 and the ensuing years.

In such a situation it would be idle to look for any major development in the realm of Socialist ideas. The Communists either said and did faithfully what Moscow told them to say and do or, breaking away from Stalinist leadership, dissipated themselves among a host of contending tiny factions totally lacking in constructive ideas. The Socialists either followed unimaginatively the patterns of European Social Democratic thought or, when they broke away, became involved in faction fights in which they sought vainly to find policies which would keep them distinct from Communism and would at the same time enable them to follow an independent course. Their misfortune was that there was no considerable body of opinion to which they could appeal, because the rising Trade Unions were not interested in such matters and left them to carry on their factional disputations without any audience that was prepared to listen to them. It is true that before long the solidarity of the C.I.O. Unions began to break down. David Dubinsky, having defeated the Communists who had for a time won control of his powerful International Ladies' Garment Workers' Union, refused to follow the rest of the C.I.O. into a definitive breach with the A.F. of L., and returned to the A.F. of L. fold. John L. Lewis, the effective founder of the C.I.O., quarrelled with it and with Roosevelt and led his miners back to a position of independence of both the rival movements. The C.I.O. turned upon the Communists within its ranks, and expelled the Communist-dominated Unions from affiliation to it. Nevertheless, the main body of the C.I.O. held together and was able to break new ground in the field of successful collective bargaining and also to pioneer in building up closer relations with the international Trade Union movement. By 1940 the United States was a country practically without a Socialist movement; but it was at the same time one in which ideas and policies commonly regarded as Socialistic had made very great progress, and the ground had been prepared for much closer collaboration with the working-class movements of other countries than had seemed possible a dozen years before. When, after the second world war, West European Socialists and Trade Union leaders met Walter Reuther and his C.I.O. colleagues, they found it much easier to talk together in terms of mutual understanding than had been the case in earlier contacts; and this was not mainly because the Europeans had become less Socialist — if they had — but rather because the Americans had reached a stage in social and economic relations much more closely resembling that of their European colleagues than had existed before the New Deal.

In Canada, where a Progressive Party formed mainly by the farmers after the first world war had disintegrated for want of any clear political doctrine, the great depression of the early 'thirties brought into being a new Party, based on an alliance between farmers and urban workers, under the name of

Co-operative Commonwealth Federation. This Party was actually constituted in 1933. After the collapse of the Progressives in 1925 there had come into being in Western Canada both an Independent Labour Party and a Farmers' Political Association, to carry on propaganda for a new Party opposed to both Liberals and Conservatives ; and in July 1932 the I.L.P. held a convention in Saskatoon and drew up a political programme. At the same time and place, the United Farmers of Canada, hitherto a non-political body, held a convention of their own and adopted a political programme. The two programmes were found to be almost identical ; and the United Farmers accordingly suggested that the two bodies should meet to discuss action in common. The result of this meeting was the decision to form a Farmer-Labour Party. So far, the movement was almost entirely limited to the province of Saskatchewan ; but at the instance of the new body, a wider conference, still mainly from Western Canada, met at Calgary in August 1932 and decided to launch the C.C.F. as a nation-wide Party with broadly Socialist objectives. Its original programme was indeed very close to those of the Social Democratic and Labour Parties of Western Europe, except that it had more to say about the need for the State to come to the aid of the farmers by measures designed to preserve or establish a fair ratio between agricultural and industrial prices. It also urged very strongly the case for social security legislation in the interests of the many whom the depression had thrown out of employment. The following year, meeting in conference at Regina, the C.C.F. issued its Regina Manifesto laying down its policy in greater detail. As a means of ending the disaster which had overtaken the Canadian economy under capitalism, it demanded 'a planned and socialised economy in which our natural resources and the principal means of production and distribution are owned, controlled and operated by the people'. More particularly, the Manifesto called for the socialisation of finance and banking, transport and communications, electric power, 'and all other industries and services essential to social planning', for security of tenure for farmers, the encouragement of producers' and consumers' Co-operation, and the restoration and maintenance of an equitable relationship between agricultural and other prices, for the regulation of foreign trade through Import and Export Boards, for a Labour Code guaranteeing freedom of organisation, effective participation of the workers in industrial management, and a wide range of social security legislation, for a socialised health service, for an amendment of the British North America Act to confer more adequate powers on the Dominion Government, for universal freedom of speech and assembly and the abolition of racial and other forms of political discrimination, for drastic amendment of the tax structure, and for an emergency programme based on the principle of work or maintenance for all, public spending on housing and other useful works, and the financing of such a programme by means of 'credit based on the national wealth'.

J. S. Woodsworth, who had been first elected as a Labour M.P. in 1921, was chosen as President of the C.C.F., which grew rapidly in Western Canada during the following years. Its first electoral successes came in 1934, when it elected five members to the Saskatchewan Provincial Legislature. These rose to 11 in 1938; and in 1944 the C.C.F. won 47 out of the 52 seats, and took office with an overwhelming majority under T. C. Douglas, who still holds that office, as provincial Premier. Progress was less rapid in other Provinces; but the C.C.F. was able to assume the position of third-party challenge to the Liberals and Conservatives who alternated in office in the Dominion. It was still relatively weak in Dominion politics: in 1940 it had only 8 members in the Canadian House of Commons. It grew much faster during the war, especially in Ontario, where in 1943 it elected 34 members to the Provincial Legislature and became the second largest party, with well over one-third of the seats. By that time the C.C.F. was the major opposition Party in four Canadian Provinces. When Woodsworth died in 1942 he was succeeded as leader by the English-born teacher, M. J. Coldwell, of Saskatchewan, who still leads the Party though no longer in Parliament, having lost his seat in the Canadian landslide of 1958. Among the elements which went to form the C.C.F. were, besides Labour and Farmers, a notable group of academics grouped round Professor F. R. Scott, of McGill University, who formed the League for Social Reconstruction and published an important report entitled *Social Planning for Canada*. Most of the contributors to this volume became active supporters of the C.C.F. That body, from the outset, laid great stress on the need for a planned economy as necessary to give a fair deal to town and country and to hold the different elements in its following harmoniously together.

Meanwhile, in Latin America, with its vast undeveloped resources and its perpetual struggles between Creole aristocracies and a wide variety of democratic and popular movements dominated by the native bourgeoisies of the towns, the working-class movements, still limited to small minorities because of the underdeveloped condition of industry, were continually involved in faction fights and remained for the most part quite isolated from the rural workers, who constituted the great majority of the population in almost every country of the continent. Only in the Argentine, Uruguay, and Costa Rica did white men make up the main body of the people : elsewhere it was composed mainly of either Indians or Negroes or of persons of mixed ancestry. In the late 'thirties, out of a total population of almost 130 million, the Indians and the Negroes each numbered about 16 million. Nearly a third of the population of Brazil were Negroes : more than half the inhabitants of Guatemala and Bolivia, and 40 per cent or more in Peru and Ecuador were Indians, and not far short of 30 per cent in Mexico were Indians of unmixed blood. Only the Argentine had a standard of living at all comparable with those of the more advanced countries, and even there average standards were a long way below those of the developed countries of Europe. Industrialisation depended mainly on the inflow of foreign capital, which came chiefly from the United States, though European enterprises — especially British — were still predominant in the public utility services of a number of countries — above all, in the Argentine. United States penetration was concentrated mainly in Central America, where the United Fruit Company, strongly backed by the U.S. Government, held a very powerful position and habitually allied itself with the most reactionary elements — the native owners of the great estates.

As we saw, Haya de la Torre had founded his Aprista movement in 1924, with its appeal to an Indo-American patriotism transcending national factions and for a union of middle classes, working classes and peasants against foreign imperialist penetration.[1] This movement had been in sharp conflict with the Communists, who were bitterly opposed to such a union of classes and were seeking to build up a united proletarian movement under their own control and to bring the rural workers under proletarian leadership. Socialist, as distinct from Communist, movements had no great strength except in a few countries, such as the Argentine and Chile; but there was a considerable working-class following for various brands of Anarcho-Syndicalism based on European models. In Mexico the Revolution, after its initial successes at the time of the first world war, had become bogged down in a bitter struggle with the Church and made no further progress until President Cárdenas came to power in 1934. Cárdenas, by reviving the process of land-distribution and by encouraging the growth of working-class organisations, gave a great fillip to Trade Unionism. Morones had founded his Labour Party in 1919, and had continued to lead it through the 'twenties with only moderate success; but in 1936 the left-wing lawyer, Lombardo Toledano, who had begun as a collaborator of Morones, became secretary of the newly formed Confederation of Mexican Workers, and from that point of vantage went on in 1938 to set up his Workers' Confederation of Latin America, which for a time exerted a very wide influence. Lombardo Toledano always denied his membership of the Communist Party; but he undoubtedly enjoyed its support and worked in close association with it, as well as acting as adviser to Cárdenas in labour matters. The Mexican Communist Party had been originally set up by the Japanese Comintern emissary, Sen Katayama, in 1922, under the leadership of a U.S. citizen, B. D. Wolfe, and had exerted only a minor influence. Wolfe and, with him, the famous artist Diego Rivera were excluded from the Party in 1930; and thereafter it became a faithful reflection of the shifting policies of the Comintern, moving over obediently to advocacy of a Popular Front after 1935 and giving its support to the reforms of Cárdenas despite his granting of an asylum to Trotsky in Mexico, where Trotsky was finally assassinated by an emissary of Stalin in 1940. But when Cárdenas ceased to be President and was succeeded by Camacho

[1] See Vol. IV, Part II, p. 761 ff.

in 1940, the impetus went out of the revived revolutionary movement, and Mexico settled down to the development of its economy under bourgeois rule. There was a considerable growth of industry and commerce, and in the countryside a development of large and middle-sized farms using improved methods of cultivation. The *ejidos*, or village communes, which Cárdenas had done much to develop, lost their character as community agencies and became simply farming villages under wholly individualist forms of ownership and control ; and before long the Trade Unions began to break up into warring factions. Lombardo Toledano gradually lost his influence, until he was finally expelled from the Mexican Workers' Confederation in 1948, keeping his position at the head of a hardly more than nominal Latin American Workers' Confederation which had lost all influence in the country of its birth. Even at the height of its influence the Mexican Trade Union movement had kept its almost complete isolation from the peasants, whom it did nothing to help in their struggles against the landowners and the Church — which was the greatest landowner of all. For a time, under the presidency of Cárdenas, the urban workers in Mexico — or at any rate the skilled workers — succeeded in building up for themselves a substantially improved position as a labour aristocracy ; but from 1940 onwards they steadily lost ground, though especially among the oil workers conditions continued to be vastly better than they had been before the nationalisation of the oil wells under Cárdenas in 1937–8.

Thus, in the second half of the 1930s, Mexican Trade Unionism appeared for a short time as the protagonist in a continent-wide movement of the industrial workers of Latin America, only to fall back swiftly when the Cárdenas epoch came to an end in 1940. Elsewhere, the Latin American working-class movements followed a chequered course, but on the whole lost ground to dictators who ousted the left wing almost as soon as it had come to power. In Chile, for example, in June 1932, when the effects of the world depression had aroused a great mass of popular discontent, there was for a fortnight a definitely Socialist Republic, headed by Colonel Marmaduke Grove, which drove out the previous dictator, Ibáñez, and threatened to introduce far-reaching reforms, but was speedily overthrown by a military *coup*. The outcome, however, was not a renewed dictatorship, but the recall to power of a former liberal President, Alessandri, and a kind of constitutional rule under which considerable social progress was made. The Socialist Revolution in Chile was clearly premature and the policies of its Ministers were vague and muddled ; but there was behind it a great body of popular feeling. Despite its failure, Chile had in the 1930s the strongest and most solid Communist Party in all Latin America and was also able to maintain a vigorous Trade Union movement which prepared the way for the decisive victory of the Popular Front in 1938.

Outside Mexico and Chile, the only Latin-American country which in the late 'thirties was under the rule of a régime with some claim to be called a democracy was Colombia, which enjoyed a long spell of constitutional liberal rule, lasting until 1949. Elsewhere a sequence of dictators had succeeded in establishing themselves in power — Trujillo in the Dominican Republic and Getulio Vargas in Brazil in 1930, Jorge Ubico in Guatemala in 1931, Tiburcio Carias in Honduras in 1933, and Colonels Toro and Busch in Bolivia in 1937. Meanwhile, in Peru, Haya de la Torre's Aprista movement, founded in Mexico in 1924, won great influence despite its leader's absence in exile till the fall of Leguria in 1931 enabled him to return to his own country, where he was elected President, but was immediately overthrown by a military *coup* headed by Sandoz Carro, who threw him into prison. Released by Carro's assassination in 1933, he resumed his activity, but was again persecuted, so that the Aprista movement had to continue its work underground, but remained strong enough to resist all efforts to stamp it out. At length, in 1946, a moderate candidate, Bustamente Rivero, was elected as President with Aprista support and several members of the movement entered the Ministry, but were unable to accomplish much in face of the strong opposition to their policy in reactionary circles. This state of affairs lasted till 1948, when a further military *coup d'état* was followed by sharp measures against the Aprista movement.

The Apristas, as we saw in the fourth volume of this work,[1]

[1] See Vol. IV, Part II, p. 765.

seemed likely for a time to become the greatest left-wing force, not only in Peru, but throughout Latin America. Nowhere, however, except in Peru did they succeed in becoming a mass-movement. They were bitterly opposed by the Communists, at first because they stood for an anti-imperialist coalition of the middle and working classes and of the peasants to free Latin America from subjection to foreign, and especially to United States, penetration, at a time when the Communists were acting under the slogan 'Class against Class' and were insisting on the need for proletarian leadership in the revolutionary movement, and latterly because, when the Communists had gone over to a Popular Front policy, the two movements were rivals for the leadership of the same elements. The Apristas, when they were approached by Communists with requests that they should join the anti-Fascist Popular Front, replied that they already were a Popular Front movement which those outside it should join in order to avoid division of the popular forces. The Apristas were also in strong opposition to the separate nationalisms of the individual Latin-American States, seeking to substitute for them a wider conception of continental nationalism transcending barriers of race and State and appealing to rural as well as industrial elements to make common cause against the Yankees and their reactionary leaders. When President Roosevelt in 1933 reversed the traditional United States policy of high-handedness in dealing with Latin America, and proclaimed his 'good neighbour' policy, the consequent relaxation of tensions with North America reacted against the Aprista policy of hostility to the United States, and the current of popular opinion was partly diverted from anti-North Americanism to State Nationalism. The Apristas, outside Peru, won wide support among intellectuals, but not among the working classes, despite the broadly socialistic programme they advanced. They were, indeed, in their essential doctrines, a long way ahead of anything that could form the basis for a mass-appeal; for their projects of socialisation on a foundation of international public ownership had necessarily an unrealistic ring; and the mass of impoverished rural workers to whom they endeavoured to appeal was quite incapable of united action on a continental scale. The Apristas, moreover, were in their methods highly authoritarian and aimed at building up a closely knit centralised Party subject to a strong central discipline which could not be enforced on the widely diverse elements they were seeking to enrol in support of a common policy. The Communists, up to 1935, were similarly handicapped; but when they went over in that year to the policy of the Popular Front they showed themselves a good deal more adaptable to the varying conditions of the different Latin-American countries, and much readier to come to terms with the separate Nationalist trends. The Apristas therefore on the whole lost out in the competition with the Communists, except in Peru, where they succeeded in building up a movement widely supported by the Indians of the villages, who had been almost untouched by previous attempts at organisation. The Communists, in their hatred for A.P.R.A., even showed themselves ready at times to collaborate with military *putsch*-ists against it; and this rivalry continued unabated into the post-war years.

In certain respects there is a good deal in common between the revised Marxist doctrine promoted in China by Mao-Tse-tung and the ideas of some of the Latin-American revolutionaries, though the latter did not lay the same stress as Mao did on the distinction between the 'new democratic' Revolution which was his immediate objective and the Socialist Revolution which would, he believed, follow irresistibly upon it. This similarity is not at all surprising; for Mao put forward his doctrine as applicable not only to China but to all countries suffering under colonial or semi-colonial régimes, and the problem of the place of the great mass of peasants in the Revolution presented itself in Latin-America no less challengingly than in China. Latin American Communism, in its earlier stages, was chiefly a breakaway from urban-minded Socialist Parties in relatively advanced countries, such as the Argentine, Uruguay, and Chile, and found great difficulty in establishing any contact with the peasants, with whom these Socialist movements had had nothing to do. The Comintern, however, soon realised that in most parts of Latin America nothing could be done without peasant support; and the Communist Parties, under its orders, set to work to establish united *blocs* of workers and peasants under proletarian leadership and control. At a time when the anti-imperialist, anti-Yankee, crusade was at its height, these tactics were successful in creating for a time considerable Communist, or Communist-led, movements in some of the peasant countries. At the out-set these movements were directed against the native capitalists and middle classes as well as against the foreigners ; but when the Communists made their decisive shift to the Popular Front in 1935, it became necessary to revise them by widening them to include the middle classes and even a part of the native capitalist class. This in itself would have made for an intensifi-cation of the anti-imperialist campaign ; but at the same time Roosevelt's 'good neighbour' policy was doing much to lessen anti-North-American feeling, and the emphasis in fact shifted from anti-imperialism to anti-fascism, especially under the influence of the events in Spain, which had a large effect in rallying opinion to the cause of the Spanish Republican Govern-ment and in stirring up anti-Nazi and anti-Italian sentiment. The Communists in the years immediately before 1939 consti-tuted themselves the leaders of a continent-wide anti-Fascist campaign, only to change front abruptly, as elsewhere, on the morrow of the signing of the Nazi-Soviet Pact in 1939 and to adopt a new anti-war policy which had to be reversed no less abruptly when Hitler attacked the Soviet Union in 1941. That these repeated changes of policy did the Latin-American Com-munists so little damage was due mainly to the remoteness of the European struggle from the affairs with which their poten-tial followers were in fact chiefly concerned.

Mao in China, as we saw, became the promoter of a national movement based on a patriotic combination of classes hostile to imperialism and, more particularly, to Japan. The Latin-American Communists sought to achieve a similar com-bination of classes against imperialist penetration, symbolised in their case by Yankee domination and support for the most reactionary elements in the Latin-American population. So far, the two policies were the same ; but in Latin America they were complicated, much more than in China, by racial differences, as well as by the division of the area into a large number of separate Sovereign States. The racial difficulty, to be sure, was not present in the Argentine or in Uruguay ; but it was acutely present in most parts of the continent, including Mexico, where it set up sharp barriers between the urban workers, who were largely European in origin, and the main body of the people, who were largely of mixed blood and included large *blocs* of purely Indian or predominantly Negro peoples. The Communists did their utmost to ignore racial barriers and to proclaim their hostility to all forms of racial discrimination ; but their doing so, though it helped them in some countries, went against them in others, including Mexico as well as Uruguay and the Argentine. Nevertheless they produced a considerable impact upon opinion, though they were usually unable to translate this influence into terms of mass organisation, and many of the Trade Unions which they founded or brought under their control had little more than a phantom existence and lacked any real mass-support. Their intellectual influence was far ahead of their organised power because, like the Apristas, they appeared with a challenging message of international hostility to the reactionary and repressive elements which continued in most countries to hold the keys to economic and political power. But, as compared with the Apristas, they enjoyed the advantage of being able to appear as the leaders of a class-movement and as the local representatives of a world-wide force of revolt against capitalist and feudal oppression. When, in the late 'thirties, they rallied to the support of President Cárdenas in Mexico and helped to create, under Lombardo Toledano's leadership, a Trade Union movement designed to cover the entire continent from its Mexican base, they seemed for a time on the point of establishing an effective continental crusade directed against imperialism. But, as we have seen, this movement melted away when the arch-imperialists, the North Americans, became involved in the war against the Fascist powers ; and it was not until after 1945 that the anti-imperialist crusade could be effectively resumed.

Of all the Latin-American countries, only the Argentine and Uruguay, with their populations of almost entirely European ancestry, maintained continuously Socialist Parties modelled closely on those of Europe or had been formally connected with the Second International prior to 1914. Side by side with these Parties there grew up Trade Union movements which were in part loosely attached to the Socialist Parties and in part under Anarcho-Syndicalist influence, as were the F.O.R.A.

in the Argentine and its counterpart, the F.O.R.U., in Uruguay. In the Argentine during the 1920s F.O.R.A. and the Socialist U.G.T. were roughly equal in numbers; but in 1929 a new body, the C.G.T., absorbed the U.G.T. and some of the F.O.R.A. Unions and assumed a position of predominance, which it retained until after the second world war. The Socialist Party suffered a left-wing secession following on the Russian Revolution, and the International Socialist Party which then broke away from the majority presently converted itself into a Communist Party. In 1927 the Socialist Party suffered a further secession, this time not from the left, but from a group headed by Antonio di Tomaso which considered its policy to be insufficiently Nationalist; and the Independent Socialist Party thus formed scored a big success at the elections of 1930, when it secured 109,000 votes and elected 10 deputies to Parliament as against 83,000 votes and only a single seat for the old Socialist Party. This was on the eve of the world economic crisis, which hit the Argentine hard and led to a considerable strike movement, which the Radical Government attempted to suppress. This action, together with the sharp distress caused by the depression, undermined the Government's popularity, and in September 1930 the military leaders deposed and imprisoned the President, Uriburu. The Independent Socialists supported the *coup d'état* and voted for its leader, General Justo, as candidate for the presidency, to which he was elected by 166,000 votes against 126,000 for the Democratic-Progressive candidate, who received the support of the old Socialist Party. Thereafter the Independent Socialists lost ground and fell to internal quarrelling, which ended by leading to the dissolution of the Party. The Socialist Party at first gained largely, and was able to raise the number of its elected deputies to 46; but it in its turn fell to quarrelling on the issue of the Popular Front, raised by the Communists, and at the election of 1938 it lost most of its seats and was reduced to a mere rump of 7 deputies. It also suffered a further split, when its Youth Section broke away to form the Socialist Workers' Party, which joined the Popular Front under Communist leadership. Thereafter, during the second world war, the old Socialist Party gradually rebuilt its influence, but still remained a minority group, especially in relation to the rising force of Argentinian Nationalism, of which Perón was emerging as the outstanding leader.

Meanwhile in Uruguay the Communists had captured the old Socialist Party in 1920, and had persuaded it to join the Comintern. The dissidents formed a rival Socialist Party, which in 1931 joined the Labour and Socialist International, but had very little popular support. The world crisis led in Uruguay to a *coup d'état*, in which the President, Gabriel Terra, maintained himself unconstitutionally in office : Emilio Frugoni, the Socialist leader, took refuge in the Argentine. In 1938, when General Baldoni stood for election as successor to Terra, Frugoni stood against him, but was heavily defeated. Baldoni, however, instead of following Terra's policy of submission to American imperialist interests, proceeded to re-establish the laws passed under President Battle twenty years before, and received Socialist support for his measures. A reactionary attempted to assassinate Frugoni in the Chamber, but did not succeed ; and the Socialist Party was allowed to carry on its activities freely, without any such repression as its counterparts suffered elsewhere.

In Brazil, where the Communists had been the predominant working-class group in the 1920s and had operated for the most part underground as an illegal organisation, a new Labour Party had been formed in 1929, and the following year achieved a membership of 130,000. In 1934 this Party became part of the National Liberation Alliance, a coalition formed to oppose the increasingly dictatorial conduct of Getulio Vargas. In the summer of 1935 the Alliance issued a manifesto calling for an advanced policy of social reform, and a few months later it declared a general strike against the Vargas régime. Vargas was able to defeat the strike, and retorted by proclaiming the dissolution of all political Parties and the establishment of a sort of corporative State, which maintained itself until Vargas resigned in 1945.

In view of these wide differences from area to area, it is impossible to make any general statements about the Socialist movements of Latin America, not because each country pursued its own course uninfluenced by what was occurring elsewhere, but because currents of opinion, however widespread their influence, took very different forms according to the environment in which they had to find means of expression. Most of the widespread currents of doctrine were of European, rather than of Latin-American, origin; but in the 'thirties these European influences, except that of Communism, were getting weaker — in particular, the once-powerful Anarcho-Syndicalist influence, which came mainly from Spain and Italy and to some extent from France, and grew weaker as fewer agitators on its behalf came to Latin America from those countries and as considerable sections went over to the Communists during the Spanish Civil War. European Social Democracy too was a declining influence, largely for the same reasons; but the Communists experienced great difficulty in getting their conception of centralised party discipline accepted by the Latin Americans, who had been accustomed to much looser forms of organisation and especially to refashioning their Trade Unions every few years to adapt them to changing currents of popular feeling. The one indigenous movement of continent-wide significance was that of A.P.R.A.; but this ran foul, not only of the Communists, but also of the particularist Nationalism which was steadily gaining strength in a number of countries, and especially in the Argentine, where for a time it almost swept Socialism away. Cárdenas, in Mexico, also pursued a policy based on indigenous conditions and, while primarily an agrarian reformer, worked closely for a time with Lombardo Toledano's ambitious projects of continent-wide Trade Union organisation. But the Mexican Revolution, after Cárdenas, turned more and more into a movement of economic development in which the State encouraged bourgeois forms of economic growth and allowed the co-operative elements in the peasant *ejidos* to be submerged.

In general, then, the principal common characteristics of the Latin-American working-class movements were theoretical immaturity and a failure, in most cases, to create any effective links between the urban workers and the peasants, who continued for the most part to subsist at very low standards of living in comparison with the townsmen, from whom they were in many cases shut off also by barriers of race and colour. These barriers were being gradually broken down as industrialisation advanced, especially in the mining districts. But except in the Argentine the number of industrial workers was in the 1930s still very small in comparison with that of the peasants, who, save where they had been attracted by some form of Communism, or in Peru by the Aprista movement, still remained mainly unorganised and were often cat's-paws in the hands of the reactionary leaders of the Catholic Church.

CHAPTER XI

THE SOVIET UNION FROM THE BEGINNING OF THE FIRST FIVE-YEAR PLAN

I N the fourth volume of this study the account of developments in the Soviet Union stopped short on the eve of the first Five-Year Plan and of the plunge in the countryside into massive collectivisation of peasant holdings. We then saw how Stalin successfully eliminated first Trotsky and then Zinoviev and Kamenev from their positions in the Communist Party, and thereafter turned on Bukharin and the former right wing. We saw how Stalin managed to consolidate his hold over the Party, so as to make himself virtually dictator of its policies, with a submissive Political Bureau and Central Committee ready to do his will. We saw, moreover, how, after appearing against Trotsky as the opponent of comprehensive planning and a speedier tempo of industrialisation, Stalin suddenly turned round and became the foremost advocate of the measures he had hitherto derided; and how he executed a similar *volte-face* in agricultural policy by launching the great campaign for collectivisation and for mass-attack on the so-called '*kulaks*'.

We must now consider in some detail what these new policies actually involved, and how they were carried out. It is a matter of general agreement that during the 1920s, after the civil war had ended and the New Economic Policy been set on foot, there had been a marked relaxation of internal tensions, and the Russian people, though still very poor, had been able to live somewhat better and under much less stringent regimentation than in the earlier years after 1917. Stalin, to be sure, had not been during these years on the extreme right wing of the Party. He had not echoed Bukharin's advice to the *kulaks* to take full advantage of the N.E.P. to enrich themselves, or positively opposed industrialisation. But he had opposed Trotsky's drive to speed up industrial development to the fullest possible extent and had stood out against Trotsky's thesis that the only possible basis for a Socialist economy was high production — higher production than could be achieved under the most advanced capitalism, and that the sole way of overcoming the antagonism between townsmen and peasants was to produce a greatly increased supply of industrial goods for exchange with the countryside. Trotsky, in asserting this, had coupled with it a recognition that it was bound to take a long time for Russian productivity to catch up with that of the more advanced capitalist countries, and had reached the conclusion that the prospects of Socialism in the Soviet Union remained dependent on the spread of the Revolution to one or more of these countries and that 'Socialism in One Country' was an impracticable and self-contradictory policy. Trotsky had denounced Stalin as a betrayer of the cause of world revolution for declaring 'Socialism in One Country' to be a practicable objective. Stalin also worked to industrialise Russia as fast as he thought safe; but throughout his dispute with Trotsky he had accused him of a readiness to antagonise the peasantry by pressing on with it at too hot a pace, in the absence of loans of capital from abroad. Stalin had clung to the N.E.P. and had been unwilling to stir up class-war in the villages in view of the weak condition of Soviet industry and the dependence of the towns on peasant supplies, especially from the more prosperous farmers. Under the Five-Year Plan the basic industrial production of the Soviet Union grew at an unprecedented rate. Coal, steel, oil, electricity were all produced at levels far exceeding those contemplated in the earlier drafts of the Plan, which were marked by a high concentration on the output of capital goods, only quite subordinate attention being given to consumers' goods, to transport, or even to housing, of which there was a terrible shortage in the rapidly increasing centres of population. The desire was to advance as swiftly as possible in the basic industries, which formed the necessary foundation of industrial power; when these had been raised to a sufficient level, but only then, would it become possible to meet the consumers' demands for a higher standard of living. Nor was it left out of the calculations that the basic industries would provide the essential production for strength in war, or that the first need was to make the Soviet Union as strong as possible against the possible armed onslaughts of the capitalist powers, which were deemed to be determined to overthrow it.

The situation in the Soviet Union, before the plunge into agricultural collectivisation, was no doubt highly precarious and unstable. Rapid industrialisation, in the existing state of Soviet industry, seemed to require a massive importation of capital goods, which could be paid for only by greatly increased exports of primary products — especially grain. But the re-distribution of land holdings following the Revolution had destroyed the basis for wheat exports on the pre-war scale. Russian agriculture in Czarist days had been largely subsistence farming, and the large exports had come mainly from the big capitalist farms and not from the main body of peasant culti-vators. The Revolution had divided up these large farms; and the peasants who took them over naturally wished to consume a greatly increased proportion of the produce rather than to hand it over either for export or for supplying the towns. Even when harvests were good, the Government found it difficult to persuade the peasants to disgorge their surplus grain; and when they were bad the export surplus completely disappeared and it was even necessary on occasion to use up scanty foreign exchange in importing grain from abroad. Moreover, if the Government resorted to forcible measures for squeezing the peasants, either by requisitions or by purchase at unduly low prices, the peasants were apt to retaliate, not only by refusal to give up their harvests, but also by restricting grain production and either leaving the land idle or diverting attention to in-dustrial crops, for which better prices were being paid. In 1926–7 the Government had done relatively well, and a sub-stantial export of grain had been possible; but in 1927–8 there was a sharp fall in the amount of grain it was able to collect, and its power to buy industrial goods overseas was sharply curtailed, with severe effects on industrial development.

The seriousness of the crisis was generally recognised : the question was how it should be met. One possible policy was to give aid to the peasants, by offering them substantially higher prices, or by allowing them to sell their produce to an increased extent on the free market. Such a policy, however, would be bound to benefit chiefly the better-off peasants, who held a large part of the surplus, and to strengthen the already existing tendency in the villages towards the growth of a *kulak* economy based on the renting of land by the richer from the poorer peasants and the increased employment of hired labour.

'*Kulak*', in the Soviet Union of that date, proved an elastic word. Originally it seems to have signified a relatively well-to-do peasant who employed some labour other than his family's. He was thus an 'exploiter' — an actual or embryo capitalist — because he extracted profit by employing wage-labour. He was also, in most cases, a cultivator of some rented land besides the plot that belonged to him — usually of one or more parcels of land too small or too poor to enable their owners to live by cultivating them for their own subsistence. He might be, in addition, a dealer in other men's produce, buying up grain which they wished to turn into immediate cash, and therefore able to take advantage of the considerable seasonal fluctuation of prices. But he could be a *kulak* even without this, if he was guilty of the sin of employing even one man's help for his own profit — at any rate if he did so regularly, and not merely at harvest time. But the definition was not clear; there was no saying exactly what made a middle peasant into a *kulak*, and the imputation of being a *kulak* could, as we shall see, be affixed to more or fewer according to the policy of those in power and of neighbours. The Soviet leaders were not prepared to stimulate production by allowing the more prosperous farmers to get into a position which would enable them to dictate terms to the towns and possibly to bring about a return of capitalism; Stalin, up to 1929, had followed a middle line, half-way between Trotsky on the left and Bukharin on the right.

Then, suddenly, Stalin, having routed his critics, changed his line, declared for a drastic upward revision of the capital investment contemplated in the earlier drafts of the Five-Year Plan, and embarked on the great campaign of agricultural collectivisation. Instead of limiting such collectivisation to at most 20–25 per cent of peasant households during the ensuing five years, he issued orders to go ahead with collectivisation at the utmost possible speed, and turned loose on the countryside a host of agents with orders to do their utmost to carry it into execution at once. There is no doubt that this *volte-face* was due immediately to a large-scale outbreak of peasant hoarding. Peasants, especially the better-off, were refusing to sell their grain unless prices were greatly increased ; and the towns were faced with the prospect of famine. One answer would have been to give the higher prices that were being demanded : another was to declare war on the *kulaks* and take possession forcibly of the harvested supplies. But it was necessary to avoid a situation in which the peasants would be united in the struggle against the Government. As many as possible of the poorer peasants had to be brought over to support the official policy. This, Stalin thought, could be done if they could be offered the prospect of taking over the *kulaks'* land and livestock, which would become merged in the new collective farms.

The Soviet leaders had a deep belief in the superior productivity of collective agriculture, which would render possible large-scale measures in the application of machinery and the adoption of higher production techniques. They had already endeavoured to demonstrate this by establishing, chiefly on virgin land, vast State farms, chiefly grain factories ; but these had covered only a very small part of the total cultivated area. The results, moreover, had been disappointing, largely because there had been a lack of farmers competent to direct such vast agricultural enterprises, and also partly because Soviet industry was ill-equipped for supplying them with the necessary machines. This, however, had not destroyed the deeply rooted Marxian faith in the virtues of large-scale farming ; but it was realised to be impossible to extend very rapidly the amount of State farming, or to transform individual peasant holdings into large State farms in face of the immense redundancy of the peasant population over the numbers such farms could employ. There had, however, been already a very rapid spread of agricultural Co-operation, both for the purchase of farm requisites and for marketing and the supply of credit, though not for actual Co-operative cultivation ; and it was deemed that this experience of Co-operation had prepared the minds of many peasants for an extension of Co-operative methods into the field of production.

Accordingly, in order to avoid this new 'scissors' crisis, it

was decided to embark on a large plan of agricultural collectivisation on a Co-operative basis, by setting up Co-operative
farms on which the peasants would be invited to pool their
land and labour and to bring their implements and livestock
into a common pool, and even, if they wished, to go further and
establish communes in which they would live and eat in common
— though it was expected that most of them would prefer to
stop short of this, and to retain their separate households and
living arrangements. The proposed *kolkhozi* were thus
intended to be, in most areas, rather Co-operative *artels*,
analogous to the artels of craft producers which were already
prevalent in small-scale industry, than fully fledged communes;
but they were to enjoy all the advantages of large-scale production, aided, as far and as fast as possible, by the supply of
machinery from Machine Tractor Stations to be set up under
State control. In addition, they were to be given a fine send-
off by being enabled to start with taking over the lands, livestock, and implements of the *kulaks*, who were to be forcibly
dispossessed and driven out, and were even to be refused
admittance as members of the *kolkhoz*. High hopes were
entertained that the change would quickly result in a great
increase in total production, and also that it would be possible
to achieve this together with a sharp decrease in the numbers
employed and with a large addition to the man-power engaged
in industry.

Some of these results did follow; others did not. There
was a large drift to the towns in search of industrial employment; for a great many villages had far more people than
could be fully employed on the land save at the busiest seasons
of the year, and industrialisation, speeded up under the Five-
Year Plan, was soon calling for a big increase in the industrial
labour force. On the other hand, there was no speedy increase
in the output per hectare of cultivated land, and there was an
immense fall in the number of livestock. This was directly
due to the methods adopted for collectivisation, and the wide
extension of the term '*kulak*'.

If the *kulaks* were to be dispossessed, and their holdings
taken over by the collectives, the temptation to swell their
numbers, and so increase the possessions of the collective, was
obvious, and under the pressure of the hordes of ardent young

Communists who were sent out to the villages to urge collectivisation there is no doubt either that collectivisation was imposed
upon many who had no enthusiasm for it, or that the name
kulak was attached to middle peasants who were not guilty of
exploitation but merely of an individualist dislike of regimentation. The entire process was supposed to be voluntary, no
doubt; but that did not mean that any individual peasant was
able to reject it if a majority in his village, or group of villages,
were in favour of it, or could be induced to vote for it by
propagandist pressure. Most certainly, an alleged *kulak* could
not stand out against the decision of his neighbours, or even,
if he was judged to be a *kulak*, have any right to share in the
decision.

Those who, as *kulaks*, were dispossessed, suffered terribly,
as is well known. They were driven in droves from their
holdings, their property confiscated, and they themselves
exiled to remote timber camps and constructional projects such
as the giant canals, in which they were forced to work under
what were in effect slave conditions, and subjected to such
inhumanities that many thousands of them and their families
perished miserably. No one — or almost no one — expressed
any sympathy for them, or even troubled to enquire what
became of them after they were driven out. It did not seem
to matter how many of them died of their hardships — and
their families with them; for were they not 'class-enemies'
who, if they had been allowed their way, would have led the
Soviet Union back along the road to capitalism; and had such
'class-enemies' even the most fundamental rights? The Communists held that they had not.

The immediate outcome might have been foreseen. The
wretched victims killed their livestock instead of handing it
over; and the number of horses, cows, sheep, goats, and pigs
in the Soviet Union fell precipitately, causing a general famine
of milk and meat.[1] Those who were remorselessly driven out,
moreover, included a high proportion of the more skilled and
progressive agriculturists; this meant that the new collectives
started very seriously short of persons capable of competent
managerial service, and a great deal of inefficient management
ensued.

[1] For the grain famine which followed in 1931–2, see p. 241.

The by-products of precipitate collectivisation were so disastrous that Stalin had to issue his famous message 'Dizziness from Success', calling a halt, re-emphasising that collectivisation was intended to be voluntary, and laying the blame on the too great zeal of subordinates in carrying out the orders given to them. When the halt was called, many of those who had flocked into the collectives flocked out again and resumed individual production; and collectivisation itself was modified by allowing the member peasants to retain small plots in their own possession and to work on these over and above their labour on the collective, and also by allowing them to keep a small number of livestock in individual ownership — provided they did not go to the length of becoming *kulaks*. But after a brief delay the process of collectivisation was resumed apace, till the greater part of the cultivated areas of the Soviet Union had passed under the control of the collectives, which were given a legal assurance that their new tenure would endure without limit. The land thus became, not the property of the Soviet State, but the possession in perpetuity of the thousands of separate collectives on a basis of Co-operative ownership; and, as there was not nearly enough work on the collectives to provide full-time employment for all their numbers, a great number were able to give a good deal of their time to the small plots and the livestock they were able to keep for themselves, and many more left the land to seek employment in the towns.

This movement of labour from the villages into the towns, and from agriculture into industry, was undoubtedly a good thing for the advance of Soviet production. There was beyond question a big surplus population on the land, for which alternative employment was needed; and industry, which had been beset by quite serious unemployment before the Plan was launched, was soon in need of a big accession to its labour force. In industry, as well as on the farms, there was a very great shortage of skilled workers and of technically trained experts and managers; for the Soviet Union was still only at the beginning of its vast activities in the fields of technical and technological education and training. The incomers from the villages were peasants unused to factory discipline and incapable of supplying the required skills — at any rate until they had been trained. But a prodigious effort was made, both to speed up the rate of training and to expand its scope, and also to ensure that the former peasants and their children got a large share in it and were given as good a chance — or a better — than any other class except the industrial proletariat, of profiting by it. In this respect at any rate the Soviet Union showed itself eager to promote to the utmost the formation of a new directing group mainly of proletarian or peasant origin, and to prefer such recruits to those of suspect class-origins.

This preference, however, went together with a sharp reversal of the tendency of the years before the Plan to seek to narrow differences of remuneration and to preserve at least relative economic equality as a socially desirable end. Stalin, in this too, made himself the foremost exponent of the new doctrine, which he professed to derive from Marx. Marx, in his *Critique of the Gotha Programme*, had laid down that between Capitalism and Communism there would lie a period of transition during which the correct formula for the distribution of incomes would be, not 'From each according to his capacity, to each according to his need', but rather 'From each according to his capacity, to each according to his *service*' — thus prescribing inequality of remuneration as appropriate to the transitional stage. This formula could evidently mean very different things according to the measure used in measuring services. For how were services of quite different sorts to be measured in relation one to another? It was simple enough to conclude from it that piecework, rather than timework, was, wherever practicable, the better way of remuneration. But that did nothing to solve the problem of relative levels of remuneration for persons engaged in quite different trades. Even if it was deemed possible to lay down relativities regarded as appropriate for different kinds of manual workers, how were such wages to be related to the earnings of technicians, supervisors, managers, and administrators? In the early years of the Revolution very strict limits had been imposed on what members of the Communist Party were allowed to earn, no matter how important their jobs might be. Marx had undoubtedly given high praise to the Paris Commune for paying the members of the Government no more than workmen's wages, and thus breaking with the idea of Governments or administrators constituting a superior class of privileged persons standing apart from their subjects. But were such practices consistent with the dire need of the Soviet Union to offer the greatest possible encouragement to higher production ? Was it not rather necessary to offer every possible inducement to high output and energetic service ; and did not this involve increasing rather than reducing the existing inequalities of remuneration, both between man and man and between group and group ? Stalin held that it did ; and, long before the Stakhanovite movement of 1935, piecework had been greatly extended and fast workers paid highly for superintending their slower colleagues. Indeed, the new element introduced in Stakhanovism was not piecework on terms highly favourable to the rapid worker so much as the provision for the Stakhanovite of special assistance designed to enable him to concentrate all his effort on his essential task, and thus to achieve productive feats that would have been utterly impossible without such help. Moreover, side by side with the deliberate widening of wage differences went a reversal of the narrow limits hitherto imposed on the earnings of the holders of what were regarded as superior jobs, until it came to be a moot point whether the distribution of earned incomes was any less unequal in the Soviet Union than in the most advanced capitalist countries. There remained of course the fact that in the Soviet Union no one could own the means of production or make a fortune by employing hired labour ; but as far as earned incomes went there came at any rate to be no great difference in distribution between the Soviet Union and Great Britain, or even the United States.

This came about, not so much because Stalin had a personal preference for high inequality, as because Soviet policy, under his influence, came to be directed almost exclusively to promoting the highest possible production. The task of the Soviet Union, as he envisaged it, was first to catch up the leading capitalist countries in aggregate production of advanced industrial goods, such as coal, steel, oil, and electricity — and, perhaps above all, chemicals — and thereafter to overtake and surpass them in production per head. When the Five-Year Plan was first launched, the promise was held forth, not only of a great increase in total production — at any rate in the heavy industries — which was actually achieved, but also of a fall in prices following on a reduction in working costs due to higher productivity — which was by no means achieved in the early stages. The reason why it was not achieved was no doubt in part that so much new labour, unused to factory work, and so much untrained supervision and management had to be employed, and also in part that the new industrial plants took considerably longer than had been expected to get finished and begin to produce, and that often when one was ready another, on which it depended for materials or components, was not, and had to be waited for. This, of course, applies mainly to the first Five-Year Plan rather than to its successors ; for by the time these were fairly launched, many of the growing pains were over and it had become possible to plan with a nearer approach to realistic accuracy. In the early stages, however, the teething troubles were severe ; and the increase in total production was achieved only by a very large addition to the numbers of the industrial labour force. The expected fall in costs was also prevented by two other factors, closely inter-connected — a sharp rise in the wages bill, due partly to increasing inequality and partly to higher prices, and a very rapid rise in currency circulation. The latter had, of course, to increase if a larger amount was to be paid out in wages ; but it grew faster than it would have done on this account alone, as the attainment of the highest possible output, almost regardless of its cost, came to be accepted as the supreme objective.

We have seen that the Five-Year Plan, in its preliminary drafts, made before the great change in policy, was for the most part a very mild affair, projecting only a quite modest increase in industrial production. Each revision of it, however, raised the targets, which were raised even further when it was proposed to complete the Plan in four instead of five years. These first targets were not, for the most part, reached, even in the heavy industries, on which the Plan was chiefly concentrated ; and in the lighter, consumers' industries they were not even approached. For, whereas the Plan was launched under what seemed to be highly favourable conditions, both at home and abroad, it had in fact to encounter a variety of highly adverse forces which might well have brought it to total shipwreck. The first of these was the world depression, which fell with the greatest force on the world prices of foodstuffs and of many key raw materials. This fall sharply reversed the Soviet Union's terms of trade as an exporter mainly of raw products and a would-be importer of capital goods. Intended imports had to be cut down to fit the reduced supplies of foreign exchange; and industrial development had to be shifted over to a greater use of materials produced at home. This may have been a blessing in the long run; for it forced the Soviet Union to intensify its search for and supply of home-produced materials, of which it had great unexploited resources. Nevertheless, in the short run it was an important delaying factor. Secondly, the expanded Plan had been based on optimistic assumptions about agricultural production. No one had anticipated the mass-slaughter of livestock, or the consequent famine of milk and meat. But over and above this came the disastrous harvest failure of 1931-2, bringing famine to the Ukraine and to other affected areas and severe shortage to the whole country. It is true that this dire calamity had been preceded by two years of fairly good harvests; but these had been used up, and, when the blow occurred, there was no accumulation of stocks to meet it. In the affected areas very many thousands — perhaps even millions — died of starvation. Nor could this be without its effect on the towns, and on industry; for the limits to industrialisation were set, in the last resort, by the supply of agricultural products. It is not surprising that great efforts were made to keep knowledge of the disaster from the people and from the rest of the world, or that its very occurrence was vehemently denied, on the plea that what had happened was not a famine due to natural causes, but mainly a widespread scarcity brought about by the deliberate opposition of *kulaks* and other opponents of collectivisation, who had either done their best to prevent the sowing of the fields or had left the grain to rot untended in them. It was hardly denied that, where this was supposed to have happened, the areas thought to be guilty of sabotage were left to suffer for it without much effort to relieve their hardships, even when these involved large numbers of deaths from sheer starvation. The Webbs, for example, in their massive work on *Soviet Communism*, resorted to this explanation, denying that there had been a famine in any ordinary sense of the word, and asserting that mass resistance to collectivisation had been the main cause of the acute scarcity in the Ukraine and in other regions. They showed remarkably little sympathy for the sufferers, and accused the nationalist leaders, such as the Ukrainian, Mazepa, from his exile in Paris, as having done their utmost to bring the 'famine' about from political motives. It may well be true enough that the shortage was largely, or even mainly, due to *kulak* and other peasant resistance to enforced collectivisation; but even that hardly justifies the callousness, as most of the resistance had been provoked by the enforcement of a process that was supposed to be in its essence voluntary.

Nevertheless, the Plan weathered the storm, and the Soviet Union achieved a massive increase of production in the heavy industries, partly at the cost of abandoning its targets for the lighter industries and postponing most of its projects for the improvement of the heavily overburdened railways and for the adequate housing of the great bodies of new town-dwellers. The Five-Year Plan had been designed to make possible an improvement in living standards, albeit at a slower rate than the heavy industries were to expand. But in fact the supply of many consumers' goods actually fell off, despite the greatly increased numbers of urban consumers, and it is doubtful whether, for the main body of the people, standards of consumption rose at all. As an expedient for dealing with the crisis, there was developed an elaborate structure of differential prices to different groups of consumers, giving preference to the manual workers, who were enabled to buy a minimum quantity of essential goods at specially low prices, while other consuming groups had either lower allocations or were forced to buy at much higher prices. These differentiations in the price structure made it impossible to say by how much the cost of living rose during the first Five-Year Plan; but there is no denying that, in the towns as well as in the country, very many consumers went exceedingly short. In the matter of food, however, a great effort was made to open industrial canteens and refreshment rooms at which the workers could buy tolerably nutritious meals at fairly low prices; and this considerably relieved the pressure on the industrial proletariat, though it did nothing to relieve the villagers and but little for the rest of the non-industrial population.

It is astonishing, as one looks back after the event, to consider how confident most economists were in those days that the Five-Year Plan would fail, and even that the entire structure of the Soviet Union was bound to collapse almost at once. I vividly remember reading a book by Professor von Mises in which he declared outright that no such structure could possibly exist — much less maintain itself durably — because of its utter flouting of all rational economic principles and laws. By 'rational' Professor von Mises of course meant obedient to the laws of the market — which I at any rate do not regard as 'rational' at all. But the point is that Professor von Mises did so regard them and could not believe in the viability of any structure built up in defiance of them — and that his opinion was widely shared. That there were some laws of the market from which the Soviet Union could not escape its own leaders had good reason for knowing. It could not, for example, import more than it could pay for with its exports, unless it could persuade foreigners to lend it the money — and its attempts to tempt foreigners to do so by granting foreign concessions had been quite markedly unsuccessful. The less it believed in the laws of market economy, the more strictly it had to observe them in its foreign dealings. Did it not follow that it would be forced to observe them in its domestic affairs also, by cutting down its investment to what it could induce its consumers to forgo in the way of immediate consumption, and thus abandoning its hopes of speedy industrial development? In a sense, this was so; but what most economists failed to see was that there remained open to it the alternative of fixing a high investment target, and thus compelling its citizens to restrict their consumption to what was left after this target had been reached. Those who drew up the Five-Year Plan in the form which it finally took did act in this spirit. They allocated an exceedingly high proportion of the productive resources to development projects which could yield only a deferred return in goods, and condemned their citizens to live as best they could on such consumers' goods as could be supplied consistently with their investment programme. How good, or how bad, the consequent standards of living would be would depend on the success of the effort to raise production to the highest possible level not in the sections to which the greatest means of capital investment were to be diverted, but rather in those other sections which would have to be starved of capital if the heavy industries were to be adequately supplied with it. Above all, there must be enough food to keep the producers alive and in good health ; yet little capital could be spared for agriculture, despite its key position in the struggle for success. The hope of increased agricultural production rested on the success of collectivisation ; but collectivisation itself required a large investment in farm machinery — especially tractors — without which large-scale farming could not be effectively carried on. Enough tractors there could not be for some time to come ; and the utmost effort must be made to ensure that what were available went as far as possible, by being concentrated in Machine Tractor Stations able to utilise them to the fullest extent.

The Bolsheviks were faced in fact with a great choice, between trying to induce the peasants to produce more by traditional inducements — which would have made a high rate of investment in industry impossible and have greatly strengthened the better-to-do villagers — and grouping the villagers, or the majority of them, into Co-operative Societies to work in common, with the aid of as much mechanisation as could be applied, in the hope that the higher productivity of collective work would raise total output and at the same time release redundant farm labour for industrial employment. The second of these policies was chosen, with the results we have already observed. Well before the famine, the number of collective farm households, which had reached about 14 million, had been reduced to about 6 million after Stalin's pronouncement on 'Dizziness from Success', but had speedily begun to grow again, and was back at 14 million, or 80 per cent of all peasant households, by the beginning of 1933, when there were over 200,000 collectives covering over two-thirds of the total grain area. To these must be added the much larger, but also much less numerous State Farms, which by 1933 employed a million workers and covered one-tenth of the grain area. Moreover, these latter were in possession of more than half the total number of tractors. The State Farms included about 500 gigantic 'Grain Factories', as they were called, and also a much larger number of smaller concerns producing specialised crops, such as tea, tobacco, or sugar beet, or engaged in rearing live-stock. Economically, they were none too efficient, and much criticism was directed against their bad management; but they did greatly reinforce the State's holdings of grain at a critical period, though it had come by 1932 to be argued that they had been established on much too grandiose a scale for effective management, and with all too little regard to the effects of using land for the continuous production of a single crop, such as wheat: so that many of them were before long divided up into more manageable units and turned over to mixed farming or at any rate to diversification of crops by means of rotation.

The combined effect of the State Farms and the collectives was, at all events, to increase the amount of grain available for the market, and thus to make possible the feeding of a rapidly increasing industrial population. When the years of crop failure were over, the Soviet Union emerged definitely into a situation in which both a rapidly increasing industrial prole-tariat and the means of supplying it with basic foods — other than milk and meat — had become assured. But, partly because of the modifications made in the first Five-Year Plan in face of the impressive difficulties, the consumers did much less well in other respects. Production had been kept up to the mark in the heavy industries only at the cost of cutting down still further the already scanty allocations of capital for the development of the consumer trades, especially textiles; and during the critical years the shortage of clothing was really acute, though the supply of boots was distinctly better. It is, however, possible to carry on without acute hardship with very few new clothes — though not without boots, especially if the quality is poor and the wear hard. At all events, whether standards of living in general rose or fell during the years of the first Plan, the people came through them without disaster — except of course the *kulaks* and the famine victims, with whose troubles there were few to sympathise — and with a greatly enhanced belief in themselves and in the high merits of the structure they were helping to build. The practicability of building Socialism in one country, without help from any of the advanced capitalist countries, seemed to have been plainly demonstrated. It was not built yet; but it seemed well on the way. No World Revolution — no spread of the Russian

Revolution to the West — seemed any longer to be a necessary condition of success. Such events would of course still be welcome if they occurred; but all was not lost even if they never did occur. At one time it had been a common article of faith among the Bolsheviks that the Revolution could not lastingly succeed in backward Russia unless one or more of the great advanced countries came to its aid, and 'Socialism in one country' had been dismissed as an impracticable dream. But by the time the first Five-Year Plan ended in 1932 this doctrine had gone quite out of fashion. It was maintained only by 'Trotskyists', who regarded the new set-up as inherently nationalistic and continued to base their hopes of Socialism on higher technological foundations than were as yet within the range of Soviet possibility.

The first Five-Year Plan was not, indeed, completely fulfilled during the $4\frac{1}{2}$ years for which it was allowed to run. In coal, in steel, and in pig iron production was seriously short of the very high targets that had been set. Coal output was nearly 65 million tons as against a target of 75 million; steel was under 6 million as against 10, and pig iron 6·2 as against 10. But the capital goods industries as a whole increased their production two-and-a-half times, slightly more than the original target fixed for them; and, among them, machinery showed a fourfold increase — considerably more than the original Plan, and oil also more than reached the planned output. Electricity, though it fell short of the planned increase, raised its output more than two and a half times.

The lagging behind of coal, steel, and pig iron was due chiefly to delays in the construction of new plants, which were not ready to begin production at the due dates. The consumers' goods industries, except boots and shoes, suffered much more from this and other handicaps, as they had their allocations of capital and of raw materials reduced in face of the difficulties which the Plan met with both at home and abroad. But the boot and shoe industry recorded a threefold increase, in part no doubt at the expense of small-scale craft production. The total factory output of consumers' goods was said to have advanced by 87 per cent, with textiles as the main laggards, chiefly because of shortages of both cotton and wool.

On the whole, then, even if the Five-Year Plan was not

fulfilled, despite all the obstacles, in four and a half years, a most impressive demonstration had been given of Soviet productive power. It is true that these results had been achieved only by an increase in the labour force far larger than had been contemplated under the Plan. The total number of wage- and salary-earners had in fact almost doubled, whereas the Plan had contemplated only a total increase of 40 per cent, including a rise of no more than one-third in industry and 58 per cent in industry and construction combined. Actually, in construction the labour force had increased fourfold — a clear indication of the immensely high concentration on factory-building and similar projects. Thus, low productivity continued, despite the very high aggregate production; and with wages rising sharply on account of the scarcity of workers in the expanding areas, unit costs of production were in most cases still very high. Indeed, this may have caused some considerable exaggeration in the estimates of the actual increases in output, which were supposed to be measured in 1926–7 prices, except in the case of new products, which were largely valued at their actual cost when they were first put on the market — when their cost was likely to be high.

Yet, even if the announced figures of the Plan's fulfilment substantially exaggerated its achievement in certain fields, its results remain impressive, especially in relation to what was happening in the rest of the world. For by 1932 the Soviet Union had become 'the country without unemployment', whereas all the others were in various degrees of depression — from the extremes of the United States and Germany to the only relatively mild slump in France and Great Britain. Admittedly, Soviet productivity was still low, by Western standards; but the Soviet Union was demonstrating the entire falsity of what had been so freely predicted of a Socialist economy — its inability to save — and was actually putting an unprecedentedly high proportion of its national income into capital goods which could yield only a deferred return in enjoyable goods and services. Those who had unwillingly to admit this, of course, explained that it was due to sheer coercion of the people by the party dictators, and predicted speedy rebellion by the discontented sufferers. Then, when rebellion failed to follow, they explained that the tyranny was too strong for it, and continued to denounce the Soviet Union as a victim of mass repression by a narrow bureaucratic clique. There was, no doubt, something in all this. There was widespread discontent among the peasants — and not only among *kulaks* or famine victims — and there was some industrial discontent; but it seems certain that among the industrial workers the predominant feeling was one of pride in the vast achievements of the régime and in the prodigious construction that was being set on foot, and that this pride so acted as to make the shortages of consumers' goods easier to bear and to prevent the growth of sentiment hostile to mass investment, or even to its concentration on the heavy industries to the detriment of other things — such as housing. The mood of these years showed very clearly that man does not live by consumers' goods alone; and the young men and women who all over the country were preaching high output and collectivisation were certainly for the most part moved by a genuine idealism, even if they were also the spokesmen of a particularly hard-headed and ruthless party bureaucracy, and of its leader, Stalin.

Nor does it appear that most workers in either town or country were conscious of being tyrannised over. In many of the collective farms many of the participants were conscious rather of an enlargement of power, especially when concessions had been made of individual plots and livestock ownership and of time off from the collectives to work for themselves. There were no doubt also many who hated the collectives and bemoaned the loss of their individual holdings; but except for the *kulaks* there was opened up for many of these the prospect of relatively well-paid employment in the growing industries or in constructional work: so that their opposition to collectivisation was neutralised by their own change of occupation. Meanwhile, for the urban workers, old and new, there were opened up prospects of individual betterment through the increasing differentiation of earnings and the greater prospects of promotion; and industrial work carried increasing prestige, as well as socially recognised privileges that were well worth enjoying — dinner tickets for cheap meals in industrial canteens and free or subsidised holidays. It was simply not the case that the Soviet working class was a slave proletariat seething with suppressed revolt. On the contrary, a large part of it was

clearly inspired by deep pride in what it was doing, and fully prepared to acquiesce in the limitations on its freedom of speech
and action that the leaders deemed to be necessary to protect
it against 'counter-revolution'. To say this is not to justify
the suppression, much less the cruelty which accompanied it;
but it does mean that, in general, neither was so widely objected
to as to engender powerful forces of revolt. In the countryside, when the famine was over, the majority of the peasants
settled down to a modified collectivisation, which allowed
steadily increasing scope for individual effort; and in the towns
employment openings were good enough to satisfy most of
the producers, leaving only reactionary groups of depressed
former bourgeois and petty bourgeois with major grounds for
grumbling.

Thus the Soviet Union passed from the first into the second
Five-Year Plan mainly in a mood of self-congratulation on the
successes already achieved, and of determination to consolidate
what had been won and to carry it further as fast as possible.
The targets for this second Plan, for the years 1933–7, were on
the whole set rather lower than those for the first Plan had
been, with projected total investment falling year by year from
24 per cent to 19½ per cent of national income, and with higher
relative allocations of capital for the consumer industries. The
broad emphasis on capital goods was retained, but more of
these goods were to be instruments for the making of consumers'
goods — spindles and power-looms, boot-making machines,
food-processing machines, and so on — and machines for
making machines or for processing basic materials. The
annual rate of increase finally laid down in 1934 was, for all
industry 16½ per cent, for capital goods 14½ per cent, and for
consumer goods 18½ per cent. Actually, in the first year of the
second Plan, the targets were not nearly reached, the overall
increase in output being only 6 per cent. But much higher
rates of increase followed in 1934 and 1935, and even in 1933
productivity increased faster than wages, so that costs began
to fall. Productivity, indeed, became much more important
as the new plants got, often belatedly, to work. According to
the Plan, four-fifths of total industrial output was to come, by
1937, from new works constructed or from older works reconstructed under either the first or the second Plan. The second

Plan was to leave the Soviet Union in a position to dispense with most forms of imported machinery and able to manufacture its own machines over the widest possible range, and also relying mainly on its own raw materials, in which a number of new fields were to be opened up. Natural rubber, which needed to be imported, was to be replaced by synthetic rubber; and the widened range of the Soviet chemical industry was to emancipate the Soviet Union from dependence on imported fertilisers.

What was allowed still to lag badly behind in the second Plan was transport — especially railways and roads. These, indeed, were becoming more and more bottlenecks, seriously limiting the possibilities of industrial growth, especially as the construction of new, remote industrial centres was on the whole lengthening the distances over which materials, foodstuffs, and finished goods alike had to be hauled by rail to reach their destinations. For canal development, large projects had already been undertaken, largely with enforced labour working under very bad conditions; but railway and road construction were given only low priorities in the first and second Plans and were allowed to fall more and more behind the tasks imposed on them. Even in 1939 the utilisation of each mile of railway track was estimated to be more than twice as high, in terms of tonnage carried, in the Soviet Union as in the U.S.A. Nevertheless, the goods were somehow transported, though not without serious delays which reduced factory output and led to local shortages even when there were in the aggregate supplies enough to go round.

When the second Plan was launched on its course, the world depression had reached its nadir and Hitler was on the eve of taking over power in Germany and destroying the German working-class movement. But the Plan was of course worked out before the final overthrow of the Weimar Republic and, apparently, without any attempt to estimate the effects of such an event. For the Soviet leaders, as we saw, completely misunderstood the nature of German Fascism and made an altogether false estimate of the effects of its rise to power. Not until 1934 were they ready to estimate the Fascist danger at all at its proper rate. But, when they did realise what it involved, they changed course rapidly, both in their political attitude and in readjusting their economic Plan. Politically, they changed first by joining the League of Nations in 1934, and by summoning the Communist Parties in all countries to a common crusade to entice the parties of the left into People's Fronts against Fascism; and economically they reacted by amending their Plan to provide for higher expenditure on armaments and on the expansion of industries that could be swiftly diverted to the making of munitions of war.

Thus there was a considerable diversion of expenditure to armaments during the second Plan, which ran till 1937. When the Soviet Union came to draw up a third Plan, to begin in 1938, the need for such diversion had become still more insistent. Budget expenditure on defence doubled in 1938; and defence needs made it necessary to maintain a high degree of concentration on the development of the heavy industries, and especially on building up the new centres of production in the Urals and in Asia, beyond the range of German bombing planes. This migration of industry, which was of course carried immensely further in and after 1941, made it the more indispensable to take the question of railway transport seriously in hand by building new lines, doubling and relaying old ones, and redesigning facilities at terminals and exchange points. These processes had begun under the second Plan, but had been allowed to lag behind. Indeed, the problem of railway development was insoluble until the shortage of steel had been overcome; for railway construction is a greedy consumer of steel, and only towards the end of the second Plan was there enough steel to enable it to be seriously tackled. In view of the increasing demands of defence and transport, the consumers' goods industries had again to take a secondary place, though it was now easier to supply them with machinery made in the new factories. Agriculture too had to take a back seat in face of more urgent claims; but this seemed the less serious because the basic food supply, except meat and milk, had already been assured and the number of tractors had become adequate for the needs of both State and collective farms. In 1937 the worst of the growing pains of the new economic structure seemed to be over.

This, however, was by no means the case, quite apart from the modifications called for by the defence programme.

For the purges of 1937 and 1938 fell heavily on the ranks of the industrial managers and caused during these years serious shortcomings in the fulfilment of the Plan. Not until 1940 were the consequences of the purges effectively overcome, and hardly had they been so when Soviet industry was plunged into the disaster of war and mass evacuation from the Western areas had to be hastily undertaken. But I do not propose to carry the record of Soviet developments into this period. It stops short, for my purpose, with the recovery of 1940–41 from the setbacks of 1938–9, which arose mainly out of dislocation resulting from the purges and from the improvisation of new managerial *cadres*.

It is indeed almost incredible that the Soviet Union should have been able to resist and to carry on as it did in 1941 so soon after the great dislocation of the purges. No one can say exactly how many of the holders of key positions in the Soviet Union, or how many of their subordinates, were affected by them ; but it has been suggested that well over half, and perhaps two-thirds, of the total number of such persons were killed, exiled, or at least driven from their posts, so that every branch of affairs — civil as well as military — had to be provided with new leaders. Of the Soviet diplomatic corps — ambassadors, ministers, and counsellors of embassy or legation — two-thirds were liquidated, in that they were either executed, or simply disappeared. The army leadership was dealt with no less severely. Out of eight high-ranking officers who were called in as extra judges in the trial of Tukhachevsky in June 1937, only one, Marshal Budenny, survived the later purges. One of the other seven died in his bed : six were liquidated. The Central Committee of the Communist Party elected in 1934 had 71 members. At the beginning of 1939 only 21 remained active. 3 died naturally, one (Sergei Kirov) was assassinated, one committed suicide, nine were announced as shot, the other 36 disappeared. In the principal cities more than half the members of the Communist Party were expelled. In 1934 the Party had over 2 million full members and 1,200,000 candidate members. At the end of 1937 members and candidates together numbered only 1½ million. In the summer of 1938, after half a million new members and candidates had been admitted, the total was still under 2 million.

Purges on such a scale were bound to cause extreme dislocation ; for even among those who escaped them, the effect was bound to be very great, when no man could trust his neighbour, and the wildest denunciations were everywhere being made. Directly, the main responsibility rested on the Commissariat of the Interior (N.K.V.D.), in which the Ogpu had been incorporated, first under Yagoda and then under Yezhov, who remained at its head until December 1938, but had been shorn of much of his power in August, when Beria was made Vice-Commissar under him. It was indeed in August 1938 that the engines were at length reversed ; and thereafter the purging died away, and the task of rebuilding the shattered fabric of Soviet society could be taken seriously in hand.

It is not easy to be sure, even now, how much substance there was behind this vast destruction of those who had been the leaders both in the great Revolution of 1917 and during the twenty years succeeding it. At one end of the affair, I think there can be little doubt that the alleged conspiracy of Tukhachevsky and the Generals was real, and that preparations had been made for a military *coup*. At the other extreme, I find it quite impossible to believe that Trotsky was really the leader and inspirer of a wrecking movement inside the Soviet Union, or was in any way acting in collusion with the Nazis. Trotsky was, no doubt, fully capable of conspiring with opposition elements inside the Soviet Union to overthrow Stalin, but hardly of promoting or identifying himself with the senseless acts of sabotage charged against the alleged conspirators inside the Soviet Union, and he was certainly quite incapable of lending himself to the plottings of the Nazis, to whom he was at least as bitterly hostile as he was to Stalin and his entourage. Between these two sets of allegations — against Tukhachevsky and against Trotsky — lies a vast middle field about which it is much harder to feel assured. Was there in truth a civil as well as a military conspiracy ? Were Zinoviev and Kamenev, were Bukharin and Radek, were Sokolnikov and the rest of the liquidated opposition, really traitors, working in collusion with the Nazis, or simply honest critics and opponents of Stalin's policies, driven underground and forced into conspiratorial activities by the suppression of the right to criticise openly, but guiltless of all collaboration with the external enemies of the Soviet Union? That most of them were in fact conspirators, prepared to go to considerable lengths in opposition to Stalin, seems undeniable: that they were agents, or even conscious abetters, of the Nazis not a tittle of reliable evidence seems ever to have been produced. To say this is not to deny, or even to doubt, that the Nazis had in Russia many paid agents who were doing their best to dislocate the Soviet economy and to sow internal dissensions wherever they could; and it has to be admitted that some of the convicted men may have become unconscious victims of the Nazi agents and have worked with them without knowing them for what they were.

What, then, of the confessions made during the trials? Almost no one, I think, now believes that these were extracted by the use of mysterious drugs, or even of torture in the extreme sense. Fears on account of their friends and families may have played a part in procuring these extraordinary demonstrations of self-abasement; but it seems unlikely that even this was a major factor. The confessions must, I think, be taken as largely genuine, in the sense that those who made them had been induced to believe in their own guilt, even of things they had not in fact done, or intended to do. If there did exist in fact both a military conspiracy — as I think there did — and a conspiracy of civilians in which Nazi agents may have taken part as the abetters and instigators of the domestic conspirators, mainly without the latter's knowledge, it becomes intelligible that conspirators wholly guiltless of conscious collusion with the Nazis should have been led much further than they intended to go, and should be struck with remorse when they found how far they had been led and have sought to save their souls by abject confession. This could not have happened in a country in which even a modified freedom of speech and criticism had existed; but in the Soviet Union of the 'thirties no such freedom existed, nor was there any tradition of it from the past. The confessions remain, even so, extraordinary; but it is unnecessary to endeavour to explain them by involving explanations in terms of a peculiar 'Russian soul', save in the sense in which the word 'soul' is no more than a reference to the peculiar tradition and prevailing atmosphere of Russian politics.

Few are likely now to doubt that a large number of the victims of the great purge of 1936–8 were absolutely innocent of the charges made against them and were convicted at most of the sin of 'guilt by association' or even on no ground at all save that someone saw fit to denounce them. But it would be unsafe to conclude that the entire purge was no more than a frame-up, with no reality behind it. There was at the least a very large body of domestic discontent, which Trotsky was doing his best to organise and stimulate from abroad ; and this mass of discontent was probably big enough to constitute a real danger to the régime. The purge did a great deal to affect adversely the opinion about Russia in the West, to encourage a belief that the régime might shortly collapse, and to cause a gross underestimation of the strength and reliability of the Red Army. This effect on opinion abroad, which Stalin seems either not to have anticipated or not to have cared about, had undoubtedly a great influence on British and French attitudes to coming to terms with the Russians for concerted resistance to the Nazis, and helped to account for the complete ignoring of the Russians in the discussions over Czechoslovakia in 1938. But, as against this, Stalin undoubtedly succeeded in his essential object — the entire elimination of opposition to him or to his régime inside the Soviet Union, and the consolidation of his own dictatorial rule. The opposition inside the Soviet Union was not merely crushed : it was eliminated in such a way as to cut the Trotskyists and other critics in exile off from all contact with forces inside the country. Nor was the population of the Soviet Union reduced by it to a state of reluctant subservience which paralysed its activity. On the contrary, as the event showed, when the immediate dislocations had been overcome, Stalin was left as the unquestioned father-figure of a people strung up to a most intense effort of collective defence and organisation : so that the fund of enthusiastic service at Stalin's disposal after 1941 was probably greater than in any other country. This does not justify the purge — much less the excesses committed under it, especially in the later stages ; but it does mean that, if nothing matters except power, and ideals are of no account, the purge must be accounted a success, though, even so, a success produced at an exceedingly high price.

Meanwhile, the second Five-Year Plan was running its course. Revised before its actual commencement in 1934 to give greater weight to the claims of defence, both by speeding up development of the heavy industries and by placing as many as possible of the new plants well out of reach of German bombers, the Plan inevitably suffered some dislocation from the removal of a high proportion of its executants in the course of the purge, but nevertheless was in the main successful in its objectives. It was fortunate for the Russians that tractor factories, which were needed in large numbers for the success of collectivised agriculture, were also capable of being turned over rapidly in case of need to producing tanks and other munitions of war, and that chemical factories for the production of fertilisers could be for the most part similarly converted to war uses. It was also possible to construct a military system of defence in depth in close connection with agricultural settlement. Thus, the damage done to production for consumer use was kept down to a minimum.

The Second Five-Year Plan, which ran from 1933 to 1937, but was considerably modified in its course by the growing attention paid to defence, did not in all its main respects reach the assigned targets, though in certain fields these were notably exceeded. The output of coal more than doubled between 1932 and 1937, but the 1937 output was only 128 million tons out of a planned output of 152 million. Pig iron output also doubled without quite reaching the planned total. Steel output, on the other hand, rising from 6 million tons in 1932 to 17·6 million in 1937, exceeded its target, while the machine-making industry increased its production threefold, as against a planned doubling. Oil, with an output of only $30\frac{1}{2}$ million tons as against a planned output of nearly 47 million, was the most laggard among the basic industries; but it was officially reckoned that these industries, taken as a group, had reached their planned output, whereas the consumers' industries as a group had failed to reach their target. The output of cotton goods had been planned to double, but had risen by only 42 per cent; and that of woollen goods, also planned to double, rose by no more than 22 per cent. For light industry as a whole output doubled between 1932 and 1937, whereas it had been planned to increase $2\frac{1}{2}$ times. During the second Plan there was a notable development of new industries, above all of heavy chemicals, the extraction of non-ferrous metals, and the making of aeroplanes, motor-cars, and farm tractors and other machines. The new collective farms were given adequate supplies of machinery: the number of tractors doubled, and the motor-car 'park' increased eight times. Of total industrial output, by 1937 four-fifths came from plants newly built or radically reconstructed since 1928.

Let us now ask what the purging meant in terms of Socialist, or of Communist, thought. First, it meant the discarding in effect of the conception of a single Revolution of the world proletariat, of which the Revolution in Russia was merely a part. For the Trotskyists, this conception was vital, because according to them Socialism could be built only on a foundation of the highest productive techniques attained under capitalism, and as an advance upon them, bringing plenty with it. Backward Russia seemed to them to be clearly incapable of leading the way into Socialism, even if it did its very utmost to industrialise itself rapidly; for it could not hope for a long time, if at all, to catch up with the productivity of the most advanced capitalist countries, so as to enjoy the plenty which alone could bring the scramble of contending classes to an end. According to Trotsky, the entire idea of 'Socialism in a single country' was untenable; and it was so most of all if the country in question lagged behind in the employment of modern techniques. But then, for Trotsky, Socialism meant popular welfare as well as power, whereas for Stalin it meant only power, or at most only power exercised in the name of the proletariat; and he was to show that power, without welfare or equality, could be achieved even by a backward country possessed of great natural resources and so organised as to use up unprecedently large proportions of its productive capacity in increasing its investment, even at the expense of a fall in its standards of living. It did not matter to Stalin if the whole people stayed poor, so long as the Soviet Union became great in world affairs — first, able to defend itself against its enemies, and thereafter to impose more and more of its will on others. He did not renounce his hopes of world revolution: that, he felt sure, would come in due time with the collapse of capitalism, which he regarded as certain in the long run. He gave up, however, his desire to foment World Revolution immediately, as a means of strengthening the Revolution already accomplished in Russia. Such reinforcement he believed he could do without, if he could make Russia strong enough to avert eclipse in war; and in the meantime he proposed to make consolidation inside the Soviet Union the supreme criterion of policy. It did not matter to him if this involved a widening, instead of a narrowing, of economic differences, or the growth of a new ruling caste in many respects resembling a new class, provided he could be sure that this new ruling caste did not rise up against him. It was also nothing to him if the main body of the people had to go desperately short of the means of satisfactory living, provided that their hardships did not find an outlet in movements of discontent leading to possible revolt. As he was well aware that the people, given freedom to express its preferences, would opt for better living conditions as against a high rate of capital accumulation, it was necessary for him to eliminate every focus for opposition, and to liquidate all possible critics of his policy. But he did not shrink back from this, whatever it involved. Moreover, like most men who think in terms of power, he also loved power and to accumulate it in his own hands, and came more and more under the obsession of personal power as an objective.

This does not mean that Stalin was utterly wrong, and Trotsky right, in the great controversy between them both before and after Stalin had driven Trotsky from the leadership. For one thing, Trotsky too was a most dangerous thinker, as obsessed with his view of World Revolution as was Stalin with his determination to build up a vastly powerful Soviet Union subject to his personal rule. The Trotskyists, where they appeared as organised minority groups, were usually most intractable doctrinaires, devotees of revolution quite irrespective of its chances of success and insisting rigidly on its proletarian basis no matter how little the proletariat showed itself in a revolutionary mood. It may be that there are always, in all situations, small groups of this sort — natural rebels and dogmatic idealists who take no account of men in determining their objectives, and refuse to compromise their ideals by adjusting their action to the circumstances; and it may be that such persons gravitated naturally into the Trotskyist camp.

258

That does not alter the fact that the Trotskyist gospel was, or became, one of world proletarian Revolution to be pursued under all conditions, and involving a denunciation of Stalin in particular as having 'betrayed the Revolution' by diverting it from its original pursuit of ideological, Socialist ends into a mere quest of power, regardless of the purposes for which the power was to be employed. But I think those who took this view of Stalin in the 1930s to some extent misunderstood him; for Stalin was not in fact then pursuing power solely for its own sake. He did genuinely believe it to be important that the Soviet Union should establish itself as a country to be reckoned with in world affairs and that it mattered that in the Soviet Union society rested on a basis of collective ownership from which private profit-making had been eliminated as a source of unearned income: so that differences of income and status, large or small, rested on a foundation of personal service and not of exploitation in a capitalist sense. It may seem to many of us not to matter greatly whether large incomes and superiority of status depend on one thing rather than another, if they actually exist; but to Stalin I think the difference did genuinely matter. As against this, personal freedom was to Stalin a matter of no account; for in considering human values his attitude was that of regarding the class, and not the individual, as the repository of rights, and even in relation to the class he thought rather in terms of the class as a whole than of the individuals who composed it, and believed its interests to require formulation and enforcement by a body of leaders rather than by all its members. He was a centralist, and not a democrat; but his centralism was a real article of faith, and not a mere corollary of his quest for power as such. This may have ceased to be so when he had enjoyed for some time the sweetness of effectively exercising absolute power on behalf of the whole society; but, whatever he became in his latter years, I believe he was in the 1930s, according to his lights, an ardent believer in the mission of Russia and of the peoples whom he had sought to unify under the new Constitution of 1936. That Constitution did at any rate play a notable part in unifying the numerous nationalistic and linguistic and cultural groups of the Soviet Union round the idea of a single Greater Russian State, in which they were all equals despite racial and cultural differences and able to enjoy their several cultures on terms compatible with that unity. The unity was also expressed in the unitary structure of the Communist Party, which obeyed a common doctrine and was not split up into separate Parties for the various constituent Republics or for the national and cultural groups making up the Soviet population as a whole. But, in matters outside politics, the Party stood for a diversity within the unity; and it can hardly be denied that in doing this it achieved a remarkable measure of success.

It is not, however, irrelevant that Stalin, with all his qualities as leader and administrator, was also an exceedingly nasty man — sly, vindictive, and utterly unscrupulous about means, cruel, perhaps even sadistic, and certainly more and more intolerant of anyone who he thought might possibly offer any challenge to his authority. Consequently, the Socialism he envisaged himself as bringing to birth was shorn of most of the qualities which have been highly valued by most of the apostles of Socialism, who have been for the most part kindly men, inspired by a strong passion for social equality and for freedom, and against suffering and injustice. Stalin cared nothing for equality or freedom, and was quite unmoved by suffering or by hatred of injustice, unless it were class-injustice in a form familiar to him. Socialism for him involved the elimination of classes in the form in which he could recognise their existence; but he neither cared how much the displaced 'enemies of the people' were made to suffer nor regarded as injustice any extreme differences of status or income that could help the new society to increase its collective power. The judgment upon him of posterity is bound, I think, to be a mixture of praise and blame. Without his leadership, it is doubtful whether the Soviet Union would have overcome the difficulties confronting its continued existence; but the new Russia he had so large a part in making emerged from his hands severely damaged, in a human sense, by his methods of action and incapable of making the best use of the great power he had helped it to win. Whether Stalin was, or was not, a great, or even a good, military leader I am not equipped to judge; but I think this verdict stands broadly valid irrespective of that particular question. He was, I think, beyond question a great man; but greatness and goodness are not necessarily found together either in private or in public life.

In comparison with Stalin, Trotsky is a humanly attractive figure; and I think he too has to be called great. He was certainly a great organiser, as well as a superb orator; but his defects lie hardly less on the surface than his qualities. No man could well have made more mistakes than he did in his long struggle against Stalin; and perhaps the greatest single mistake of his life was his failure, even if ill, to appear at Lenin's funeral, to which he could certainly have got in time had he been minded to make the effort. On this occasion, as on others, he seems to have allowed his conduct to be ruled by his mood of the moment, and to have assumed that he could afford, because of his personality, to dispense with concessions. In the ensuing struggle for power, he undoubtedly allowed Stalin to make rings round him by a refusal to meet his opponent on the battle-ground of backstairs intrigue, and was too proud, till it was too late, to make any effort to build up a personal following. He was imperious and headstrong in action, and far too apt to despise collaborators to whom he felt himself intellectually superior. He could indeed inspire deep devotion; but he was never good at working with other men on equal terms. Devoted to his conception of Socialism as a stage in social evolution in which the scramble for shares in an unduly small cake would have already disappeared, he envisaged a permanent Revolution that should on no account be halted short of this; and, unable to envisage the prospect of completing such a Revolution in backward Russia alone, he became the arch-apostle of World Revolution just at the time when other men were admitting that the time for it had, at any rate for the immediate future, gone by. He could not, as one of the chief makers of the Revolution of 1917, say that that Revolution had been a mistake, or admit that there had existed no real chance of its speedy extension to the advanced countries of the capitalist world. Instead, he had to go on pursuing his object, even though no chance of success existed; and he had to go on blaming Stalin for not pursuing it and for persisting in his attempt to build a sort of Socialism devoid of the real spirit of Socialism in a single backward country. He said much that was highly pertinent by way of criticism of Stalinist Russia — above all, of its bureaucracy and of Stalin's part in creating it. But Stalin had largely borrowed Trotsky's actual policies, while adapting them to a different purpose; and Trotsky had not much to offer by way of an alternative. Cut off from direct contact with the Soviet Union, he understood less and less what was happening there; and after the great purge he lost what contacts he had previously maintained. That he ever consciously co-operated with the Nazis is a ridiculous supposition, with not a jot of evidence behind it. But that he used what opportunities he had to make trouble for Stalin inside the Soviet Union is equally beyond question. Stalin was therefore able to build him up into a symbolic figure of evil: so that even to-day it is nearly impossible for his name to be mentioned there without execration, and his immense part in the Revolution and the Civil War has been almost completely wiped out of memory by a deliberate falsification of history which, in this connection, is still maintained. Trotsky was self-willed, headstrong, and personally vain of his powers; but that does not prevent his having been a great man. I should hesitate to call him a good man too; but he is at any rate not personally repulsive as Stalin is, and his *History of the Russian Revolution* is, I feel sure, a great book — though I should not be prepared to say the same of any of his other writings, even of those admirable pamphlets, *The Lessons of October* and *The New Course*. He had also, much more than either Stalin or Lenin, an understanding of the West and of Western ideas, even though he repudiated them. Finally, in his dealings with men, he was by nature a conciliator, despite his imperiousness and impetuosity; for in general he saw differences as things to be overcome by rational argument rather than magnified into unbridgeable conflicts of principle. That was one of his major sins in the eyes of the Old Bolsheviks, of whom he was not one; but it was rather in reality one of his supreme merits, though it was used as a weapon to bring him down. If Trotsky rather than Stalin had become the arch-maker of the new Russia, it is very doubtful whether it would have come through its struggles to its present position of world power; but I feel sure, if it had survived, it would have done so with very much cleaner hands. For Trotsky, whatever his defects, did dislike needless cruelty and oppression and did believe in social equality as an indispensable Socialist objective.

Regarding Bukharin, the principal victim in 1938, it will

be remembered that Lenin, in his famous Testament, had both paid high tribute to Bukharin as a member of the Central Committee and at the same time thrown doubt on his understanding of Marxism. By this he meant, I think, that Bukharin's interpretation of Marxism was not his own, in that it assigned a lesser rôle to the industrial proletariat and insisted on fairer treatment for the peasants, and wished to push the New Economic Policy to a still further point. Through the 'twenties and 'thirties Bukharin remained on the extreme right of the movement, but did not deviate far from it until after the rise of the Nazis, when he became associated with Zinoviev and Kamenev, and later to some extent with Trotsky out of growing hostility to Stalin. But it is sheerly nonsensical to regard him as a paid stooge of either the Nazis or British imperialism. Indiscreet he may have been ; but what else could he have been unless he was prepared to give way entirely — which he was not ? As for the many less important Bolshevik opponents who were liquidated with him, most of them had in all probability done nothing at all — at any rate not beyond a little indiscreet talking, if even that. They were got rid of because they were suspected, rightly or wrongly, of being less than 100 per cent loyal to Stalin's Russia — and for nothing else.

CHAPTER XII

COMMUNISM IN CHINA IN THE 1930s

IN the fourth volume of this history I carried the record of Chinese Communism, in bare outline, right up to the 'Long March' by means of which Mao Tse-tung, driven out of his base in Southern China, transferred his headquarters to the north-west and set up his new Soviet Government with its centre at Yenan, in Shensi. I must now, however, go over some of this ground again, in order to connect it with the developments at Yenan during the later 'thirties. As we saw, in 1927–8 Chinese Communism had been all but destroyed by the campaigns waged against it by Chiang Kai-shek and his Kuomintang supporters; and in 1928, at a Congress held far away in Moscow under the eye of the Comintern, the Chinese Communist Party had attempted to work out a new policy suitable to the changed conditions, and had put the entire blame for the disaster, except as far as it rested on Chiang and the Kuomintang right wing, on the errors of the Chinese Communist leadership, despite the fact that what it had attempted to do had been in all respects authorised and even instigated by the Comintern. It was no longer possible to persist with the policy of alliance with, and infiltration into, the Kuomintang, which had been ruthlessly expelling the Communists from its ranks, breaking up the labour organisations, such as the Trade Unions, that were under Communist influence, and executing wholesale such Communist or near-Communist leaders as it was able to catch. After 1927 the Communists in the cities had been driven underground and almost annihilated as an organised force; and the C.C.P. had lost almost the whole of its membership among the industrial workers. Attempts to retrieve the situation by sporadic risings in a number of cities had only served to complete the eclipse; and all that remained of the once-powerful Communist movement were a few centres of peasant revolt in the countryside and small underground groups in the cities made up largely of intellectuals, with little contact with the mass of the people. In these circumstances, the Moscow Congress had been driven to recognise the key importance of the rural problem and of land reform; but they had been severely hampered in seeking solutions by their dogmatic belief that the revolutionary leadership must be taken by the industrial proletariat, without which the peasants would be incapable of any constructive revolutionary effort, and by their deeply rooted hostility to peasant agriculture and to the tendency of movements among the poorer peasants to take as their objectives the equal redistribution of the land among peasant families. Holding, as they did, that China was not yet ripe for Socialist Revolution, and that the immediate aim must be to bring about a Revolution that would stop short, for the time being, at a bourgeois-democratic stage, the Communists could not press for immediate nationalisation or even for immediate collectivisation such as the Russians were just embarking on; for either would be a measure appropriate to the Socialist rather than to the bourgeois-democratic Revolution. Nor could they take unequivocally the side of the poorer peasants against the better-to-do; for this would, at any rate in many areas, disastrously break up the unity of the peasant movement of revolt. Consequently, the Moscow Congress was able to give no clear guidance on the agrarian issues, and continued in theory to insist on the primacy of the industrial proletariat and to deny the constructive rôle of the peasantry.

Actual conditions were, however, soon too strong to be resisted on grounds of orthodox Marxist theory. Driven out of the major towns, the Communists had either to give in altogether or to make the most of such opportunities as were still open to them in the countryside, and particularly in those rural areas where there existed both powerful movements of rural discontent and terrain difficult of access by the armed forces of the Kuomintang and the war-lords who had come to terms with it. In these circumstances there developed inside China a number of areas, large or small, in which the peasants, having risen against their local oppressors, refused to pay rents and interest on debts, confiscated and redistributed the land owned by unpopular landlords, or even by landlords generally, and in many cases inflicted fines and humiliations on landlords and usurers, and in some cases cut off their heads. In some areas similar action was taken against the wealthier peasants, who employed labour on the lands they owned or rented, whereas in other cases the peasants as a whole took action against landlords and usurers as a class. For the most part the peasants had only improvised arms and no military equipment; but there was a good deal of irregular fighting between guerrilla peasant bands and the armed guards maintained by the landlords and the local governments, and more or less organised forces of 'Red Guards' made their appearance in many areas. Most of these peasant uprisings achieved only a short-lived success; but in a few cases, in favourable terrain, there grew out of them definite local Soviet administrations which completely replaced the previous government authorities. Such uprisings had been occurring throughout the 1920s — even during the years of Communist collaboration with the Kuomintang; but after 1927 they assumed a new importance and came more definitely under Communist control.

Much the most important of these Soviet areas was the area in Kiangsu, Hunan and the neighbouring provinces of South China which came under the control of the forces led by Mao Tse-tung. There, in mountainous and difficult territory, Mao was able to establish control over a fairly extensive and populous area from which landlords were driven out, rents abolished or greatly reduced, and the nucleus of a regular Red Army created out of and side by side with the peasants' irregular forces. This Red Army set to work not only to train officers for devoted revolutionary service, but also to indoctrinate its entire rank and file in revolutionary principles. Animated strongly by equalitarian ideas and living under conditions of acute scarcity of almost all kinds of supplies, the Red Army insisted on a combination of strict military discipline with a strong emphasis on social equality and the equal sharing of hardships by men and officers, as well as by the holders of civilian posts.

Chiang Kai-shek, having consolidated his hold on the major cities, turned his attention, in 1930, to a determined attempt to eliminate these areas of rebellion. In many cases he succeeded without much difficulty in repressing the local Soviets, though not as a rule in destroying underground resistance; but in the case of the Kiangsu-Hunan area, where Mao was in control, one great military expedition after another, after achieving initial successes, was beaten back and routed by Mao's forces, which captured large quantities of war material and enlisted large numbers of deserters in the Red Army. Mao's strategy in these campaigns was that of organised withdrawal before the attack and gradual retirement to prepared positions well within the Soviet area. Then, as the enemy's lines of communication were lengthened and the difficulties of operating in hostile country increased, the Red Army, having waited its chance, would launch a counter-offensive, drive back the enemy and regain the lost territory, and under favourable conditions, pursue the retreating forces into areas not previously under Soviet control — less with the object of holding such areas permanently than of establishing guerrilla organisations in them and thus making them less usable as bases for a renewed attack. This policy of withdrawal followed by counter-attack not pursued too far was exceedingly successful; and in 1930–32 the Red Army succeeded in beating back four major campaigns launched by Chiang Kai-shek on an ever-increasing scale, with attacking forces varying from 200,000 to half a million or more. During his counter-offensive Mao made no attempt to capture, or at any rate to hold, major cities, reckoning that his forces were inadequate for such operations and could hold their own only if the terrain was definitely favourable to their defensive strategy. There was always opposition to this policy from Communists who, continuing to believe that the revolutionary impetus needed direction by the industrial workers, were urgent for the seizure of major towns; but Mao steadily resisted such a policy. There were also Communists who were against his policy of initial withdrawal because of the temporary sacrifice of territory which it involved, and urged that the Red Army should stand firm in holding what it had won, even when it had to face forces greatly superior to it in numbers. Mao stood out against this, insisting on the need to draw on the enemy's forces until they could be separated into groups far enough parted for the Red Army to concentrate in superior force against each in turn.

Finally, in Chiang's fifth major offensive, in 1933, Mao was overridden, and an attempt was made to resist the attack without yielding territory to the initial onslaught. The consequence was that the Red Army was driven back none the less, and was unable to consolidate its forces for a successfully placed counter-offensive : so that, although the attack was beaten off, the lost ground was not successfully regained, and the Red Army suffered serious losses. In these circumstances, Chiang's sixth offensive, in 1934, succeeded in making the main bases of the Soviet area no longer tenable ; and it was decided to evacuate the entire region. Chiang failed, however, to encircle and annihilate the Red Army, which was able to embark on the 'Long March' and, surmounting almost incredible difficulties, to re-establish itself in North-West China, where it consolidated an existing guerrilla régime into a regular Soviet Republic, which presently set up its headquarters at Yenan, in the province of Shensi, early in 1937, and was able to maintain itself despite all Chiang's efforts to dislodge it.

Two years before this, early in 1935, Mao had become Chairman of the Central Committee of the C.C.P., in which his unquestioned ascendancy dates from that time. He had been elected a member of the Central Committee at the Moscow Congress of the Party in 1928, but had been up to 1935 only one among its leaders, and not the most influential in its general councils. He had indeed fallen foul of his fellow-leaders on more than one occasion, as a critic of both right- and left-wing deviations from what he regarded as the correct policy for Chinese Marxism, which from the first he regarded as necessary to be differentiated in certain vital respects from what had been appropriate in the Soviet Union or in other countries. Most of all had he differed, after the disaster of 1927, from the view that it was expedient under the circumstances to set out above all to reconstitute Chinese Communism as a mainly urban movement, resting on the support of the main body of the urban proletariat and, in order to do this, to make onslaughts on the major cities and attempt to seize and hold them against the Kuomintang. Such attempts had seemed to him to offer no prospect of success in the prevailing conditions ; and he had denounced them as mere 'adventurism' or 'putsch-ism'. He had fallen foul of Li Li-san during his period of ascendancy in the Party's councils on this account. Even when

Li Li-san was driven to resign from the Politbureau in November 1930, after having been censured for his 'deviations' by the Comintern, and had recanted and been sent to Moscow early the following year, and when the Secretary-General of the C.C.P., Hsiang Chung-fa, had been caught and executed by the K.M.T. in Shanghai in June 1931, Mao was still only one leader among many, till in November 1931 he was elected to preside over the first All-China Soviet Congress at Juichin and there took the leading part in proclaiming the Chinese Soviet Republic and in enacting its Constitution and basic laws. Thereafter, as Chairman of the Central Executive Committee of the new Republic, he held a more authoritative position. In 1932, when Ch'en Shao-gü ceased to be Secretary-General of the C.C.P. and went to Moscow, his successor was not Mao, but Ch'in Pang-hsein. When the second All-China Soviet Congress met at Juichin in January 1934 Mao was again elected as Chairman; but Chang Wan-t'ien became Secretary-General in succession to Ch'in. Only in January 1935 did Mao become Chairman both of the C.C.P. and of the Politbureau — that is to say, after the evacuation of the Kiangsu area, which had begun in October 1934.

Mao had fallen foul not only of Li Li-san and the so-called 'adventurists' of the C.C.P. left wing, but also of certain right-wing deviationists who, arguing with him that the time was unpropitious for adventurous action, had gone to the other extreme, and had wished to lie low and wait for a more favourable conjuncture to present itself. For Mao in abstaining from adventures that were certain to culminate in defeat by no means meant that nothing should be attempted. Nothing, he felt sure, could prevent the K.M.T. and its allies from holding the bigger towns; but it was quite beyond their power to police effectively the whole of the vast Chinese countryside, which was seething with local grievances against landlords, usurers, tax-gatherers, and local war lords, and against all forms of foreign imperialist exploitation — which he thought he saw everywhere at its evil work. He believed in the possibility of using this predominantly peasant unrest, not merely to stir up local revolts that would be quickly suppressed, but in certain areas to expel the landlords and usurers and establish local Soviets which would be able to maintain themselves for considerable periods in favourable terrain and might, by spreading over an increasing area of the countryside, undermine Chiang Kai-shek's authority and prepare the way for an uprising that would in due course become strong enough to resume its onslaught on the towns and to regain the industrial proletariat for the Revolution. In order to achieve this, it was of course necessary to do as the peasants wanted — to drive out the landlords and to divide up the land into peasant holdings, and to renounce for the time being — and for a considerable time to come — all attempts to organise the peasants in collective farms or to bring the land under public ownership. But this Mao was fully prepared to do if he could thereby strike an effective blow at the Revolution's enemies. To act in this way was not, in his view, to be in any respect false to Marxism or Communism; for the starting-point of his thinking about immediate policy was that China was still unripe for the Socialist Revolution, and that it was necessary first to complete the bourgeois-democratic Revolution, in which the middle classes and the intellectuals would be ranged on the side of the workers and peasants against the feudal and militarist elements in the existing society. He therefore set to work, in common with a number of other leaders — among them P'eng Pai and Chu Teh — to establish, chiefly in country mountainous and difficult of access, independent areas under the rule of local or regional Soviets mainly led by peasants and devoting themselves to the reform of the land system and the taxes and to the building up, not merely of Red militia — guerrilla forces — but also, as speedily as might be, of a disciplined and trained Red Army thoroughly indoctrinated with Communism and forming cadres which could be reinforced above all by deserters from the K.M.T. forces.

True, in describing what he had in mind, Mao always insisted that the peasants would be acting under the doctrinal inspiration of the industrial proletariat, and that the latter alone could serve as the vanguard of the Socialist Revolution. He insisted too that, though the immediate task was the completion of the democratic Revolution and not the making of the Socialist Revolution, the latter must always be kept in mind as the long-run objective and the Communist Party must maintain its independence in order to prepare for it, and must by no means allow itself to become merged with its allies in support of the democratic Revolution as an end in its own right. It is, however, difficult to be quite sure in what sense Mao assigned this necessary position of leadership to the industrial proletariat in any real shape ; for he was apt to speak of the industrial proletariat and the C.C.P. in the same breath, as if they were in effect identical, even at a time when the main part of the C.C.P.'s membership, and of its leaders, certainly did not consist of industrial workers, of whom there were, for a long time after the 1927 disaster, quite few in its ranks. In Mao's eyes the C.C.P., whatever elements might in fact comprise it, was by notion and definition at least the 'vanguard' of the industrial proletariat, as the most advanced social-economic class. Heavily outnumbered as they might be, not only by the peasants, but also by the artisans engaged in small-scale occupations, the industrial workers were none the less the class in the name of whose ideology the Socialist Revolution would have to be won, and the C.C.P. was the vanguard of this class even if very few of its members belonged to it.

It may, I think, be fairly held that, in advancing this doctrine, Mao was guilty of unclear thinking and was using words in illegitimate and misleading senses. But there is no doubt that he did regard an independent C.C.P. as the indispensable leader of the Revolution both in its bourgeois-democratic phase and in its destined development into a Socialist Revolution ; and that in his mind the Soviets which he and other leaders set up, first in Kiangsu and Hunan and subsequently in Shensi and the North-West, were no more than provincial and preparatory organisations, destined to lose their rôle of leadership when the Communists had become strong enough to resume their control of the greater cities and to bring the main body of the industrial workers once more into their ranks or into auxiliary organisations, such as the Trade Unions, in which the Communists could exercise effective control. For the time being, however, the leading rôle in the Revolution rested with the peasants, and it was necessary to take the fullest advantage of the opportunities presented by the country areas for helping the Revolution through its season of adversity. By the beginning of 1935 the C.C.P. leadership had been thoroughly converted at least to this point of view ; and thereafter Mao held almost undisputed sway as both ideological and practical leader of Chinese Communism.

Deeply rooted in Mao's thought was the essential difference which it made that China was neither an economically advanced nor a politically independent country, but was the prey of foreign imperialism. This partly accounted for its backwardness and for the continued sway of the feudal elements in it; for the feudalists were the subordinate allies and abetters of the imperialists, without whose help they could not hope to maintain their rule over the Chinese people. Accordingly, the feudalists were at all times ready to betray the people to the imperialists, and to do the imperialists' bidding. There was, however, fortunately for China, dissension in the imperialist ranks. Japanese imperialism, at all events from 1931 onwards the most immediate and pressing danger, was sometimes at loggerheads with British and American imperialism; and even the two latter sometimes fell out among themselves. It was necessary to fight all the imperialists; but it was also necessary, wherever possible, to take advantage of their dissensions, and even on occasion to use the less immediately dangerous in fighting the more so. Of the different imperialisms, the most dangerous throughout the 1930s was unquestionably the Japanese, for Japan had launched its attack in Manchuria in 1931 and thereafter had proceeded to spread its power southwards into China proper, until in 1937 its aggression had developed into full-scale war extending over all the principal areas of China. The failure of the League of Nations from 1931 onwards to take any effective measures to check the Japanese aggression had been regarded as showing clearly the fundamental unity of imperialism as the enemy of the Chinese people, and British and American imperialists had been assigned their share of the blame; but the main resentment and anger of the Chinese people had naturally been directed against the Japanese, whose aim and intention of subduing the entire country became increasingly manifest. The newly established Chinese Soviet Republic actually declared war on Japan as early as February 1932, and called upon all groups and classes in China to join in measures of resistance to Japanese aggression; but as long as the Soviet headquarters remained in Kiangsu the Soviet Republic was cut off from direct contact with the Japanese, and only small-scale guerrilla measures could be taken against them in the Japanese-occupied areas in the North. Only when the Soviet headquarters was removed to the North-West in 1935, after the 'Long March', did the Soviet forces come into regular conflict with the Japanese invaders and begin to play a leading part in the anti-Japanese struggle. It was in December 1935 that the Central Committee of the C.C.P. issued its first call for a national united front against Japan and called upon the K.M.T. to collaborate with it in organising a national movement of resistance.

This call for united action, which was reiterated during the ensuing years, involved fundamental changes in C.C.P. policy and in Mao's presentation of the Communist case. After the earlier co-operation with the K.M.T. had utterly broken down in 1927–8, the Communists had denounced the bourgeoisie as having betrayed the Revolution and had sought to reconstruct their movement as an alliance of peasants, intellectuals, and petty bourgeoisie under the leadership of the industrial proletariat — or rather, of the C.C.P. itself as its vanguard. But by the middle 'thirties it had become plain that the opposition to Japanese imperialist penetration extended not only to these classes, but also to a large section of the 'national bourgeoisie'. In these circumstances Mao and the C.C.P. became willing to recognise what they called the 'national bourgeoisie', in order to distinguish them from yet more reactionary elements, as possible collaborators in the anti-Japanese struggle, and to urge the creation of a United Anti-Japanese Front broad enough to include them as well as the other classes to whom they had been appealing in their calls for united action.

A great deal was said in China by way of justification of this apparent return to the policy of class-collaboration which had broken down so disastrously in 1927. This time, of course, the advocacy of the United Front coincided with the new policy of the Comintern for United Fronts against Fascism in Europe ; and in the summer of 1935 the Seventh World Congress of the Comintern called specifically for such a Front in China against Japan. The question was how far rightwards the Front should extend and what should be its organisational basis. There is, as we have seen, a sense in which Communism is always in favour of the United Front; but the meaning of the term can range from the 'United Front from below', which is in effect a call from the Communist Parties to the masses to desert their reformist leaders and rally under Communist leadership, to the 'United Front from above', which implies collaboration with these same leaders in a common campaign for a particular objective. By 1935 the Comintern, having become aware of the Fascist danger, which it had previously underestimated grossly, especially in Germany, had passed over from the first of these attitudes — 'Class against Class' — to the second, and was calling upon every group it could hope to attract into an anti-Fascist crusade. China, as a semi-colonial country, was, however, differently situated from the countries of the West; and in China the correct equivalent of the United Front against Fascism appeared to be the United Front against Japan, as the most dangerous representative of imperialism and the present enemy of the national independence of the Chinese people. In view of the strong feeling aroused by Japanese aggression, it was evidently possible to raise up a mass-movement of resistance, and to denounce and isolate Chiang Kai-shek and those of his supporters who, instead of putting out their main effort against Japan, had shown themselves determined to carry on the civil war in the hope of destroying the Chinese Soviet Republic. The industrial workers, the peasants — well-to-do as well as poor — the intellectuals, and the petty bourgeoisie were all unquestionably in a mood to respond to such an appeal; but what of the greater bourgeoisie, who had joined Chiang in defeating the Revolution in 1927? Many of these too were strongly anti-Japanese and were suffering from the impact of Japanese imperialism; and it was therefore possible to appeal to them as well to join the Anti-Fascist Front, especially if it took the form of a general, patriotic, Chinese national Front against the wicked foreigners. Mao and his fellow-activists accordingly produced a new analysis of Chinese class-structure, in which the 'national bourgeoisie' made its appearance as one of the patriotic classes to be included in the anti-Japanese Front, thus leaving outside the Front only those sections of the bourgeoisie and the feudal classes which had shown clearly their readiness to collaborate with the Japanese, or at all events to subordinate the struggle against Japan to the civil war against the Chinese Soviets. The United Front, in this sense, involved a conditional preparedness to co-operate with the K.M.T. and with Chiang himself, the conditions being that the civil war should be given up in order to concentrate all possible forces against the Japanese, and that the K.M.T. should agree to reintroduce some sort of democracy and to take part in convening a National Assembly to work out an agreed programme for the future; and also that concessions should be made to the workers and peasants by immediate improvements in the standard of living. Given the acceptance of these conditions, the C.C.P. declared itself ready to stop confiscation of land from the landlords, to merge the Red Army with the K.M.T. forces, and to discontinue the use of the name 'Soviet' and accept the dissolution of the independent régimes in the Soviet areas and the inclusion of these areas in an All-China democratic structure.

To the C.C.P. Manifesto putting forward this programme of action and calling on the K.M.T. to accept it, the K.M.T. made no reply. The civil war continued; but the Communists, having set up in March 1937 their Shensi-Kansu-Ninghsia Soviet Government with its headquarters at Yenan, waged more and more open war against the Japanese in the North-Western provinces and intensified their campaign for the United Front. In August 1937 the C.C.P. issued its 'Ten Great Policies for Resistance against Japan and for National Salvation'; and in September its 'Manifesto on K.M.T.-C.C.P. Co-operation', sent to the K.M.T. in July, was made public by the Central Government. Also in September the Red Army, renamed the 'Eighth Route Army', advanced into northern Hopei and Shensi to harass the Japanese by guerrilla warfare, and the name of the Shensi-Kansu-Ninghsia Soviet Government was changed to 'Border Region' Government, thus dropping the word 'Soviet'. In December a new 'Border Region Government' was set up in the Shensi-Hopei-Chahar region, and before then a new Fourth Army had been organised out of Communist and other elements in Kiangsi and Fukien and had moved into Kiangsu and Anwhei to harass the Japanese rear.

The attitude of the C.C.P. in face of the open war between China and Japan which began in July 1937 can best be seen in the 'Ten Great Policies' of the following month. These were : (1) Overthrow of Japanese Imperialism. (2) Total Military Mobilisation of the Nation. (3) Total Mobilisation of the Entire Nation. (4) Reform of Political Mechanism (by convening a National Assembly to draft a democratic Constitution and by setting up a National Defence Government containing the revolutionary elements of all parties and groups, but excluding pro-Japanese factions). (5) Support for the Peace Camp, and opposition to the aggressors' camp of Japan, Germany and Italy. (6) Reform of the tax system, confiscation of traitors' property, expansion of production, and elimination of Japanese goods from the market. (7) Improvement of economic conditions for workers, peasants, civil servants, teachers, and anti-Japanese soldiers, reduction of rents and interest rates, unemployment relief. (8) A new educational system, general, compulsory and free, and a new curriculum to save the country and fight the Japanese. (9) The wiping out of traitors, puppets, and pro-Japanese groups. (10) On the question of all-out co-operation between the K.M.T. and the C.C.P., the building up of an anti-Japanese national united front of all parties, groups, classes and armies to lead the fight against Japan and to cope with the national crisis by sincere unity.

In putting forward this programme the C.C.P. strongly stressed its compatibility with the 'Three Principles' laid down by Sun Yat-sen — Nationalism, People's Rights, and People's Livelihood — which were nominally accepted by the K.M.T. At the same time, the 'Three Principles' were declared to be fully compatible with the standpoint of Communism and to embody Communist demands at the stage of the bourgeois-democratic Revolution. The Communists made no attempt to conceal their intention of advancing in due course beyond this stage to that of the Socialist Revolution or of maintaining the independence of their own organisation in order to leave it free to work for this further advance when the time came ; but they emphasised the point that they were working immediately, not for Socialism, but only for a democratic stage transitional to it, which would necessarily develop in the direction of Socialism.

This was the gospel which Mao set forth in his work, *On*

the New Democracy, published in 1941, but largely anticipated
in his writings of the previous years. *On the New Democracy*
was put forward not merely as an amplification of the declarations and manifestos in which the policy of the United Front
had been expounded from 1935 onwards, but also as a new
contribution to Communist theory, worked out in China and
in accordance with Chinese conditions. Up to 1935 the
Comintern had put forward a series of policies for applying its
general policy to Chinese circumstances, which were recognised
as having special historical characteristics of their own. But
from 1935 onwards the Comintern, having endorsed the policy
of the United Front in China as well as elsewhere, ceased to
advance policies of its own to be accepted by the C.C.P., which
was left to work out its own line in accordance with the general
United Front directive. This is what Mao was essentially
attempting to do.

On the New Democracy begins with an emphasis on China's
status as a semi-colonial country, which has been living under
feudal conditions for about three thousand years. It then lays
down that what his ideal for China is, *i.e.* revolution divided into
two stages, democratic and Socialist, which are different in
nature. But the democratic Revolution, which is the first of
these stages, is to establish a New Democracy, essentially
different from the old democracy as well as from feudalism.
The Chinese democratic Revolution, it is said, can be traced
back in its beginnings to the Opium War of 1839–42; but at
that point and right up to the Russian Revolution of 1917
it remained within the orbit of the old bourgeois-democratic
World Revolution, of which it was a part. From 1917 onwards,
however, the Chinese democratic Revolution came within the
orbit of the new bourgeois-democratic Revolution, and became
part of the World Proletarian-Socialist Revolution. What this
means is that, though the immediate objective continues to be
bourgeois-democratic, the Revolution, even at this stage, is no
longer of the old type, under bourgeois leadership for the
building of a capitalist society under bourgeois dictatorship,
but is a new kind of Revolution led, wholly or in part, by the
proletariat, with the immediate aim of setting up a new State
based on the joint dictatorship of all revolutionary classes. In
other words, since 1917 the World Revolution has entered on

a new phase : it has become 'the Proletarian-Socialist World Revolution, in which the proletariat of the capitalist countries is the main force, and the oppressed natives in the colonies and semi-colonies are their allies'. In the latter, all revolutionary classes, no matter whether conscious of it or not, become part of the Proletarian-Socialist World Revolution and allies of the proletariat in its furtherance. Accordingly, the bourgeois Revolution in such countries becomes a bourgeois-democratic Revolution of a new type, essentially different from the old. If the Chinese bourgeoisie is incapable of leading such a Revolution against feudalism and imperialism, the responsibility for doing so belongs to the Chinese proletariat, to the peasants, and to the intellectuals and other petty bourgeois elements. These classes, it is said, 'have awakened or are awakening, and are bound to be the basic parts of the State and government framework in the Democratic Republic of China', which can only be 'a dictatorship of all anti-imperialist and anti-feudal people'. Thus the new Democratic Republic differs in essence from the old, weaker type that is under the dictatorship of the bourgeoisie. Three kinds of State are recognised under the general category of Republics : those under bourgeois dictatorship, those under proletarian dictatorship, and those under a joint dictatorship of social revolutionary classes ; and the third of these is the transitional form in colonial and semi-colonial areas. In such a Republic there will be an economic policy corresponding to the political structure. Banks, big industries, and other forms of big business, including former foreign-owned enterprises, will be owned and reorganised by the State ; but other forms of enterprise will be allowed to exist where they cannot 'manipulate the people's livelihood'. The tillers of the soil will own it : the land of big landlords will be confiscated and redistributed among the peasants ; but rich peasants will be allowed to continue in possession.

Mao goes on to speak of the place of the peasant in the Chinese democratic Revolution. 'The Chinese Revolution is in essence a revolution of the peasantry, the peasant war of resistance is in essence a war of resistance of the peasantry. The policy of new democracy is in essence the transfer of power to the peasantry. The new, genuine Three Principles — alliance with the Soviet Union, alliance with the Communists, and support of the peasants and workers — are in their essence the principles of a peasant Revolution. . . . The anti-Japanese war is in its essence a peasant war. . . . Everything that we do is for the peasantry.' But Mao adds that this does not mean the overlooking of other classes, though more than 80 per cent of the population of China is peasantry. 'The force of the peasantry is the main force of the Chinese Revolution. But there are also several millions of industrial workers, who are essential to the life of the people ; and without them the Revolution could not succeed, for it is they who are the leaders of the Revolution and have the highest revolutionary spirit'. Thus Mao, after appearing to assert the primacy of the peasants, comes back to the notion of the industrial workers as in some deep sense the necessary leaders of the Revolution ; but by the 'industrial proletariat' does he really mean the workers in industry or the Communist Party regarded as necessarily their vanguard ? I think there is confusion here ; but clearly the two are closely identified in his mind.

Mao then goes on to speak of the 'cultural Revolution' which reflects and serves the purpose of the political and economic Revolution. A Socialist culture, he says, is impossible for the time being, because it must reflect a Socialist politics and a Socialist economics, which do not and cannot yet exist. It is, however, an indispensable task to expand the propaganda of Communist thought and the study of Marxist-Leninist teachings, because without this not only the Socialist but even the democratic Revolution cannot succeed. The Communists must prepare the people for the coming Socialist stage of the Revolution ; but they must keep this preparation distinct from the building up of a new popular culture appropriate to the democratic stage. The essence of the latter is its national character : 'it belongs to our own nation and bears the characteristics of our own nation'. The new culture must absorb a great deal from the cultures of other nations, but must avoid absorbing them wholesale. 'The thesis of "wholesale Westernisation" is a mistaken viewpoint.' Just as the body takes food, separating what it takes into what it can absorb and the residue, and excreting the latter, so China must deal with foreign cultural materials. Formal Marxism is of no use to China until it has been adapted to the national form appropriate to

Chinese culture. The new culture must be, too, predominantly scientific, rejecting all forms of feudal and superstitious thought and seeking truth through the study of concrete facts. It must recognise the greatness of China's cultural tradition and take from it whatever is more or less democratic or revolutionary in character, but should never absorb it indiscriminately. Finally, the new culture must be popular : it must appeal directly to the people, and never isolate itself from them in an ivory tower ; and for this it is necessary to reform and simplify the language and to use simple words. 'The combination of new democratic politics, new democratic economics, and new democratic culture is the Republic of the New Democracy.'

This is no doubt an inadequate summary of Mao's argument, which is by no means clear at all points ; but I think it fairly presents the essence. The main new factor in it is the assertion of the possibility, and of the necessity for China, of a joint dictatorship of several classes. No possibility of anything except a dictatorship of some sort is recognised at all, the democracies of the Western world being treated simply as forms of bourgeois dictatorship. But, whereas Communists had been accustomed to argue that every form of State must rest on the dictatorship of a particular class, bourgeois or proletarian, Mao advanced the theory of a dictatorship shared between the classes participating in the Revolution and thus extending to all except the allies of the feudalists and imperialists. Such a dictatorship he regarded, however, not as resting on the whole people, irrespective of class, but on a sharing of power between classes. This was indeed the fundamental character of his New Democracy, as applicable not to all the world, but to countries not yet ready for Socialism and especially to feudal and imperialist-dominated countries such as China. It was essentially a conception of transition ; for such countries were destined to press on from the democratic to the Socialist Revolution, and the Communist Parties had in them the dual function of playing their part in the former and at the same time preparing men's minds for the latter : so that in working in a United Front with other elements they must on no account give up their independence or allow themselves to become merged in it to the detriment of their long-run task. Mao attacked as right-wing dissidents those who so acted as to foster such absorption, while he attacked with equal vehemence the extremists of the left, who denied the legitimacy of co-operation with other classes in the immediate task of accomplishing the democratic Revolution — attacking on this score especially the Chinese Trotskyists, who had set up their own organisation, with Ch'en Tu-hsin (1880–1942) at its head, at a Conference held at Shanghai in 1931, but whose leaders had been arrested and imprisoned by the K.M.T. in the following year. Mao had bracketed the Trotskyists with the imperialists as the Revolution's chief enemies in his report to the C.C.P. in November 1938, when he had denounced Han Lin-fu's Third Front with special vehemence. The Chinese Trotskyists, who continually harked back to the 1927 disaster as the outcome of alliance with the K.M.T., were the strongest critics of the United Front and of Mao's New Democracy, and were denounced as bitterly as were the followers and alleged followers of Trotsky in Europe.

The Communists, as we saw, had offered in 1937 on certain conditions to give up their independent Soviet Governments, to abandon the use of the word 'Soviet', to merge the Red Army in a unified anti-Japanese national army, and to stop confiscating and redistributing land in the areas under their control, as part of a general bargain with the K.M.T. for common action against Japan. How far did these conditions actually come about? Some change in relations with the K.M.T. had begun after the 'Sian Incident' of December 1936, when Chiang Kai-shek, after being kidnapped by Chang Hsueh-liang, was released on the advice of the C.C.P. The K.M.T. did not make any official answer to the C.C.P.'s proposals of 1937 for a United Front; but various negotiations took place between the two Parties, and for a time the civil war between them was actually called off and the armies of both worked together in resisting Japan. In 1937 and 1938 relations between the two Parties substantially improved, at any rate on the surface. Then, after the fall of Hankow in October 1938, there was a gradual deterioration, and conflict again became open after the K.M.T. attack on the Fourth Army in January 1941. We have seen that, during the period of improved relations, the Communists did actually change the official designation of the Soviet areas; and in July 1938 a group of C.C.P. delegates, headed by Chou En-lai, met the K.M.T. leaders for negotiations at Chungking. But by the summer of 1939 Chiang Kai-shek had ordered a complete blockade of the Communist-controlled areas in Shensi and Kansu. Nevertheless, the Communists persisted in their efforts for united action, introducing in July 1940 in the areas under their control the system called the 'Three Thirds', of government by coalitions made up in equal numbers of Communist, K.M.T., and 'non-party' representatives. This policy was continued even after, in January 1941, the K.M.T. general, Ku Chu-t'ung, had attacked the Fourth Army, capturing its commander and killing its vice-commander in battle, and dislocating the entire force, of which remnants escaped to join the Communists in Kiangsu and Shantung. So matters continued, with a mixture of collaboration in some areas and actual fighting between the rivals in others, right up to the end of the war in Europe. Then came, in April 1945, the seventh C.C.P. Congress at Yenan, which revised the Party Constitution and received a report from Mao on the question of Coalition Government. In revising the Constitution the Congress inserted a Preamble, which is notable as describing the 'ideas of Mao Tse-tung' as 'the guiding principles of all the party's work', and as taking them, together with the fundamentals of Marxism-Leninism, as basic in defining the course of the Revolution in China. The C.C.P. describes itself as 'a unified, compact organisation, built on the principles of democratic centralism, and held together by the discipline which all party members must observe conscientiously and voluntarily'.

The C.C.P., in thus erecting Mao Tse-tung to a position of equality — or almost equality — with Marx and Lenin and placing him, at any rate by implication, well above either Engels or Stalin, was doing its leader great honour, if not precisely as an original theoretician, at least as a master of tactics and strategy who had seen clearly how to adapt the creed of Marx and Lenin to the circumstances of China as a feudal and semi-colonial country — and perhaps to the circumstances of other such countries. But was the doctrine of Mao not, in effect, more than an adaptation of the Marxist-Leninist creed? Mao himself said not; for he professed, no less than Marx or Lenin, to regard the industrial proletariat as the class destined to lead the Revolution, not only at the Socialist stage to which he looked forward as certain, but also to a great extent in the preceding 'new democratic' phase. If his words were to be taken literally, the Revolution could succeed at either stage only under proletarian leadership. True, he had said also that, at the 'new democratic' stage, it was bound to be mainly a peasant Revolution and had throughout his career been mainly a leader and organiser of peasant revolt. There was, none the less, a feeling in his mind that the peasants, though they might *make* the Revolution at its earlier stage, could not *lead* it except under guidance, as well as a deep belief that they could not in any sense make the Revolution in its second, Socialist stage. What he called 'proletarian' leadership was therefore necessary at both stages, and necessary at the first stage in order to ensure that due preparation should be made at once for carrying it on to the second, and that the Party should not be allowed to degenerate into a mere peasant Party, or to become merged with the other forces with which it needed, for the time being, to act in alliance. On this ground, Mao insisted with all his force and throughout his career that the errors of the 'twenties should not be repeated — that the C.C.P. should not infiltrate into the K.M.T. or lose its power of independent action and policy-making through collaboration with it, or with the classes for which it endeavoured to speak. Mao saw the impossibility of effective working-class leadership — in the sense of actual leadership by a mass-party based on the industrial workers while the greater cities were held by the K.M.T. — or indeed even until the industrial proletariat had become considerably larger and more concentrated through the progress of industrialisation. But he was able to his own satisfaction to reconcile the actual pre-eminence of the peasants in the revolutionary struggle and the absence of any large influence of the C.C.P. among the industrial workers by his belief that the C.C.P. was the natural, the inevitable, the only possible leader and vanguard of the industrial proletariat, even if but few of them belonged to it or were able to fulfil the necessary conditions of doing so by playing an active part in its work. For Mao, the very ideas 'Communist Party' and 'industrial proletariat', were inseparably connected, so that it was impossible to conceive of the one without the other or to contemplate the possibility of division between them. This was the very basis of his Marxist-Leninist philosophy ; and nothing that he said was intended as a departure from it. For the present, it was necessary to rally against imperialism and above all against the Japanese every class and group that could be induced to play its part in the United Front and in the making of the New Democracy. But the 'New Democracy' was only a transitional step on the road to Socialist Revolution, and when the time became ripe for Socialist Revolution the leadership would be bound to rest with the C.C.P. alone, as the vanguard and representative spokesman of the industrial workers. A joint dictatorship of several classes was held possible and necessary at the stage of the democratic Revolution ; but Mao never said, or I think supposed, that it could endure into the subsequent Socialist stage.

How, then, did Mao suppose that if, at the Revolution's first, democratic stage, the peasants were placed in individual, or family, possession of the land, it would be possible for it to pass on to its subsequent, Socialist stage ? Assuredly, he did not believe that individual peasant cultivation could itself provide a basis for Socialism, or be even compatible with the functioning of a Socialist society. But he spoke hardly at all of the conditions of the transition from New Democracy to Socialism, except in predicting that it would necessarily occur in due course. He seems in fact to have believed as thoroughly as Marx or Lenin in the superiority of large-scale enterprise and in the inseparable connection between it and Socialism as to have held as a fundamental article of faith that the Socialist Revolution, conceived of in terms of it, would necessarily triumph when the imperialist incubus had been removed. He was strong in advocacy of industrial development, as became plainer than ever when the C.C.P. launched its drive for increased production in February 1943, but had been sufficiently evident long before. But how peasant agriculture would be transformed into collectivised or nationalised farming he never felt called on to explain, his chief concern being always with two things — the requirements of immediate revolutionary strategy and the maintenance by the C.C.P. of its essential doctrines unimpaired by the exigencies of compromise for the time being.

On this latter point, as we have seen, he always insisted with the utmost vehemence. In advocating alliances with all anti-imperialist groups, he never concealed, or wished the C.C.P. to conceal, its further Socialist objectives. On the contrary, he regarded the C.C.P. as a school of Socialism and Communism no less than as a leading force in immediate affairs, and laid at all times great stress on its educational rôle and on the duty of all its members to make themselves adepts in Marxist-Leninist doctrines. He was very insistent too on the importance of what he called 'democratic centralism' as the indispensable method of party organisation and control. Mao insisted that the C.C.P.'s policy should be carried out in disciplined fashion by all the members, and that this policy should emanate from the Party's central organisations rather than be transmitted to them from lower down in its ranks. Therewith he stressed the need for the fullest discussions among all members and branches of policy issues on which no officially binding decisions had yet been reached; but he also emphasised that such discussions should take place only inside the Party and among its members and that there was no corresponding right of free discussion extending beyond the Party. This restriction was of particular importance when the Party was being called on to act in co-operation with other elements in a United Front; for it ruled out any right of free discussion in the joint organisations extending beyond the Party.

Provisions along these lines were included in the Party Constitution adopted in 1945, as most of them had been in that drawn up in 1928 at the Moscow Congress. The new Constitution, however, laid increased stress both on the central determination of policy and on the discipline confining discussion and free expression of opinions concerning party matters to party members in internal debate. Article 25 lays down that 'Prior to their determination by the Central Committee, the local and other party organisations or their responsible officers shall discuss matters of a national character only among themselves, or submit their proposals respecting such questions to the Central Committee. In no case shall they make a public announcement of their views or decisions.' This, to be sure, applies only to 'matters of a national character'; but there are corresponding provisions concerning 'intra-party democracy' in the clauses dealing with regional and local organisation. The Chapter dealing with the structure of party organisation opens with the words, 'The party structure is organised on the principle of democratic centralism', and lays down an elaborate hierarchy determining the relative precedence of the various bodies within the Party, up to the National Congress as the highest authority. It is also laid down that, in the case of each body, 'when these are not in session, the committees elected by them are the supreme authorities at the various levels of party organisation'. This clearly establishes the superior authority of the Central Committee except during actual sessions of the National Congress. A Regional Congress, for example, has no rights as against the Central Committee. Local party organisations are accorded a 'right to make decisions concerning questions of a local character'; but these 'must not be inconsistent with the decisions of the Central Committee or of higher organisations'. Party Cells are declared to be 'the basic organs of the Party', and 'Party Nuclei' are to be set up in 'government organisations, labour unions, peasants' associations, co-operatives, and other mass organisations in which three or more party members hold responsible positions', but these Nuclei are put under the direction of the corresponding party committees at the various levels, and have no independent authority. Finally, there are provisions for disciplining members who offend against party discipline, up to the sanction of expulsion from the Party; but there are stringent procedures for appeal by either party organisations or individual members against any sentence passed upon them, and it is laid down that the purpose of the disciplinary measures is educational, and that 'it is by no means intended . . . to enforce any principle of mass punitivism within the Party'. Party organisations are definitely discouraged from taking up an unduly rigid attitude : in general, warning or advice rather than expulsion seems to be regarded as the appropriate method of dealing with first, or fairly mild, offenders. There is, however, no doubt about the duty of strict conformity by all members to decisions reached by the Central Committee or, subject to it, by the lower party organisations, or about the emergence of policy from the top level and its transmission downwards rather than the other way, from the members and branches to the centre.

We have seen that the C.C.P., in putting forward its programme for the United Front, declared its readiness to stop confiscating land for redistribution to the peasants. This was actually done during and after the Sino-Japanese War which began in 1937; but it did not mean that the C.C.P. deprived itself of its principal appeal to the peasants. It remained free, while leaving the remaining landlords in possession, except where they could be driven out as definite traitors to the national cause, to take action for the reduction of rents and rates of interest on loans and for the reversal or reduction of oppressive taxes levied on the peasants. In a policy decision issued in January 1942 the Central Committee of the C.C.P. laid down in detail its land policy in the basic areas under Communist control. Under this policy, rents were to be heavily reduced and interest rates brought down; but land-lords who accepted the reduced rents, and even feudal gentry doing so, were to be assured of receiving the reduced sums due to them and in the possession of their land and capital. The C.C.P. called on its members to 'recognise that most of the landlords are anti-Japanese, and that some of the enlightened gentlefolk also favour democratic reform'. Accordingly, the C.C.P.'s policy is 'only to help the peasants in reducing feudal exploitation, but not to liquidate feudal exploitation entirely, much less to attack the enlightened gentlefolk who support democratic reform. Therefore, after rent and interest rates have been reduced, the collection of rent and interest is to be assured; and it is laid down that, in addition to protecting the civil liberties, political, land, and economic rights of the peasants, we must guarantee the landlords their civil liberties, political, land, and economic rights, in order to ally the landlord class with us in the struggle against the Japanese. The policy of liquidating feudal exploitation should only be adopted against stubbornly unrepentant traitors.' Disputes between landlords and tenants are to be settled, wherever possible, by concilia-tion; and the 'Three Thirds' system of government is to be 'carried out resolutely, strictly and extensively in councils and governments at various levels'. Government regulations must not be 'partial', but should bind peasants as well as landlords.

There is no doubt that on the basis of this very moderate land policy the C.C.P. continued able to make an effective appeal for peasant support. In doing so, it relied in part on the actual gains secured under it, but also very greatly on a direct appeal to nationalist feeling. From the moment when the C.C.P. began to call for an Anti-Japanese United Front the tone of its appeals was strongly nationalist, and internationalism, which had been a strong characteristic of its earlier attitude, receded more and more into the background. The entire effect of Mao's doctrine was to differentiate the case of China — and also of other countries subject to imperialist domination — sharply from that of other countries, and accordingly from that of the Soviet Union : so that the Soviet Union's example ceased to be a thing for deliberate imitation and the need for China to work out an appropriate policy for itself was heavily emphasised. Basically, the doctrine was not nationalistic, since it was held to be applicable to all colonial or semi-colonial countries, and not to China alone ; but, as the question was mainly one of how the Chinese could act most effectively under the conditions of their own country, it became mainly a matter of working out the strategy of action appropriate to China. When this had been so defined as to give the leading place to a rallying of all possible forces inside China against Japanese imperialism, there ceased to be any immediate difference between Chinese Communist policy and Chinese democratic nationalism ; and such nationalism became more and more a part of the official policy of the C.C.P. This estranged the C.C.P. from the Comintern, despite the latter's ardent advocacy of the United Front against Fascism ; and in practice the Comintern almost ceased to intervene in Chinese affairs long before Stalin abolished it in 1943. Mao continued to affirm as principles of action alliance with the Soviet Union and the regarding of the Chinese Revolution at both its stages as essentially part of the World Proletarian Revolution ; but this did not mean that he was prepared to accept any dictation of Chinese policy from Moscow, or to move on towards World Revolution while the national 'new democratic' Revolution in China had still to be fully achieved. In becoming much more nationalistic in tone, and invoking much more readily the glories of past Chinese history and culture, the C.C.P. was following a course in the main parallel to that of the Soviet Union, at any rate after 1941, and of other Communist Parties, such as the French, in the late 'thirties; but the course it followed was its own and was not forced upon it by the Soviet Union.

Broadly, then, what emerged in China during the 1930s, mainly under Mao Tse-tung's influence and inspiration, was a distinctively Chinese Communism in which a much greater rôle was assigned to the peasants than in Communism in most other countries; for, though the leadership of the industrial proletariat continued to be asserted in principle, it was recognised that the Revolution was, and must be, in practice primarily a peasant Revolution both immediately and for a considerable time to come, and the nominal leadership of the industrial proletariat meant in effect little, if anything, more than the leadership of the C.C.P. over the peasants. The peasants would, in Mao's view, be necessarily the major actors in bringing about the new democratic Revolution, within which the C.C.P. would be at work not only to assist in bringing it about, but also in preparing the minds of men for the Socialist Revolution that was destined to follow in its train. Moreover, in view of China's semi-feudal, semi-colonial status it was indispensable to rally to the side of the Revolution every element of the people that could be induced to take part in the anti-imperialist crusade and to accept the need for a 'democratic' political and social structure; and this involved a strong insistence on national solidarity as a means of rallying support. How far the C.C.P. became a convert to nationalism in theory it is not easy to say: at any rate it became highly nationalistic in practice, and it must be borne in mind that the unity of theory and action was among the Marxist principles which Mao himself most vehemently affirmed. Mao gave, in 1937, a lecture *On Practice*, which was subsequently published, asserting most strongly that 'Marxism is not a dogma, but a guide to action', and his entire contribution to Socialist thought is in accordance with this assertion.

I have dealt in this chapter entirely with Chinese Communism, and have said nothing of the development of other forms of Socialism in the China of the 1930s. There is, indeed, little to say about developments outside the Communist Party, which, as soon as it began to recover from the disaster of 1927, had a near-monopoly of the advocacy of Socialism and stood alone in working for it in a practical way. Outside the C.C.P.

there were at all times groups which opposed the United Front strategy and called for a more limited proletarian policy based on an alliance of workers and peasants only and for closer identification with the cause of World, as distinct from merely Chinese, Revolution. These were the groups Mao denounced as 'Trotskyists', as some of them professedly were, but others not. To these groups belonged those who took part in the Shanghai Conference of 1931 and set up a rival Central Committee headed by Ch'en Tu-hsin as Secretary-General, Han Lin-fu's 'Third Front' and Liu Jen-ching's 'Lenin Front' denounced by Mao in 1938, and a number of other 'opposition' movements. Mao also denounced as *putsch*-ists' and 'adventurists' those who followed Li Li-san's leadership in 1930, prior to his recantation and removal to Moscow the following year. There were also right-wing dissidents, denounced as 'opportunists', such as T'an Ping-shan, who was expelled from the Party at the end of 1927 for continued collaboration with the K.M.T. and subsequently organised a 'Third Party', and Ku Shan-chung, who went over to the K.M.T. after his arrest in 1932.

Apart from these 'deviationists' there were in China a good many intellectuals in sympathy with Socialism, but unconnected with the C.C.P. or with its dissident offshoots. To most of these the policy of the Anti-Japanese United Front made a strong appeal and, without espousing Communism, they were ready to collaborate with the C.C.P. and largely to accept its leadership in immediate policy. Until the rise of the Democratic League after 1945 these elements lacked a central organisation round which they could cohere; and most of them either worked in the United Front or became active in such non-political bodies as the Co-operative League — or, of course, both. The non-Communist intellectuals, however, did not at any time possess a mass following and were not able to exert any considerable influence. Nor do they appear to have been fertile in the realm of Socialist thought, though some of them made some attempt to adapt European Socialist Pluralism to Chinese conditions, and their influence in the Co-operative movement continued to be substantial right up to 1949 — mainly outside the areas under Communist control.

Mao Tse-tung, however, is the only figure of real Socialist

status who emerged in China between the wars, as the preacher and practical executant of a notable variant of the Communist attitude, assigning a much larger place than Communists elsewhere were ready to give both to the peasantry and to the nationalistic implications of the United Front in a semi-feudal, semi-colonial country, which he sought to make the ally both of the Soviet Union and of the democratic nationalist movements in other countries subject to imperialist penetration. How his policies developed after the Communists had won power in 1949 is a matter lying far beyond the scope of the present volume.

————

An excellent collection of translated source material is C. Brandt, B. I. Schwartz, and J. K. Fairbank, *A Documentary History of Chinese Communism* (Harvard, 1952). See also P. H. Clyde, *The Far East* (New York, 1948); J. K. Fairbank, *The United States and China* (Harvard, 1948); H. Feis, *The Chinese Tangle* (Princeton, 1953); H. R. Isaacs, *The Tragedy of the Chinese Revolution* (Stanford, 1938); Mao Tse-tung, *China's New Democracy* (1941, English translation, New York, 1945); and *Selected Works* (in course of appearance, Vol. I, 1954); R. C. North, *Moscow and the Chinese Communists* (Stanford, 1953); D. B. Rose, *China among the Powers* (New York, 1945); B. I. Schwartz, *Chinese Communism and the Rise of Mao* (Harvard, 1951); R. H. Tawney, *Land and Labour in China* (1932); J. Stalin, *Stalin on China* (Bombay, 1951); H. A. Steiner, *Maoism* (Los Angeles, 1952); Hu Ch'iao-mu, *Thirty Years of the Communist Party of China* (Pekin, 1951); R. C. North, *The Kuomintang and the Chinese Communist Elites* (Stanford, 1952); Edgar Snow, *Red Star over China* (1938); P. Thurber, *American-Russian Relations in the Far East* (New York, 1949); F. Moraes, *Report on Mao's China* (New York, 1953); W. W. Rostow, *The Prospects for Communist China* (1954).

CHAPTER XIII

LOOKING BACKWARDS AND FORWARDS

I BRING this study of Socialist thought to an end in 1939, with the outbreak of the second world war; for the developments which come after the war are still too recent for the historian to evaluate with any confidence. But I cannot end my summary without some attempt to estimate where Socialism as a world movement stood in 1939, or what then seemed to be its prospects. For more than twenty years it had been sharply divided into two contending movements — Communism and Social Democracy — of which the former held absolute power in the Soviet Union and the latter formed the constitutional Government in the three leading Scandinavian countries, albeit without the support of a clear majority of the electors in any of the three. Both Communism and Social Democracy had been extinguished, except for certain underground activities, in Italy, Germany, Spain, and most of the States of Eastern Europe. There was a powerful Communist, as well as a Social Democratic, minority in France; and in Great Britain, where Communism had little following, the Labour Party had been slowly recovering from the disaster of 1931, and was challenging the Conservative supremacy that still existed after the election of 1935. In the United States the American Socialist Party, never a real force since 1914, was far gone in disintegration, whereas the Trade Unions had increased their strength very greatly under the New Deal. In Latin America, Communism was the creed of active, but not very large, minorities in most of the Republics, whereas Social Democracy was nowhere a predominant force; and both were at loggerheads with the Aprista movement, which was powerful in Peru, and in Mexico President Cárdenas had done much to raise and carry on the tradition of the primarily agrarian Revolution. Australia and New Zealand had Labour Governments; and the latter had made notable advances towards the Welfare

State. In Canada the traditional Parties still held the predominance; but the Social Democratic Co-operative Commonwealth Federation had begun to challenge their authority, especially in Saskatchewan. In South Africa the Labour movement was still in a condition of disintegration, and racially intolerant Nationalism was a rising force. In India a Congress Socialist Party had come into being but still operated within the framework of the Congress Party, and in developing rivalry with the Communist Party. In Japan Socialism of all sorts had been for the time eclipsed by the development of nationalist militarism. In China, Mao Tse-tung had established his ascendancy in the counsels of the Communist Party, and had put himself at the head of a Popular Front to resist Japanese imperialist penetration; but the central government of China was still in the hands of Chiang Kai-shek and the Kuomintang. There were nascent Communist and Socialist movements in a number of countries in the Middle East; but they were still small and ineffective. Finally, among the lesser European countries, Belgium, Holland, and Switzerland possessed large Social Democratic minorities which showed no sign of becoming majorities, Portugal was firmly under Dr. Salazar's dictatorial rule, Czechoslovakia had powerful Communist and Social Democratic minorities, neither strong enough to control the country, Poland had passed under the semi-dictatorship of the colonels who had succeeded Pilsudski, and in Finland the Socialists had recently fallen from office.

Taken as a whole, this was a disappointing situation for Socialism as a world force. The Communist World Revolution, so confidently predicted in the early 'twenties, had not merely failed to occur, but had been put for the time being almost out of mind by its Russian protagonists, who were devoting their energies, under Stalin, to building up 'Socialism in a single country' and were throwing their influence on the side of anti-Fascist Popular Fronts designed to protect the Soviet Union against the dangers of Nazi aggression. Meanwhile, Social Democracy, though in a few countries its supporters had been able to make substantial advances in the direction of the Welfare State, showed a marked tendency to settle down as a permanent large minority in most of the constitutionally governed countries of the West and, even when it held the government in its hands, showed little zeal for any rapid advance towards Socialism as an alternative basis to capitalism for the economic ordering of society.

The Social Democratic and Communist movements of 1939, though sharply opposed to each other, professed to derive their inspiration mainly from a common original. Save in a few countries, of which the most important was Great Britain, where Marxian doctrines had but little hold, both Communists and Social Democrats were by profession followers of Marx, whose essential doctrines they interpreted in essentially different ways. Both schools expressed their belief in the Marxian theories of value and surplus value, and agreed in holding that the property-owning classes exploited the proletariat by buying the commodity, labour-power, at less than the value of its product. Both believed in an economic interpretation of history which held forth to the proletariat the prospect of becoming the ruling class in society and using its power to abolish itself, as well as other classes, in the coming classless society. Both believed that capitalism, once a pioneer of advanced methods of production, was destined to be superseded by a system of public ownership of the means of production under which the exploitation of men by men would disappear and give place to production for use, instead of profit. Where they differed was that, whereas the Communists proclaimed the need for revolution and for proletarian dictatorship in the hands of an essentially new kind of State which would thereafter proceed to abolish itself and to replace the government of men by the administration of things, the Social Democrats held that the existing State could be transformed by degrees into a democratic instrument of Socialist construction and accordingly needed not to be overthrown but to be captured by winning a majority of its electors over to the Socialist side. The Social Democrats, organised chiefly in countries which, at any rate after 1918, possessed universal or at least manhood suffrage for the main legislative Chamber, proclaimed parliamentary democracy and majority rule as indispensable foundations for Socialism ; whereas the Communists, organised mainly in countries where parliamentary democracy did not exist, thought in terms, not of individual voters or majorities, but of organised classes as repositories of power and were wholly

prepared to deny voting rights to members of the opposing
classes and to rest their prospects on a dictatorship that would
exclude all 'class-enemies' from any share in political influence.
The dictatorship urged by the Communists was, however,
always that of a class, the proletariat, or of combined classes of
workers and peasants acting under proletarian leadership. The
dictatorship of the class became that of the class-party only
because the latter was regarded as the essential representative
of a class-vanguard, embodying the aspirations of the class as
a whole and therefore entitled to govern in its name. Social
Democrats, on the other hand, denied that Marx had ever
advocated dictatorship in the sense given to it by the Communists. Marx, they said, had only contrasted the dictatorship
of the proletariat with that of the bourgeoisie in the sense of
standing for majority against minority rule and regarding the
proletariat as consisting of the great majority of the whole
people, including the exploited countrymen as well as the town-
dwellers engaged in modern industry. The Communists, for
their part, habitually used the word 'proletariat' in two
different senses, one embracing the exploited classes as a whole
and the other only the industrial wage-earners, or even only
those engaged in large-scale industry; and their attitudes to
the peasantry ranged from regarding the great mass of poor
peasants and landless rural workers as the natural allies of the
proletariat against the wealthier classes, to looking down on
peasants as persons engaged in obsolescent forms of small-
scale production, to be brought out of their primitiveness by
the industrialisation of agricultural methods under strictly
proletarian leadership and control.

From the beginning of the Communist movement, its
quarrel with Social Democracy manifested itself in acute form
in relation to the treatment of colonial territories under the
rule of the imperialist powers. In such territories, Social
Democrats for the most part urged the need for better treatment of the native peoples and for a gradual development of
self-governing institutions towards full internal autonomy —
tendencies in harmony with their own gradualist home policies;
whereas the Communists, as the declared enemies of imperialism and colonialism, went all out to foment colonial revolt and
the complete liquidation of imperialist rule. Reformist and

revolutionary policies thus came into strong opposition in any colonial area in which the Communist movement was able to strike roots.

It is easy to see, if one looks at the matter from a comprehensive world standpoint, that neither Communism nor Social Democracy had in reality a practical message for all countries. On the one hand, there was never any real prospect that certain countries — Scandinavia, for example, or Great Britain — would wish to embark on Communist revolutions in order to overthrow their existing systems, which could be at any rate substantially amended if a majority of their peoples were prepared to vote their reforming Parties into power. On the other hand, in Russia before 1917, no path was open save that of revolution, primarily because the will of a majority to reform was not recognised and there was no constitutional method of promoting democratic advance. Some countries, notably Germany, stood midway between these contrasting situations, in that they possessed Parliaments, elected on a wide franchise and with considerable powers, but these Parliaments had no control over the executive Government, which remained in irresponsible hands : so that a vital clash between the popular Chamber and the executive Government would have to be either compromised or settled by an appeal to force. France, for different reasons, also stood poised between the extremes, because it had a tradition of revolution derived from 1789 and because it contained within it large elements which had never accepted the institutions of the parliamentary Republic. Italy too, because of the weakness of its parliamentary tradition and of the long-standing quarrel between Church and State, stood in an ambiguous position between the parliamentary democracies and the countries subject to authoritarian rule ; while in Japan the parliamentary Parties had never established themselves as entitled to issue orders to the military or to reduce the divine ruler to the status of a constitutional monarch.

Viewed from a world standpoint, the manifesto issued from Berne in 1919 by the revived Second International had a distinctly parochial sound. It had no message at all for the Russians, or the Chinese, or the Japanese, and not much for the Germans or the Italians, except in terms of the as yet untried institutions of the new Weimar Republic. But the

almost simultaneous Manifesto of the newly founded Comintern, issued from Moscow a month or so later, was at least as
parochial, resting as it did on a dogmatic assertion that the
proletariat in all countries had before it a plain duty to travel
in all respects the Moscow road — which was in fact quite
unrealistic in relation to Great Britain, or Scandinavia, or the
United States, and not much less so in relation to France and
Italy or, as the events showed, to Weimar Germany — to say
nothing of Australia and New Zealand, Canada and Mexico,
or indeed India and Ceylon. Only the Centrals of the Vienna
'Two-and-a-half' International were able to see how absurd
it was to lay down a single method as applicable to all countries,
regardless of their circumstances and traditions or of the
opportunities open to their peoples ; and the Vienna attempt
to reconcile the disputants by recognising both these points of
view as of limited application was swept aside by the rival
advocates of intolerance.

Let us now look back for a while much further, and try
to see how Socialist thought had developed from its first
beginnings at the end of the eighteenth century into the movements of the years before the second world war. In this
retrospect, the earliest Socialist projector of whom we need to
take note was Gracchus Babeuf and his Conspiracy of the
Equals of 1796. For, though the word 'Socialism' was still
unborn, Babeuf has a clear title to be regarded as the first
Socialist thinker to put himself at the head of a movement of
broadly Socialist intention ; and it is significant that he began
as a revolutionary conspirator seeking to carry the great French
Revolution on to a further, equalitarian stage. Out of Babeuf
and his conspiracy comes a long line of Socialist conspirators —
Blanqui and Barbès, the extreme left wing of the British
Chartists, the Paris Commune, and, in certain aspects, the
leaders of the Bolshevik Revolution of 1917 itself, though the
charge of 'Blanquist' made against Lenin has been often and
hotly denied. One tradition among several in the Socialist
record is beyond question that of the insurrectionary uprising
of an *élite*, of a devoted body of revolutionaries aiming at
drawing the less active mass behind them into the new society
by the power of example as well as precept. At all times and
in many countries there have been groups of persons whose

instinctive conception of Socialist revolution has been in terms of such an uprising; and probably this will always be so, even in countries where such insurrectionary upheavals stand less than a dog's chance. For such insurrectionism is mainly a matter of temperament and of constitutional inability to think in any other terms, though of course there are times and places when many persons not temperamentally so minded are induced by peculiar circumstances to resort to insurrection as a political weapon.

The second stream of the Socialist tradition is essentially different. It takes its rise in the early community-projectors — in Robert Owen and Charles Fourier, with their projects of small communities, withdrawn from the competition around them to pursue the good life in little, for the most part self-sufficient, groups of producer-consumers, co-operating instead of contending for the means of living, and animated by social philosophies of mutual goodwill. Fourier's appeal to natural human inclinations and Owen's to the moral principle of communal solidarity were no doubt widely different and appealed to different social groups; and Owen had, what Fourier lacked, a close connection with the working-class movement at a certain phase of its development. But they were both Utopians, seeking to refashion the existing societies on a basis of face-to-face association in small communities, with which each hoped in course of time to cover the entire earth, the relations between them resting on a broadly federal basis, and the whole question of power becoming irrelevant and meaningless in face of the entire freedom enjoyed by each constituent community. Their successor, Cabet, differed from them both in that he sought to found a larger community bound together by a much stricter equalitarian discipline, in which the face-to-face voluntarianism of Owen and Fourier gave place, at any rate in intention, to a wider band of association. But Cabet too belongs to the camp of the Utopians, who conceived of the new society as coming about by a voluntary withdrawal from what Owen called the 'old, immoral world' of competitive disorder into a harmony of national association resting on an appeal to the better qualities of human nature.

The third early school was essentially different from both the others. Henri Saint-Simon was neither an insurrectionary equalitarian nor a utopian visionary, but a planner with a considered doctrine of historical development. He saw the mission of the nineteenth century in the emancipation of mankind from the rule of '*les oisifs*' — the kings, aristocrats and militarists who dominated affairs both before and after the great Revolution — and their replacement by '*les savants*' — the men of scientific knowledge, who would re-establish the lost unity and order of society by developing the means of production in the service of all, and above all others, of '*la classe la plus nombreuse et la plus pauvre*'. In Saint-Simon's eyes, what was coming was not a class-conflict between employers and workers, but a collaboration of both to make an end of war and exploitation together and to create a planned economy under which the production of wealth would advance by leaps and bounds. Under their beneficent rule would arise a 'New Christianity' from which all theological dogma would have been refined away and only scientific truth would find honour. Saint-Simon's disciples added to the doctrine of the 'master' a declaration of the illegitimacy of all inherited wealth and of the need to allot social and economic functions in strict accordance with men's capacity to put them to good use in the common interest. Some of them, particularly Enfantin, launched out into strangely mystical interpretations of the master's religious doctrine, which brought discredit on the movement and helped to destroy its social importance. But to Saint-Simon and his followers is to be traced back that strand in Socialist thought which ranges Socialism with the advocates of planned economy, and also that tendency which ranges it on the side of technological development and large-scale industrialism as the necessary foundations of a Socialist order.

The fourth major development of Socialist thought came with the work of Louis Blanc, subsequently developed in certain of its aspects by Ferdinand Lassalle. Louis Blanc's greatest contribution was the idea of the 'Right to Work' — of the obligation resting on the State to provide employment for all willing workers, as expressed in his *Organisation of Labour*, first published in 1839. Blanc stood for a system of self-governing National Workshops, to be established and financed by a reformed democratic State, but to be left free to manage their own affairs subject only to a general co-ordinating and planning control by the representatives of the whole people. Lassalle, in the 1860s, took over this notion and applied it to the conditions of Prussia, demanding that the Prussian State should provide capital for the development of self-governing producers' Co-operative Societies, working under a political régime of universal suffrage, which would convert the State from an enemy of the people into the essential instrument of their emancipation.

Louis Blanc and Lassalle between them had much to do with the growth of the idea that Socialism required State intervention, not merely to regulate social and industrial conditions, but to make the State actually responsible for the conduct of industry through associations of workers formed and encouraged under its auspices. This conception of Socialism, however, ran directly counter both to the new 'Scientific Socialism' proclaimed by Marx and Engels in the 1840s and to the radically different doctrine worked out by P.-J. Proudhon at approximately the same time. For Marx and Engels, in their version of the Materialist Conception of History, advanced a doctrine in which they summed up the history of mankind as the record of a sequence of class-struggles, in the latest phase of which the main contending classes had been reduced to only two — capitalist and proletarian — between whom the contest would continue with growing acuteness until the bourgeois, the capitalists, were finally overcome by the revolt of their proletarian exploitees and society was reorganised on a basis free from classes and from economic and social contradictions. All other classes than these Marx regarded as in process of disappearing under the impact of technological advance — feudalists as the capitalists replaced them more and more in the seats of power, and petty bourgeoisie, small-scale artisans, and peasants as large-scale production drove them out of the market by its superior economic efficiency. Large-scale capitalism was thus, in Marx's view, essentially up to a certain point a force working for progress; but it contained within itself contradictions that fatally barred its advance beyond this point and brought the proletariat, swollen by its growth, into the field against it as a more and more menacing force. The outcome, Marx held, could be predicted with scientific certainty as the overthrow of capitalism and the socialisation of the means of production under proletarian control.

Marx undoubtedly expected this *dénouement* to come quite soon, as the outcome of one of the recurrent crises to which the capitalism of his day was subject. He both underestimated capitalist resilience and the ability of capitalist-controlled States to come to the rescue of the threatened capitalist class, and over-estimated the force of proletarian solidarity and the possibilities of enrolling under the proletarian banner the social groups flung down into it by the advance of large-scale capitalism and the peasants pauperised by the progressive industrialisation of agriculture. But he was correct in foreseeing the struggle between workers and capitalists as the outstanding conflict of the late nineteenth century in the advanced capitalist countries and also in predicting an advance of the trend towards production on a larger and larger scale. Marxian Socialism made its first great impact on the workers of the advanced countries in the days of the First International in the 1860s. He published the first volume of his great work, *Das Kapital*, in 1867, and under his influence his followers founded the Eisenach Social Democratic Party of Germany in the same year, in sharp opposition to Lassalle's Universal German Workmen's Association, which had been established a few years before. The great bones of contention between Marxists and Lassallians during the ensuing years of conflict concerned first the iron law of wages, which the Lassallians upheld but Marx denied and, of greater immediate significance, the attitude to be adopted by Socialists in their dealings with the State. On this issue, whereas the Lassallians looked to the State, refashioned on a basis of universal suffrage, to act as the promoter of workmen's productive enterprises in opposition to the capitalists, the Marxists proclaimed the need to destroy the capitalist State root and branch and to build on its ruins a new State based firmly on the workers' power.

This was a sharp conflict of doctrines ; but it did not avail to prevent the fusion of the Marxist and Lassallian German Parties at the Gotha Congress of 1875, on the basis of an agreed programme which Marx roundly denounced as making too large concessions to the Lassallian point of view, especially in relation to the State. His German followers nevertheless

ignored his protest, and went ahead with the fusion, which they
regarded as essential for the successful struggle against Bis-
marck's anti-Socialist crusade. The United German Social
Democratic Party, emerging successfully from this struggle,
thereafter became a model for Socialist Parties over most of
Europe, except in Great Britain, where H. M. Hyndman's
S.D.F. never commanded more than a very small support and
was soon reduced to insignificance by the growth of non-
Marxian Parties, first Keir Hardie's I.L.P. of 1893 and then
the L.R.C. of 1900, which became the Labour Party in 1906.
But in most of the countries of Western Europe — Scandinavia,
Holland, Belgium, Spain, Italy, and Austria among them —
Marxian Social Democratic Parties came in the 1880s and
1890s to play a predominant rôle in working-class politics,
while in France and in Russia the field was divided between
Marxian and non-Marxian Parties of varying complexion.

Marxism, in the form given to it by the German Social
Democratic Party, thus came to be the predominant influence
in the Second International, founded at Paris in 1889, and so
continued up to the breakdown of the Second International in
1914. This Marxist influence, however, did not at any point
go unchallenged, though it appeared again and again to prevail
against the forces opposed to it. The fundamental challenge
to Marxism had indeed been made in the 1860s, in the First
International itself, when Marx had to do battle first with the
disciples of Proudhon and then with the formidable opposition
of the Russian, Mikhail Bakunin, whose hold on certain sections
of the International was so strong as to cause Marx to condemn
it to death by a removal of its headquarters to the United States
rather than risk the danger of its falling into Bakuninist hands.

Proudhon and Bakunin have often been grouped together
because their followers were equally opposed to Marx; but
they were in fact widely different in their outlook, though they
had in common a bitter hostility to centralisation and to the
State as an engine of bureaucratic control. Proudhon was in
fact a strong believer in the virtues of an independent peasantry,
made up of small producers tilling their own land, and of small-
scale artisans similarly producing goods individually or in co-
operation directly for the consumers' market. He wanted such
producers to be supplied with gratuitous credit by a People's

Bank which would ensure them the means of employment ; and he wanted each producer to receive a reward, on a basis of free contract, corresponding to the success of his personal, or family, effort. The Proudhonists in the First International were accordingly opposed to public ownership of the means of production, including land, and were supporters of free Co-operative enterprise aided, not by the State, but by Credit Banks under their own control. They were, in effect, Anarchists rather than Socialists, if Socialism is taken to involve State ownership ; and their defeat in the First International by the advocates of public ownership was in effect the first clear identification of Marxian Socialism with such ownership. But no sooner had the Proudhonists been defeated than the followers of Bakunin appeared as a new opposition to Marx, backed by the bulk of the Spanish and Italian following of the International and by a large section of the Swiss, centred in the Jura watch-making area round Le Locle and La Chaux-de-Fonds. This new opposition met the Marxists with a fundamental challenge, by denying the right of the London General Council, which Marx controlled, and indeed of any authoritative body, to lay down a policy or programme binding upon the national and local sections of which the International was loosely made up. Bakunin, in his general social philosophy, laid stress on the primary independence of the local face-to-face group and on its right to determine its own policy without being subjected to any authoritarian control from outside. He wished to reduce the International to the status of a merely consultative body, with no power to bind the national and local sections, and he declared outright war on States in all their forms as organs of bureaucratic authority over the people. There was, Bakunin maintained, a natural solidarity of the local group, which could manage its local affairs on a basis of free co-operation of men with men, whereas larger political units, such as national States, were necessarily made up of rulers and ruled, between whom no such solidarity could exist. There was also a rift between Bakuninists and Marxists over the issue of property claims. The Bakuninists wished to concentrate on a campaign for the abolition of inheritance, whereas Marx contended that inheritance was merely a symptom of the disease of private property itself, and held that the attack should be directed to the disease rather than to the symptom. This dispute, however, though it loomed large in the actual conflict between Marx and Bakunin, was in fact superficial in comparison with their major difference on the question of authority and centralisation. For whereas Marx regarded the establishment of centralised working-class political parties as the essential next step towards the Socialist Revolution, Bakunin saw in them rather instruments for the betrayal of the workers' interests through the inevitable growth within them of bureaucratic tendencies and of propensities to come to terms with the authoritarian State instead of making its utter destruction the fundamental objective of social policy.

At the Hague Congress of 1872 Marx, in the absence of the Italians, who had refused to attend, succeeded in bringing about Bakunin's expulsion from the International, and thereafter the removal of its headquarters to the United States, where it expired a few years later after a period of inactive moribundity. But his opponents carried on a rump International in Europe for some years, mainly under Anarchist and Syndicalist auspices, till it too expired in the course of a renewed attempt at unification of forces at the Ghent Unity Congress of 1877. A skeleton, purely Anarchist, International was constituted at a secret Congress in 1881, but apart from this there was thereafter no formal international Socialist link, apart from a few occasional Congresses, till the foundation of the Second International in 1889. Therein, the struggle between Socialists and Anarchists was at once renewed, with the solid weight of the German Social Democratic Party thrown against the Anarchists, who were repeatedly expelled from the Congresses of the International, only to reappear with a renewed challenge at each successive meeting. In the Second International, the existence of a regularly constituted Socialist Party, contesting parliamentary elections where there were such elections to contest, became the criterion of eligibility for membership, which was restricted to Socialist Parties carrying on their work on a basis of class-struggle. This was by no means always easy to interpret — for example, the British Labour Party made no profession of class-struggle in its declarations of policy, but was admitted as a party actually engaged in the class-struggle whether it said so or not, whereas

Anarchist groups which proudly declared their class principles were firmly excluded if they refused to engage in parliamentary action. In countries such as Russia, where until after the 1905 Revolution there was no Parliament with seats to contest, the will was taken for the deed, and the Russian Social Democrats — Mensheviks as well as Bolsheviks, and also the non-Marxist Social Revolutionaries — were admitted to affiliation, as were both the bitterly hostile parties of 'Broad' and 'Narrow' Socialists in Bulgaria.

In the Second International the German Social Democrats appeared as a solid and united Party. Not so the French, until they were forced into unity by hard pressure from the International in 1904. For in France the Socialists were sharply divided into several contending groups. Jules Guesde led the oldest of them, the Parti Ouvrier, in strict conformity with Marxian tenets and in close alliance in most matters with the Germans; while Jean Jaurès, of the Independent Socialist group, gathered round him a large following pledged to the defence of the bourgeois Republic against its anti-democratic and anti-semitic enemies, and prepared, if need arose, to collaborate with the radical bourgeoisie in such defence, which the Guesdists disclaimed as contrary to Socialist principles of independence. A third Party, led by Édouard Vaillant, continued the intransigent tradition of the Blanquists, and yet a fourth, under Paul Brousse, proclaimed itself as 'Possibilist' and concentrated mainly on measures of social reform and municipal activity. Moreover, the situation in France was complicated by the attitude of the Trade Unions organised in the C.G.T., which declared in favour of abstention from all association with political Parties — while leaving its members free to join them if they wished — and favoured a Syndicalist variant of Anarchism which consciously looked back for its inspiration to Proudhon rather than to Marx.

Indeed, Syndicalism, which struck roots in Italy and Spain as well as in France, and had its analogue, in some respects though not in all, in the I.W.W. movements in America and Australasia, was in the early years of the present century the new challenge to Marxian Socialism, in both its revolutionary and its reformist aspects. European, as distinct from American, Syndicalism was the direct successor of Anarchism, and delivered its onslaughts on the traditional Socialists from the same localist and federalist standpoint. Political Parties, it was argued, inevitably led their adherents into the evils of oligarchy and destroyed the spontaneous solidarity which arose locally out of common everyday experiences in the workshops. 'La lutte de classe ne peut être menée que sur le terrain de classe' — that is, in the industrial field — they argued. Politics led not only to bureaucracy and oligarchical control but also to compromise in order to conciliate marginal groups of electors. Political action thus blurred the class-struggle and was fatal to the revolutionary *élan* of the working class. Lenin, indeed, took an opposite view, regarding politics as the chief field of revolutionary activity, and demanding political control over the Trade Unions, which were liable in its absence to be content with merely reformist activities. But Lenin was thinking of Russia, where political action had almost of necessity a revolutionary character, whereas the Syndicalists were thinking of parliamentary politics of the Western type. The Syndicalists were, however, opposed to Lenin's kind of political Party as well as to Parties of a parliamentary kind. For they were hostile to all forms of centralised control which undermined the spontaneous solidarity of workers in the local industrial conflict, and would have nothing to do with the 'democratic centralism' which was an essential characteristic of Bolshevism. The Comintern, at the time of its formation in 1919, did no doubt issue its appeal to revolutionary shop stewards and other elements of the left which shared the Syndicalists' hostility to centralised discipline; but it was soon made clear that there was no room in it for such elements, however left-wing, unless they abandoned their hostility to central discipline and accorded the Party and the Comintern Executive the right to direct Trade Union as well as political policy. Those Syndicalists, or non-Syndicalists, who rallied to the Comintern at the outset were very soon at loggerheads with its Moscow leadership. Such men as Rosmer and Monatte in France and Ángel Pestaña in Spain speedily found themselves outside the Comintern and among its strongest opponents; and the same fate befell the Norwegians under Martin Tranmael and the section of the Italians that followed Bordiga into the Communist Party.

The case of the American Syndicalists of the I.W.W. was

somewhat different; for the I.W.W. stood not so much for local autonomy as for Industrial Unionism on a national scale, corresponding to the greater integration of American Big Business. But the Americans, or at any rate some of their chief leaders, such as W. D. Haywood, were also repelled by the highly centralised discipline of the Soviet Union, and reacted strongly against it; for in practice the I.W.W. in America had been a highly localised body, throwing up its own local leaders in localised industrial struggles, such as the great Lawrence textile strike, and officered largely by immigrants from Europe who had brought thence their Syndicalist outlook and found themselves at odds with the highly organised bureaucracy of the Unions attached to the American Federation of Labor. Many of these I.W.W. supporters found their way into the Communist ranks in 1919, but were speedily disillusioned and either dropped out or became attached to one or another of the almost infinite number of splinter movements that appeared on the American left.

The Syndicalists, particularly in France, had a further criticism to offer of the working-class political Parties. These, they said, instead of uniting the workers on a class basis, divided them into adherents of rival ideologies and thus destroyed natural solidarity. This criticism came easily in France, in view of the French experience of numerous contending political sects, whereas in most countries there was one clearly outstanding Socialist political Party, even if there were small dissident groups outside its ranks. The reasons for this difference between France and other countries were mainly historical. The rivalries of the French Socialist sections went back a long way, and no one group had ever succeeded in establishing itself in a position of predominance; whereas in Germany Marxists and Lassallians had united to form a single Party, and in many other countries predominance had gone to Parties founded mainly on the German model. There was indeed no such Socialist unity in Spain; but there the Trade Unions too were divided between rival movements of broadly equal strength, whereas in France the C.G.T. had no effective rival during the period of Syndicalist activity in the early years of the twentieth century.

Syndicalism had no great hold in Europe outside the Latin

countries, though it was of considerable influence for a time in Holland and in post-war Norway. In Great Britain it developed some activity during the years of industrial unrest before 1914, but was relegated to a position of secondary importance by the rise of Guild Socialism during the first world war. The Guild Socialists echoed many of the Syndicalist arguments, without going to the same lengths of opposition to the State, which most of them wished to keep, in democratised form, as an agency of general government side by side with the Guilds. But, while highly critical of the Labour Party for its reformism, the Guild Socialists never fully endorsed the essential localism of the continental Syndicalist movement. This was largely because in Great Britain the Trade Unions were firmly organised on a national basis, and national was rapidly replacing local collective bargaining. The Guild Socialists as a rule took this industrial centralisation for granted, and aimed at establishing national guilds based on the national Trade Unions rather than local communes such as the French, Italian, and Spanish Syndicalists had chiefly in mind. Despite the presence of a small group round Prince Peter Kropotkin, who lived in England, British Anarchism was very weak and had no influence at all in Trade Union circles, and the tradition of parliamentary government was very strongly entrenched. The Guild Socialists were accordingly rather critical of those definitely hostile to the institutions of parliamentary democracy and concentrated their propaganda on the need for extending democracy to the industrial sphere as well.

The localism of the European Syndicalists reproduced in a later form the federalism which had been the opposing trend to Marxism in the thought of Proudhon and Bakunin. This was a source of both strength and weakness — of strength because the growth of large-scale organisation and of centralised bureaucracy with it had set up in many men's minds a reaction against the depersonalising tendencies of the modern world and had induced a mood favourable to what the Americans call 'grass-roots democracy', and of weakness because the working-class movement itself had necessarily been much affected by the growth of scale and tended to regard large-scale organisation, whatever its human disadvantages, as necessary for fighting purposes and therefore to be accepted as a condition of the struggle with large-scale capitalism. It was no accident that the Syndicalist gospel found its main following in countries, such as France, Italy, and Spain, where large-scale capitalist enterprise, though it existed, was less advanced and much less pervasive than in the foremost capitalist countries, such as the United States, Great Britain, and Germany. The Latin countries, on the whole, still had in the early years of the twentieth century working-class movements in which the bonds of local solidarity were stronger than those of each separate industry as a national unit : so that the French, Italian, or Spanish *syndicat* was still a local body, and the national organisation in each industry usually only a federation of local bodies which felt their attachment to local Chambers of Labour federating the local Unions to be at least as strong as to the national industrial centres. Syndicalism as a movement tended to die down as national unification developed, and also as the question of nationalisation came to the front in the public utility services and in basic industries such as coal-mining. It was obviously much easier to devise realistic projects of local workers' control for enterprises that were local than for mere local sections of nationally organised concerns. Even when it was urged that a high degree of decentralisation should be aimed at in industries subject to large-scale national organisation, the attempt to do this was apt to encounter the hostility of national Trade Union leaders, who feared loss of authority if responsibility and power were widely diffused.

Up to 1914, in the recurrent activities within the working-class movements between centralisers and federalists, the latter had usually got the worst of the battle, because the factors of economic and political development alike favoured centralisation. The more Trade Unions grew, and achieved recognition as bargaining agencies, the more were they impelled to seek collective bargains extending over wide areas and to replace local by national bargaining ; while the growth of highly organised Socialist Parties, seeking representation in national Parliaments, moved in the same direction and rendered it more difficult for sectional groups or sects to maintain positions of independence. The emphasis in both the Trade Union and the political fields was more and more on unity, and dissent from the majority opinion was regarded more and more as a crime because it broke the solidarity of the movement. This did not prevent splinter groups from appearing; but it made their position more difficult and increasingly substituted national for local action. This was the case whether the national bodies tended to the left or to the right, though it applied more obviously when they moved rightwards, as most of them did; for in Western Europe at any rate the trend was definitely rightward as the growing parliamentary Socialist Parties accommodated themselves to the conditions of day-to-day parliamentary action and mass-electioneering. The same tendency, however, could manifest itself even when the trend was to the left. In Russia, for example, where the defeat of the 1905 Revolution had left the road open for a renewed revolutionary advance, the Bolshevik section of the Social Democratic Party, working underground as a revolutionary conspiracy, adopted almost perforce a most extreme form of centralised discipline and developed this into a matter of principle by the theory of 'democratic centralism' which it professed to derive from Marx. The Mensheviks went much less far in the direction of rigid central discipline; but they too were centralisers in comparison with the much more loosely organised Social Revolutionaries, whose movement, spanning the whole range of opinion from right to extreme left, allowed scope for large local differences and imposed no uniform doctrine on its individual members or on the groups which made it up. The Social Revolutionaries indeed can hardly be said to have possessed a common doctrine beyond a broad support for revolutionary action in the field of land reform and the overthrow of the autocracy which upheld the vested interests of the landowning classes. But, except for a very short period in 1905–6, while the revolutionary movement in Russia was at its height, the Social Revolutionaries hardly counted in the affairs of the Second International, in which the Germans, who were centralisers almost to a man, were throughout the predominantly influential force.

The Germans, for their part, were centralisers mainly because they were up against the highly centralised autocracy of Prussia, as the leading element in the German Reich. Whether they agreed with Kautsky or with Bernstein in the great Revisionist controversy, they were at one in seeking to build up a strong and closely knit Socialist Party, behind which they hoped to rally a majority of the German electors, with a view to the overthrow of the autocratic régime. So set were they on maintaining the unity of the Party that almost nobody wished to drive Bernstein and his supporters out of the Party, so as to enforce a split. It was indeed the less difficult to maintain party unity because the differences between Kautsky and Bernstein, though wide in theory, had very little bearing on the actual behaviour of the Party in the current situation. For, though Kautsky and the majority which supported him spoke and thought in terms of what they called a revolutionary break with the existing régime, whereas Bernstein emphasised the likelihood of a gradualist progress in the direction of Socialism, neither faction seriously intended any early action of a revolutionary kind, and the Kautskyites as much as the Revisionists looked on the task of the Party as the winning of an electoral majority and therefore regarded unity as an indispensable condition of success. The growing weight of the Trade Unions in party affairs also made for increasing centralisation ; for the Unions could hope to establish themselves as effective agencies for collective bargaining only on a basis of united industrial action over a wider and wider field, and success in industrial bargaining evidently required a readiness of minorities to comply with majority decisions even when they disapproved of them. Trade Union insistence on the requirement that minorities should accept this form of majority rule was easily carried over into the field of politics where Trade Unions engaged in political action as the allies of the Socialist Party — a trend which manifested itself even more clearly in Great Britain than in Germany, because the British Labour Party, unlike the S.P.D., was built up mainly on a Trade Union basis and its policy decisions were made, in the last resort, by Trade Union block voting at the Labour Party Conferences.

Up to 1917, however, the Socialists were always and everywhere in a minority, without apparent prospect of any early conquest of political power. Splits and factional movements might appear to the party leaders as obstacles to the advance of the Parties along the road to power ; but even in their absence there was little prospect of power being achieved in the near future. The situation became radically different after 1917, when a Government professing Socialist objectives had actually become the ruling power in a great State and had to face the responsibilities of its new authority. For there arose for the first time as a practical issue the question whether the centralised discipline which had characterised the victorious Party in its road to power was to be carried over into the institutions of the new State, or whether opposition Parties were to be tolerated and accepted as necessary elements of the new order. This question was in fact twofold; for it arose in connection both with Socialist groups and Parties which dissented from the victorious Party and with non-Socialist groups and Parties which represented forces fundamentally hostile to the Revolution. The Bolsheviks without hesitation settled both parts of the question negatively. They did not even consider recognising any rights of opposition as belonging to open counter-revolutionary elements; and though for a short time they shared the Government of the new State with the Left Social Revolutionaries and allowed the Mensheviks to remain in existence as an organised Party, it soon became clear that there was to be no place for Socialist dissidents, any more than for a non-Socialist opposition, under the new régime. The Right Social Revolutionaries, many of whom became heavily implicated in the civil war in armed opposition to the Bolsheviks, were broken up immediately when the Constituent Assembly was dispersed. Only a very few Mensheviks took up arms against the Bolsheviks in the civil war, whereas many did their best to collaborate with the Bolshevik régime. But, although the Bolsheviks made use of many Mensheviks, especially in diplomatic posts and in the economic institutions of the new State, it soon became clear that the Menshevik Party was to be deprived of all power of independent action and that its spokesmen were to be driven from the points of vantage held by them in many local Soviets and in many of the Trade Unions, and that no scope was to be left for any Socialist Party which was not prepared to identify itself completely with the Bolshevik point of view. As for the Left Social Revolutionaries, the Bolsheviks set to work to bring their rank and file members over *en masse* to the Bolshevik Party, but allowed its leaders no opportunity to press their own points of view by any collective action.

What emerged in Russia, then, on the morrow of the Bolshevik Revolution, was a one-party State that was not prepared to tolerate any possible focus of opposition, or to accept the collaboration of any organised Party outside itself. Nay, more than that; for it soon appeared that factions within the Party were to be suppressed as completely as factions outside it, and the 'Workers' Opposition' and presently other dissident factions, or alleged factions, were relentlessly broken up. The doctrine of 'democratic centralism', which had come into being as a necessary condition of the successful carrying on of conspiratorial opposition to the old régime, became a dogma of the new rulers, first as necessary for the defeat of the foreign interventionists and of the counter-revolutionary elements inside Russia, but presently as the very basis of the new proletarian democracy which was to provide the driving force of World Revolution. In this spirit the Comintern set out to establish its disciplinary control over the Communist Parties of all countries, even to the extent of ordering them to adopt what policies and what leaders it approved. Moreover, whereas democratic centralism had allowed in theory full freedom of discussion up to the moment at which a binding decision was made, the scope of such discussion was more and more circumscribed by denouncing as factional all attempts to organise groups in support of any policy of which the party leaders disapproved, and it was made clearer and clearer that the right of discussion was confined strictly to intra-party gatherings and carried with it no right to publish or propagandise sectional views differing from those of the party leaders, and further that policies were intended to emerge from the leadership and to be transmitted downwards to the rank-and-file members, rather than to proceed upwards from the lesser to the higher levels of the Party.

In effect 'democratic centralism' turned into centralism without the democracy. There was supposed to be a correct party answer to all possible questions, a scientifically correct class answer to which the party leadership, as the vanguard of the vanguard, held the key; and absolute conformity to the views of the leadership became the acid test of party loyalty. Though there was in Russia in theory no Führer or Duce holding a position analogous to Hitler's or to Mussolini's, the authority claimed for the collective leadership was no less absolute than theirs, and the structure of Bolshevism soon came to bear close analogies to the totalitarianism of the Fascist States — so much so that many of the critics of both treated them as mere variants of a single type, totally ignoring the elements in which they differed *toto caelo*. Prominent among these critics were many of the Social Democrats of the Western countries, who had as their guests exiled Socialists from Russia and its border States and admitted such guests to the counsels of the Labour and Socialist International as representing Socialist Parties in exile. These exiles were, naturally, for the most part vehement in their denunciations of the Bolshevik régime, and their presence inevitably acerbated relations between the Western Social Democrats and the Soviet Union, till it sometimes seemed as if the Social Democrats were setting a higher value on their conception of democracy than on the cause of Socialism — an attitude which the Communists did nothing to discourage until their belated conversion to Popular Front policies in face of the menacing advance of Fascism. Even this change of front, coinciding as it did with the great Stalinist purge in the Soviet Union, was unaccompanied by any modification of the extreme Bolshevik doctrines of one-party monopoly and rigid party discipline : so that there were immense obstacles in the way of the acceptance and harmonious working of any Popular Front in which the Communists played a part. For the Social Democratic leaders could not be expected to forget in a moment what the Communists had been saying about them, or to feel any confidence that party policy might not before long take a turn back to similar denunciation of right-wing and Centrist leaders — as indeed, it did between 1939 and 1941.

A staggering blow was the 1939 Nazi-Soviet Pact, when the Soviet Union turned abruptly from its years of effort to build up anti-Fascist Popular Fronts to check Hitler's and Mussolini's repeated aggression and lack of faith, and entered into a compact with Nazi Germany on terms apparently quite irreconcilable with these efforts and thus set the Germans free to launch their onslaught on the West without immediate danger of being exposed to an attack from the East. In retrospect, it is not difficult to appreciate Stalin's reasons for this action. At the least he was gaining time; and after the dislocation of the Soviet forces arising out of the condemnation of Tukhachevsky and his fellow-commanders and so many of the lower officers and the troubles due to the accompanying civilian 'purges', time was of great account for reorganisation and revising of both military and economic power. Besides, the Pact offered an opportunity for partitioning Poland and thus covering the Soviet Union from a direct advance from the West, and also of coercing Finland when the West would be unable to come effectively to its assistance. Moreover, experience of negotiations with the Western powers had clearly shown both how little reliance they were prepared to place on Soviet military aid and how different their point of view was from that of the Soviet Union. The refusal of the West to come to the help of Czechoslovakia at the time of the Munich crisis served to show, if not that they were deliberately encouraging Hitler to 'go east' with their tacit blessing, at least that they would do nothing to stop him.

Nevertheless, the signing of the Nazi-Soviet Pact came as a serious blow to many Communists who were still busily engaged in the anti-Fascist Fronts they had been building up in many countries, and found themselves compelled either to reverse their policy in mid-stream or to renounce their Communist allegiances. So firmly had most of them been induced to regard the defence of the Soviet Union as the permanent duty of every Communist that most of them took the former course, in some cases after a period of uncertainty which cost some, for the time being at least, their places in the Communist hierarchy. In doing so, they were under the necessity, not only of opposing the 'phoney war' of 1939–40, but also of following Molotov into an attitude of outspoken hostility to the Western powers, and of denouncing the war as a struggle between rival imperialisms, with which the Socialist Soviet Union could have nothing to do. This, at least, was sharply inconsistent with the line the Soviet Union had been taking in its anti-Fascist phase, and indeed with the plain truth; for even if the Western powers were predominantly capitalist in outlook, they were at any rate much less anti-Socialist than the Fascists. But this did not deter the Bolsheviks, who had been so used to denouncing the Social Democrats as enemies of Socialism, and to regarding the Soviet Union alone as embodying true Socialism that they reverted without hesitation to their former attitude and sloughed off their Popular Front with no sense of more than a passing inconsistency.

I can see why the Soviet Union, under Stalin's rule, signed the Nazi-Soviet Pact, but I cannot believe him to have been justified, even in the circumstances of 1939 ; for I believe that Fascism and Nazism were bestial cults that had to be resisted and overthrown at all costs. Even if the Soviet Union was justified in not entering the war in 1939, it does not follow that it was justified in partitioning Poland with the Nazis or in attacking Finland, or indeed that it was justified in still keeping out of the war at the darkest hour for the West, after the fall of France. It could, moreover, even in 1939 have adopted a much more neutral attitude than it did actually adopt and enforce on the Communist Parties in the belligerent and neutral countries right up to 1941, when its and their attitudes were changed abruptly by the Nazi attack on the Soviet Union. Thereafter, no doubt, the Communist Parties of the various countries were among the most determined anti-Fascist fighters ; but even then their loyalty was more to the Soviet Union than to the combined forces of which it thereafter formed a part.

It is pertinent to ask what were the sources of this deep and enduring loyalty to the Soviet Union as the centre of world Socialism — a loyalty which remained proof against every disclosure of the dictatorial ruthlessness of the Stalinist régime and largely remains to-day, when that régime is still in power, though greatly modified in its day-to-day working. The main source was a feeling that the Communists had at any rate fought for many years practically alone against the world forces making for war and for the maintenance of capitalism, whereas the Social Democrats had offered nothing more than fine words and had surrendered, in Italy, Germany, and even Austria, almost without striking a blow in defence of the working-class movement. There was a great fund of goodwill towards the Russian Revolution, if not towards Communism as an ideology ; and letting down the Soviet Union did appear as a betrayal to many who were not at all prepared to uphold its actual behaviour — especially towards deviationist Socialists within or without. There had been widespread popular response to the movement for United Fronts against Fascism, among rank-and-file militants, if less among Social Democratic leaders. But the Communists, even in their most accommodating mood, had shown themselves difficult to work with because the United Fronts they sought were always, at bottom, Fronts which Communists would lead and control, and not genuine alliances with non-Communist elements in the working class, which according to Communist theory could have but one genuine and uniting policy — that of the Communists themselves.

There was no practicable bridge between Communism and Social Democracy as they existed in the 1930s. Evident though the need was for working-class unity in the struggle against Nazism, only Hitler, by wantonly invading the Soviet Union in 1941, could bring the Western democracies and the Soviet Union into an enforced partnership in the second world war ; and even then, as the collaboration was between Governments rather than peoples, and as the Social Democrats did not control, even where they took part in, the Governments of the Western countries, nothing effective was achieved towards bridging the gulf that lay between Social Democrats and Communists ; with the consequence that it was all too easy for the old antagonisms to break out afresh when the war was over and the common enemy had suffered decisive defeat. This, indeed, is the situation in which the world still stands to-day, with Western Social Democrats ranged in alliance with the United States against the Soviet Union in a cold war which, if it ever 'hots up', threatens the human race with absolute destruction.

Can, then, nothing at all be done to bridge this calamitous gulf ? Despite the death of Stalin and the partial repudiation of Stalinism by the present leaders of the Soviet Union, very little beyond an agreement to live and let live and a mutual renunciation of war as no longer a usable instrument of policy, but henceforward a form of mutual suicide fatal to all the combatants : so that no one in his senses can look forward to it with anything except horror and a determination to avoid it at almost any cost. I say 'almost any'; for there are still all too many persons who, declaring that they prefer death to slavery and accusing the Soviet Union of sinister designs to enslave all Europe, see no alternative to continuing to pile up armaments as deterrents to such an attack, even though they admit that if these armaments ever came to be used, nothing could avert a mutual slaughter which it is horrifying to contemplate. In these circumstances, agreed disarmament and the total prohibition of atomic weapons have come to be first priorities on the agenda of the embattled nations; but even the passing of the war danger and the liberation of mankind from the fears which it arouses would of itself do nothing to narrow the gulf between Communist and Social Democratic points of view. Indirectly, however, it might do much; for the removal of the war danger would put an end to one great force that makes for totalitarian forms of government and might well open the way to a gradual liberalisation of the régimes at present dominant in the Soviet area of the world.

It is, however, quite unreasonable to expect such liberalisation to take the form of an adoption by the Communist controlled areas of institutions modelled on the parliamentary systems of Western Europe or on the presidential-parliamentary structure of the United States; for it can by no means be taken for granted that such institutions, even in their modern near-democratic forms, are articles of export, which can be reproduced in countries so widely different in their traditions and social structures as Russia and China. We have therefore to ask ourselves, not whether Russia or China can be induced to imitate or reproduce our Western political institutions, or to govern themselves in closer accord with our ideas of what constitutes good government for ourselves, but rather what can properly be regarded as universal, and not merely particular, in the political values which have been established among us as the outcome of a prolonged evolutionary struggle, and accordingly as necessary for that régime of democratic co-existence which must come into being if the entire race of mankind is not to perish, before long, in utterly devastating warfare. Are we, for example, so entirely satisfied with the system of two or more party government through nationally elected Parliaments with their Cabinets, or through Presidents dividing power with Congress, as in the United States, as to insist that these are the only possible basis on which democracy can be built? Or do we admit that democracy can take alternative forms which can claim equally with ours to express the primal values of society ?

Instead, then, of calling on the Russians or the Chinese to adapt their institutions to ours, let us rather attempt to state what are the essential values which we are attempting to realise in our political structures, and then attempt to discover in what alternative institutional forms it is possible for these values to be embodied. And let us further, in as far as we are aware of real values which our institutions have so far failed to embody, be on the look-out for such values and for any sign of their embodiment, actual or potential, in the institutional structures of the Communist countries or of others which are uncommitted to Western forms of political organisation.

The value for which, above all others, the battle of the Western world has been fought has been personal freedom. This was asserted first as an aristocratic claim, on behalf of those who belonged to a superior class claiming a monopoly of power, and did not extend to any corresponding claim on behalf of the great majority of inhabitants of the territories over which it was made. Its extension to these others occurred earliest in the special sphere of equality before the law, as a challenge to the exclusive claim of a minority to a privileged legal status. This application of it made an end of slavery and serfdom and brought all men to a formal equality of legal status, while leaving untouched the inequalities both of political rights and of social and economic standing. With some overlap, the recognition of equal legal status was followed by the demand for political equality, in the sense of an equal human right to participate in the determination of government, at any rate to the extent of the right to vote in choosing the holders of legislative, and indirectly, of executive authority. But this claim to equal political citizenship was granted, not as a human right, but rather by a gradual extension of civic rights to a growing proportion of all the people. The extension of this claim from men to women was in most cases long delayed ; and even when the right to vote was widely extended, there was in many cases a lag before it was accepted as applying not only to the main legislative body, but also to the executive authority which had previously been in the hands of the Crown. In Great Britain the crucial phase in the transition occurred when the power of the Crown to appoint and dismiss the executive government was taken over by the elected legislature, so that those who had till then been the servants of the Crown became in effect the representatives of a parliamentary majority and came to owe their authority to a popular mandate. This happened in Great Britain long before the electoral machinery had been so amended as to make the legislative authority in any sense representative of the entire people, whereas in some other countries — notably Germany — a mass electorate for the legislature was achieved long in advance of the recognition of the legislature's right to control or choose the executive. In one way or another, however, parliamentary democracy came to be regarded as involving both the election of the responsible legislature by the whole people and the choice of the executive government either by a similar method, as in the U.S.A., or by the verdict of the whole people given at a parliamentary election, as in the British system.

In theory, the extension of political rights to all the people, so as to give them the power to choose both the legislature and the executive government, could take place without any parallel recognition of social and economic rights. In practice, however, the purely political rights of all could hardly be conceded without large repercussions on the economic and social structure ; for a mass electorate controlling the executive government as well as the legislature could hardly be expected to refrain from using its power for economic and social ends. Accordingly, with the extension of voting rights went an increasing tendency to use the power of the State to influence the distribution of wealth both by more progressive taxation and by using the product of such taxation to promote a less unequal distribution of purchasing power. This process led by gradual stages towards the development of the idea of an economic minimum, which the State ought to secure for all its inhabitants in the form of social security services, such as the effective guarantee of full employment and the provision of social benefits for the sick and disabled, for the aged, and for children, especially in large families. Thus, out of the institution of political democracy arose the so-called Welfare State, in which a minimum standard of social security came to be applicable to all the inhabitants. But it is of the very nature of such security that it may be conceded at any level each particular society is able to afford, so that it is not so much conceded absolutely or not at all, but so far or so far only, and that the demand for more of it is insatiable as long as any substantial economic inequality continues to exist.

Thus, in the societies of the West, there have been on the whole three successive stages in the development and extension of social rights. In the first stage the achievement has been mainly of civil rights as extending to all, and therewith towards the extinction of claims to minority privilege in the realm of social status in relation to legal rights. In the second stage the claim to political rights has been gradually affirmed and extended both by the concession of voting rights to more of the people, and ultimately to practically all, and by the transference of executive power from the Crown to bodies of persons owing their position to popular assent and responsible for the use of power to popular opinion. In the third stage, this political power has been used to impose the concession of social and economic rights by the institution of some sort of Welfare State guaranteeing a measure of social security to all the citizens.

In these societies, with or without the aid of revolution, there has been a gradual broadening and extension of the realm of rights by which more and more social rights have been effectively extended to more and more people. The values that have been achieved, at any rate in part, consist of these rights ; and the battle still to come seems to centre round their further development into the conditions of a classless society. There is opposition to this process, as there has been at each previous stage ; but it seems reasonable to expect it to continue in view of the driving forces for further change embodied in modern institutions and in the existing distribution of basic social power. We have doubtless good cause to know that the process does not advance uninterruptedly and that there can be calamitous throw-backs, as there were in Italy and in Germany in our own day. But, even as these have been successfully removed, we can with fair confidence expect a removal of similar tendencies if they reappear — not indeed as a thing certain and irresistible, but as a probable outcome of common man's determination to hold fast to what has been achieved and to use it as a stepping-stone to further advances.

What we have gained in varying degrees in various parts of the West can be summed up as follows — first, a pretty general recognition of all men and women as having certain basically equal claims to be treated as persons in their own right, and therewith a negation of the claims of some men to be treated as superior to the rest in respect of these rights; secondly, a pretty general recognition that among these universal rights is a right to basically equal participation in deciding under what government each society shall be carried on, and therewith a right to change the government by majority vote — which implies the existence of a possible alternative government; and thirdly, some guarantee to each citizen of a measure of social security, necessarily limited to what a society can afford at any particular stage of its development, but tending to grow with each growth in the means of making it effective. In general, the recognition of these three rights has come about by successive but overlapping stages, and the struggle to give full effect to the earlier has continued after the main contention has been transferred to the later. In Great Britain, for example, though equality before the law has long been recognised in principle, it is still necessary to take further measures to make it fully effective in face of the high cost of legal remedies and the advantage these confer on the wealthy in their contentions with the poor; and, in the second of the three spheres, though universal suffrage has been recognised, basically undemocratic institutions such as the House of Lords and the Monarchy still survive, albeit with greatly attenuated powers, and the entire social structure is still dominated by class-divisions, though these have become much less rigid and oppressive than formerly.

When, from our own point of view, we survey the institutions that have been established in the Communist countries we are at once aware that these fail in many vital respects to satisfy our standards of achievement. In the first place, there is in these countries no basic equality of all men and women in respect of civil rights because the régime is one of dictatorship wielded by a single party as the representative of a single class, equality of basic rights being explicitly denied to all persons who do not belong to, or successfully identify themselves with, this ruling class. Moreover, even among the members of the ruling class, recognition of right is accorded not to the individual as such, but to the class as a whole; and any individual who is regarded as acting contrary to collective class interests is treated as forfeiting his share in the collective right. The basis of these new societies is in fact class-right and not individual right. It is no doubt expected and intended that in course of time class-distinctions will disappear and all citizens will come to be members of a single class by the merging of other classes in the proletariat : so that the very notion of class will become obsolete and no one will be excluded on class-grounds from the basic equality of the classless society. But, even if and when this happens, the basic right recognised will, according to the Communist philosophy, be that of the whole society rather than that of the individuals who make it up ; so that there will still be no recognition of the basic rights of the individual.

Secondly, in respect of participation in the work of government and of decision what the government is to be, Communist societies do indeed recognise the right of each individual to vote and the right of a majority to choose the government, but in practice the absence of any alternative potential government robs the right to vote of its real value and reduces it to a mere endorsement of a government which is in fact chosen, not by the electors, but by a single dominant party which arrogates to itself the exclusive right to determine what the government is to be and even claims the right to perform acts of government by its own fiat : so that legislation can be enacted by the party itself equally with the Soviets which constitute the formal government structure. This double assumption of authority by the party is held to be justified because the party in some sense represents the proletariat, of which it is the vanguard, and is accordingly authorised to govern the whole society on its behalf. Moreover, though the party has a mass membership, the formation of policy within it is conceived along the line of what is termed 'democratic centralism', under which the initiative in this formation rests with the central leadership and not with the broad mass of party members, who are compelled by the rigid party discipline to obey the orders emanating from the central leadership and are forbidden to form 'factions' for the furtherance of divergent points of view. This amounts to a sheer denial of democracy as it is understood in the West, and involves a complete exclusion not only of non-party persons but even of the great majority of party members from any share in determining who shall constitute the government or what policies are to be pursued. At the root of this oligarchical system lies once more the belief that what counts is the class rather than the individual, and that true democracy consists not in the participation of every individual in the democratic process but in the supremacy of a single organ representing the dominant class as a whole and itself dominated by a central leadership which is deemed to express the correct collective class view.

When we pass to the third group of rights — those of a socio-economic nature — the same discrepancy appears. These rights are indeed for the most part granted in fuller measure than in the West, in relation to the ability of the Communist societies to concede them ; but they are again conceded not to the individuals as such, but rather in relation to their ability to serve the collective interests of the society. Thus, consumers' needs have been systematically postponed to those of economic development, in order to build up the collective strength of the society ; and in the realm of education, where the achievement of the Soviet Union has been most impressive, the stress has been laid on the contribution which a highly educated people can make to the collective service of the society rather than on the effects of education in furthering individual character and achievement. The Soviet educational system is fundamentally utilitarian : it is a part of the collective effort of Soviet society to achieve the highest possible productivity, and cultural values are systematically subordinated in it to this fundamental purpose. In other social services too the main emphasis is on the contribution these can make to the all-round efficiency of the society rather than on the benefits they confer on the individual.

In short, in all three spheres of action the contrast between Western and Communist societies is between a basic individualism which asserts, and a basic collectivism which denies, the priority of individual values. There is, and can be, no way of transcending this fundamental difference : the only question that matters is whether, in the world of to-day and to-morrow, it is possible for societies resting on these conflicting principles to co-exist and to collaborate despite the basic differences in their pattern of values.

In the more advanced Western societies, this basic individualism has shown itself to be compatible, up to a point, with an approach to democratic equalisation. In such societies, all three groups of individual rights have been extended, to a considerable and real extent, to the entire people, so that for almost everybody there exist certain basic freedoms, a certain right to participate in the making of political decisions, and certain guarantees of social security — though these rights fall short of full recognition and the achievement of social and economic rights is still particularly incomplete and precarious. But in most of the less developed societies none of these rights exist to any considerable extent — neither the basic civil rights, nor the political, nor the social and economic. These countries are set on establishing for themselves new institutions which need to embody their aspirations towards a way of life that will emancipate them from their long stagnation — and in many cases from long subordination to colonial rule. They find themselves confronted broadly with two alternative models for the construction of these new institutions, the one that of the West and the other that of Communism. If they elect to follow the Western model, they are under the necessity, not merely of constructing certain particular forms of government, imitated mainly from those of the West, but, much more formidably, of developing ways of thought and behaviour that will allow such forms of government to function with success — notably tolerably efficient and uncorrupt administrative systems and a high degree of literacy to promote the free interchange of opinions. On the other hand, if they adopt the Communist model they can hope to achieve, unless the Western powers prevent them, a much more rapid tempo of collective social and economic advance and a form of government which calls for much less in the way of widespread participation in the actual conduct of governmental processes.

It cannot be expected that among peoples which have never experienced, for the great majority, the benefits of individual freedom and participation in government these things will have an overriding appeal. Nor is there in these days the possibility of a gradual evolution through which a tradition of personal freedom and political participation could be built up by stages among larger and larger sections of the people. It is sheerly necessary to make a much more rapid leap in the concession of popular claims and to give a high immediate regard to economic and social rights, as well as to the political claims, of the common people. It may be possible, under specially favourable conditions, for territories to emerge from colonial status and set up their own forms of self-government without social revolution — as has occurred already in Ghana and Malaya and, to a more limited extent, in Tunisia and Morocco, as well as in India, Pakistan, and Burma ; but the chances of this are poor in areas in which there exists any substantial population of European settlers living at a standard greatly superior to that of the native inhabitants, as in Algeria, Kenya, and Central Africa, and in the latter the road to self-government appears to be that of revolution rather than of peaceful change. In such areas the strong support given by the Communists to colonial nationalism seems bound to evoke a lively response in face of the intransigent attitudes of the settler minorities, which can hope to maintain their privileges only by naked force. For where progress can be achieved only by fighting for it in armed conflict, there can be little prospect of the growth of a tradition resembling that of the West, and the stress is likely to be laid on collective rather than on individual advances. Similar considerations apply to other underdeveloped countries which are emerging not from colonial rule but from feudal despotisms of native rulers. For the ruling classes of such countries can be expected to stand obstinately in the way of developments which threaten their powers and privileged status, so as to drive their peoples into mass rebellions leading to the establishment of some form of dictatorship rather than to democracy in its Western form. Communist dictatorship, rather than Western democracy, established itself in China under Mao Tse-tung ; and the Bolshevik Revolution in Russia brought with it the victory of a single, highly disciplined party which showed itself no more regardful of individual rights than the Czarist autocracy which it replaced.

Nevertheless, disregardful as the Communist States are of the claims of the individual as such, it must not be left out of account that in the realm of collective rights and achievements they have brought with them very large satisfaction to a great many individuals. Though the main motive behind the extraordinarily rapid development of education in the Soviet Union may have been that of improving the capacity of the citizens to serve the State, the education is none the less an unquestionable achievement by which a vast number of individuals have profited; and similarly the new social security services, whatever the motives underlying them, have helped to transform the social texture of the society and have carried with them a great extension of real liberty. Even if the individual is left helpless in his dealings with the State, the number of individuals who actually suffer under, or are keenly conscious of this oppression, is much less than the number who benefit by the advantages conferred by the new society for its own purposes. When there is no popular tradition of individual freedom or political participation the absence of them may not be at all widely felt, and most people may be much more conscious of the benefits most of them derive from the new institutions than of the repression to which, as individuals, they stand exposed. Most of them are, moreover, very much more aware of the appeals made to them to play a part in the great work of social construction than of the extent of their subordination to a small governing *élite* in possession of exclusive authority.

Socialism, up to the rise of Bolshevism in Russia, was almost exclusively a current of opinion within Western society, having its home mainly in Western Europe. In almost all its forms it was a part of the radical tradition in Western Europe seeking to carry further the victories of the common people over the ruling classes, and voicing its protest against the *laissez-faire* capitalism which had established itself in the leading countries of the West. This capitalism was its enemy, but was nevertheless regarded as standing higher in the course of social evolution than the forms of society which had preceded it and as having formed a necessary stage in the process of social evolution which was to culminate in the establishment of a classless Socialist structure. Revolutionary no less than gradualist Socialism held to this theory of evolutionary change from lower to higher forms. There was, accordingly, a strong tendency to think of capitalism as preparing the way for Socialism and of the growth in the scale and concentration of economic enterprise as contributing to the making ready of society for Socialism. The fewer the hands in which the control of capitalist enterprise became concentrated, the nearer it was to readiness for being taken over on behalf of the whole people. Thus, while capitalist concentration might increase the power of the capitalists to exploit the workers, capitalism could not avoid bringing into being a mass revolt of the class it subjected — a class which would before long become strong enough to wrest this control from capitalist hands and take it into its own.

The first effective challenge to this view of Socialism as the necessary successor to capitalism came from the Russian Narodniks who, faced with a native capitalism much less powerful and pervasive than that of Western Europe, raised the question whether it was necessary in Russia to pass through a stage of developed capitalism before advancing to Socialism, or whether it might not be possible in Russia to found a Socialist society directly on the ruins of the Czarist autocracy. Why, the Narodniks asked, should we overthrow the Czar merely in order to replace his authority by that of another, and perhaps a more formidable, enemy of the people, in the shape of capitalism ? Can we not, by using the large communal element in Russian society, proceed immediately to the construction of Socialism without enduring the pains of Capitalism ? Marx, the arch-prophet of Western Socialism, showed himself in his later years not unfriendly to this notion, though he never fully espoused it. His followers in Russia, however, broke sharply away from it, insisting that the rapidly growing forces of Russian capitalism must be allowed to take their course and that Russia too must pass through its phase of capitalist domination before Socialism could be ready to take its place. The Russian Mensheviks became the chief upholders of this doctrine, contemplating a fairly prolonged period after the overthrow of Czardom during which the Socialists would constitute the main opposition to a predominantly capitalist Russian society ; whereas the Bolsheviks, more keenly alive to the weakness of Russian capitalism and to its involvement with Czardom, contemplated a much shorter transition period or even a very rapid passing of the Revolution from its bourgeois to its Socialist stage. Lenin, however, always insisted strongly on the fundamental difference between the two Revolutions — bourgeois and Socialist — and on the need for the one to precede the other ; whereas Trotsky maintained that the capitalist class would be unable to establish itself as the effective ruler of Russia, so that the first revolution would have to be brought about under mainly proletarian leadership and would therefore have to develop directly into the second — a view which came near to denying that there would have to be a capitalist phase before the proletarian Revolution could arrive. It was Lenin who attempted to solve the riddle by propounding the alternative of a bourgeois Revolution under proletarian control, resulting in the establishment of State Capitalism as the form of transition from Czardom to Socialism, and thus propounding a doctrine which required a capitalist stage in the evolution without the necessity of a capitalist State régime.

If, however, the control of the State machine was to pass directly or with hardly an appreciable interval into the hands of the proletariat, this could hardly be done except under a dictatorial régime ; for the industrial proletariat, being no more than a small minority of the whole people, could not hope to establish its rule on any basis of majority voting. It would need, no doubt, to come to terms with the peasants, and to make any concessions that might be needed in order to enlist peasant support ; but it would need to guard itself against the danger of being outvoted by the vast peasant majority and to keep the ruling power firmly in its own hands. Hence, on the one hand, the reluctant adoption of a broad policy which allowed the peasants to become individual owners of the land, and on the other the dismissal of the Constituent Assembly in which the peasants were the predominant element.

In any case, the Russian Revolution of 1917 could not have been primarily an anti-capitalist Revolution ; for Russian capitalism was much too weak to be the chief opponent of the revolutionaries. Of the two Revolutions of 1917 the first was against Czardom and brought to an end the age-long autocracy of the Czars without putting any viable alternative structure in its place. The fall of the Czar brought down with it the power of the landed aristocracy and the bureaucracy through which the Czars had governed, leaving a void which was filled for the time being by local peasant revolts and by the assumption of authority in the towns by the workers' Soviets. The successive Provisional Governments under Lvov and Kerensky were quite unable to govern, and increasing disintegration set in during the summer months. This prepared the way for the Bolshevik Revolution, in which power was seized by the leaders of the Bolshevik Party, with the Left Social Revolutionaries in alliance, against the other Socialist Parties — the Mensheviks and the Right Social Revolutionaries — and without the support of the main body of the people, though probably with that of a majority of the industrial workers. This almost bloodless victory was won because the forces arrayed against the Bolsheviks were hopelessly divided and unable to provide any sort of Government capable of holding the country together. Its main opponents were certainly not the capitalists, who played hardly any part in the events of 1917, but were simply swept aside by the movement of events. It resulted, no doubt, in their certain disappearance from the scene; but the main achievement of the double Revolution was not the defeat and liquidation of the capitalist class, but the final disappearance of the old, predominantly feudal and agrarian society and its replacement by the rule of a single party — for the Left Social Revolutionaries speedily dropped out of the picture after the *coup*.

Socialist control was thus established in the Soviet Union as the successor not to capitalism, but to autocratic and feudal rule, and in opposition to a large body of Socialist opinion. The Bolsheviks then set out to build up the new Russia on the ruins of a mainly pre-capitalist society, but with an armoury of ideas in which Socialism was regarded as essentially the successor to capitalism and as resting on the basis of the relatively undeveloped industrial proletariat. Plunged at once into civil war and involved before long in a struggle against foreign intervention, the Bolsheviks had to use such scanty forces as they possessed for these struggles. A high proportion of the industrial workers had to be mobilised for the armed forces, and many of them were killed in the fighting. Meanwhile, industry had to be rebuilt almost from nothing with a largely improvised unskilled labour force drawn mainly from the ranks of the peasants, and the machinery of administration had to be improvised afresh by a vast recruitment of new elements on whose devotion little reliance could be placed. The Red Army had to be created by an immense effort of recruitment, for which Trotsky bore the main responsibility. Under all these influences there emerged a new kind of Socialism, which owed little to the European Socialist traditions and a great deal to the initiative and driving force of one man — Lenin.

The European Socialist tradition could, indeed, be of little help to the Bolsheviks during the critical early years of the new régime ; for the situation they had to face was one which had never been contemplated either by Marx or by his successors in the European Socialist movement. The German Socialists and above all their leading theoretician, Karl Kautsky, had always contemplated that Socialism would come to power by conquering and taking over the economic institutions of a fully developed capitalism, so that the change would consist mainly in the coming of a new high command, which would henceforth conduct these enterprises in the service of the whole people. Speculation about the form which the new control was destined to assume had been dismissed as utopian, and the question deferred till power had been won, the more readily because it had been tacitly assumed that the capitalist structure could be taken over and changes in it thereafter introduced at leisure and in accordance with democratic terms. It had been assumed that Socialism would come, with or without violent Revolution, in response to the manifest desire of a majority of the people, whose collaboration with the new order would therefore be assured. Democracy, in the form of universal suffrage and the determination of policies by general vote of the people, had been taken for granted.

This was a situation totally different from that in which the Bolsheviks assumed power ; and the European Socialist tradition gave them no guidance as to their behaviour. Universal equal suffrage plainly would not serve their ends ; for it would place power in the hands of the peasant majority, which was largely untouched by Socialism and was set, above all, on gaining individual, or family, possession of the land and but little interested in the forms of government or in finding means of holding the vast country together. Some sort of

dictatorship was the only practicable alternative to the dissolution of Russia into a large number of separate peasant
Republics, or to the re-conquest of parts of the country by
counter-revolutionary elements. Accordingly the question on
the morrow of the Bolshevik Revolution was not whether or
not there should be a dictatorship, but rather what sort of
dictatorship there should be. This question, however, was
really settled by the nature of the party which had been the
prime mover in seizing power; for this party possessed both
a highly centralised discipline and a doctrine of 'democratic
centralism' and a high intolerance of all who did not agree
with it and accept its lead. Consequently, though the Revolution had been made in the name of the Soviets, which though
dominated by the Bolsheviks in the principal towns included
also representatives of other Parties, the real direction of policy
passed into the hands of the Party, which claimed the right to
exercise it as the true representative of the industrial working
class and the sole properly authorised expositor of a proletarian
viewpoint. From the moment when the Left Social Revolutionaries seceded from the Government in opposition to the
Brest-Litovsk Treaty, the Bolshevik Party was in effect the
Government, and the opposition elements in the Soviets were
rapidly weeded out, so that the Soviets ceased to be bodies
recruited by free popular elections, even among the industrial
workers, and came to be mere emanations of the Party, accepting without question its lead in matters of policy and, in effect,
forced so to do because, as against their loosely federal structure,
the Party constituted a closely unified and disciplined force
operating over the entire territory of the Russian empire. This
unitary structure of the Party over the entire State was essential
to the Party's authority, and served as the main prop of its
dictatorship. The exigencies of civil war at home and of the
struggle against foreign intervention compelled the Party to
resort to higher and higher centralisation and bureaucratic
control. As long as Lenin remained effectively at the head
of affairs this centralisation remained compatible with some
measure of free discussion inside the Party *élite*; but with his
removal by illness Stalin's chance came. Trotsky denounced
the rapid growth of bureaucracy within the Party, only to be
swept aside and driven into impotent opposition and, before

long, exile. Stalin used his position as Party secretary to make himself full master of the bureaucracy and presently to elevate himself to a position of personal dictatorship. The collective dictatorship of the proletariat had never been a reality; for from the first the Party, rather than the class, had been the holder of dictatorial power. But the dictatorship of the Party passed into the hands of an even smaller body of Party leaders and thereafter into those of a single individual, who proceeded to use his power remorselessly in the liquidation of his erstwhile comrades. Only after Stalin's death was there a denunciation of the so-called 'cult of personality', and therewith some attempt to revert to a condition of collective leadership; but even thereafter the realities of power continued to be confined to a small body of leaders, between whom internal struggles for power and influence arose, albeit in less extreme forms than those of the Stalinist epoch.

Through all these changes the major objectives of Soviet policy remained, with one exception, largely the same. In the early years after the Revolution the Bolsheviks took it as certain that their Revolution could not survive unless the advanced capitalist countries could be induced to follow their example, and thus to convert the Russian Revolution into a World Revolution on the Russian model. The Third International was founded in 1919 with this end in view and continued to pursue this end until its impracticability had to be recognised. Then Stalin adopted the slogan, 'Socialism in One Country' and converted the International into an agency, no longer of World Revolution, but of universal trouble-making for the non-Communist countries and of appeal to workers everywhere to subordinate their own immediate interests to the claims of the Soviet Union as the protagonist of Socialism in a hostile world. The victory of Nazism in Germany brought, belatedly, a change of front, and forced the Communists into an attempt to create anti-Fascist Fronts; but in face of the failure of these efforts Stalin again changed course and came to terms with the Nazis, only to change front again, perforce, when Hitler launched his attack on the Soviet Union in 1941.

In this one respect, Soviet policy underwent drastic changes, though the objective of World Revolution was never abandoned, but only deferred. In other respects, the objectives of policy remained mainly the same through all the changes. The Bolsheviks' task, as they saw it, was to raise Russia as speedily as possible from its economic and social backwardness into the foremost place among advanced industrial societies, so as to beat the capitalists at their own game. The foundations of this attitude had been laid in Lenin's day by his grandiose plan of electrification; but Lenin had shown his appreciation of the need to advance with caution by adopting the New Economic Policy of 1921 and by his behaviour towards the projects of the planners of grandiose schemes of industrial development. Only after Stalin had successfully liquidated most of the remaining leaders of the 1917 Revolution, or at all events driven them from power, came the sharp change in policy embodied in the first Five-Year Plan and in the enforced collectivisation of agriculture despite widespread peasant resistance. These immense economic changes, however, involved no alteration in the fundamental objective of economic development, but only an intensification. The Soviet Union, after the initial setback of the famine, proceeded faster than ever with the development of the heavy industries, to which the advance of the lighter industries catering directly for consumers' needs was definitely postponed and continued to be so through a succession of further Five-Year Plans. Meanwhile, in agriculture there was, after the famine, an advance in total arable production; but the vast slaughter of livestock which had accompanied the collectivisation could not be at all rapidly made good. Indeed, a number of its effects remain operative even to-day; and the growth of agricultural output as a whole has lagged badly behind that of industrial production, despite a large increase in the cultivated area by the breaking-up of 'virgin lands', mainly through the spread of State farming.

Undoubtedly, the changes made at the end of the 'twenties involved a great increase in the severity of State-imposed economic discipline and an offering of financial inducements to high individual output which ran counter to the previous tendencies towards a lessening of economic inequalities. Stalin put himself at the head of this movement and, in the course of the 1930s, established his dictatorial rule on a personal basis by further liquidation of his critics and by converting the vast Communist Party machine into a subservient instrument of his personal rule. This was the system that came to an end with Stalin's death in 1953 and was belatedly denounced by Khrushchev at the 1956 Congress of the Party. But, though Beria was duly liquidated and discipline somewhat relaxed after Stalin's death, there was no fundamental change of objective, or even of method. A collective control of policy was to some extent substituted for Stalin's personal rule; but the objectives and to a great extent the methods remained as before, though the latter were in a limited degree relaxed. There was no alteration in the one-party structure of Soviet society; and the power of the Party became in some respects even greater. Molotov and Malenkov were indeed driven out of the leadership without being liquidated — which seemed to indicate some softening of the régime; but the Soviet Union's action in crushing the Hungarian revolt of 1956, even without the subsequent execution of Nagy and Maleter in June 1958, showed that there had been no fundamental change, and the renewed onslaught on 'Titoism' in 1958, after the *rapprochement* with the Yugoslavs in 1956, plainly indicated that the Soviet leaders were not prepared to relax their grip on the satellites, despite the concessions they had been forced to make to Poland in 1956.

In short, even in 1958 the Soviet Union remained essentially a one-party State, entirely controlled from above by the Communist Party leadership and allowing almost no scope for the expression of dissident, or even deviating opinion. In this respect Communist China followed its lead, after great hopes had been raised by Mao's apparent encouragement for the 'blossoming of a hundred flowers' in the ideological garden. Mao sided with the Soviet Union in the Hungarian affair and went even beyond Moscow in the attacks on 'Titoism' in 1958; and, except in Poland, there was little or no sign of relaxation in the satellite countries.

Over the same period, however, the Soviet Union was doing its utmost to appear as the foremost advocate of peace and co-existence in opposition to the alleged war-making politics of the United States and of the Western countries generally. It can, I feel sure, be taken as true that the Soviet leaders — and at least equally the Soviet peoples — sincerely desire to avoid a war in which the destruction on both sides would of necessity be incomparably severe, and would greatly prefer to be left to pursue their aims by other means. But, unfortunately, it does not follow that they are prepared to reverse, or even to modify, their aims or to accept any terms which they hold would place them at a disadvantage in relation to the United States. As for the latter, though most people and most leaders in the U.S.A. also doubtless hope that war can be avoided, many of them are not at all prepared to be content with any position that falls short of clear military superiority or to give up the hope not merely of containing but of actually defeating Communism and of helping to bring about the overthrow of some at any rate of the existing Communist régimes. In these circumstances the contest for military superiority, especially in atomic weapons, continues unabated, and instruments of destruction are piled up on both sides to an extent that has become sheerly absurd, as well as economically disastrous to any lesser country, such as Great Britain, that attempts to keep pace with them. Indeed, the only terms on which any real progress can be made involve an abandonment by both parties of all hope of being able to defeat each other in war and to survive. This means a real willingness to co-exist in peace despite the acute differences that divide them. It involves that the Soviet Union shall give up the hope, if it has ever been entertained, of bringing about by armed force the triumph of Communism as a world system ; but it also involves that the Americans shall give up their hopes of military superiority and shall reverse their ambitions to overthrow Communism in every country by armed force — which at present they seem still very reluctant to do.

We have to leave the world Socialist movement, then, in a state of great weakness, eclipsed for the time being in Italy, Germany, Austria, Spain, and most of Eastern and Central Europe, and hardly less so in the United States, where the upsurge of working-class consciousness connected with Roosevelt's New Deal had failed to take at all a Socialist form, whereas Communism had dissipated itself in a series of faction fights with very little impact on the main body of the working class. I leave the story there, right in the middle because the later phases of it are not, in my view, yet finished or ripe for the pen of the historian. I have not indeed been able to avoid carrying the story, at certain points, well beyond 1939; but I make no pretence in these occasional glimpses of later developments, of telling a complete or comprehensive story, or even of giving a current theoretical account. My own standpoint has, I think, emerged sufficiently throughout these volumes. I am neither a Communist nor a Social Democrat, because I regard both as creeds of centralisation and bureaucracy, whereas I feel sure that a Socialist society that is to be true to its equalitarian principles of human brotherhood must rest on the widest possible diffusion of power and responsibility, so as to enlist the active participation of as many as possible of its citizens in the tasks of democratic self-government.

INDEX OF NAMES

Adler, F., 169
Alessandri, A., 221
Alfonso XIII, King of Spain, 119, 126, 146
Alter, V., 199
Antonescu, Gen., 200, 204
Araquistain, L., 142
Attlee, C. R., 65, 68, 69, 78, 79
Auriol, V., 109
Azaña, M., 120, 122, 126, 129, 130, 138, 141, 146
Aznar, Admiral, 119

Babeuf, G., 297
Bakunin, M., 123, 302, 303-4, 308
Baldoni, Gen., 227
Baldvinsson, J., 185
Baldwin, S., 77
Barbès, A., 297
Barrio, M., 131, 141
Barth, K., 58
Bartlett, V., 87
Bauer, O., 153, 157, 164
Beales, H. L., 67
Berenguer, Gen. D., 119
Bernstein, E., 310, 311
Besteiro, J., 124, 142, 148
Bevan, A., 81, 84, 88
Bevin, E., 68, 78, 89
Blagoev, D., 204, 205
Blair, W. R., 67
Blanc, L., 299-300
Blanqui, L. A., 297
Blatchford, R., 68
Blum, L., 17, 79, 93, 101-14 passim, 117-18
Bohlen, Krupp von, 51
Bohlschwingh, F. von, 57
Bondfield, M., 65
Bonnet, G., 104
Bordiga, A., 306
Bottai, G., 7
Bracke, A., 118
Branting, H., 177
Braun, O., 49
Braunthal, J., 169
Briand, A., 93
Brousse, P., 305

Browder, E., 212, 213
Brüning, H., 35
Budenny, Marshal, 252
Bukharin, N., 230, 233, 262-3
Busch, Col., 221

Caballero, F. L., 123, 124, 125, 131-42 passim, 147-8
Cabet, E., 298
Caillaux, J., 93
Calvet, L., 122
Camacho, Pres., 220
Cannon, J. P., 212
Cárdenas, Pres., 219, 220, 225, 228, 292
Carias, T., 221
Carol, King of Rumania, 199, 200
Carro, S., 221
Casanovas, J., 142
Chamberlain, N., 16, 17, 23, 88, 89, 104, 105, 115
Chang Hsueh-liang, 281
Chang Wan-t'ien, 269
Chautemps, C., 93, 95, 103, 104, 109, 112
Ch'en Shao-gü, 269
Ch'en Tu-hsin, 281, 290
Chéron, H., 94
Chiang Kai-shek, 264, 266-8, 270, 274, 281, 282
Chiappe, J., 95
Ch'in Pang-hsein, 269
Chou En-lai, 282
Churchill, W., 16, 89, 90
Chu Teh, 270
Clynes, J. R., 65, 86
Cojander, A. K., 184
Coldwell, M. J., 217
Comorera, J., 142
Companys, L., 122, 128, 129, 142, 143-4
Cripps, Sir S., 65, 68, 69, 74, 80, 84, 85, 86, 88

Daladier, É., 17, 23, 93, 94, 95, 105
Dalinier, 95
Dalton, H., 65, 68, 74, 75
Danneberg, R., 155, 168

339

Darré, R. W., 53-4
Daudet, L., 94
Déat, M., 94, 117, 191
Desrousseaux, A., 118
Deutsch, J., 153, 164
Dewey, J., 214
Díaz, J., 142
Dimitrov, Dr. G., 213
Djaković, D., 201
Dmowski, R., 10
Dobrogeanu-Gherea, C., 204
Dollfuss, E., 71, 72, 98, 150, 159-
    160, 161, 162-3, 164, 165
Doncas, Dr. J., 128, 141
Dorgères, H., 97, 98
Doriot, J., 117
Douglas, T. C., 217
Doumergue, G., 72, 95, 96, 97
Dubinsky, D., 215
Durruti, B., 137

Echevarrieta, H., 142
Eden, A., 99, 104
Ehrlich, H., 199
Elliott, S. R., 87
Engels, F., 26, 300
Erlander, T., 177

Faure, P., 107
Feder, G., 37
Fey, Major, 159, 163, 165, 166
Fierlinger, Z., 198, 205
Fimmen, E., 192
Flandin, P.-É., 97
Foster, W. Z., 212, 213
Fourier, C., 298
Franco, Gen. F., 79, 100, 113, 130
Frick, Dr. W., 46, 48
Frugoni, E., 227

Gaitskell, H., 68
Georgiev, K., 205
Gerhardsen, E., 182
Gidev, 202
Giral, J., 131, 138
Gitlow, B., 212
Gollancz, V., 83, 84, 148
Göring, H., 45, 46-7, 48, 54, 57
Gorkić, M., 201
Greenwood, A., 65, 69, 79
Grossmann, 50
Grove, Col. M., 220
Guesde, J., 116, 305

Halifax, Lord, 105
Han Lin-fu, 290

Hannington, W., 67
Hansson, P. A., 176, 177
Hardie, K., 302
Hassenfelder, 57
Haywood, W. D., 307
Henderson, A., 65, 68, 69
Hernández, J., 142
Herriot, É., 94
Hilferding, R., 156
Hillquit, M., 211
Hindenburg, Field-Marshal von, 35,
    45, 46, 54, 56
Hitler, A., 3, 7, 13, 16, 29, 35, 41,
    44-6, 52, 55, 56, 57, 58, 78, 79, 81,
    99, 100, 104, 162, 165, 166, 314,
    315, 317
Hlinka, Fr., 198
Hoare, Sir S., 78-9, 99, 166
Horner, A., 85
Hornsrud, C., 182
Horthy, Admiral, 5, 199
Hsiang Chung-fa, 269
Hugenberg, Dr. A., 36, 46, 53, 54
Hyndman, H. M., 302

Ibáñez, C., 220
Iglesias, P., 124
Ivanov, Z., 205

Jäger, 57
Jaurès, J., 104, 117, 118, 305
Johannsen, A., 172
Jovanonić, D., 202
Jowett, F. W., 65, 85
Justo, Gen., 226

Katayama, S., 219
Katz, C., 204
Kautsky, K., 156, 310, 311, 331
Keppler, W., 51
Kerache, J., 212
Kerensky, A. F., 330
Kestl, 51
Khrushchev, N., 335
Kilbom, K., 25
Kirkwood, D., 65
Kirov, S. M., 72, 105, 252
Kropotkin, P., 308
Krupp von Bohlen, 51
Ku Chu-t'ung, 282
Kun, B., 10, 199
Kunsinen, O., 184
Ku Shan-chung, 290

Lansbury, G., 65, 69, 78
Laski, H. J., 83-4, 85, 86, 90, 148

Lassalle, F., 299, 300, 301
Laval, P., 17, 77, 93, 98-9, 117, 166
Lawrence, S., 65
Layret, F., 122
Lee, A., 211
Leipart, T., 49, 50
Lenin, V. I., 261, 262, 263, 297,
    306, 329, 331, 332, 334
Lerroux, A., 120, 122, 127, 128,
    145
Lewis, J. L., 215
Ley, Dr., 50, 51, 52
Li Li-san, 268-9, 290
Litvinov, M., 23, 88, 106
Liu Jen-ching, 290
Lloyd, C. M., 67
Lloyd George, D., 76-7
Longuet, J., 80, 118
Louis, P., 96
Lovestone, J., 212
Lucacz, G., 204
Lvov, Prince, 330

MacDonald, R., 64, 77, 78
Maček, V., 202
Machow, R., 44
Macia, Col. F., 122
Malatesta, E., 123
Malenkov, G., 335
Maleter, P., 335
Malinov, 202
Malvy, L., 93
Man, H. de, 187-8, 189-91
Mann, T., 85
Mao Tse-tung, 223, 224, 264, 266,
    267-73, 274-5, 276-81, 282-5, 288,
    289, 290-1, 335
Marković, S., 200
Marquet, A., 94, 117, 191
Martinović, R., 201
Marx, K., 26, 238, 295, 300-5, 328
Maura, M., 120
Maurin, J., 125, 141
Maurras, C., 94
Maxton, J., 65, 85
Mazepa, 242
Middleton, J. S., 70
Mikhailović, D., 205
Mises, Prof. von, 243
Mitchison, G. R., 67
Moch, J., 118
Molotov, V. M., 335
Monatte, P., 306
Morones, L., 219
Morrison, H., 65, 74, 75, 86
Mosley, Sir O., 64, 83

Müller, L., 57, 58
Mussolini, B., 6, 7, 77, 99, 161,
    162

Nagy, I., 335
Negrín, J., 131, 137, 138, 142
Neickov, D., 206
Neumann, H., 25
Neurath, Baron K. von, 46
Nin, A., 125, 137, 138, 141
Noel-Buxton, Lord, 65
Norman, M., 66
Nygaardsvold, J., 182

Orwell, G., 148
Owen, R., 298

Papen, F. von, 35, 36, 44, 45, 46,
    49, 58
Parker, J., 69
Pastochov, K., 205
Paul-Boncour, J., 94
P'eng Pai, 270
Pestaña, Á., 123, 306
Pétain, Marshal, 17
Pethick-Lawrence, Lord, 75
Philip, A., 118
Pilsudski, Marshal J., 10, 198
Pivert, M., 102
Poincaré, R., 93, 98, 110, 111
Pollak, O., 169
Pollitt, H., 85, 89
Prieto, I., 125, 138, 141-2, 144, 148
Prince, A., 96
Proudhon, P.-J., 300, 302-3, 308

Quiroga, C., 130, 131

Radić, S., 202
Rakosi, M., 199
Remmele, 25
Renaudel, P., 94, 118, 191
Renner, K., 160, 161, 168
Rentelen, Dr. von, 52
Reuther, W., 215
Rintelen, A., 165
Rivera, D., 219
Rivera, J. A. P. de, 128
Rivera, P. de, 19, 119, 123
Rivero, B., 221
Robles, G., 128, 129, 146
Robson, W. A., 68
Rocque, Col. de la, 94, 97, 112
Röhm, E., 7, 54, 55
Roosevelt, F. D., 14, 207, 208, 209,
    211, 213, 215, 222

Rosmer, A., 306
Ruthenberg, C., 212

Saint-Simon, H., 298-9
Salazar, 5
Sanjurgo, Gen., 21, 126, 127
Sarlo, 202
Schacht, H., 53
Schachtman, M., 212
Schleicher, Gen. von, 35, 44, 45
Schlucher, Dr., 51
Schmidt, 53
Schmitz, Dr., 165
Schober, Dr., 155-6, 157
Schuschnigg, Dr. von, 72, 150, 165-
    166, 167-8
Scott, Prof. F. R., 217
Seipel, Dr., 150, 151, 152, 154-5,
    156, 157, 158, 159, 160, 162
Seiss-Inquardt, von, 167
Severing, K., 49
Shinwell, E., 65, 78
Sinclair, U., 211
Sotelo, C., 128, 130
Souza, G. de, 142
Spaak, P. H., 187
Stalin, J., 22, 25, 26, 29, 89, 106, 200,
    230-1, 233, 237, 239, 244, 255,
    257-63, 314-15, 316, 332-3, 334-5
Stambolisky, A., 196
Starhemberg, Prince E., 154, 156,
    159, 166
Stauning, T., 179
Stavisky, S. A., 72, 95, 96, 97
Steeg, T., 93
Stefensson, S. J., 185
Steincke, K. K., 179
Strachey, J., 83, 148
Strasser, G., 44, 45
Strasser, O., 7
Stresemann, G., 47
Sun Yat-sen, 276

Tanner, J., 85
Tanner, V., 183, 185
T'an Ping-shan, 290
Tardieu, A., 93
Terra, G., 227
Thaelmann, E., 25

Thomas, J. H., 77
Thomas, N., 208, 212
Thorez, M., 107, 116
Thyssen, F., 50, 51
Tito, J. B., 21, 200, 201, 202, 205
Toledano, L., 219, 220, 225, 228
Tomaso, A. di, 226
Topalović, Ž., 21
Toro, Col., 221
Torre, H. de la, 218, 221
Tranmael, M., 181, 183, 306
Trevelyan, Sir C., 88
Trotsky, L., 29, 214, 219, 230-1, 233,
    253, 255, 257-8, 261-2, 329, 331,
    332
Trujillo, 221
Tukhachevsky, Marshal M., 252,
    253, 315

Ubico, J., 221
Uriba, V., 142
Uriburu, Pres., 226

Vaillant, É., 305
Vandervelde, E., 187
Vásquez, M., 142
Vaugoin, K., 156
Vargas, G., 221, 227
Vayo, Á. del, 142

Wagner, Dr. O., 51
Wallas, G., 84
Warwick, Countess of, 68
Wauters, A., 187
Webb, B., 68
Webb, S., 65, 68
Wels, O., 48
Wigforss, E., 172, 176, 177
Wilkinson, E., 65
Winter, Dr. E., 164, 165
Wise, E. F., 68
Wolfe, B. D., 219
Woodsworth, J. S., 217
Woolf, L., 68

Zamora, N. A., 19, 119, 120, 121,
    127, 130
Zeeland, van, 188
Zyromski, J., 102

GENERAL INDEX

Abyssinia, 77, 78, 99, 132, 166-7
Action Française, 94
Agrarian League (Austria), 151, 154
Agrarian Party (Bulgaria), 202, 205
Agrarian Party (Czechoslovakia), 197, 198
Agrarian Party (Sweden), 176, 180
All-China Soviet Congress (1931), 269
Almería, 139
Alpine Montan-Gesellschaft, 158
American Federation of Labour (A.F. of L.), 207, 209, 210, 212, 213, 215, 307
Anarchist Federation, Iberian, see *Federación Anarquista Ibérica*
Anarchists, 303-5
 in Great Britain, 308
 in Latin America, 219, 225-6, 228
 in Spain, 20, 119, 122, 123, 125, 128, 132, 136, 140
 in Yugoslavia, 201
 see also *Confederación Nacional de Trabajo* (C.N.T.)
Anarcho-Syndicalists :
 in Latin America, 225-6, 228
 see also Syndicalists
Andalusia, 122
Anschluss, 156, 159, 163
Anti-Comintern Pact, 23, 81
Anti-semitism :
 in Germany, 37, 38, 40, 41, 59-60
 in Hungary, 203, 204
 in Italy, 203
 in Poland, 203, 204
 in Rumania, 203
Anwhei, 275
Aprista Movement, 218-19, 221-3, 228
Argentine, 218, 219, 224, 225-6
Association for the Preservation of Economic Interests in the Rhineland and Westphalia, 51
Asturias, 129, 144
Australia, 2, 292
Austria, 1, 62, 71-2, 104
 and Germany, 62, 100, 156, 167-8
 Austrian Legion, 165

Austria—*contd.*
 Communism in, *see* Communist Parties
 Constitution, 154-5
 economy, 157-8
 Nazis in, 158-9
 Socialism in, *see* Socialist and Labour Parties
 Trade Unions in, 158, 160, 163, 164
Authorisation Bill (Germany, 1933), 48, 49
Automobile Workers' Union (U.S.A.), 212

Bank of England, 66
Barcelona, 124, 128, 130, 137-8, 144
Basque provinces, 136, 144
Belgium, 19, 100, 187-91
Berchtesgaden, 105
Bilbao, 124, 126, 131, 136, 142, 144
'Black Coffin' demonstrations, 67
Boden Credit Anstalt, 157
Bolivia, 218, 221
Bolsheviks, 310, 312, 328-9, 330-3
Brazil, 218, 221, 227
Bulgaria, 72, 195, 196, 202, 204, 205-6, 305

Camelots du Roi, 94, 97
Canada, 2, 215-18
Capital (Marx), 301
Catalonia, 121-8 *passim*, 131, 135, 136, 137, 140, 141, 143
Catholic Church, 5
 in Austria, 151, 154, 159, 162
 in Belgium, 19, 187, 190
 in Czechoslovakia, 198
 in France, 110
 in Germany, 36, 56, 58-9, *see also* Centre Party
 in Holland, 19
 in Latin America, 220, 229
 in Spain, 10, 20, 112, 120, 121, 127, 130
 in Switzerland, 194
Centre Party (Germany), 44, 45, 46, 47, 48, 51, 58

Chile, 219, 220-1
China, 335
 and Japan, 272, 273-6, 284
 and U.S.S.R., 288
 bourgeoisie in, 273, 274-5, 277,
  278
 collectivisation in, 270
 Communist Party in, *see* Communist Parties
 peasants in, 269-70, 274, 278-9,
  283, 284, 287-8, 289
 proletariat in, 267, 268, 270-1,
  273, 277-8, 279, 283-4, 289
 Red Army in, 266, 267-8, 270,
  275, 281
 United Front in, 273-5, 277, 281,
  285, 288, 290
C.G.T. (Argentine), 226
Christian Social Party (Austria),
 151-61 *passim*, 168
Christian Social Party (Belgium),
 187, 188, 190
Christian Trade Unions (Germany),
 44, 50, 56
Collectivisation in the U.S.S.R.,
 232-7, 241, 244-5, 248, 334
Coming Struggle for Power, The
 (Strachey), 83
Comintern (Third International),
 21-2, 24-5, 62, 297, 313, 333
 and China, 264, 269, 273-4, 277,
  288
 and C.N.T. (Spain), 123
 and Czechoslovakia, 198
 and France, 107, 115
 and Germany, 42, 43
 and Latin America, 219, 223
 and Norway, 181
 and Syndicalism, 306
 and U.S.A., 212, 214
 and Yugoslavia, 200-1
 Popular Front Policy, 22-3, 106,
  205, *see also* Popular Front
 United Front Policy, 24-5, *see
  also* United Front
Committee for Industrial Organisation (U.S.A.), 207
Communism :
 and Nazism, 4, 12-13, 42-3, 274
 and Social Democracy, 294-6,
  312, 314, 316-17
 see also Communist Parties
Communism (Laski), 84
Communist Parties :
 Argentine, 226
 Austria, 152

Communist Parties—*contd.*
 Belgium, 189
 Bulgaria, 202
 China, 264-5, 267, 268-9, 270-1,
  273-6, 281-90
 Czechoslovakia, 197, 198
 Finland, 183, 185
 France, 16, 17, 61, 72, 93, 95, 96,
  101-2, 106-7, 108, 114, 115-18
 Germany, 4, 25, 35, 36, 42-3, 45,
  47, 48, 49, 60-1
 Great Britain, 64, 67, 72, 73, 76,
  82, 84, 85, 86, 114
 Greece, 202-3
 Hungary, 199
 Iceland, 185
 Latin America, 219-29 *passim*
 Norway, 182
 Poland, 198, 199
 Spain, 20, 124, 128, 129, 131-2,
  134-5, 136, 138, 140, 141, 142,
  145-6, 147
 Sweden, 25
 Switzerland, 192
 Uruguay, 227
 U.S.A., 207, 208, 211, 212-13,
  214, 215
 U.S.S.R., 26-7, 28-9, 230, 238,
  252, 260, 312-14, 330, 332-3,
  334-5
 Yugoslavia, 21, 200-2
*Confederación Española de Derechas
 Autónomas* (Ceda), 128, 146
*Confederación General de Traba-
 jadores Unitarios* (C.G.T.U.),
 124
Confederación Nacional de Trabajo
 (C.N.T.), 123-4, 125, 126, 129,
 132, 135-42 *passim*, 147-8
Confédération Générale du Travail
 (C.G.T.), 17, 72, 95-6, 305,
 307
*Confédération Générale du Travail
 Unitaire* (C.G.T. Unitaire), 95-
 96
Confederation of Mexican Workers,
 219, 220
Congress of Industrial Organisa-
 tions (C.I.O.), 14, 207, 208,
 210, 213-14, 215
Conservative Party (Gt. Britain), 15
Conservative Party (Spain), 119,
 120, 121
Co-operation and co-operative
 movement, 298
 in Denmark, 179

Co-operation and co-operative movement—*contd.*
  in Eastern Europe, 196, 197
  in Gt. Britain, 87
  in Prussia, 300
  in Sweden, 172, 173, 178
  in U.S.A., 211
  in U.S.S.R., 234-5, 237, 244
Co-operative Commonwealth Federation (Canada), 215-17
Co-operative League (China), 290
Co-operative Party (Gt. Britain), 64, 87
Co-operative Union (Gt. Britain), 72
Costa Rica, 218
Credit Anstalt, 33, 157
Critique of the Gotha Programme (Marx), 238
Croatia, 201-2
Croix de Feu, 94, 97, 98, 111, 117
Czechoslovakia, 81, 88, 105, 195, 197-8, 203, 205, 255, 315

Daily Herald, 83
Das Kapital (Marx), 301
Dawes Plan, 32, 34, 36
Democratic centralism, 285, 313
Democratic League (China), 290
Democratic Party (U.S.A.), 208, 213
Denmark, 1, 179-81
Dominican Republic, 221
Doriotists, 115, 117

Ecuador, 218
Einheitsgewerkschaft, 164, 166
Eisenach Social Democratic Party, 301
End Poverty in California (E.P.I.C.), 211
Esquerra, 122, 124, 128, 137, 138, 141, 143-4
Estat Català, 128, 141, 142, 143

Fabian Society, 68, 69, 83, 91
Falange Española, 19, 128
Fascism, 3, 5-15, 24, 63
  and Spanish Civil War, 112-13
  in Austria, 1, 158-9, 162
  in Belgium, 189
  in Croatia, 202
  in France, 94-5, 97, 111, 117
  in Germany, 1, 5-9, 12-13, 62-3
  in Hungary, 199, 204
  in Italy, 1, 5, 6-8
  in Poland, 204

Fascism—*contd.*
  in Rumania, 200, 204
  in Spain, 10, 128, 146
  in U.S.A., 14-15
Federación Anarquista Ibérica (F.A.I.), 125, 128, 130, 135-43 *passim*
Fighting Association of the Industrial Middle Classes (Germany), 52
Finland, 183-5, 315, 316
Flemish National Movement, 189, 190
F.O.R.A. (Argentine), 225-6
For Socialism and Peace, 73-4, 85
For Soviet Britain, 76
F.O.R.U. (Uruguay), 226
France, 1, 16-17, 296, 305
  and Abyssinian crisis, 78-9, 99, 166
  and Czech crisis, 105
  and Germany, 100, 104
  and Spanish Civil War, 15, 79, 80, 100-1, 103-4, 112-14, 132-3
  and U.S.S.R., 105-6
  Blum Government, 17, 79, 93, 101-14
  Catholic Church in, 110
  economy of, 102-3, 108-11
  election of 1932, 93-4
  fascism in, 94-5, 97, 111, 117
  Matignon Agreements, 102-3, 108, 109
  Popular Front in, *see* Popular Front
  Socialism in, *see* Socialist and Labour Parties
  Syndicalists in, 115, 306, 307, 308
  Trade Unions in, *see* Trade Unions
Franco-Soviet Pact (1935), 105
'Free' Trade Unions (Germany), 44, 50
Frente Popular, 129-30
Front Populaire, 17, 79, 101-3, 105, 106-14, 145
Fukien, 275

German Industrial and Trade Committee, 52
Germany, 1, 3, 100, 310-11, 320
  and Austria, 162, 165
  and Italy, 165, 167
  and Nazis rise to power, 35-7, 44-50, 54-5

345

Germany—*contd.*
and reparations, 32, 33, 34
and Spanish Civil War, 15, 79,
80, 100-1, 133, 144
and Sweden, 171
and U.S.S.R., 89, 205, 213, 253,
254, 314-16
annexation of Austria, 100, 104
anti-semitism in, *see* Anti-semitism
capitalists and the Nazis, 50-4
Churches in, 36, 56-9
economic crisis (1931), 32-3, 34-5
Socialism in, *see* Socialist and
Labour Parties
Trade Unions in, *see* Trade
Unions
see also Fascism *and* Nazi Party
Gijon, 136
Gleichschaltung, 8, 36, 41, 55, 57, 58
Godesberg, 105
Gotha Congress (1875), 301
Grammar of Politics (Laski), 84
Grand Confederation of French
Production, 108
Great Britain, 100, 296, 320, 322
and Abyssinian crisis, 77, 78-9,
99
and China, 272
and Czech crisis, 105
and Latin America, 218
and Spanish Civil War, 15, 79, 80,
100-1, 103, 132-3, 148-9
and the Fascist threat, 15-16
election of 1931, 64-5
election of 1935, 77-8
Labour Party, *see* Socialist and
Labour Parties
Popular Front in, 82, 84, 87-8
rearmament, 78-82
Trade Unions in, *see* Trade
Unions
unemployment in, 67, 70-1, 76
United Front in, 72, 73, 82, 84,
85, 86-7
Greece, 202-3
Grossdeutschland, 37
Guardias de Asalto, 127
Guatemala, 218, 221
Guild Socialism, 308

Heimwehr, 150-67 *passim*
Hirtenberg, 161
Histadrut, 21
History of the Russian Revolution
(Trotsky), 262

Hoare-Laval Agreement (1935), 78-
79, 166
Holland, 19, 191-2
Honduras, 221
Hoover Moratorium (1931), 34
House of Lords, 74, 322
Hunan, 266, 267, 271
Hungary, 5, 9-10, 195-6, 199, 203,
335
Hunger Marches, 67, 71

Iceland, 185-6
Independent Labour Party, *see*
Socialist and Labour Parties
India, 2, 293
Industrial Recovery Act (U.S.A.),
209
Industrial Relations Act (U.S.A.),
209
Industrial Workers of the World
(I.W.W.), 306-7
International, First, 301, 302-3
International, Second, 153, 296,
302, 304-5, 310
International, Third, *see* Comintern
International Brigade, 132, 134,
136, 144-5, 148
International Labour Office, 75
International Policy and Defence
(National Council of Labour), 80
International Transport Workers'
Federation (Holland), 192
Iron Guard (Rumania), 200, 204
I Say NO (Barth), 58
Italy, 1, 100, 296
and Abyssinia, 77, 78-9, 99, 132
and Austria, 162, 165
and Germany, 165, 167
and Spanish Civil War, 15, 79,
80, 100-1, 133, 144
anti-semitism in, 203
Fascism in, 1, 5, 6-8

Japan, 296
and China, 81, 272
Socialism in, 293
Jeunesses Patriotes, 94
Jews, *see* Anti-semitism
*Juntas Ofensivas Nacional-Sindica-
listas*, 128

Kansu, 275, 282
Kiangsu, 266, 267-8, 271, 272, 275,
282
Kibbutzim, 21
Kolkhozi, 235

Kooperativa Forbundet, 172
Kulaks, 233-4, 235-6, 241, 245
Kuomintang (K.M.T.), 264, 265, 268, 269, 270, 275, 281-2, 290

Labour and Socialist International, 48, 61, 107, 182, 193, 314
Labour and the International Situation (National Council of Labour), 81-2
Labour Front (Germany), 36, 50, 51
Labour League of Youth, 85
Labour's Immediate Programme (Labour Party), 85, 86
Lapuan Movement, 183, 184
Lausanne Agreement (1932), 34
League for Social Reconstruction (Canada), 217
League of Nations, 16, 23, 75, 80, 85, 100
  and Abyssinia, 77, 99, 166-7
  and Japanese aggression in China, 272
Left Book Club, 83, 84
Lessons of October, The (Trotsky), 262
Let Us Face the Future (Labour Party), 91
Liberal parties (Gt. Britain), 64, 78
Liberal Party (Belgium), 187, 189
Linz, 163
London County Council, 71
'Long March' (of the Red Army), 264, 268, 273
'Loyal Grousers', 68

McCarthyism, 14
Madrid, 128, 130, 131, 132, 134, 136, 143, 144
Magyar nationalism, 10
Málaga, 131
Manchukuo, 72
Manchuria, 272
'Marburg' manifesto, 58
Marxism, 294, 300-5
  and China, 279-80
Matignon Agreements, 102-3, 108, 109
Means Test, 71
Mensheviks, 305, 310, 312, 328, 330
Mexico, 2, 142, 218, 219-20, 224, 225, 228

Narodniks, 328
National Association of German Industry, 51

National Council of Labour, 74, 79, 80, 81
National Democratic Party (Czechoslovakia), 197
Nationalisation, 294
  in France, 96, 103
  in Gt. Britain, 66, 73, 74, 75, 85, 92
  in Sweden, 172-3
Nationalist Party (Germany), 35, 36, 45, 46, 47, 48, 51, 54
National Liberation Alliance (Brazil), 227
National Socialist Industrial Cell Organisation, 44
National Unemployed Workers' Committee Movement, 67, 76
National Unemployment Assistance Board, 70, 71, 76
Nazi Party (Austria), 158-9, 161, 163, 165
Nazi Party (Germany), 3-9, 12-13
  aims of, 37-44, 55
  and the capitalists, 50-4
  and the Churches, 56-9
  and the Jews, 37, 38, 40, 41, 59-60
  and working-class movements, 42-44, 48-50, 60-1
  lack of resistance to, 49-50
  rise to power, 35-7, 44-50, 54-5
Nazi-Soviet Pact, 23, 89, 205, 213, 314-16
New Course, The (Trotsky), 262
New Deal, 1, 14, 62, 71, 111, 207, 208-11, 214
New Economic Policy (N.E.P.), 230, 334
New Fabian Research Bureau, 66, 68, 69, 91
New Party (Gt. Britain), 64, 83
New Zealand, 2, 292
N.K.V.D., 253
'Non-Intervention Pact', 2, 15, 79, 80, 100-1, 103-4, 113-14, 132-4, 145
North-Western Employers' Association, 51
Norway, 1, 181-3

Old World and the New Society, The, 90
On Practice (Mao Tse-tung), 289
On the New Democracy (Mao Tse-tung), 276-81
Organisation of Labour (Blanc), 299
Oviedo, 129

Pacifism :
  in Danish Social Democratic
    Party, 179
  in French Socialist Party, 104
  in Labour Party, 15, 78
Pact of San Sebastián, 119
Pan-German Nationalist Party
  (Austria), 151, 161
Paris Commune, 297
*Partido Obrero de Unificacíon Marx-
  ista* (P.O.U.M.), 124, 135, 136,
  137-8, 140, 141, 143, 147
Parti Populaire Français, 117
*Partit Socialista Unificat de Cata-
  lunya* (P.S.U.C.), 125, 135, 137
Party of Proletarian Unity (France),
  96
Peace Ballot (1935), 77
Peasant Front (France), 98
Peasant League (Austria), 154
Peasant Party (Croatia), 202
People's Front (France), see *Front
  Populaire*
People's Party (Germany), 47, 51,
  58
Personal freedom, 319-27
Peru, 218, 221-2
Plan du Travail (de Man), 187-8,
  189-91
Poland, 5, 88, 89, 195-6, 198-9, 203,
  205, 315, 316
Popular Front, 314
  in Bulgaria, 202
  in Eastern Europe, 205
  in France, 17, 79, 96, 105, 106-14
  in Gt. Britain, 82, 84, 87-8, 145
  in Iceland, 185
  in Latin America, 219, 221, 222,
    223, 224, 226
  in Spain, 23, 129-30
  in Switzerland, 193
Progressive Party (Canada), 215, 216
Proletarian Party (U.S.A.), 212
Protestant Church :
  in Germany, 36, 56-8
  in Holland, 19

Rabassaires, 122, 124, 137
Radical Party (Denmark), 179, 180
Radical Party (France), 93, 94, 96,
  97, 101-2, 103, 104, 105, 109-10,
  111
Radical Party (Spain), 119, 120,
  127, 145
Rassemblement Populaire, 101
  see also *Front Populaire*

Red Army (China), 266, 267-8, 270,
  275, 281
Red Army (U.S.S.R.), 331
Reichsbanner, 49
Reichswehr, 49, 54
Reparation payments to Germany,
  32, 33, 34
Republican Parties (Spain), 114,
  115, 119, 129-30
Rexiste Movement, 189, 190
Reynolds News, 84, 87
Rhineland, Hitler's invasion of, 79,
  100
Rumania, 195, 199-200, 203, 204,
  205
Runciman Mission, 105
Russia, *see* Union of Soviet
  Socialist Republics

Santander, 131, 136
Saskatchewan, 216, 217
Schutzbund, 150, 151, 154, 163
Serbia, 195, 202
Shenai, 268, 271, 275, 282
Slovak People's Party, 198
Social Democracy and Communism,
  294-6, 312, 314, 316-17
Socialism, development of, 297-
  317
Socialism and the Defence of Peace
  (National Council of Labour),
  79
Socialist and Labour Parties :
  Argentine :
    Independent Socialist Party,
      226
    Socialist Party, 226-7
  Austria :
    Social Democratic Party, 150-
      164, 168-9
  Belgium :
    Labour Party, 187, 188, 189,
      190
  Brazil :
    Labour Party, 227
  Bulgaria :
    Social Democratic Party, 202,
      205-6
  Canada :
    Co-operative Commonwealth
      Federation, 215-17
    Farmer-Labour Party, 216
    Independent Labour Party, 216
  Czechoslovakia :
    Social Democratic Party, 197-8,
      203

Socialist and Labour Parties—*contd.*
  Denmark :
    Social Democratic Party, 179,
      180
  Finland :
    Social Democratic Party, 183,
      184, 185
  France :
    Neo-Socialist Party, 94, 190
    Socialist Party, 61, 93, 94, 95,
      96, 101-2, 104, 106-7, 115-
      118
  Germany :
    Social Democratic Party, 4, 35,
      36, 43, 47, 48, 49, 60-1, 302,
      304, 305, 311
  Great Britain :
    Independent Labour Party, 64,
      65, 67, 68, 72, 76, 80, 82, 85,
      86, 302
    Labour Party, 1, 15, 61, 64-70,
      71, 72-82, 85-92, 133, 145,
      148-9, 302, 304, 311
    National Labour Party, 64
    see also Co-operative Party
  Holland :
    Labour Party, 191
    Social Democratic Party, 191,
      192
  Hungary :
    Social Democratic Party, 199
  Iceland :
    Social Democratic Party, 185-6
  India :
    Congress Party, 22
  Mexico :
    Labour Party, 219
  Norway :
    Labour Party, 181-2
    Social Democratic Party, 181,
      182
  Palestine, 21
  Poland :
    Socialist Party, 198-9, 203, 205
  Rumania :
    Social Democratic Party, 199,
      205
  Spain :
    Socialist Party, 119, 123, 124-5,
      126, 129, 131, 141, 142, 144,
      145, 148
    United Socialist Party of
      Catalonia, 125, 135, 137
  Sweden :
    Social Democratic Party, 18,
      61, 170, 175, 176, 177, 178

Socialist and Labour Parties—*contd.*
  Switzerland :
    Social Democratic Party, 192-3
  Uruguay :
    Socialist Party, 227
  U.S.A. :
    American Labor Party, 214
    Socialist Party, 207, 208, 211-
      212, 213, 214-15
  Yugoslavia :
    Social Democratic Party, 21,
      200, 205
Socialist League, 66, 67, 68, 69, 73-
  75, 76, 82, 85, 86
Socialist United People's Party (Ice-
  land), 185-6
Social Revolutionary Party (Russia),
  305, 310, 312, 330, 332
Society for Socialist Inquiry and
  Propaganda (Gt. Britain), 68
South Africa, 293
Soviet Communism (Webb and
  Webb), 241-2
Soviet Union, *see* Union of Soviet
  Socialist Republics
Spain, 1, 19-21
  agriculture and agrarian reform,
    121, 122
  Anarchists in, *see* Anarchists
  Asturias, 129
  Barcelona (May, 1937), 137-8, 139
  Caballero's Government, 133-4
  Catalonia, *see* Catalonia
  Catholic Church in, 10, 20, 112,
    120, 121, 127
  Communism in, *see* Communist
    Parties
  Constitution (Republican), 120-1,
    131
  economy, 122, 126-7
  election of 1936, 129-30
  elections of 1931-3, 119, 121-2
  Fascism in, 10, 128, 146
  Socialism in, *see* Socialist and
    Labour Parties
  Syndicalists in, *see* Syndicalists
  Trade Unions in, 122-4, 125,
    126, 129
  workers' control in, 135, 139-40,
    143
  see also Spanish Civil War
Spanish Civil War, 112-14, 130-1,
  144-5
  and 'non-intervention', 2, 15, 79,
    80, 100-1, 103-4, 113-14, 132-4,
    145

Spanish Civil War—*contd.*
British Labour Party and, 79, 80,
148-9
France and, 79, 80, 100-1, 103-4,
112-14, 148
Stahlhelm, 49
Stakhanovism, 239
Stavisky scandal, 72, 95, 96, 97
Stresa Conference (1935), 77
Sweden, 1, 18-19
and Finland, 184
and Germany, 177
co-operative movement in, 172,
178
economy, 171, 175-6
elections, 175, 178
socialism in, *see* Socialist and
Labour Parties
social security in, 172, 173-6, 177
Trade Unions in, 173, 178
unemployment relief, 174-6
Switzerland, 19, 192-3
Syndicalists, 304, 305-9
in France, 115, 306, 307, 308
in Latin America, 219, 225-6,
228
in Spain, 20, 123, 125, 132, 136,
139, 140, 141, 143, 308, 309

Teruel, 137
Toledo, 131
Trades Union Congress (T.U.C.),
66, 67, 72, 76, 77
Trade Union Federation (Finland),
184
Trade Unions, 11, 309-10
in Austria, 158, 160, 163, 164
in Belgium, 190
in Chile, 221
in China, 264
in Finland, 183, 184
in France, 16, 17, 72, 95-6, 106,
107, 108, 109, 305
in Germany, 32, 35, 36, 42, 43-4,
49-50, 56, 311
in Gt. Britain, 15, 64, 66, 70, 76,
308
in Holland, 191-2
in Hungary, 199
in Iceland, 185
in Latin America, 225, 228
in Mexico, 219, 220
in Norway, 183
in Palestine, 21
in Spain, 122-4, 125, 126, 129
in Sweden, 173, 178

Trade Unions—*contd.*
in U.S.A., 1, 2, 14, 207-8, 209-
210, 213-14, 215, 306-7
*see also under names of individual
unions*
Trotskyists, 257-8
in China, 281, 290
in France, 115
in U.S.A., 212, 214
in U.S.S.R., 253, 255

U.G.T. (Argentine), 226
Ukraine, 241
Unemployment in Gt. Britain, 67,
70-1, 76
Unemployment Insurance Act
(1934), 70
Unión General de Trabajadores
(U.G.T.), 123-4, 126, 129, 136,
137, 138, 139, 140, 147
Union of Soviet Socialist Republics,
1, 2, 25-31, 296, 310, 312-18,
328-36
agriculture and collectivisation,
232-7, 241, 244-5, 248, 334
and China, 288
and Czechoslovakia, 82, 105, 198
and Finland, 184
and France, 105-6
and German Fascism, 250-1
and Hungary, 199
and League of Nations, 75, 106
and Poland, 198, 199
and Spanish Civil War, 79, 80,
101, 114, 133, 135, 142-3, 146
and U.S.A., 317, 318, 335, 336
armament programme, 251, 256-7
education in, 324, 327
Five-Year Plan, first, 230-49
passim, 334
Five-Year Plan, second, 249-51,
256
incomes in, 238-9
industrialisation, 230-2, 237-40,
242, 243-4, 245, 246-51, 256-7
investment in, 243, 247, 248, 249
Nazi-Soviet Pact, 23-4, 89, 205,
213, 314-16
N.E.P., 230, 231
Popular Front policy, 22-3, 251,
314, *see also* Popular Front
Socialist attitude to, 27-30
Treason trials, 25-6, 114, 252-5
United Front, 24-5, 317
in China, 273-5, 277, 281, 285,
288, 290

United Front—*contd.*
  in France, 72, 106
  in Gt. Britain, 72, 73, 82, 84, 85-87
  in Spain, 72
  in U.S.A., 213
United German Social Democratic Party, 302
United Peace Alliance (Gt. Britain), 87
United Socialist Party of Catalonia, see *Partit Socialista Unificat de Catalunya*
United States of America, 1, 84
  and China, 272
  and Germany, 32, 33
  and Latin America, 218, 222
  and U.S.S.R., 317, 318, 335, 336
  economic crisis, 33, 34, 62, 208-209
  Fascism in, 14-15
  New Deal, 1, 14, 62, 71, 111, 207, 208-11, 214
  Socialism in, see Socialist and Labour Parties
  Trade Unions in, see Trade Unions

Unity Manifesto, 85-6
Universal German Workmen's Association, 301
Uruguay, 218, 224, 225, 227

Valencia, 131, 132
Versailles, Treaty of, 36, 38, 77
Vienna, 150, 153, 157, 164

Washington Naval Treaty, 72
Welfare State, 320-1
Workers' and Peasants' Party (Poland), 198
Workers' Confederation of Latin America, 219
Workers' control in Spain, 135, 139-140, 143, *see also* Syndicalism
Workers' Party for Marxist Unification, see *Partido Obrero de Unificación Marxista*
Working People's Party (Croatia), 201

Yenan, 264, 268, 275, 282
Young Plan, 33, 34
Yugoslavia, 21, 200-2, 205, 335

END OF VOL. V

PRINTED BY R. & R. CLARK, LTD., EDINBURGH